ORGANIZING FOR SCHOOL CHANGE

Improving education is a key priority for governments around the world. While many suggestions on how best to achieve this are currently under debate, years of academic research have already revealed more about how to encourage change than is sometimes assumed. This volume brings together for the first time some of the most significant work of Karen Seashore Louis, one of the foremost thinkers and researchers in the field. *Organizing for School Change* presents a unique variety of research-based results from studies conducted over the past 25 years. What emerges is not a simple blueprint for change, but a realistic picture of what needs to be done if we want to make schools better.

The book is organized into the following four sections, each of which has a different specific emphasis:

- The course of change: what we know about how to enact it.
- The central role of teachers as both innovators and keepers of a school's culture.
- How schools function as organizations, and the organizational characteristics that need to be addressed as part of effective and lasting change.
- The gap between research and practice, and what needs to be addressed in order for effective policies to be developed and put into practice.

Drawing on a wide and comprehensive list of sources, the ideas brought together in this collection will prove invaluable and insightful reading for practitioners of school change and academic researchers alike. Pulling together the themes that are threaded throughout Karen Seashore Louis' work will stimulate both newcomers and veterans of the field of school change and improvement to consider research and craft in new ways.

Karen Seashore Louis is the Rodney S. Wallace Professor of Teaching and Learning, Department of Educational Policy and Administration, at the University of Minnesota. She has more than 30 years' experience of studying school improvement.

CONTEXTS OF LEARNING
Classrooms, Schools and Society

Managing Editors:

Bert Creemers, *Faculty of Psychology, Education and Sociology, University of Groningen, The Netherlands.*
David Reynolds, *School of Education, University of Exeter, Exeter, UK.*
Janet Chrispeels, *Graduate School of Education, University of California, Santa Barbara, USA.*

ORGANIZING FOR SCHOOL CHANGE

Karen Seashore Louis

Routledge
Taylor & Francis Group

LONDON AND NEW YORK

First published 2006 by Routledge
2 Park Square, Milton Park, Abingdon, Oxon OX14 4RN.

Simultaneously published in the USA and Canada
by Routledge
29 West 35th Street, New York, NY 10001

Routledge is an imprint of the Taylor & Francis Group

Typeset in Bembo by Bookcraft Ltd, Stroud, Gloucestershire
Printed and bound in Great Britain by Biddles Ltd, King's Lynn, Norfolk

British Library Cataloguing in Publication Data
A catalogue record for this book is available from the British Library

Library of Congress Cataloging in Publication Data
Louis, Karen Seashore.
  Organizing for school change / Karen Seashore Louis.
    p. cm.
  Includes bibliographical references and index.
    1. School improvement programs–United States–Case studies. 2. Educational
    change–United States–Case studies. I. Title.

LB2822.82.L69 2006
371.2'00973–dc22   2005013138

ISBN10: 0-415-36226-1
ISBN13: 978-0-415-36226-19

This book is dedicated to my daughters, Margit and Erica, who were still at home when much of this work was being conducted but who rarely complained when Mom was busy writing, and to my husband, Dan, whose keen editorial eye and slashing red pen have consistently improved my prose.

Contents

Illustrations

Tables

Acknowledgements

The following chapters are reproduced with the permission of the Taylor & Francis Group (www.tandf.co.uk/journals):

- Chapter 5   Louis, K.S. (1994) "Beyond 'managed change': Rethinking how schools improve." *Journal of School Effectiveness and School Improvement* 5: 1–22.
- Chapter 8   Louis, K.S. (1998) "Effects of teacher quality of work life in secondary schools on commitment and sense of efficacy." *Journal of School Effectiveness and School Improvement* 9(1): 1–27.
- Chapter 13   Detert, J., K.S. Louis, and R. Schroeder (2001) "A culture framework for education: defining quality values for US high schools." *Journal of School Effectiveness and School Improvement* 12(2): 183–212.

The following chapter is reproduced with the permission of Blackwell Publishing Ltd:

- Chapter 1   Louis, K.S. and R.A. Dentler (1988) "Knowledge use and school improvement." *Curriculum Inquiry* 18: 32–62.

The following chapter is reproduced with the permission of Uitgeverij Zwijsen b.v:

- Chapter 2   Louis, K.S. (1986) "Permanent innovations: Theoretical and administrative issues in institutionalizing change." In J. Voogt and A. Reints (eds), *Naar beter onderwijs*: 128–43. Tilburg: Zwijsen.

The following chapters are reproduced with the permission of Teachers College Press:

- Chapter 3   Louis, K.S. and M.B. Miles (1990) "Planning improvement efforts." In *Improving the Urban High School: What Works and Why*. New York: Teachers College Press.
- Chapter 7   Louis, K.S. and B. Smith (1990) "Cultivating teacher engagement: Breaking the iron law of social class." In F. Newmann (ed.), *Student Engagement and Achievement in American Secondary Schools*: 119–52. New York: Teachers College Press.

The following chapter is reproduced with the permission of Corwin Press:

- Chapter 4   Louis, K.S. and J.A. King (1993) "Reforming schools: Does the myth of Sisyphus apply?" In J. Murphy and P. Hallinger (eds), *Restructuring Schools: Learning from On-going Efforts*: 216–50. Newbury Park, CA: Corwin.

The following chapter is reproduced with the permission of The University of Chicago Press:
- Chapter 9   Louis, K.S. and H. Marks (1998) "Does professional community affect the classroom? Teacher work and student work in restructuring schools." *American Journal of Education* 106(4): 532–75.

The following chapters are reproduced with the permission of Elsevier:
- Chapter 11   Wahlstrom, K. and K.S. Louis (1993) "Adoption revisited: Decision making and school district policy." In S. Bacharach and R. Ogawa (eds), *Advances in Research and Theories of School Management and Educational Policy, Vol. 1*: 61–119. Greenwich, CT: JAI Press.
- Chapter 15   Louis, K.S. and R.G. Corwin (1982) "Policy research in a policy vacuum." In *Sociology of Education and Socialization Research, Vol. 3: Policy Research*: 121–49. Greenwich, CT: JAI Press.

The following chapter is reproduced with the permission of Transaction Press:
- Chapter 16   Louis, K.S. (1995) "Improving urban and disadvantaged schools: Dissemination and utilization perspectives." *Knowledge and Policy* 13: 287–304.

The following chapter is reproduced with the permission of Springer Science and Business Media:
- Chapter 17   Louis, K.S. (1998) "Reconnecting knowledge utilization and school improvement: Two steps forward, one step back." In A. Hargreaves, D. Hopkins, M. Fullan, and A. Lieberman (eds), *International Handbook of Educational Change*: 1074–95. Dordrecht: Kluwer.

Preface

In all English-speaking nations, and in other countries too, we live in a world of accelerating and intensifying educational reform. Economic competitiveness, international comparisons in educational test results, and parents' growing concern for their children's futures feed and fuel political senses of urgency and panic about how to raise educational standards, cut educational costs, or do both at the same time within single election terms. The modern result is successive waves of, and sometimes ideological and political wars over, top-down educational reform initiatives and directions. Some of these reforms have benefited schools and students to greater or lesser degrees, but cumulatively their impact on the educators responsible for implementing them has been to subject them to what management expert Eric Abrahamson (2004: 2–3) terms *repetitive change syndrome*, which has two components:

- *Initiative overload*: "the tendency of organizations to launch more change initiatives than anyone could ever reasonably handle."
- *Change-related chaos*: "the continuous state of upheaval that results when so many waves of initiatives have evolved through the organization that hardly anyone knows which change they're implementing or why."

The consequence is what Seymour Sarason (1990) calls "the predictable failure of educational reform."

It is clear that most reformers just do not understand the reformed, or the political and organizational realities of the work that the reforms disturb. Yet it is not as if this failure of reformers to improve teaching and learning is a recent affliction. In other periods and times, the tone of reformers may sometimes have been softer, and their political intentions may not always have been quite so suspect, but there is no Golden Age of successful and sustained educational change to which we can or should return.

The 1960s and 1970s witnessed the proliferation of many innovation movements and projects across the world, but the dissemination was uneven and few of the projects ever fully spread. In the 1980s, and in some places into the 1990s, efforts to focus on the school as the center of change, by altering the structures and cultures of teachers' work, succeeded where leadership was strong, resources were abundant, and teachers' capacity for improvement was sufficiently high. But success in spreading improvement beyond a few such centers of promise in particular schools or districts to places where teachers were less qualified, leadership was weak or resources were in short supply, was less impressive. Across the years, through different historical periods of reform, most educational change efforts have either been unsuccessful, or their successes have been localized or short-lived.

The reason for this ultimate tragedy of change in education has best been captured by the educational change field's most widely known theorist, Michael Fullan. Over the years, Fullan has identified and communicated many important lessons about change that have deeply affected the world of practice. However, the insights and strategic directions for which Fullan is famous would not be possible or credible without the existence of an extensive body of rigorous research on educational change, on which his and others' syntheses draw.

Foremost among the researchers who have produced this evidence base for the field of educational change is Karen Seashore Louis. Over a quarter-century, working alone and in collaboration with a range of research partners, Louis has created a prodigious body of quantitative and qualitative research on educational change in elementary, middle, and high schools that has marked her out as a leading thinker and front-line researcher in this distinguished field. Working at all levels of policy development and implementation, and (with her Swedish ancestry and as a speaker of Dutch) outside her native USA as well as within it, Louis' work makes a profound contribution to the knowledge base of educational change and school improvement that stretches across time and space.

This long overdue book brings together some of Karen Seashore Louis' most important work, for the very first time in a single place. It is work that is always empirically solid and often strategically inspired. With her background and training in organizational studies, Louis fully understands and persistently communicates how reform efforts impact on schools and school systems as complex organizations, and how these organizations and the reform processes meant to change them can be redesigned to create better learning and higher standards of achievement for the students they ultimately serve.

The work of Louis' that has been collected in this book addresses six key areas of educational change: knowledge utilization, planning and implementation, organizational learning and development, collaboration and community, teacher commitment and capacity, and overall sustainability.

Contemporary improvements and reform efforts pay increasing (but not politically consistent) attention to the evidence-base for intended reforms, and to ways in which teachers might and should make use of evidence-based practices (Hargreaves and Giles, in press). The historical precursor to this movement is the less fashionably labeled field of "knowledge utilization". In her earlier chapters especially, Louis' foundational research in this area demonstrates how people do not adopt or reject research knowledge in a technical or rational way based on the general dependability of the evidence. Rather, knowledge is a social process, shared and distributed among communities whose perceived practicality of the evidence, credibility of sources, impact on opinion leaders, and fit with current norms of work all influence how and whether research-based practice will ever be adopted in the ways their developers wanted.

The planning and implementation of education change efforts, Louis shows, is equally imprecise and non-rational. Successful planning, her research reveals, is flexible enough to respond to the complexity and uncertainty of organizations and the contexts that surround them. Successful planning is evolutionary, not linear; improvisational rather than pre-fixed or locked-in. In a world of prescribed programs, and overconfident top-down reform, Louis' encouragement for reformers to think "beyond managed change" remains timelessly important.

In opposition to purportedly teacher-proof processes of top-down change, Louis takes the research on organizational learning and adaptation to ask "how can we get knowledgeable, well-educated, professional people to cooperatively obtain, share, and act on information effectively in increasingly uncertain settings" (Chapter 6). Her answer is to be found in her work on professional communities in the mid-1990s, which set the early foundation for another current movement to develop schools as professional learning communities. The structures, cultures, and leadership of schools that work as professional communities, she shows, enable outsider and insider knowledge of effective practices to be accessed, shared, cross-fertilized, and adapted in ways that lead to improved quality of teaching and learning.

Collaboration is a central component of professional communities, and Louis pays close attention to it, especially in her research on teaming and team-building. Shared values, a focus on student learning, transparency of practice, and reflective dialogue to evaluate it are essential elements of effective professional collaboration, as her research clearly demonstrates.

No reform will ever be effective unless the teacher can do or learn to do what the reform requires. Louis' research therefore points to important connections in the relationship between student achievement, student engagement, and teacher engagement. Part of this engagement, in turn, depends on the quality of work life that teachers experience. Once again, on the basis of her evidence, Louis appeals to reformers who want to raise student achievement by asking them to also attend to the quality of the work life of teachers who are responsible for bringing about these improvements. Reform designs and implementation processes that respect teachers, opportunities to participate in improvement efforts, experience of stimulating professional interaction, helpful feedback about performance, and having sufficient resources are among some of the key factors behind the professional engagement that will ultimately lead to sustainable school improvement.

Sustainability is one of Louis' remaining key themes. Few reforms are sustainable in the deep environmental sense (Hargreaves and Fink 2006). They do not last, they do not spread, and while they benefit some schools this is often at the cost of other schools around them. Louis' early work on "permanent innovation" gives some warning signs about the threats to sustainability – especially excessive or ill-considered turnovers in school leadership.

In the early years of the twenty-first century, America epitomizes arrogance and over-confidence in war (Johnson 2004) and arrogance and overconfidence in educational reform (Hargreaves and Fink 2006). It is not entirely alone in either domain, but in other parts of the world there is a realization that just as political overconfidence cannot secure the long peace that follows a deceptively swift war, so can overconfident, heavy-handed reform initiatives fail to secure lasting improvement in real learning after initial, then quickly plateauing surges in superficially tested performance. Other nations and organizations are therefore beginning to combine the rightful sense of political commitment and urgency to improve public education, with a recognition that the means for achieving this must address and include the professionals responsible for delivering the results, along with the complex organizational realities in which they must do their work.

The extensive evidence base of Louis' long-lasting work reminds us that organizational change is not simple, but neither is it ineffable. Organizations can be made to work for improvement, not against it, but for that to happen we must work respectfully with the very organizations that themselves need to change. Students matter, people matter, organizations matter. Their undeniable agency can be harnessed to bring about the improvement we need, or that agency will perversely and persistently defeat all change efforts that ignore it. Learning is not just the goal of change, but also its soul and its spirit. This is the essential message of Louis' book and also of her impressive research legacy.

Andy Hargreaves,
Boston, August 2005

References

Abrahamson, E. (2004) *Change without Pain: How Managers can Overcome Initiative Overload, Organizational Chaos, and Employee Burnout*. Boston, MA: Harvard Business Schools Publishing.

Hargreaves, A. and D. Fink (2006) *Sustainable Leadership*. San Francisco: Jossey Bass.

Hargreaves, A. and C. Giles (in press) "The sustainability of innovative schools as learning organizations and professional learning communities during standardized reform." *Educational Administration Quarterly*.

Johnson, D. (2004) *Overconfidence and War*. Cambridge, MA: Harvard University Press.

Sarason, S. (1990) *The Predictable Failure of Educational Reform*. San Francisco: Jossey Bass.

Foreword

In this impressive book, Karen Seashore Louis bridges two of the yawning gaps in educational reform.

The first is the gap between the desire to carry out reforms and the capacity to put them into lasting practice. The second is the gap between the vast amount of valuable academic research on this topic, and the very limited amount of time that busy educational practitioners have to learn the lessons of this research.

Policy-makers on both sides of the Atlantic will find this book an essential guide to the distilled academic wisdom on how to improve schools.

The unique quality of this book is that Karen applies her rigorous approach as an organizational sociologist to the problem of applying the reforms that she espouses as a passionate educationist. She does not waste time repeating the many, many bright ideas for school reform that have emerged since the 1970s. She focuses on the questions about how to implant them effectively in schools, and how to ensure that they take root and continue to flower perennially in those institutions.

Several of the most impressive chapters are drawn from papers or articles she has published since the mid-1980s. But these chapters are in no way dated. They acknowledge that Karen and her co-contributors have already found some of the answers, that some of the wheels do not need to be re-invented.

The retrospective mode also enables us to witness how Karen's thoughts and perceptions have developed as she helped to assemble the building blocks that go towards a secure foundation for lasting educational reform.

She does not claim to have found all the answers yet. But she rules out simplistic notions, for example, that the key just lies either in individual teachers, or in schools only, or in central directions from the state. She knows that all these elements have to be included in a successful strategy.

Most important of all, she is convincing in her belief that a successful strategy is possible. One of her chapters is entitled "Reforming Schools: Does the Myth of Sisyphus apply?". She believes that, for educationists, it can indeed be only a myth. Reformers are not necessarily doomed eternally to struggle to push the boulder of reform up the steep sides of the canyon of institutional resistance. They can get over the top and onto the plateau of real and lasting school improvement.

Kathryn A. Riley,
Institute of Education,
London, November 2004

Section I
The Process of Change and Innovation

An unintended consequence of compiling a book from my more than 25 years of research and publication on education and schools is the opportunity for overview and reflection. The process of parceling my work into four sections and arranging them in chronological order revealed themes that I had somehow been oblivious to.

My interest in school improvement developed rather gradually, and actually came after my self-identification as an organizational sociologist. My doctoral dissertation, which was published in 1979 (*Bureaucracy and the Dispersed Organization: The Educational Extension Agent Experiment*), was based on a study of the use of the ERIC (Education Resources Information Center) system by teachers, but I chose to emphasize the problem of developing innovative organizational units to accomplish new goals rather than focusing on school change. At that time I planned to move into medical sociology, where I figured the prestige and the ability to raise funds would be greater than in education. I quickly discovered, however, that interviewing doctors and studying clinics was much less interesting to me than working with teachers and schools. As I moved, very early in my career, from an academic teaching position into a policy research institute, I became a member of a large team studying "comprehensive change" in rural schools. It was one of the most exciting experiences of my career, and resulted in a life-long collaboration with Sheila

Rosenblum, as well as a book and several articles. Hooked on school improvement by the late 1970s, I did not turn back.

My focus on school improvement has consistently drawn on theories from the social sciences to analyze data gathered in my studies. One of these relates to the sociology of knowledge. The first chapter in this section, "Knowledge Use and School Improvement," emerged from research conducted with Bob Dentler in the early 1980s, and foreshadows a theme that has become even more apparent in the last decade. How knowledge and information contribute to educational change appears in my later writing on leadership and school improvement (Chapter 5, "Beyond 'Managed Change'"), and even more so in my interest in applying organizational learning theory to school improvement theories (Chapter 6, "Organizational Learning and High-performance Learning Communities").

From the beginning of my career I have been more influenced by the organizational writing of James March, and later Karl Weick, than rational decision theorists or structural sociologists. My empirical observations of schools (all of my research has included both interviews and survey methods) strongly suggest that, while teachers and administrators try to "do the right thing," they are often deeply affected by factors that either interfere with or prevent optimizing decisions. The process of change and the resulting incremental decisions are thus central to an understanding of how schools improve.

These assumptions are implicit in Chapter 1, but are more fully developed in Chapter 2 ("Permanent Innovations"), where I discuss a problem that still causes policy-makers and administrators to tear their hair out: the tendency for new practices to disappear as quickly as they are adopted. When this chapter was written in the mid-1980s we knew, from the influential Rand Change Agent Studies, that "mutual adaptation" between a planned innovation and the exigencies and preferences of a specific adopting school eroded the potency of school change efforts. This observation was complemented by a large national study I had just completed that looked at adoption and institutionalization of new programs (the RDU study, referred to in Chapter 15). As part of that study, I became convinced that, in order to understand the problem of disappearing innovations, we needed to bring in organizational theories that help us to understand the positive outcomes that are often associated with behavior that appears, on the surface, non-rational or even deliberately opposed to the reform policies that provide the funding and opportunities for local change. My position then and now is that there are inherent tensions in the intersection of policy intent and local practice that cannot be overcome solely with better professional development, more organized incentives, or better models of practice.

The argument that we need to modify rational change models to correspond to practice rather than constraining practice so that it conforms to rational models is particularly evident in Chapter 3 ("Planning Improvement Efforts"), which is taken from the urban high-school research that I conducted with Matt Miles. This chapter, based on both case studies and survey data from urban high schools, argues that we need to turn planning models on their head. We observed that effective planning was often only marginally goal directed – or at least that the goals of improvement shifted so regularly over time that planning had to be evolutionary rather than a rigid blueprint for action. Michael Fullan, drawing on our work, has given this perspective pungency by calling it the "ready, fire, aim" change force.

Social scientists have long debated the value of theories that emphasize radical change (paradigm shifts) versus incremental change (reflective practice). Most studies of school improvement in the 1970s and 1980s emphasized small-scale changes that had little impact outside of the classroom. While I have conducted some of these studies, my work has always addressed the problem of larger-scale school improvement as well. The rural comprehensive change study that I encountered at the beginning of my career as an educational researcher introduced me to the idea of "changing everything at once" rather than having teachers improve through gradual shifts in practice. This emphasis on the whole-school change process continued through the work that I have carried out with data collected as part of the Wisconsin Center for the Organization and Restructuring of Schools. The Wisconsin studies led directly to the framework that I propose in Chapter 6, where I lay out a model that brings together variables that, over the course of my research on large-scale change, have had the greatest impact on improving student learning (see Chapter 9 for another analytic effort emerging from this work).

While I believe that comprehensive change is possible and sometimes desirable, I have often found it necessary to challenge policies that assume that novel ideas can be easily introduced and sustained. As the title implies, Chapter 4 ("Professional Cultures in Reforming Schools: Does the Myth of Sisyphus Apply?") addresses this aspect of my work directly. The chapter borrows from my dissertation's theory about "the liabilities of newness," but adds empirical information about how radical educational innovation, even when it is well supported, also encounters powerful forces that press toward the status quo. Chapter 4's theoretical perspective owes a great deal to "new institutionalism" scholars such as John Meyer, who argue that radical change can only be successful when external social pressures correspond to the goals and means of change. However, it combines this perspective with micro-level change theories, looking at how decisions that appear sound and conditions that look manageable on the surface can, when combined, result in a tangle of expectations that lead back to the status quo. The failure of the two schools in this chapter to sustain radical change is not attributable to lack of competence, flawed design, or to resistance to "difference," but to cumulating conditions that can thwart great expectations.

In addition to the role of knowledge and the quasi-rationality of the change process, a third theme runs through the chapters in this section: the importance of interpersonal influence in understanding change. Rather than thinking about change as an individual endeavor, I have consistently opted for theoretical frameworks that emphasize the importance of social interaction. This perspective appears in Chapter 1, where the idea of "social processing" of information is introduced as a major factor affecting whether change will take place, returns in Chapters 3 and 5, where the role of the school leaders in "greasing the wheels" of social interaction and exchange of new ideas is emphasized, and continues in Chapter 6, in which the importance of social structures that support informal discussions about change are central to the model presented. The importance of social relations among teachers and administrators is central to my ever-evolving theories about how change happens, and also feeds other foci of my work. Not surprisingly, this theme applies also to Section II, where I explore the nature of teachers' work.

A final theme, emerging in the late 1980s, concerns leadership in change. I fell into leadership studies rather than pursuing them. In the mid-1980s, when my colleagues and I began a study of urban high schools, we had no intention of focusing on principals, except as the logical respondents to our survey of urban-school efforts to implement change programs based on "effective schools" models. When we began to analyze the case study data, however, the importance of principals became apparent and the book that finally emerged placed a great deal of emphasis on the influence that they had over the change process. While I still consider myself to be a reluctant expert on leadership, and never design my own studies to look at leadership per se, I have come to see the importance of examining leadership as a distinct topic. My increasing involvement with colleagues in the University Council for Educational Administration, and the Educational Administration Division of the American Educational Research Association influenced my move in this direction, but much of my increasing interest was data-driven: leadership was the elephant in the school change closet that could not be ignored. This theme is reflected in Chapters 3, 5 and 6.

Before this brief introduction is concluded, if you read further in this book you cannot help but notice that almost every empirical chapter is co-authored. In addition to preferring to work with both qualitative and quantitative data simultaneously, I hate working alone. My best ideas have always come when I am talking to a colleague about a theory, or when we are debating an interpretation of some tidbit of data. Thus, this entire volume should be dedicated to my friends and collaborators over the years, each of whose fingerprints are evident in these chapters.

1

Knowledge Use and School Improvement

Introduction

Elementary and secondary education has recently become the object of intense and widespread attention in the United States of America. Despite calls for "leadership" at the school level, the shape of the reform movement is increasingly determined by the state. We suggest that state-directed reform efforts often ignore the important contribution of more school-focused policies to encourage and support improvement efforts in the school and classroom. In this article we summarize data from a study of the dissemination and use of educational knowledge in the USA to support the contention that there are a variety of paths leading to the goal of improved education. In our conclusion we make recommendations about the role for school-focused knowledge-use strategies.

Reform and School Improvement

Recent public debates have often been couched in terms of major reform initiatives. The recommended policy aim include all public schools in the nation or in one state and, in addition, the proposals are most often mandatory and complex, encompassing a "bundle of innovations" from the perspective of the system that is to be changed (van den Berg and Vandenberghe 1984). In the United States, the reform movement has emphasized new standards for both educational inputs (curriculum offerings, length of the school day and year, teacher qualifications) and outputs (competencies at various levels and graduation requirements), and has most often focused singularly on the role of the teacher. A recent major report from the Carnegie Forum (1986) centers on ways to attract more talented teachers to the profession, to change preservice or inservice education, and to provide different kinds of incentives and supports to motivate higher teacher performance.

The desire to reform the educational system in response to high levels of public concern is not surprising. However, research on the implementation of large-scale educational reforms suggests that they rarely achieve the many subgoals that they aspire to, and seldom serve as a stimulus for measurable changes at the societal level (UNESCO 1965; Van den Berg and Vandenberghe 1984). There are several reasons for this, which may be deduced from research on program and policy implementation. On a relatively mechanistic level, there is plenty of opportunity for "slippage" in the implementation of a major reform as it passes through the administrative levels between a central government agency and a school or classroom (Berman 1978; Yin et al. 1979). Van den Berg and Vandenberghe (1984) argue that the sheer complexity of major reforms makes them likely to suffer from administrative implementation problems. This is increasingly the case the longer the period of implementation (Louis 1987). Louis also argues that virtually all case studies of school improvement efforts show that unpredictable "normal crises," such as strikes, superintendent or principal turnover, or the introduction of new and competing change programs from outside of the school can both sidetrack successful programs and bolster lagging efforts.

In addition, centrally initiated educational reforms often represent symbolic aspirations rather than realistic programs for change (Dentler 1984; Louis and Corwin 1984). As Deal (1984: 59) puts it, "research, policies and guidelines may not be as adequate or powerful as we would like to believe." Cohn and Distefano (1984) use case materials to demonstrate that the major recommendations of the United States "Nation at Risk" report (United States Department of Education 1983) have little relevance to the underlying problems of a district that they studied. They pessimistically conclude, however, that the poor fit will be overlooked and that "In all probability the commission's ill-fitting recommendations will be applied. ... The results will either be the blocking of legitimate progress, or the creation of new and more serious problems" (Cohn and Distefano 1984: 219). The potential negative impacts of imposing symbolic input and output goals on schools is also documented by Alexander and Pallas (1985) and McDill et al. (1985).

Criticisms based on an institutional analysis of the implementation process are supported both by substantial empirical data from a variety of settings in the United States (Berman 1981) and by less well-documented evidence from other countries (Louis 1986). The implication is that top-down reform policies rarely match the varied and often unpredictable contexts in which they must be applied. If this is the case it is appropriate to think about alternative models for designing school improvement programs.

The School-focused Knowledge Use Alternative

Evidence suggests that leaving the responsibility for improving schools totally in the hands of local educators is not a viable alternative to the reform paradigm. Sarason (1971) argues that the culture of schools is inherently conservative and an unlikely source for ideas that will transform education. Others (Huberman 1983; Hargreaves 1984) demonstrate that there are many pressures on teachers, in addition to learned modes of interaction and thinking, that prevent them from integrating theory and practice effectively. Furthermore, when left to their own devices, school staffs often choose innovations of low quality (Nelson and Sieber 1976). Mann (1978), commenting on the inappropriateness of a reform/implementation paradigm, remarked that educators seem doomed to recreating the wheel in perpetuity.

We disagree, finding that there are middle roads between top-down paths of educational renewal and those which are dominated by local practitioners. One alternative, the school-focused knowledge use strategy, is premised on two elements. First, the school is assumed to be the most appropriate unit of change. This assumption may be distinguished from typical recent reform legislation, which attempts to increase uniformity within districts or states by introducing identical changes in all schools, and a bottom-up strategy which focuses on meeting the needs and improving the performance of individual teachers. Second, within a school-focused approach, the strategy for inducing change is based in the accumulating dissemination and knowledge use studies in education (Mort 1964; Carlson 1965; Sieber et al. 1972; Louis et al. 1981; Crandall et al., 1983). A school improvement strategy based on dissemination and knowledge use is conditioned by research about the circumstances under which educators at policy and practice levels will attend to and act on new information that is made available to them from the outside. Rather than relying on blunt and often inappropriate (although well-meaning) sanctions or administrative mechanisms for creating widespread change, a knowledge use strategy assumes that there are many positive incentives for educators to change and improve the ways in which they do things (Sieber 1981). As a consequence, genuine improvement is possible from below, but instead of simply hoping that schools will resonate to "good" ideas, the strategy is premised on the assumption that improvement is more likely to occur if they are provided with outside assistance and support at a modest level.

Proponents of a knowledge use strategy also assume that knowledge has certain characteristics that make it more or less likely to be used, irrespective of the scientific basis or validity of the ideas that are presented (Rogers and Shoemaker 1972; Lindblom and Cohen 1979); and that knowledge is not an objective "thing" to be used in the way that we use a tool to achieve a clear and fixed purpose, but a set of cognitive understandings that are changed and developed during the process of applying them (Weiss 1979). Because knowledge use is inevitably a social process in educational settings, the opportunities for spread and impact of new ideas beyond an original recipient are substantial, and diffusion will increase the impact that a single intervention can make upon practice (Rogers and Shoemaker 1972).

In summary, the main elements of a knowledge use model for school improvement involve:

- capitalizing on known or identifiable incentives for change;
- providing information or knowledge that has characteristics that make it "usable" by the relevant practitioners;
- creating or supporting opportunities to create shared understandings of how new ideas could help to improve local practice; and
- stimulating increased diffusion of new ideas within and between educational agencies.

Again, a major feature of this model is that it is neither "top down" nor "bottom up," but a mixture of the two. It is school-focused in the sense that local conditions within specific schools are expected to influence the course of knowledge use and improvement in all the phases of change.

The Knowledge Use Study

These elements of a knowledge use model were explored in a three-year study of activities that were undertaken in Regional Educational Laboratories and State Education Agencies (SEAs) in the United States. The results of this study have been extensively reported elsewhere (Louis *et al.* 1984), and this article will summarize some of the main findings relevant to the framework presented above.

The study's objectives were to develop a method that would permit increased understanding of the dynamic processes of the flow and use of knowledge among educators, to study the extent of knowledge diffusion, and to explore the degree to which different dissemination strategies resulted in more or less diffusion and use of knowledge beyond the initial recipient. Although the study looked at knowledge use in general, the primary criterion for assessing the impact of knowledge was the degree to which it fed into activities and plans that would result in changes and improvement in schools.

These objectives implied several design features. First, it was necessary to arrange for flexible data collection so that the nature of individual activities and their potential effects could be understood. Second, a component of more broadly representative, standardized data collection was needed in order to compare the amount and scope of effects across events and strategies.

Some of these goals might have been better addressed by several separate studies, but the effective use of available resources demanded a single study. A new approach, which we have called the "tracer case study," was therefore developed to take advantage of the simultaneity of several components of the study. There were three basic features to this design (given here in the order in which they were carried out).

1. *Systematic sampling* of a limited number of dissemination events. A set of twelve "events" or instances in which a laboratory or SEA attempted to disseminate information for the purposes of educational improvement were selected from a universe

of all of the activities that the eight laboratories and nine SEAs in our study nominated as having some potential for significant impacts on practice or policy. The criteria for choosing the events were detailed (see Louis *et al.* 1984: 22–4), but the sample was designed to maximize variation on (a) the degree to which information was provided directly to the school-based individuals who were expected to use it, versus indirectly, where school personnel were reached through some intermediary such as a SEA; and (b) the emphasis in the change effort on tailoring information to local contexts.[1] Some of the events were:

- *Skills Inventory*: A laboratory provided information about a program that could be valuable in helping local school districts to meet a new state requirement for curriculum articulation and individualization to an SEA Associate Superintendent. A number of district superintendents attended workshops or visited the laboratory, and distributed information to their principals.
- *Effective Schools:* A laboratory developed a program to train individual schools in applying concepts from the effective schools literature. A number of schools in several states volunteered to participate in training by laboratory personnel over a two-year period. We traced the impact in two schools.
- *Teaching Writing:* A laboratory developed a research-based review of the literature on oral and written communication organized around questions solicited from teachers. The distribution of the book was traced through a regional conference which featured the volume. The conference was attended by SEA staff and some local school district staff who were expected to design strategies for further distribution.

2. *Field interviews* with the providers of information, and primary (initial) recipients and secondary recipients (those to whom initial recipients passed the information). Site visits were conducted by two senior researchers who were familiar with the organizational and educational context in which the "event" took place. Extensive interviews, using the standardized case method (Yin 1984), were conducted with between ten and twenty people. Every effort was made to follow the "best leads" in terms of finding utilization and impact of knowledge. Interviews were unstructured, permitting respondents to define issues in their own terms.

3. *Tracer surveys* of a sample of the universe of recipients. A two-stage telephone survey of primary and secondary recipients was conducted in each of the twelve cases. The survey gathered standardized data on patterns of knowledge use and other outcomes. The sample was generated by asking the laboratory or SEA to provide a list of all people who received the information directly from them. A random sample of twenty people (or the universe, where fewer than twenty were nominated) was selected for the first wave of interviews. Primary recipients provided us with lists of names of individuals that they had given the information to, and the union of these lists for each case defined a population from which a second random sample of secondary recipients was drawn. A total of 620 people were sampled, and 566 interviews were completed. Response rates were not significantly different between cases.

This methodology has advantages and limitations. It enabled us to tie our study to real information and to settings with which we became very familiar through our case work, while developing a sample of potential users that was far larger and more diverse than is typically encountered in a comparative case study. However, our relatively large sample of respondents still represents a small number of preselected stimuli. There are, therefore, some limitations on the conclusions that we can draw about the role of information in schools and other educational agencies. In the end, the study consists of twelve cases that combine qualitative and quantitative data collection techniques in the multisite/multimethod tradition (Smith and Louis 1982). We must emphasize that the analysis on which this chapter is based gives equal weight to qualitative and survey data. In this chapter we illustrate our arguments primarily with survey findings because of the difficulty of presenting a lot of compelling qualitative findings in a short paper. Case material will be used illustratively.

Measures of Use and Impact

Survey questions were used to obtain three scales relating to knowledge use. First, salience was measured by asking the degree to which respondents actually remembered receiving information, and the content of its message. Even with extensive probing by the interviewers, 22 per cent of the respondents did not remember getting any information, and an additional 24 per cent indicated that they had not used it in any way. Those who did not receive information were eliminated from all further analyses; those who claimed not to have used it were eliminated from analyses of use. Second, we assumed that use could take place either at the individual or organizational level and therefore developed indicators for each type. Nine items, measured on a four-point scale, were developed for personal use. Sample items include "(It) assist(ed) you in developing materials for your own use" and "(It) convince(d) you to stop doing something that you had been doing in your job." Seven organizational use items were included, such as "(It) help(ed) in initiating a new program policy or practice" and "(It) help(ed) in preparing a position or concept paper that could be used in the future." Scales were developed by adding items within the personal and organizational use scores.

A distinction was also made between personal and organizational level gains that could occur as a consequence of knowledge use. Twelve indicators of personal gains, measured on a four-point scale, were included in the survey. Sample items included: "An opportunity to improve your own professional skills," "Achieving greater control over activities in your agency," "Gaining support for ideas or plans (that) you already had," and "An improved chance for career advancement." Eight organizational gains, measured on a three-point scale, included items reflecting an increased ability to deliver services, improvements in staff morale, improved operating effectiveness, and agency reputation, among others. Gain scales were computed by counting the number of instances where the extreme positive score was indicated. The personal gain scale thus could range from zero to twelve, while the organizational gains score could range from zero to eight. In some analyses we use a summary "impact scale," computed by standardizing and adding the four gain scales.

Findings

User Incentives

A wide range of incentives for innovation in schools has been suggested by Sieber (1981). In this study we examined several that might be associated with individual internalized values, personality, or predisposition, and several others that might be characterized as extrinsic or external motivations that can be affected through organizational or policy decisions. Personal incentives (such as personal gains) included:

- *professional performance*, including such things as achieving greater efficiency in one's job, or gaining opportunities to try out new ideas;
- *increased influence or authority*, including achieving greater visibility in one's work or gaining opportunities for increased professional networks; and
- *material rewards*, including increased job security or career advancement.

Organizational incentives included:

- mandates from either the state or local level;
- pressures from colleagues to get and use information;
- general pressure in the work environment to "solve problems";
- negative previous experiences with knowledge use and innovation that create organizational disincentives; and
- organizational rewards for knowledge use, such as positive support from supervisors, or other career incentives for innovations.

An examination of the relationship between incentives and use or gain based on Pearson correlations and a canonical correlation indicates several key findings. To begin with, *both personal incentives and organizational incentives are strongly associated with gains and use* (can. corr. = 0.72 and 0.45). These coefficients may be interpreted as the strength of the association between the first principal component representing the incentives variables and the first one among all of the outcome measures. We may also conclude that *organizational incentives appear to be less potent than personal incentives in stimulating knowledge use*. To expand upon this point, the presence of mandates is correlated with organizational use of information at a very low level ($r = 0.09$, P >0.05), as compared with a desire to improve professional performance ($r = 0.37$, P <0.01). It is particularly important to note that the presence of organizational mandates and general pressures to "solve a problem" (conditions that clearly characterize the current status of most schools) are not strongly correlated with organizational improvements. Together these findings suggest that *external stimuli alone will have only limited impact in producing an openness to new ideas in educational settings*. Rather, knowledge use is most likely to occur when personal incentives are mobilized.

The canonical coefficients for individual outcome measures provide insights into which variables are contributing most to the overall relationship between the two sets of variables. The association is largely due to the effects of five incentives – improved professional performance, increased authority and influence, state or local mandates, general pressure in the work environment, and organizational rewards for knowledge use – and the personal gain impact measure. This leads to the conclusion that *personal gains tend to be maximized under a wide variety of types of incentives.* This was unexpected since we had hypothesized that personal incentives would lead to higher personal gain, while organizational incentives would lead to higher organizational gain. We interpret the finding, however, as additional support for the observation that it is difficult to achieve major organization-wide change with small or indirect stimuli (Berman and McLaughlin 1977; Louis *et al.* 1981).

If we examine some of the qualitative findings from the case studies, an understanding of these findings is increased. For example, of the three cases that had the highest reported impact on the survey respondents, two combined a strong mandate with a very high level of personal incentives. In both cases, the mandate was flexible enough that building-level participants could choose an emphasis within the program that seemed to "fit" them. The third high-impact case, an Effective Schools Program studied in a single building, did not have a mandate from outside the school. Teachers, however, reported strong pressure from the principal to participate in the training, and the training was viewed as a way of coping with a district mandated curriculum change.

In all these cases participation provided significant opportunities for professional growth and, for the schools and individuals involved, a chance to attack issues that they themselves were concerned about within the context of the mandate. Although educators were directed to participate, they decided what to do and how to do it. Thus, local and individual goals were blended with the external requirements.

Another case in which external pressures were high but personal incentives were low shows some of the reasons why new information may fail to gain attention. At the time of this study (1981–83), most school districts were under pressure to develop programs to use microcomputers in classroom and other activities. However, a booklet prepared to help schools develop a microcomputer program failed to have much impact among those who received it. Interviews in a number of the districts included in the microcomputer booklet case revealed that individuals who were assigned the responsibility for overseeing the introduction of microcomputers often did not see this activity as central to their job. Thus, the booklet tended to join a variety of other publications on their bookshelf, or to be circulated to others who felt a similarly limited sense of responsibility.

These cases illustrate some of the reasons why personal incentives are an essential supplement to external pressures for change. *If information is proffered in a situation where individual empowerment or significant professional development is promised, significantly greater personal incentives are mobilized.* In cases where these conditions did not exist, information was typically routed elsewhere with little or no explanation, or permanently filed. In cases with better results, participants were often deliberately selected to ensure that some personal motivations would be high. An equally important conclusion is that *mandates may stimulate strong personal incentives under certain conditions: namely that professional rewards are visible, concrete and personally meaningful.* It is these conditions that generate energy to cooperate, to listen to new ideas, and to create actual change rather than merely symbolic conformity.

Social Processing

But initial personal and organizational incentives such as those discussed above are not the only factors that account for use. Use implies action of some sort, and once information has been obtained, individuals and groups must digest it, comprehend it and decide what to do with it. As that set of actions unfolds, an initial incentive may be reinforced or undermined. Thus, if we hope to understand the potential for school improvement using a knowledge exchange model, we must examine local decision-making activities.

Theories of decision-making and organizational change have a venerable history in the social sciences. There are rational models (Katz and Kahn 1966), quasi-rational models (Anderson, 1983), and nonrational models (March and Olsen 1976). Common to all of the different models are two key notions. First, decision-making involves assessing and analysing whatever information happens to be available to the individual or group making the decision. Second, decision-making often occurs in a social context. Often it involves a group, but even when it does not the individual making the decision weighs the information and options against the demands and constraints of the social context.

Although social processing is common, it is not necessarily the norm in many work settings. For example, in organizations where professional autonomy is highly valued and a collegial climate is absent, information use may occur by individuals without any reference to others. Or, in a hierarchically structured organization, the top executive may frequently get information and make subsequent decisions without consulting with subordinates. *Assessment and social processing both involve further analysis of the information, and they transform information by customizing and personalizing it for local use.*

Our survey findings indicate that social processing occurs commonly in these knowledge exchange settings: 87 per cent of those who remembered getting information reported engaging in some social processing activities; 60 per cent said they were involved in both informal discussion and formal meetings to consider the information. It should be emphasized that these figures are probably higher than is typical in schools, because the nominated events addressed critical issues in education, and the providers frequently attempted to stimulate meetings to discuss the information. The reports of formal and informal discussions were combined to form a scale indicating the amount of social processing.

The influence of group social processing on use is also high. We asked people to indicate how important the meetings and discussions were in affecting the way they thought about the information. Nearly 40 per cent said the social interactions were "very important" in forming their assessments of the information; 48 per cent said they were "somewhat important"; and less than 12 per cent said they were "not very" or "not at all" important. In addition, when asked whether the meetings or discussions were influential in encouraging others to use the information, 81 per cent said that they were. Because we felt that respondents could more accurately assess the influence of social processing on their own patterns of use, this variable was used by itself in our analysis.

We expected that both the amount and influence of social processing would be associated with use and gains. A canonical correlation using the survey data strongly supports this hypothesis. Here we see that social processing appears to have a potent effect on the organizational use and gain variables as compared with personal incentives.

This indicates that they are important components of a knowledge-based improvement strategy: *unless new ideas are widely discussed in an agency or organization, it is unlikely that coordinated, measurable changes will take place.*

The case materials help to locate some of the mechanisms by which social processing occurs and affects use. All three of the "events" that had the highest impact had a built-in social process imposed either by the state or by the laboratory that was providing assistance. All three required participation by both administrators and teachers, and the collection and interpretation of data at the local level. Thus, local educators became involved in action research, which many regard as a good vehicle for motivating and empowering teachers (Hopkins 1985). All of the activities required formal meetings, the assignment of teacher groups to work on parts of the activities, and other structures that reinforced participation and discussion. Thus, we suggest that *mandates stimulate reform most effectively when they emphasize organizational processes that must be followed rather than particular inputs or outcomes. The result is to blend local and externally imposed goals in the context of knowledge exchange.* In addition, we found that social processing was more likely to occur when the relationship between the agency communicating the information and the recipient was characterized by some intensity. The issue of intensity will be discussed in more detail below. Here we will simply note that where information was accompanied by some personal assistance in interpreting its utility and applicability to the recipient's own context, it was more likely to motivate further discussions with colleagues. In other words, talk breeds more talk in schools.

In some low-impact cases, the group that was targeted to change involved only one or two people in an agency. This approach failed to generate a social mass at the local level that facilitated discussion and interaction, except in instances where the individual recipient was very highly motivated. Giving information to a single individual seemed to inhibit social processing irrespective of organizational status; librarians, superintendents, teachers, and specialists all tended to keep the information to themselves when they were the only recipients in their agency. And where information was extremely complex or abstract, local educators were often too impatient to spend a great deal of time working with it in group settings, or were reluctant to pass it on for fear that it would irritate colleagues. (This point will be returned to later.)

Taken together these findings suggest that *the process of interacting with colleagues about the information is a critical determinant of whether new information is used and that one of the major determinants of social processing is a sense of pressure from the outside.* Although collegial exchange may be satisfying in itself, most of the schools or other agencies in which we conducted interviews exhibited high levels of social processing primarily because they sought to achieve a goal that was defined from above. To give an example, the two cases that were top-ranked in terms of impact – Long Range Planning and Educational Renewal – were also highest in the amount of influence and social processing, and were stimulated by state-sponsored projects that mandated a planning process with high levels of representation and committee work. It should be recalled, however, that we did not attempt to study the full range of social and professional interactions in these agencies; rather, we looked only at how the information-use settings that we studied were similar to or different from what typically occurred in the school or agency.

How does social processing help educators to use information more effectively? First, it helps local educators to test the value of the information, in terms of its "fit" to the local setting. Often an assessment of "fit" began during the initial transmission of the information, and affected the probability that further consideration would occur. For example, an instance in which a laboratory provided research findings about the roles of principals in effective schools stimulated considerable initial discussion about the applicability of information initially developed for a rural state to a single, urban district. Second, social processing engages local educators in whatever adaptation or development activities are required. Through these activities additional incentives are created for use. In the event just described above, the effective schools findings that were provided were limited, but the staff used the materials to develop a questionnaire that was used as part of the program to strengthen the principal's role.

Perhaps the most important function of social processing is that it helps to build or affirm commitment to information use. Because it represents an investment by a group, it may stimulate increased attention on the part of individuals as to how it may improve their own situation. In addition, because it draws attention to the information, it enhances personal incentives, particularly those relating to increased visibility and influence in the organization. Social processing leads not only to increased impact among those who first come in contact with new ideas, but can also be a vehicle for further transmission. Since a knowledge-exchange strategy is based in part on the stimulation of secondary diffusion of ideas, we will now turn to this topic.

The Diffusion Dilemma
The survey and case materials shed light on the question of whether the knowledge reached practitioners who were in positions to make use of it for improvement. Two possible correlates of diffusion behavior were examined: the strategy used to transmit the information, and the personal characteristics of the recipients. Two different types of diffusion behaviors were defined: a five-point "brokering behavior" scale reflecting the level of initiative taken to pass on information, and a simple "amount of diffusion" or the total number of people to whom information was given.

Strategies and Diffusion
Three of the twelve events employed a direct diffusion strategy of giving the knowledge to the targeted users. In five cases, knowledge was diffused indirectly by sharing it with educators trained or situated to convey it to others. And in four cases, a mix of direct and indirect strategies was tried. The survey findings invite the inference that diffusion is greatest when an indirect strategy is used . This holds, however, only where steps were taken to guide the brokering behavior. The case described earlier in which individuals were haphazardly assigned to pass on a booklet about microcomputer applications shows how indirect approaches can collapse if poorly planned.

An important addendum to this finding is that diffusion behaviors tend to damp out as they move further from the initial source of communication. Analysis of variance was used to determine whether there was a difference in diffusion between those respondents who were nominated by a laboratory or SEA as initial recipients, and those who were located at later stages in the diffusion chain. Both diffusion behaviors showed a significant difference between the initial recipients and those who received it later in the diffusion chain, and the damping out persisted between the second-level recipients (those who received it from an initial recipient) and third-level recipients (those who received it from a second-level recipient).

Personal Characteristics and Diffusion

Many factors such as social status, education, cosmopolitanism, and exposure to communication channels have been shown to be associated with adoption of innovations and with effective opinion leadership (Rogers and Shoemaker 1972). However, less is known about what kinds of people make effective knowledge brokers (see Granovetter 1982). The planned change and knowledge-use literature contains proposals to improve communication networks (Miles 1978; Glaser et al. 1983) but does not reveal much about who should occupy what nodes. In this study we investigated two types of personal characteristics: professional status and incentives for knowledge use. The data yielded an association between the position of an educator in a crude status hierarchy of educational agencies, and his or her diffusion behavior. Teachers and school-based administrators have relatively low rates of diffusion behaviors while SEA staff have the highest levels on three of the four diffusion behaviors. The relationship between status and diffusion behavior is particularly pronounced in the case of amount of diffusion. Thus, if an increase in the rate of knowledge flowing within a system and between related systems is sought, it would probably be effective to start with high-status professionals in state agencies, research and development (R&D) laboratories, or universities. However, as we point out below, reaching the classroom from this level may be difficult.

On the other hand, there is evidence in our findings to suggest that neither individual nor organizational incentives are powerful factors in determining diffusion. A regression of the personal and organizational incentives variables on the two diffusion behaviors produced squared multiple correlations of only 0.10 to 0.05. While the equations are statistically significant, they have little theoretical or practical interest because the effects are so small.

Who Talks To Whom?

Since the goal of a school improvement program based on knowledge exchange is to get information into the hands of people who may play a key role in school improvement efforts, the direction that the information takes after the first recipient matters a great deal. Getting information into a setting where it could conceivably have an impact on classroom practice is also important and underscores the need to understand the "who talks to whom" question. Because of their size and complexity, tables based on the survey will not be presented here (see Louis et al. 1984).

Firstly, in this type of dissemination context, information tends to move down the educational hierarchy. People at lower levels are much less likely to transmit information to their superiors. Information often crosses organizational boundaries between agencies, moving from an organization that is more removed from the local school to one that is closer. Secondly, people outside of schools, particularly those located outside of school districts but also those in district offices, rarely send information directly to teachers, even when the information is intended for use in the classroom. Rather, teachers tend to be reached through intermediaries located within the schools (such as school-based specialists or administrators). Finally, principals, although they serve a central role in mediating communication within schools, are the least likely role group to engage in frequent communication behavior: they receive lots of information, but they rarely send it on – even to teachers. Thus, both case and survey findings indicate that *the educational hierarchy often functions to insulate teachers from outside information useful to their formal responsibilities. However, when teachers do get information, they are likely to share it with their peers.* Among those teachers who sent information on to someone else, two-thirds sent the information to one or more teacher colleagues.

These findings may also be linked to the earlier discussion of social processing. We noted that social processing tended to occur most frequently in cases where there was a strong stimulus from above. In the case of teachers, our findings indicate that such stimuli are not necessarily frequent. If teachers do not regularly receive information with positive pressures to use and discuss it, the opportunities for school-focused strategies for improvement are clearly limited.

Knowledge Properties

We found that in many instances the main reason information did not diffuse was because it was perceived to be inappropriate or not useful. Our study went beyond user assessment to examine the extent to which the form and content of the available knowledge in each of the twelve cases affected its impact and use. A measure of the *reality of knowledge* was created based on our ratings of six features of the materials used in the twelve cases:

1. *Craft legitimation.* Is there evidence of reality testing in the construction of the knowledge product? For example, were practitioners involved as consultants or active participants in development? Was the product extensively field tested and did feedback from this testing influence the final product?
2. *Compatibility.* Is the social context of prospective users, particularly in regard to their opportunities and incentives for action, incorporated into the knowledge product?
3. *Accessibility.* Is the knowledge product designed to be accessible to a person who does not already share the same assumptions or frame of reference?
4. *Observability/Imagery.* Is there opportunity for the prospective user to assess the knowledge in light of his or her own reality? For example, is there opportunity to see the ideas or practices at work in normal settings, or are there vivid descriptions of the ideas or practices at work?
5. *Adaptability.* Does the knowledge product encourage local adaptation, and was it specifically designed for local adaptability? (A low rating is given if the product assumes or requires fidelity to a particular model and all its component parts.)

6. *Inspiration.* Does the knowledge product have a strong inspirational thrust? Are ideal-istic-altruistic values an important component of the message?

All six components were independently rated on a 1 (low) to 4 (high) scale, by two or more members of the research team, each of whom was familiar with all of the cases and information materials from the study. For each of the cases the total possible score on the "reality" scale was 6 to 24. The two raters had few disagreements; differences were resolved through adjudication with a third staff researcher. Finally, ratings were reviewed for consensus by all staff who had familiarity with the knowledge on which the case was based. The scores for our twelve cases ranged from 7 to 23.

In addition, the research staff used similar procedures to rate each of the twelve cases on the dimension of *intensity of the dissemination process*. Included were indicators of:

- the frequency of contact between disseminators and users;
- the length of the change of event or project; and
- the degree of face-to-face communication between users and disseminators.

The scored intensity scale values ranged from 3 to 10 along a measure that could range from 3 to 12.

Other knowledge properties and process factors were also rated and scaled, but these two proved to be most indicative of what affects user impact. The reality scale correlated with the scale of impact ($r = 0.88$), and the process intensity scale correlated with impact ($r = 0.73$). A regression of impact on these two variables indicated a very strong associa-tion, and other variables did not add appreciably to the equation. The findings thus strongly support the idea that the impacts of knowledge are highest when the content has been shaped to fit the reality constructs and concerns of practitioners, and that when strong reality features are augmented with high intensity of interaction, impacts are further reinforced.

To give an example, the case of a laboratory-developed effective schools program, which had both the highest impact and reality scores, shows evidence of abundant reality testing during and after preparation. The training program had been tried out in a number of schools prior to its application in the site that we studied. Even then it was still considered a pilot program and the laboratory was continually modifying it in light of new training experience. The overall design was meant to be adapted to the charac-teristics and priorities of each site. The district in our tracer case study had just initiated a comprehensive redesign of its curricula and instructional management systems and requested special emphasis on this in the training. The developer also expected outcomes to vary across sites due to variations in local priorities. The knowledge presented was practical and highly motivating according to the teachers and administra-tors. But perhaps most important, it seemed to make good common sense. As the super-intendent said, "Even if there were no data ... how can you argue with time on task?"

The case of a well-researched book that attempted to answer real questions from classroom teachers about ways to improve oral and written communication skills also shows the importance of reality and intensity. The developers resisted suggestions that a guide to action be included because they believed that understanding should precede classroom changes, and although teachers helped to generate questions and a few reviewed drafts, the interplay between teachers' needs and ways of using information was deemed by them (and us) as relatively low. Although the book was made widely available to schools, it was passively distributed at this level. Where it was discussed in workshops, it tended to be covered in brief sessions where the main agenda was devoted to other items. The book thus received only average scores on the intensity indicators, and had an impact on teachers that was well below average despite consensus among our research staff that the quality of the ideas presented was very high.

These findings reinforce the measurement approaches taken toward incentives and social processing. They are not different in implications, let alone divergent; rather the reality scale extends the logic of incentives backward into the knowledge properties themselves, and the intensity scale tests how responsive users are to a process which assists them face-to-face over a reasonable length of time.

The Place Of School-focused Knowledge Strategies

A mandated or "top-down" approach to educational improvement presupposes implementation as a result of extrinsic rewards, such as increased financial aid or improved pay, and of the threat of sanctions to be used for noncompliance. A "bottom-up" approach presupposes a self- or group-generated disposition to seek new knowledge. The "middle-out" approach inherent in state or laboratory assistance may carry some features from both of these approaches; however, its power stems from the quality of mutual exchange relations developed among participants. This paper has catalogued some reasons why state mandated reforms, operating in isolation from other organizational events, cannot improve educational practice. Strictly local reforms, even where they are supported by state or federal funds, seem even shorter-lived, prone to waste of resources, and extremely confined as to diffusion across boundaries (Berman and McLaughlin 1977). The knowledge use strategies we examined also cannot generate improvements when isolated from a host of preconditions discussed above. When the three approaches are sensibly combined, however, the prospects for deep improvements are greatly increased.

Like many other organizations, the culture of schools is not naturally innovative. Yet, attempts to change schools that do not take the characteristics of teachers and schools into account cannot succeed. In our view, the power of a knowledge use strategy lies in its ability to capitalize on both external and internal pressures for improvement. As the research of Huberman (1983), Hargreaves (1984), and Little (1984) implies, lack of locally developed change in schools does not stem from lack of interest, but from an incapacity to move between the role of innovation developer and colleague, and "classroom coper." Mandates cannot change this condition, but they can increase the incentives for change. Information, where it is appropriately framed to fit the realities of schools and accompanied by increased exchange and discussion among peers, can help to provide a bridge between individual incentives and external organizational pressures.

The evidence that knowledge-based strategies focused on schools can lead to school improvement is solid and growing (Love 1985). State mandated reforms that incorporate these strategies are rare, however, because neither voters, governors, nor legislators are familiar with, let alone interested in, the organizational complexities entailed in schooling. Researchers seldom collaborate with disseminators in efforts to give new knowledge the properties we have called "reality," moreover, and laboratory planners sometimes fail to design a pathway of diffusion and social processing that culminates in classroom utilization.

Policies governing dissemination strategies in the United States since 1965 have evolved in a way that supports the importance of our argument, but the evolution still lacks continuity, let alone synthesis. Information service activities tend to assume that educators will make their own moves toward new knowledge, and this has been true for a handful of information-rich local systems. The evolving dissemination programs at the federal level were based on the assumption that supporting SEA technical assistance initiatives would improve the rate of spread and the amount of assistance going to schools. Both phases stimulated an ever-improving variety of combinatorial or mixed strategies in which laboratories and a few state agencies learned to design mediated, collaborative projects that actually reached teachers in poor as well as rich schools. Between 1975 and 1980, the power of school-focused knowledge strategies grounded in good linkage practices and strong interactive assistance began to be understood.

Our findings do more than affirm the value of carefully mixed strategies. They also begin to identify the design terms and organizational conditions under which knowledge will best lead to improvements. A state legislature, for example, may change the graduation requirements for every public high school in a state, but this change will have no effects, or damaging effects, if high-school faculties do not have the time, the resources, or the knowledge with which to put the new requirements into each school's own context in ways that are meaningful rather than mechanical. What is more, if time, money and knowledge resources of the right sort are available, school staff can often make good improvements without a restrictive and potentially damaging new state statute.

Note

1. A longer version of this chapter, including tabular presentation of the data, was published as K.S. Louis and R.A. Dentler (1988) "Knowledge use and school improvement." *Curriculum Inquiry* 18: 32–62.

References

Anderson, P. (1983) "Decision-making by objection and the Cuban missile crisis." *Administrative Science Quarterly* 28: 201–22.

Alexander, K. and A. Pallas (1985) *Curriculum Reform and School Performance*. Baltimore: Center for the Social Organization of Schools, Johns Hopkins University.

Berman, P. (1981) "Educational change: An implementation paradigm." In *Improving Schools: Using what we Know*, ed. R. Lehming and M. Kane: 253–86. Beverly Hills, CA: Sage.

—— and M. McLaughlin (1977) *Federal Programs Supporting Educational Change*, vol. 9. Santa Monica, CA: Rand Corporation.

Carlson, R. (1965) *Adoption of Educational Innovations*. Eugene: University of Oregon Press.

Carnegie Forum (1986) *A Nation Prepared: Teachers for the 21st Century*. New York: Carnegie Corporation.

Cohn, M. and A. Distefano (1984) "The recommendations of the national commission on excellence in education: A case study of their value." *Issues in Education* 2: 204–19.

Crandall, D. *et al.* (1983) *People, Policies and Practices: Examining the Chain of School Improvement* (vols I–X). Andover, MA: The Network.

Deal, T. (1984) "Searching for the wizard: The quest for excellence in education." *Issues in Education* 26: 56–67.

Dentler, R. (1984) "Ambiguities in state-local relations." *Education and Urban Society* 16: 145–64.

Glaser, E., H. Abelson, and K. Garrison (1983) *Putting Knowledge to Use*. Beverly Hills, CA: Sage.

Granovetter, M. (1982) "The strength of weak ties: A network theory revisited." In *Social Structure and Network Analysis*, ed. P. Marsden and N. Lin. Beverly Hills, CA: Sage.

Hargreaves, A. (1984) "Experience counts, theory doesn't: How teachers talk about their work." *Sociology of Education* 57: 244–54.

Hopkins, D. (1985) *School-based Review for School Improvement*. Leuven, Belgium: ACCO.

Huberman, M. (1983) "Recipes for busy kitchens: A situational analysis of routine knowledge use in schools." *Knowledge* 4: 478–510.

Katz, D. and R. Kahn (1966) *The Social Psychology of Organizations*. New York: Wiley.

Lindblom, C. and D. Cohen (1979) *Useable Knowledge*. New Haven, CT: Yale University Press.

Little, J. (1984) "Seductive images and organizational realities." *Teachers College Record* 86: 84–102.

Louis, K.S. (1986) "Reforming secondary schools: A critique and an agenda for administrators." *Educational Leadership* 44: 33–6.

—— (1987) "Permanent innovations: Theoretical and administrative issues in institutionalizing change." In *Naar beter onderwiis* (*Toward Better Education*), ed. J. Voogt and A. Rients. Tilburg: Zwijsen.

—— and R. Corwin (1984) "Organizational decline: How state agencies adapt." *Education and Urban Society* 16: 165–88.

——, S. Rosenblum, and J. Molitor (1981) *Strategies for Knowledge Use and School Improvement*. Washington, DC: National Institute of Education.

——, R. Dentler, and D. Kell (1984) *Exchanging Ideas: The Communication and Use of Knowledge in Education.* Boston, MA: Center for Survey Research.

Love, J. (1985) "Knowledge transfer and utilization in education." In *Review of Research in Education,* vol. 12, ed. E. Gordon. Washington, DC: American Educational Research Association.

Mann, D. (1978) "The user driven systems and a modest proposal." In *Making Change Happen,* ed. D. Mann: 285–307. New York: Teachers College Press.

March, J. and J. Olsen (1976) *Ambiguity and Choice in Organization.* Oslo: Universitetsforlaget.

McDill, E., G. Natriello, and A. Pallas (1985) *Raising Standards and Retaining Students: The Impact of the Reform Recommendations on Potential Dropouts.* Baltimore, MD: Center for the Social Organization of Schools, Johns Hopkins University.

Miles, M.B. (1978) *On Networking.* Washington, DC: National Institute for Education. Unpublished Manuscript.

Mort, P. (1964) "Studies in educational innovation from the Institute of Administrative Research." In *Innovation in Education,* ed. M. Miles. New York: Teachers College Press.

Nelson, M. and S. Sieber (1976) "Innovation in urban secondary schools." *School Review* 27: 101–19.

Rogers, E. and F. Shoemaker (1972) *Communication of Innovations.* New York: Free Press.

Sarason, S. (1971) *The Culture of the School and the Problem of Change.* Boston: Allyn & Bacon.

Sieber, S.D. (1981) "Knowledge utilization in public education: Incentives and disincentives." In *Improving Schools: Using What we Know,* ed. R. Lehming and M. Kane: 115–67. Beverly Hills, CA: Sage.

——, K.S. Louis, and L. Metzger (1972) *The Use of Educational Knowledge.* New York: Columbia University, Bureau of Applied Social Research.

Smith, A. and K.S. Louis, eds (1982) "Multimethod policy research: Issues and applications." *American Behavioral Scientists* 21: 1–144.

UNESCO (1965) *Educational Reform: Experiences and Prospects.* Belgium: UNESCO Press.

United States Department of Education (1983) *A Nation at Risk.* Washington, DC: US Government Printing Office.

van den Berg, R. and R. Vandenberghe (1984) *Grootschaligheid in de onderwijsvernieuwing. (Large-scale Innovation in Education).* Tilburg: Zwijsen.

Weiss, C. (1979) "Research for policy's sake: The enlightenment function of social research." *Policy Analysis* 3: 531–45.

Yin, R.K. (1984) *Case Study Research: Design and Methods.* Beverly Hills, CA: Sage.

——, M. Gwaltney, and K.S. Louis (1979) *Quality Control and Product Information Systems: An Interim Report on Implementation, Use and Effects in the R&D Utilization Program.* Cambridge, MA: Abt Associates.

2

Permanent Innovations: Theoretical and Administrative Issues in Institutionalizing Educational Change[1]

Introduction

I recently ate dinner in a Chinese restaurant where (as is customary in the USA) I was served a cookie with a small fortune in it, which said: "it is easy to open a shop, but very difficult to keep it open." I was immediately struck by the similarity between this folk wisdom and a research problem that has intrigued me for some time. A translation of the fortune into educational language would read this way: it is easy to get a school to try an innovation or curriculum (and perhaps even to implement it well), but very difficult to keep it operating for a long time.

Since the mid-1970s applied researchers, administrators and policy makers have been increasingly concerned with the general question of how one moves between a policy or plan for educational improvement and actual change in school structure and behavior. We have come to know this issue by a clearly recognized code word: implementation. The research on this topic is rather extensive. Many think we have a pretty good grasp of how to design, introduce and support innovations in ways that increase the likelihood that they will be implemented reasonably well, and have an impact on the quality of education (Lehming and Kane 1981; Crandall *et al.* 1986).

But it is hard to ignore the frequency with which schools (and other organizations) that are effectively implementing new programs – even major innovations – simply drop them. If I return after a few years to a school that has been a star innovator, I often can't find a trace of the activities that impressed me so much. The problem of getting innovations to stick over the long haul is beginning to be referred to as the "institutionalization problem." In the remainder of this paper, I will point to a variety of theoretical and practical issues that face us as we try to unravel and understand this problem.

A few initial remarks about my perspective are in order. First, by institutionalization I mean the stabilized assimilation of new practices, products, processes, or capacity by an institution. This paper argues that a poor understanding of the institutionalization process limits our ability to consider ways in which administrators may affect it. Some needed modifications in our theoretical assumptions will be suggested in three areas: the "manageability" of institutionalization, the distinctiveness of institutionalization as a stage in the change process, and the desirability of institutionalization as an outcome of reform. Each theoretical problem will be illustrated with case materials or references to published cases that show its actual effects on administrators who are responsible for designing and carrying out change programs.

Second, institutionalization is assumed to be a process that emerges over time (Janis and Mann 1977) and thus may vary depending on the nature of the organization being studied. However, the process is also often similar in organizations of different types. The issues raised in this paper are relevant to educators at national, state/regional or local levels and the problems of institutionalization in non-educational settings would look rather familiar to an educator.

Third, we need to understand how educational reforms are institutionalized at the policy level, as well as formulating a theory of institutionalization of innovations in schools. Tornatzky et al. (1983) point out that we need theories that integrate what we know about "macro-implementation" (implementation of a policy) and "micro-implementation" (implementation of a new program or practice in a specific organization). The same can be said for institutionalization, and this discussion is premised on the belief that basic processes at these two levels are not dissimilar. Thus, examples to support the discussion are drawn from national, state, and local-level studies.

Finally, I anticipate that this analysis will apply in an international context. My own research is based on only one country, but because of my involvement in the Organization for Economic Cooperation and Development's International School Improvement Project I have a broad (if somewhat superficial) understanding of the context of school improvement efforts in other countries.

What Do We Know?

The institutionalization problem is clearly not a new one. In the educational literature, it has been current since Berman and McLaughlin (1977) undertook a follow-up of the schools involved in their well-known "change agent study" and found major modifications or discontinuation of new programs in many of them. Recent work by Yin

(1979), Huberman and Miles (1984) as well as my colleagues and myself (Louis *et al.* 1981; Rosenblum and Louis, 1981) has contributed to our knowledge. More recently, Miles and Louis (1987) have attempted to synthesize these and other studies. There is a risk of being superficial by summarizing a summary, but it is possible to list some of the key factors influencing institutionalization:

- *The centrality and quality of the innovation.* Improvement programs that are closely tied to core educational activities – for example, curriculum and classroom practice, or reorganizing to improve the learning environments in schools – are more likely to be retained than peripheral improvements. Innovations that are significant improvements over past practice are also more likely to survive.

- *The scope and complexity of the innovation.* Improvement programs that require significant changes on the part of members of the organization and that involve a relatively large proportion of the staff are more likely to persist than activities that involve trivial modifications or small, isolated pockets of activity.

- *Support and pressure from administrators (but not necessarily active involvement).* Perhaps the most critical initial aspect of support is the creation of a generalized sense of urgency and excitement. However, during the initial transition from an experiment to a modus operandi, resources from the top may be crucial. Support may be of many types: ideological, material, motivational, or integrative. Mandates (demands for change) may also motivate.

- *Supportive environments and structures.* Educational organizations that exist in highly turbulent or troubled environments have a difficult time sustaining new activities, no matter how valued they are internally. Similarly, the organization must value and protect organization-wide commitment to the new activities, and must have decision-making structures that permit such a commitment to be made.

- *A change process that invites and sustains commitment.* Research does not support the need for broad participation in all phases of an improvement program: mandated innovation is often as effective as innovation that percolates upward through the system. However, people in a change process need to be provided with public opportunities to affirm and "buy in" to the change, perhaps at the point of deciding how to implement the program, or in decisions about specific programs to implement. They also need to feel that participation will be rewarded, either symbolically or by improved performance.

- *Assistance, particularly diverse and repeated training.* In order to achieve the perceived and actual mastery of new skills or the familiarity of operating within new structures and programs, external reinforcement from experts located either within or outside the organization is often critical at several points.

- *Skilful and stable leadership for change.* Leaders must be sensitive to the organizational setting and the need to make important transitions to a more permanent status. Also important is an ability to deal with delay and ambiguity. The latter may diminish an emphasis on strict fidelity to initial goals, but supports more long-term persistence.

- *Supportive organizational settings.* A recent review of the institutionalization literature (Miles and Louis 1987) found commonality across fields as diverse as economic development, education and private-sector organizational studies, suggesting that agencies that have a history of innovation, particularly similar types of innovation, are more likely to institutionalize successfully, as are organizations that have a generally decentralized authority structure.

- *Stable organizational settings.* Many improvement projects that appear to be destined for continuation are thrown off track due to significant shifts in policy (often due to turnover of the chief administrator), dramatic changes in resources, union-management conflict, or other crises. Although instability provides an opportunity for chance, it deflects changes that are in process.

These represent a good set of generalizations about institutionalization that are likely to hold up under further examination. However, we are far from having theories that will withstand the test of practice: they do not help us to explain why the rate of institutionalization of reasonably well-implemented innovations is so low. The remaining sections of this paper do not pretend to offer a complete theory, but outline some nagging concerns that emerge from available case studies of educational innovation, and the frustrations that are expressed by managers of change programs and educational policy makers.

Policies and Theories: "Manageable" or "Non-Rational"?

One striking tension is apparent in many of the studies, although it is explicitly raised in only a few (Louis and Rosenblum 1981; Jansen 1987). As policy analysts and/or organizational theorists, we are caught up in a set of "rational-managerial" perspectives, including (1) a belief in a quasi-science of organizational behavior, and (2) an expectation that research findings can be applied in a top-down fashion within government and educational agencies (Schön 1983; Astley and Van de Ven 1984). We admit, of course, that administrators are constrained by environmental pressures, the loose coupling of educational organizations in general, and by the tendency for "slippage" to occur when programs are implemented in a hierarchically structured organizational setting (Yin *et al.* 1980). Nevertheless, we tend to suggest ways for administrators to cope with these inevitable problems as if they could be eliminated (Goodman *et al.* 1980). Unfortunately, as we shall explore below, an examination of real-life experiences tends to undermine this sense of manageability.

Institutionalization as Highly Decentralized Decision-Making
Institutionalization is a very school-specific process. As noted in Miles and Ekholm (1985: 53), "School improvement requires the school as an organization to 'learn' to reorganize itself, to change its own internal conditions and to become better at the process of managing change". Thus, it is not plausible to expect uniform results from an educational reform effort even where policies are specific about goals and means, and decisions about institutionalization are inevitably made at lower levels of the hierarchy

than those relating to planning or implementation (Louis 1986). Variability in results is inevitable because interest in any particular program or reform is often brief for policy-makers and top administrators. In the long run their interest must turn to other pressing matters – priorities shift, and resources are reallocated. When this happens, the decision to maintain new practices will depend on the internalized interests and concerns of those who are responsible for carrying them out. These individual motivations are not easily subject to manipulation by the elaborate system of positive and negative incentives that often accompanies well-designed reform programs. Thus, in many cases the decision to maintain programs over the long haul will be left to the individual users, although in more tightly coupled systems it may be an organization-wide phenomenon.

Normal Crises

Most of the studies mentioned above (or at least their unpublished data) reflect another equally important theme: the essential unpredictability of many aspects of significant reform efforts. Because they extend over time they allow for the intrusion of external factors too numerous and varied to be accommodated either in theory or in the actual program plans. In the study of the R&D Utilization Program, my colleagues and I developed the notion of "normal crises" that diminish administrative control over the course and outcomes of a change program. These range from "acts of God" to unantici-pated agency or school reorganizations (Louis *et al.* 1981; see also Huberman and Miles 1984).

The important point about normal crises is that we know that they will happen, but we do not know which ones will occur or how they will affect a school improvement effort until after they happen. In one situation a teacher's strike may completely elimi-nate the improvement effort, diminishing commitment and preventing any possibility of institutionalization. In an urban school district in the USA, on the other hand, we found that a planned change effort was viewed as a welcome vehicle for eliminating wounds that developed during a strike – it was a chance to work together for things that mattered to everyone (Desmond *et al.* 1981). Similarly, in some organizations a change in the top administrator is cause for alarm when it comes to program stability, while in others it makes little difference or even resolves smoldering grievances. Whatever their eventual impact, such events demand rapid coping behaviors that deviate substantially from the kind of recommended long-range or strategic planning models that we usually associate with good change management (Keller 1983).

Internal Turmoil

Finally, significant attempts at change seem to breed their own internal instability. A number of case studies have noted the "disappearing leader" problem that occurs when talented people (for example, those most likely to spearhead a reform) are promoted or move on (Louis and Rosenblum 1981; Huberman and Miles 1984). In addition, stability among the implementing staff (teachers or others) can be an issue: where levels of turnover are moderate to high, innovations can erode simply because of the demands to train and socialize new people very frequently (Miles *et al.* forthcoming). Finally, in

many cases a thoughtful innovation simply may "fit" with the local cultures or organizational structures: some rate of non-institutionalization is to be expected simply because
people are too ambitious in their aspirations (Louis and Rosenblum 1981). This last
issue is of sufficient importance that it will be discussed in further detail later.

Implementation and Institutionalization: Sequential, Complementary or Competing Processes?

We tend to be locked into a linear model of the change process and few have questioned
the fact that institutionalization is a "stage" that follows something called implementation. Yin's (1979) formulation of "passages and cycles" further reinforces the view that
making new practices a permanent part of the routine requires decisions by administrators and policy-makers. But in reality institutionalization is part of the implementation
process and it is not possible to determine exactly where implementation ends and
institutionalization starts. In fact, recent empirical investigations of institutionalization
using both quantitative and qualitative data suggest that the variables most strongly associated with implementation and institutionalization are identical (Berman and
McLaughlin 1977; Louis *et al.* 1981; Rosenblum and Louis 1981; Miles 1983;
Vandenberghe 1987).

Identifying the overlap between institutionalization and implementation is not
merely semantic gymnastics. If they must be managed simultaneously, each design or
implementation decision must be examined not only for its short-term effects on
program operations but also for its long-term implications for maintaining the new
structures or practices. A variety of case materials can suggest an inherent tension
between the processes: the best decision for the short term may be the worst for the long
term, and vice versa. In the remainder of this section I will first illustrate some tensions
that can be easily extracted from existing case studies and then point to the implications
for the design of school improvement policies whose objective is to induce similar
changes in a large number of schools.

Status Versus Integration

One strategy for improving early implementation is to give a new activity a special
status, and high visibility. This demonstrates the organization's commitment and also
protects against early dilution of the activity. But special status often makes it difficult for
a policy or program to become part of the normal practices of the agency, and activities
that are more visible and more distinct are easier to excise under the chronic conditions
of financial stress in which most public agencies find themselves.

To illustrate: teachers in a Dutch secondary school initiated a complex curriculum
reform project known as open project education, which rapidly recruited a substantial
minority of the staff. The staff, administration and parents became split over the value of
the innovation, and external actors were drawn in as peacemakers. The resolution gave
the innovation an official status as a national curriculum experiment. Although over a

ten-year period conflict subsided, and the experimental period ended, the involved teachers failed to gain equal status in the school's program. The innovative curriculum activities are still part of the school's program, but are voluntary for both students and teachers. Longer-range persistence is doubtful as committed staff members gradually leave the school and the struggle over resources during a period of economic cutbacks becomes more intense (Jansen 1987). The open project education case illustrates the dilemma posed above: if the innovating teachers had not organized themselves into a special group, they would not have survived the first period of conflict. However, once they became identified as an experiment, it became very difficult to make the transition back to being part of the school's regular program.

This story is not a new one: Berman and McLaughlin (1977) note that giving the project a "special status" accounted for much of the discontinuation behavior that they observed in schools that participated in a variety of federally funded change programs. Holly (1983) points out that this dilemma is particularly acute for school-based review activities, which often become "stuck" as a valued school-wide analysis activity and fail to become incorporated into classroom behaviors. Bromlinsi's (1986) analysis provides additional indications that special status may prevent institutionalization even when the innovation persists over very long periods of time. But other case studies of school innovation show that housing the project in an existing department and appointing a project director who is deeply immersed in the organization is in many cases likely to lead to lower levels of innovativeness, and adaptations that may trivialize the innovation (Huberman and Miles 1984).

Change Versus Organizational Fit

Another major tension in most projects is that of finding an appropriate balance between a change that is substantial enough to be worth making, and one that "fits" well enough with the current state of the organization to be acceptable and feasible. In general, research indicates that small innovations are often discontinued because they are not perceived to be worth the effort, and innovations that are too massive are often distorted or retained in a very piecemeal fashion (Berman and McLaughlin 1977; Rosenblum and Louis 1981; Crandall et al. 1982).

Fit should be thought of as a psycho-cultural phenomenon, rather than some objective match between agency and innovation. What is a major change for some individuals and organizations is a trivial one for others, depending on current practices and culture. More importantly, however, there is no such thing as an immediate fit between a planned change of any locally perceived magnitude and the existing culture, structure, and practices of an organization.

A preoccupation with organizational fit in the early stages of an organizational innovation is likely to lead to rapid "downsizing", as Levinson (1986) noted in his study of community-service programs in private schools, and Huberman (1983) observed in his conclusions about institutionalization of innovative programs in public schools. Conversely, lack of "mutual adaptation" (Berman and McLaughlin 1977) leads ultimately to low institutionalization. This is particularly true for complex innovations.

where an initial set of plans often intentionally evolves throughout the early implementation phase until the organization has reached some understanding of the core configuration of chances that constitute its new program. The innovation is like an amoeba, changing shape dramatically.

Political abilities (as opposed to more standard planning skills) are often critical to achieving a balance between change and fit. Where program managers are not well integrated into the culture of the organization the opportunities for appropriate political management of the fitting process are poor. An interesting case occurred in a Florida school improvement program: although it was externally evaluated as successful, its detractors were convinced, based on their beliefs about how the agency should operate, that it was not working well, and was not liked in the participating schools – "facts" that harder evidence could not dispel. These "facts" were then used to justify scaling down the program. Because the project director did not share the common belief system of the organization, she had not anticipated this problem and had no way to counteract it (Louis and Rosenblum 1981).

The importance of fit between project management and the organizational culture to achieving some final program fit is apparent in other contexts as well. Elkins (1985) describes a case where a radical curriculum innovation was successfully institutionalized in a conservative private school. In her view, the success was attributable to the program sponsor's position as both an insider (he had once been a teacher in the school and returned as an administrator) and an outsider (he left to spend several years administering a very different kind of organization, from which he borrowed ideas for the innovation). This illustrates the tensions between being different and the same that are the essence of the change versus fit problem.

Leadership for Implementation Versus Institutionalization

As the Elkins case suggests, an organizational change manager must be more than someone who cares and is willing to invest the effort to develop and protect the program. For programs to survive in most organizations the project leader must also be professionally placed to create informal support for project activities as well as formal integration. The dilemma is that these two skills rarely occur together in the same individual. For example, Louis and Miles (1990) conducted case studies of five urban high schools that were selected because they appeared to be rapidly improving as a consequence of major reform programs. In only two did the school leaders who were spearheading the program appear to perform equally well in both roles. In fact, Louis and Kell (1981) find that individuals who are highly innovative and able to develop and maintain exciting program designs make poor change agents during implementation and institutionalization. The mastermind of an innovation is often an eloquent spokesperson who can create enthusiasm and a desire to change among a staff. Program designers are, however, often blind or resistant to the constraints and concerns that implementers face – concerns that may prevent the development of a real fit at the individual and organizational level. Unfortunately, most organizations don't have the resources to appoint (or find) a series of program directors whose skills match the needs and requirements of different stages in the implementation/institutionalization process. Using teams to provide different leadership skills is one option often used in industry, but this is expensive, increases coordination problems, and may result in divided leadership.

The leadership problem is aggravated when the program manager is selected from outside the agency, as is often the case where specialized expertise or a new vision is important to make the effort work better. As one recently burned change agent put it: "If you are thinking of going into a State Education Agency as an 'internal-external' agent, your life there is likely to be short. For one thing, you won't be able to stand it. For another, they won't be able to stand you."

Other Tensions
Certainly these are not the only dilemmas that face change managers in schools and other educational agencies, but they demonstrate that getting good programs in place and keeping them there is a difficult task. A key requirement of further studies of institutionalization is to generate a more exhaustive list of incompatible decisions and non-linearity in the change process, for without them it is unlikely that we will make much progress in developing useful guidelines for agencies that want to develop policies that help to stabilize their programs.

Summary and Implications

The above sections have raised some questions about the adequacy of our theories of institutionalization. I have argued that institutionalization and implementation are part of the same process and are both conceptually and practically difficult to distinguish. Even where they can be distinguished, institutionalization (like implementation) is at best a quasi-rational process, only partly subject to administrative control at any level. The evolution of an "innovation" that is ultimately stabilized at the local level is a difficult process that often results in a final set of behaviors that are loosely related to the original goals of the reformers. Because final decisions about institutionalization tend to be made at the level of the school (or even of the teacher) it is not plausible to expect uniform results from school improvement policy even where that is the desired goal. Furthermore, I have argued that although uniform results may appear socially desirable in the short run, the concept of institutionalization may be antithetical to the effective functioning of the educational system.

It is not necessary to fall back on extreme theoretical positions regarding the non-rationality of organizational behavior to incorporate the above observations. It is true that organizations often pay more attention to strategies and symbols that will ensure their stability and survival rather than thinking about their overall effectiveness (Meyer and Rowan 1977). This is exacerbated in education due to the turbulence of the policy environment (Louis and Corwin 1984). Because the mix of actors making decisions is typically less stable and well-defined than in the private sector, the decisions are much more likely to include consideration both of educational goals and of symbolic factors (March and Olsen 1976). Recognizing the occasional genuine chaos of life in organizations is not the same as saying that they never behave logically, but to ignore it is to ensure that our practice will be designed to fail.

A significant implication is that the potential influence of non-school-based decision-makers over the process of institutionalization within a given school is rather limited: the effects of state or national programs ultimately depend on the efforts of schools and individuals within them. These observations also have significant implications for the educational reform strategies that are currently being debated in virtually every developed country, as well as for researchers who care about the quality of education. The first implication is obvious: we need planned change research that incorporates specific attention to the persistent and irresolvable dilemmas, and attends to how incongruities are handled. It is difficult to obtain funding for this kind of research. Governments are less interested in hearing about paradoxes than in getting information that they can use immediately to "make schools better." This kind of research is also by its nature exploratory and qualitative, and difficult to conduct because, if the ideas expressed in this paper are valid, making progress toward better theories will be a slow slog. Yet we will not make much progress in developing better change models until we better understand why change so often seems unmanageable.

In addition to more research on planned change, we also need a different kind of research: intensive studies of schools that appear to be self-renewing (perhaps along the lines of recent studies of "excellent" schools). We also need what Campbell (1987) calls "local molar validity": intensive, longitudinal studies of complex interventions that are designed to make schools self-renewing. Campbell argues that, in the absence of such studies, little progress will be made in a valid applied social scientific knowledge about complex progam interventions.

This brings me to a final implication: as part of the educational process we should become more involved in pressuring policy-makers to design small-scale programs and interventions that serve both research and reform ends. I am not talking about educational "demonstrations" that, at least in the US and Dutch contexts, often fail to influence policy or spread to new contexts very rapidly (Glennan *et al.* 1978; van den Berg and Vandenberghe 1984). I am, rather, talking about strictly development research programs that are intended to contribute primarily to better applied social science so that what we learn can then better inform policy development.

Note

1. Adapted from a chapter of the same title that appeared in J. Voogt and A. Reints (eds), *Naar beter onderwijs*: 128–43. Tilburg: Zwijsen.

References

Astley, G. and A. Van de Ven (1983) "Central perspectives and debates in organizational theory." *Administrative Science Quarterly* 1: 245–74.

Berman, P. and M. McLaughlin (1977) *Federal Programs Supporting Educational Change, Vol. VII. Factors Affecting Implementation and Continuation.* Santa Monica, CA: RAND.

Bromlinsi, C. (1986) "The Politics of Opportunity and Limited Choice." Unpublished seminar paper. Harvard Graduate School of Education.

Campbell, D.T. (1987) "Guidelines for monitoring the scientific competence of Preventative Intervention Research Centers." *Knowledge: Creation, Implementation, Diffusion* 8(4): 389–430.

Corwin, R. and K.S. Louis (1982) "Organizational barriers to the utilization of research." *Administrative Science Quarterly* 27: 623–40.

Crandall, D. *et al.* (1982) *People, Policies and Practices: Examining the Chain of School Improvement.* Andover, MA: The Network.

——, J.W. Eiseman, and K.S. Louis (1986) "Strategic planning issues that bear on the success of school improvement efforts." *Educational Administration Quarterly* 22: 21–53.

Desmond, P., K.S. Louis, and D. Kell (1981) "Ogden junior high school." In K.S. Louis, D. Kell, K. Chabotar, and S. Sieber, eds, *Perspectives on School Improvement:* 149–58. Washington, DC: National Institute of Education.

Elkins, P. (1985) "Innovation Out Back: Creating Change in an Institutionalized Setting." Unpublished course paper. Harvard Graduate School of Education.

Glennan, T., W. Hederman, L. Johnson, and R. Rettig (1978) *The Role of Demonstrations in Federal R&D Policy.* Santa Monica, CA: RAND.

Goodman, P., M. Bazerman, and E. Conlan (1980) "Institutionalization of planned organizational change." In B. Staw and L. Cummings (eds), *Research in Organizational Behavior:* 215–46. Greenwich, CT: JAI Press.

Holly, P. (1983) "The Institutionalisation of Action Research in a Comprehensive School." MA thesis, Cambridge University.

Huberman, M. (1983) "Recipes for busy kitchens." *Knowledge* 4: 478–510.

—— and M. Miles (1984) *Innovation Up Close.* New York: Plenum.

Janis, I. and L. Mann (1977) *Decision Making.* New York: The Free Press.

Jansen, H. (1987) "Open project education: institutionalization in a conflict setting." In M. Miles, M. Ekholm, and R. Vandenberghe (eds), *Lasting School Improvement: Exploring the Process of Institutionalization.* Leuven: ACCO Press.

Keller, G. (1983) *Academic Strategy.* Baltimore: Johns Hopkins University Press.

Lehming, R. and M. Kane (1981) *Improving Schools: Using What we Know.* Beverly Hills, CA: Sage.

Levison, L. (1987) "Community service programs in independent schools: The processes of implementation and institutionalization of peripheral educational innovations." Unpublished EdD dissertation. Cambridge, MA: Harvard University.

Louis, K.S. (1986) "Reforming secondary schools: prospects and issues." *Educational Leadership* 44(1): 33–6.

—— and R. Corwin (1984) "Organizational decline: how state agencies adapt." *Education and Urban Society* 16: 165–88.

—— and D. Kell (1981) *Linking R&D with Schools: The Human Factor in Dissemination: Field Agent Roles in their Organizational Context.* Cambridge, MA: Abt Associates.

—— and M.B. Miles (1990) *Improving the Urban High School: What Works and Why.* New York: Teachers College Press.

—— and S. Rosenblum (1981) *Designing and Managing Interorganizational Networks.* Washington, DC: National Institute of Education.

——, D. Kell, K. Chabotar, and S. Sieber (1981) *Perspectives on School Improvement.* Washington, DC: National Institute of Education.

——, S. Rosenblum, and J. Molitor (1981) *Strategies for Knowledge Use and School Improvement.* Washington, DC: National Institute of Education.

March, J. and J. Olsen (1976) *Ambiguity and Organizational Choice.* Bergen: Universitetsforlaget. (reprinted: Harvard Business School).

Meyer, J. and B. Rowan (1977) "Institutionalized organizations: Formal structure as myth and ceremony." *American Journal of Sociology* 83: 340–63.

Miles, M. (1983) "Unraveling the mystery of institutionalization." *Educational Leadership* 41: 14–17.

—— and M. Ekholm (1985) "What is school improvement?" In W. van Velzen *et al.* (eds), *Making School Improvement Work.* Leuven: ACCO Press.

—— and K.S. Louis (1987) "Research on institutionalization: a reflective view." In M. Miles, M. Ekholm, and R. Vandenberghe (eds), *Lasting School Improvement: Exploring the Process of Institutionalization*: 25–44. Leuven: ACCO Press.

——, M. Ekholm, and R. Vandenberghe (eds), *Lasting School Improvement: Exploring the Process of Institutionalization.* Leuven: ACCO Press.

Rosenblum. S and K.S. Louis (1981) *Stability and Change: Innovation in an Educational Context.* New York: Plenum Press.

Schön, D. (1983) *The Reflective Practitioner.* New York: Basic.

Tornatzky, L.G., J.D. Eveland, M.G. Boviand, W.A. Hetzner, E.C. Johnson, D. Ritman, and J. Schneider (1983) *The Process of Technological Innovation: Reviewing the Literatures.* Washington, DC: National Science Foundation.

Yin, R.K. (1979) *Changing Urban Bureaucracies: How New Practices Become Routinized.* Lexington, MA: Lexington Press.

——, M. Gwaltney, and K.S. Louis (1980) *Quality Control and Product Information Systems: An Interim Report on Implementation, Use and Effects in the R&D Utilization Program.* Cambridge, MA: Abt Associates.

Van den Berg, R. and R. Vandenberghe (1984) *Groorschaligheid in de onderwijsvernieuwing.* Leuven: ACCO Press.

Vandenberghe, R. (1987) "The renewed primary school in Belgium: the local innovation policy and institutionalization of innovations." In M. Miles, M. Ekholm, and R. Vandenberghe (eds), *Lasting School Improvement: Exploring the Process of Institutionalization*: 25–44. Leuven: ACCO Press.

3

Planning Improvement Efforts[1]

Can planning work? School-based educators occasionally look at district, state, or federal administrators and wonder what it would be like to spend one's work life planning and monitoring rather than doing. Not far behind is the realization that a substantial chunk of their own time is required to tinker with programs that have been planned at the district or state level, but don't quite seem to "fit" their own school or classroom.

Planning – particularly planning for change – has also been carefully scrutinized by educational researchers, many of whom believe it makes an insignificant contribution to real school improvement. Whether or not real change and improvement occur depends more on implementation, or what happens after a reform actually gets put to the test in classrooms (Berman and McLaughlin 1974; Berman 1981; Louis *et al.* 1981). Studies of unsuccessful experimental programs initiated in the 1970s implied that planning, along with a "top-down, technological" model of change in education, should give way to a more fluid model, in which the ideal of planning for school-wide goals is abandoned in favor of letting "a thousand flowers bloom" (Clark *et al.* 1980).

But in our view, the role of planning is not as easily dismissed as these critiques imply. Furthermore, there are many different ways to go about planning. Our study suggests very strongly that the presence of good planning helps to determine whether urban schools actually change for the better. To give an example from our survey of principals, there is a strong statistical association between the use of good planning techniques and cross-role involvement on the one hand, and the actual quality of the plan that was produced and the consensus in the school about the goals expressed in the plan. These in turn affect the number of implementation problems that arise, and the level of coping effort that school people make to grapple with and solve those problems.

Yet our study also suggests something else: "Good planning" in the high schools that we studied looked very little like the planning models that are most commonly advocated in textbooks on administration and management. The goal of this chapter is to look at the reality of planning in urban high schools, and to derive some principles for action from what we observed.

Alternative Planning Models

There is no single right way to plan, but there are a great many ways to go wrong. The choice of how to plan, however, is not something that needs to be left to chance. The most appropriate model will depend on a range of factors discussed in previous chapters, including:

- the amount of consensus within the school and among the school, the community, and the district about the nature of the school's problems and desirable strategies for solving them;
- the complexity and difficulty of problems facing the school;
- the level of energy for change;
- the turbulence of the school's context; and
- the amount of autonomy and flexibility available to the school.

We'll review some common, familiar planning models, and some promising newer ones.

Long-range Planning, or "The Blueprint Model"

This model views the human actor as rational, but imperfect (Allison 1971). Ideally, planning involves regular analysis of performance problems, careful setting of measurable goals both annually and for the long term (a five- to ten-year period), exhaustive searches for alternative ways of meeting the goals, and a reflective selection process resulting in a detailed plan for implementing the chosen alternatives. Because human beings are not machines, we fall short of the ideal planning model; constrained timeliness difficulties in getting (and processing) information, and the need for immediate response to unanticipated pressures from outside competitors or regulators throw our decisions off course. Nevertheless, effective leaders should attempt to approximate the approach of the rational planner.

This model does not always apply very well to real organizations and people. For example, studies of decision-making in successful organizations indicate that strategic decisions are often made without a careful, analytic process (Donaldson and Lorsch

1983; Daft and Lengel 1984). In schools, the blueprint model usually means that planning – particularly long-range planning – is done in the district office, which may make principals and teachers feel disenfranchised, and slow their acceptance of the changes.

"Muddling Through"

A second common model involves an incremental strategy: making only decisions that cannot be avoided, letting each decision be made at the lowest possible level, and even then making a plan that has the least chance of rocking the boat (Lindblom 1959).

There are three arguments in favor of incremental planning. First, those who believe in teacher empowerment point out that an accumulation of decisions made by intelligent professionals is just as likely to result in a good direction for a school as any centralized plan. Because incremental plans are short term, and confined to a small part of the school, there is opportunity to ensure that they "work" before they are used more broadly (Weick 1976). Second, there may be no viable alternative: Because long-range planning is largely a myth, it is preferable to accommodate to the essential non-rationality of life in organizations rather than to perpetrate false standards (March and Olsen 1986). Finally, decentralized decision-making helps to promote creativity at all levels (Kanter 1983).

"Muddling through" may work for a school performing reasonably well in a relatively stable setting. However, it is often insufficient when schools face pressure to make major shifts in policy or practice. The more complicated the demands, and the larger the number of outside constituencies, the less likely it is that letting individual professionals plan for themselves and their units will result in productive change (Anderson 1989).

Strategic Planning, or Renewing Commitment to Mission and Goals

The burst of interest in strategic planning (Steiner 1979; Tichy 1983; McCune 1986) is a response to the problem of how to shift an organization's course relatively rapidly. This model departs from the previous two by emphasizing the involvement of key administrators in realigning mission and goals to the claims of relevant constituencies and trends in the environment. Emphasis is placed on creating a unified understanding among organizational members of an image of "what this organization should look like." The emphasis is on a middle-range plan – generally less than five years – and on decision-making by intuition rather than by detailed quantitative analysis. Finally, strategic planning moves beyond just acknowledging environmental forces. Instead, it focuses on the need for proactive strategies that enhance the organization's ability to deal with these pressures. When a strategic plan is in place, other levels in the organization engage in traditional planning activities to carry out the centrally determined mission.

Emphasizing coherent strategy works well where the organization is able to choose distinctive strategies to increase its competitive position in the environment. But it does not necessarily have the same effect in organizations that are highly regulated, such as schools (Snow and Hrbiniak 1980). Schools also have many legitimate goals that are difficult to prioritize, which makes it hard for top administrators to develop a clear vision that is sufficiently specific to be meaningful, yet accepted by all.

Evolutionary Planning, or "Getting There is Half the Fun"

The newest ideas about planning try to strike a compromise among the previous models. The evolutionary perspective rests on the assumption that the environment both inside and outside organizations is often chaotic. No specific plan can last for very long, because it will become outmoded either due to changing external pressures, or because disagreement over priorities arises within the organization. Yet there is no reason to assume that the best response is to plan passively, relying on incremental decisions. Instead, the organization can cycle back and forth between efforts to gain normative consensus about what it may become, to plan strategies for getting there, and to carry out decentralized, incremental experimentation that harnesses the creativity of all members to the change effort.

This approach is evolutionary in the sense that, although the mission and image of the organization's ideal future may be based on a top-level analysis of the environment and its demands, strategies for achieving the mission are frequently reviewed and refined based on internal scanning for opportunities and successes. Strategy is viewed as a flexible tool, rather than as a semi-permanent extension of the mission: if rational planning is like blueprinting, evolutionary planning is more like taking a journey. There is a general destination, but many twists and turns as unexpected events occur along the way.

No one planning model will ever suit the needs of a school under all conditions. However, our cases suggest that the evolutionary model may be the best for schools undertaking a major renewal and change effort.

Getting Started With Planning

Our advocacy of new and less rational models does not provide an answer to a very reasonable question: how should we start? How can a improvement program begin under the difficult conditions discussed earlier? More specifically, how can a demoralized and often apathetic staff come to feel that they can control the fate of the school and the students who move through it? Even more specifically, what should they do first?

Finding Energy: Building an Initial Team

Planning experts in education frequently advocate the use of a broadly based, representative planning team. Some go so far as to advocate the involvement of every employee in planning (Lotto *et al.* 1980). The requirement for broad participation was, for example, built into the California School Improvement Program that formed the initial basis for Alameda's activities. Let's look more closely at Alameda High School in order to see how planning is "supposed to look" from the perspective of an ideal process.

A first step was to constitute an ad hoc School Site Council with representatives from administrators, teachers, other staff, parents, and students … The first coordinator … proceeded [with] formal elections for a site council … The procedural plan … was to have the entire faculty meet as a large body. [Planning] was not to be an isolated process engaged in by a small group … A list of task groups were set to plan in different areas, and faculty joined up: 'These groups met monthly for one-and-a-half hours of planning … Simultaneously, a goal-setting process was conducted by the Site Council based on surveys of students, faculty, and parents … In this process, the faculty developed ownership of the program.[2]

This description illustrates elements that are believed to lead to good planning activities: a coordinating group representing all stakeholders in the school, a broadly based process in which most school members have the opportunity to contribute, and a clearly defined planning period focusing on the development of specific goals and action steps. In Alameda, many proposed activities were generated from this process, and were blended together to form the plan for the first year of implementation. As one person put it, "everyone worked without hidden agendas."

But a broadly based, participatory planning process does not always work so well in a school where faculty are divided and skeptical about change. Chester is a case in point.

A district-wide steering group was appointed to develop a plan for the proposal to the state's More Effective Schools program. The district's group included 87 people, representing all schools and community groups. During the planning period task forces … met as often as twice a month to develop ideas. However, commitment of energy was low, and actual planning documents were usually prepared by the central office staff. The high school's chronic mistrust of the district office increased when the superintendent chose a major component of the program before the participatory planning process was completed: Comments from the school indicated widespread agreement … that "downtown is ramming this down our throats." Although there was supposed to be a school-level task force … low morale at the school level made it difficult to sustain involvement.

On the surface, the initial approach to planning in Chester appeared to be rather similar in design to that in Alameda. However, broadly based planning is not a panacea in a school with a history of conflict. Chester was full of teachers who were interested in change, but the long list of recently failed innovations made them skeptical about making a commitment to the district's planning effort. They also perceived that district-office planning and any planning that they might do were largely decoupled, which reinforced their sense of powerlessness and lack of interest in getting involved.

The paradox is that participation can increase alienation under less than ideal circumstances, by increasing the profound conviction of many urban teachers that they are manipulated by administrators who do not understand the circumstances of their work.

Survey evidence about the effects of broadly based planning activities in improving high schools also shows mixed results. Schools that included more diverse groups on their planning committees tended to encounter more problems during the planning process. (Of course, the involvement of many stakeholders may have been a response to a divided or conflictful situation rather than a cause.) Planning group diversity is also associated with reduced influence of both teachers and principals over the final shape of the plan. As we will discuss in more detail later in this chapter, reduced influence of school-based participants has serious consequences for implementation and change.

But there are alternative approaches to developing an initial plan that do not require broadly based intensive participatory planning. One strategy used in three of our schools – Agassiz, Burroughs, and Bartholdi – was to find a small group of people who, for a variety of reasons, were committed to school improvement and saw themselves as able to carry out some coordinating activity. In these schools, energy had to come from a few people who had time as well as interest. Rather than beginning with a school-wide activity, the initial planning in these schools began small – even invisibly.

In Burroughs, for example, the impetus for involving the school in E2 (the school's name for their change initiative) clearly came from Margaret Storm, the principal. As Storm began to plan, she turned toward faculty volunteers. Storm told her faculty about E2, and "eight people stepped forward who were really willing to put forth for it. I felt that was enough support to go ahead." During the early months, E2 consisted largely of that committee; meetings scheduled after school hours were attended by few faculty. Miss Storm was reflective about the reason why she chose to run fast with a few players.

> The number one thing is to build a support base. You can't think you have a fantastic dream and expect people to accept it. You have to have gradual movement; you have to build support ... You have to know your staff, who are the good teachers, who are interested in working with children and parents, who are committed and non-punitive.

Although Burroughs relied on teachers rather than administrators as the early source of energy, it is not surprising that most of them were unmarried, and had fewer conflicts with the many late afternoon and evening meetings.

Early Planning: School-focused, Administrator-dominated

Our study began by assuming that principals are rarely charismatic leaders who become "turnaround managers" based on personal magnetism and vision. Nevertheless, in three of our most successful schools, the early planning process was dominated by the principal, while in the two schools that were initially less successful, principals played a less dynamic and central role. Let us begin by taking a look at the latter.

In both Bartholdi (originally rated as a school with a weak change program) and Chester, where early planning was controlled outside the building, there were real problems in implementation and gaining consensus. However, the role of the principal in each of these schools and the consequences for planning and program outcomes were quite different.

> Chester's principal, Carol Hayes, took little active initiative in planning for or coordinating the school renewal program, nor did she actively invite other school administrators to take charge … But [her] tendency to avoid a visible leadership role was not due entirely to her somewhat tentative management style: The decision to adopt the Instructional Program Leadership program as a major component of the district's improvement effort was made [by the superintendent] without any enthusiasm on her part; she was also aware that some components of the program, such as classroom scanning, were very controversial among her teachers.
>
> In Bartholdi, the principal also exhibited low investment in the district's change program, and did not participate in the initial summer planning sessions. New to the job, principal Martinez was struggling with the need to learn a variety of new skills in addition to change management. Unlike Principal Hayes, however, he clearly delegated responsibility for the program to another experienced administrator. The first person appointed to the task was unequal to it, but when Martinez was faced with the need to restaff the position he chose a respected associate principal, who was encouraged to take on a strong planning and coordinating role.

Thus, although his initiative in the early planning efforts was limited, attempts were made to compensate for this later in the program. In both schools, however, there were noticeable results of limited administrative leadership in planning. Neither Bartholdi's nor Chester's staff viewed the program as legitimate: It was initially an "outsiders" program regarded at best as irrelevant to solving problems that teachers thought were most pressing, and at worst as a significant distraction from the school's main job. Similarly, in neither school was there a clear mandate for any individual or group to resolve conflicting views about the program, or deal with problems of coordination among related efforts. People at Bartholdi and Chester could recite long lists of innovation efforts that were logically connected to the planned reform that we studied, but no early effort was made to consider how these could work together to meet school needs. In contrast, the principals of Agassiz, Burroughs, and Alameda gave active sponsorship to the Boston Compact (the first city-side business partnership to support school improvement), E2, and the mentor teacher program – all of which also originated outside the school. Teachers – even the skeptics – knew that the school's leaders cared about the program and actively engaged teachers in planning that would make it fit the school's agenda and needs. These programs could be grumbled about, but they could not be ignored.

Early principal involvement has enduring consequences for school improvement that are demonstrated through our survey data. In schools where principals reported that they had a great deal of influence over the school's plan for change, 55 per cent also indicated that they grappled with implementation problems in a wide variety of ways. Among the principals who reported that they had less influence on planning, only 35 per cent reported a wide variety of coping activities. In most schools it is the top admin-istrators who must spend the most time coping with unanticipated problems: if they don't "own" the plan, perhaps they feel less inclined to invest their time this way.

Conclusion

Effective evolutionary planning must be built on the direct involvement of the principal or some other key leader in the school. The involvement of official leaders in planning gives value to the expenditure of effort on the part of others, increases the legitimacy of those who argue for change, and increases successful problem coping.

Action Before Planning: Defusing Skepticism

Active principal sponsorship of the program and the recruitment of a small enthusiastic team were not always enough to galvanize broad action in the depressed settings. Planning theory suggests that there should be a number of distinct stages in a change effort, and planning (or mobilization) is considered an antecedent to actual implementa-tion or activity. But in Agassiz and Burroughs, we see the opposite. First there was action, and then detailed planning began. In Agassiz, for example,

> Principal Cohen ... realized that if the Compact ... was to succeed he would need to "deliver to the skeptics." The school was not ready for a real commitment to program change. Rather it had to be encouraged in that direction: "In the first year, my main concerns were with safety and climate." One of his first ... battles was with ... the phys-ical plant staff over the use of a budget for repairs ... The central Office proposed replacing the heating plant, wiring, and pipes, but Cohen reasoned that these would hardly boost the morale of the staff and students ... After a hard fight the school received all of the internal cosmetic repairs ... Cohen utilized the victory to its fullest advantage, holding a special dedication ceremony in the newly redecorated auditorium.

The case goes on to describe other programs and activities that were initiated during Cohen's first year – a new magnet program, junior Reserve Officer Training Corps (ROTC), a special program for teenage parents, and various efforts to reduce truancy. All began without the benefit of any formal school-wide planning at all. Although Cohen was verbally committed to participatory planning, the second year of his tenure also involved more action than planning, as a variety of new activities were initiated by various faculty and administrators.

At Burroughs a similar process unfolded. The school received a small planning grant from the supporting foundation at the end of the school year, and the summer was devoted primarily to reading and locating possible consultants. In the fall,

> project planning continued, but Miss Storm and the E2 committee also began to implement some of their ideas. They used some of their [planning] money to

contract with a professor at [the local] state university to conduct seven workshops during the year on reading in the content areas. And Miss Storm organized a seventh grade team of … teachers and arranged their teaching schedules so that they could meet together to coordinate their curricular units and discuss problem students. Weekly meetings began with a guidance counselor and Miss Storm participating.

In each of these cases, major activities, including restructuring and the initiation of significant (and sometimes costly) new programs, took place without committee meetings, and with no written plan supporting that action. Was this bad administration? An error in judgment on the part of the principals and cooperating teachers? Our cases suggest not, and there is theoretical evidence from other settings to support this assertion.

Action to Create Energy

Many educational researchers agree that starting an innovation program with an effort that centers on curriculum and instruction is the most effective strategy for getting teachers interested and involved (Crandall *et al.* 1986). Even where organizational variables, such as morale or climate, need to be worked on, these should usually come after teachers have been excited about an innovation that reaches into the pedagogic core. In the urban high schools that we studied, however, the collective sense of efficacy on the part of teachers was exceptionally low. The "depressed" quality of the schools required a frontal attack on organizational problems first.

Early activities should not, under these conditions, require broad teacher involvement. Making the transition to a teacher-owned effort from an administrator-owned effort is critical, but sometimes very slow. Notice that in both Agassiz and Alameda, the attack on morale and energy was not initially direct: Training programs to improve these were not instituted until the program was under way for some time. Rather, the importance of giving the whole school a sense of "being a winner" – new facilities, improved climate, and more order – is critical.

Action to Create Learning

A profound transformation in a school usually precedes increases in achievement, retention, or other outcomes. People in the organization need to learn how to act in different ways to produce the desired results. Old patterns need to be changed, new ones learned. The greater the anticipated behavioral change, the more learning must occur and the more difficult the process. More important, the development of a consensus in the school that a new way of doing things is "right" cannot occur until the new behaviors have been tried and tested. This observation does not mean that planning is irrelevant to learning. Instead, it means that in some circumstances planning cannot be carried out very effectively until people already find themselves in a "learning mode."

Change is Learning

Learning occurs when we gather information and reflect on it. Donald Schön (Schön 1987) argues that the most effective professional learning occurs not through logical analysis (plan-then-do), or random accumulation of data (trial-and-error) but through reflection-in-action, a more intuitive way of analyzing and dealing with issues that face us in our own behavior. Other research suggests that where doing comes before planning, it takes the organization longer to produce results, but that there is more collective commitment than when classical plan-then-do models are used (Miles and Randolph 1981).

Thus, in some (perhaps even many) circumstances, rational planning theory and even strategic planning models are simply inappropriate. If we know the general direction we want to go in, we may discover more if we start walking than if we spend the morning studying maps, listening to weather reports, and plotting out the precise route.

A note of caution: this works only if the do-then-plan action takes place at the school level, and at least a core group of faculty are already supportive of change. In Chester, district action and training on Instructional Program Leadership preceded planning at the school level, and this was viewed as a threat. Action in the district office does not produce learning in the school.

How Important are Data for Planning?

As a sympathetic codicil to our assertion of the primacy of action, we note that effective planning strategies are supposed to involve active data collection on the part of schools' staffs. Traditional rational planning models and strategic planning models put much emphasis on formal data collection and feedback – "finding the best information to help analyze your problem and develop the most appropriate solution."

The more successful schools in our study sometimes collected data in a formal way – but in no case was it considered very important in planning, and in some cases people didn't tell us about the data collection effort until we had interviewed them about planning on several occasions. (As we'll see, data were sometimes important in assessing the effects of action, however.)

In Burroughs, for example, significant data-collection efforts accompanied planning. The first, which occurred at the beginning of the 1982 foundation-funded planning period, involved "a faculty-wide needs assessment keyed to the characteristics of effective schools." Although that school year was full of action, there was no apparent tie between activities – which focused on reading across the content areas, parent involvement in supporting reading and study skills, and rewards for student reading – and the assessment. In the next school year,

> a school-wide assessment (Middle Grades Assessment Program) [was] carried out by a faculty/parent group trained ... at the Center for Early Adolescence in North Carolina ... The results ... indicated that the school needed more structure and clearer limits for students; increased parent participation; closer personal relationships between staff and students; teacher training in a wide variety of instructional methods; better coordination within and across departments; and more faculty effort to promote student competence and achievement ... According to one teacher, "We didn't systematically do something about these results once the study was released. But everyone got a copy of the report..."

The Middle Grades Assessment Program was saved from obscurity in Burroughs because the assessment was accompanied by suggestions for activities to remediate areas of weakness, a number of which were incorporated into the school's future plans. It was not exactly the data (which reportedly confirmed what the staff already knew), but the "how to do it" tips that helped the school.

A similar but even more extreme phenomenon can be observed in Agassiz, where a needs assessment was conducted during Cohen's first year as principal, but never analyzed or explicitly used in the later planning process. Cohen was certainly analytical, spending his years as an assistant principal observing the needs of the school. "When I came back (after the appointment of an interim headmaster), I had a good idea of what needed to be done." In fact, in Agassiz the main focus of the reform effort after the first two years was on improved "bottom-up planning." As the business liaison to the school stated,

> before the Compact there was no planning ... the focus has been on improving long-range planning and strategic planning ... I have been trying to move people away from thinking only about money, toward a research utilization perspective in the school.

This is not an ironic comment on the disjuncture between what the actors in the school wanted to happen, and what was actually happening. Agassiz was moving toward a research utilization perspective; it was incorporating planning activities at all levels. But good planning practices in this and other schools diverged from popular planning theories.

We might compare our findings with those of recent advocates for school-based review as a precursor to a major change effort (Hopkins 1985). In contrast to data-for-planning models, school-based review portrays the teachers in a school as researchers, formulating and collecting data that will help them to think about action. In this way the data collection is an important symbol – and support – for the teachers' engagement with the reform effort. The goal of school-based review is not simply to produce technical information to undergird a plan, but a way of organizing and celebrating the need for all staff to reflect upon common practice, and to contrast it with an emerging shared image of ideal practice.

It is significant that both Bartholdi and Chester were plagued by a repeated history of prior data-collection and planning efforts that went nowhere. Data collection energized faculty, named school problems, and aroused hope that "this time things would be better." But when no action ensued, despair and cynicism grew. The issue is connecting understanding (based on formal data or not) to action in the service of a shared vision.

Conclusion

In "depressed schools" one of the few ways of building commitment to a reform program is for successful action to occur that actualizes hope for genuine change. Effective action by a small group often stimulates an interest in planning rather than vice versa. Collecting data about school problems and new programs to solve them may energize people and provide a vehicle for a group's reflection about practice, but does not automatically lead to a better plan. Making the data-planning-action connection is critical.

Setting Goals – or Finding Themes?

Strategic planning manuals advocate developing a strong statement of mission prior to program planning (McCune 1986). In later planning, all possible strategic goals and courses of action should be assessed against their potential for achieving that mission. In general, while the mission statement should reflect the broad, long-term objectives of the system, change goals should be explicit and concrete.

But in none of our schools did planning behavior correspond exactly to this image. That does not mean, however, that these schools were operating under a "goal-free" or ad hoc approach to planning. Let's look at the way in which goals and school missions seemed to operate in the five schools.

Goals for Change

The main differences in the schools lie in (1) the specific change goals, and (2) the scope of the goals and program. The contrast among Bartholdi, Burroughs, and Agassiz is instructive.

Bartholdi began the program with decidedly narrow goals. The main focus was on dropout prevention, and the intervention was expected to be focused on students who were chronic absentees. The claim to be improving Bartholdi as an overall system was not supported with school-wide activities, nor did most staff view the program as anything other than a dropout program.

Burroughs came closest to designing a major reform effort around a mission, due to Principal Storm's unswerving commitment to the middle-school concept. In her mind, the program centered on changing the teachers' role patterns of student guidance and grouping. At Burroughs, however, middle-school objectives were mixed in with the language of the effective schools research (the basis for the foundation support). And even at Burroughs other themes, such as reading improvement, that were not explicitly linked to either the middle school or effective schools thrusts were prominent.

In Agassiz, goals were broad and poorly specified – the initial planning document conformed to the umbrella Compact program, including specific statements about reducing truancy, increasing achievement and graduation rates, and other critical student outcomes. There were also unrecorded objectives that were known only to the headmaster (although some were shared with close colleagues, and some were widely recognized within the school after a few years). These ranged from improving social services, to curriculum reform, to changes in planning and supervision in the school. Unstated goals provided more drive for the school than did the Compact-related goals.

Conclusion

The conclusion that we draw fits with other studies of implementation (Farrar *et al.* 1980). But it also goes against the thrust of the planning literature. The more narrow and specific the goal, the more likely the school is to run into problems in creating an environment for school reform. In schools with broader or vaguer goals, the multiplicity of moving parts and the overarching nature of the reform movement permits lots of positive action to generate support for reform.

The need for specific goals is probably true where the "innovation" is a single program. But if broad reform of the school is needed, it may be more appropriate to think about "targets of change" – classroom teaching, department functioning, whole-school climate – rather than about goals.

Mission – or Themes?

The more successful of our schools had no a priori mission statements for the program or the school itself. Instead, multiple improvement efforts coalesced around a theme or set of themes only after activity had begun. The themes, as they became linked, gradually reflected an image of what the school could become, and thus served to motivate staff members.

We use the term "theme" rather than "vision" deliberately. Themes in the more successful schools were typically not as specific and vivid about the desired future of the school as is usually implied by the term "vision." Themes were, in effect, interim change goals that helped to organize and direct energy. They were more general than specific program activities (such as implementing an in-school suspension program), but certainly were not "end-state" goals (such as "reduce dropout rate"). A "theme" is an answer to the implicit question, "What are we trying to do to improve things right now ... what are we working toward?" Thus, themes served as vehicles to coordinate disparate improvement efforts within the school. Rather than being deduced from an explicit examination of values and goals, themes were arrived at intuitively and inductively, by looking at what needed to be done in the name of reform. And they shifted over time.

In Agassiz, for example, themes reflected a maturation of the improvement program: initial themes focused almost exclusively on superficial improvements in facilities and school climate, then moved to programs to serve the needs of the "whole child," incorporating social service, self-esteem, school-to-work experience, and dropout intervention. As staff became more accustomed to the program, and as principal Cohen became versed in planning theories, they shifted toward a general vision of school-wide decentralized planning and accountability. Each alteration in the main themes involved more staff, beginning with administrators, then a small number of teachers, and finally moving to the whole staff.

In Chester, on the other hand, the themes began with the need to implement the externally imposed change programs; the curriculum alignment work proved to have usefulness and meaning. Subsequent change themes were driven by state testing and remediation requirements, the district remediation program, and the incredible demands posed by the mandated reorganization. None of the themes really added up to a vision, and most were reactive rather than "owned."

Conclusion

Effective school improvement involves a succession of change themes that are interim goals growing out of the effort itself. Sometimes these are derived from a general "vision" of what the school should become; more often, a vision emerges as themes become more linked, successful, and owned by people at all levels in the school. Themes that result from programs imposed from outside the school may galvanize effort, but leave little in the way of coherent improvement.

The Process and Content of Evolutionary Planning

Arriving at the conclusions "first act then plan" and "themes are more important than missions and goals" does not provide school-based change agents with a very specific handle on what they should do to improve the planning process. As one writer puts it, "Normative vision is ethereal; it is a mental event. Action is concrete; it is effort in the manifest world. The interpolation of these two realms is vital for change in social systems" (Pava 1986: 625).

In the remainder of this section we will review some of the adjustments that need to be made between the mental and the concrete.

Letting the Themes Form the Program

As we have suggested, following a "good planning process" is not too important. None of the schools that we looked at are textbook cases of good planning – if, by good, we mean the rational, explicit model. But an alternative view that incorporates the evolutionary planning approach we have begun to describe is worth looking at. One of the best ways of illustrating the management of evolutionary planning is to look at how the schools adapted their programs during the first few years.

All of the reform programs we studied were initiated outside the school, but the degree to which they were specified in detail varied. In Agassiz, we described the Boston Compact program as an "empty vessel," which imposed a few goals for student achievement, but said nothing about how the school should achieve those goals. In contrast, Alameda's programs specified some of the process of change (having a school site council for planning, using mentor teachers), but left the school improvement objectives up to the school. In the other three sites, the outlines of the change program were initially clearer, and were derived from outside the school. In Chester, the program was designed in some detail at the district and state level. The Bartholdi program was locally designed, but within a specific district-generated framework. In Burroughs, the basic thrust of the middle-school concept was derived from the extensive literature on middle schools. In none of these cases were all staff members comfortable with basic program assumptions.

Where a program doesn't "fit" initially, there is a great deal of extra coordinating work to keep it alive (Bartholdi); or it will simply be put off (Chester), or perhaps "downsized and blunted" in some aspects (Burroughs). Where the program is controlled outside the school (Chester), lack of fit is more likely, but may not be addressed. But no program fits perfectly. What do schools have to do to adjust over the longer haul?

Segmentation and Experimentation

It has been noted that schools are "loosely coupled" or segmented – what happens in one classroom or department may have little or no impact on what happens in the rest of the building (Weick 1976). This has the advantage of permitting small-scale innovative activities to flourish without requiring shifts in the whole school. On the other hand, when incremental planning processes dominate, moving to the large-scale improvement effort that is necessary to truly reform high schools may be impeded.

It has also been noted that the field of education is very uncertain; that for many of the most difficult problems that schools face, we cannot choose remedial strategies that have a known probability of succeeding. This uncertainty has a negative effect on motivation (Brunsson 1985).

In Alameda and Agassiz, we saw common patterns of dealing with this double-edged problem. In both schools, program descriptions involved a long list of different efforts. For example, Alameda's first year in the California School Improvement Program culminated in funding thirty separate curriculum development proposals; in Agassiz, the first year of action generated efforts to refurbish the school, improve attendance monitoring, reorganize the disciplinary and guidance system, develop a health services magnet program, and introduce junior ROTC and a teen-parent counseling program. For the most part, early efforts were spearheaded by a single individual, or a small group of highly motivated staff.

This may be contrasted, for example, with Burroughs, where early planning occurred all at once. The planning process and the first phase of implementation dropped an avalanche of new ideas and activities on the school. It was the biggest event to hit Burroughs since the school library burned down. Among some of the faculty, it was just about as welcome. "There was a great deal of resistance in the faculty," one said. "They just wouldn't get involved."

The "start small and experiment" approach has another important evolutionary planning feature: it permits schools to take advantage of unanticipated opportunities that might be overlooked or viewed as distractions if a master plan were being followed. Agassiz, for example, made little progress in thinking about inventive programs to support students with college potential. By happenstance they learned of programs in two branches of the state university that gave students opportunities to spend time on campus and, for successful participants, preferential admission status. These became a main thrust in their efforts to increase college application rates.

Expanding the Successful, Contracting the Less Successful

When the "incubation period" for new projects was well underway, schools were able to assess the value and potential impact of what was being done in the segmented activities. Rather than facing high-risk public scrutiny, the program components would be locally (and rather invisibly) tested, and evidence of their potential value could be produced on the basis of effective fit with the school as well as impact. In Alameda,

> Faculty were skeptical that students could do well in Advanced Placement courses. In one department's experimental AP courses it became apparent that students were passing the exams, and the program was expanded to include five departments. At the other end of the student spectrum, a rock climbing/wilderness course initiated to deal with gang violence was expanded, with faculty support, to include positive as well as negative student leaders, and is viewed as a symbol of their success in creating a climate of cooperation among the student body. Other, less successful programs were not continued or remained small in scale.

Conclusion

The objective of evolutionary planning is to capitalize on the "low-risk" quality of smaller-scale innovation (acting) to increase certainty (a mental event). This in turn increases motivation and the possibility of concerted, more "tightly coupled" action across the school.

Creating a Story

The potential danger of segmented experimentation and sifting through the success and fit of each piece is that the reform effort will deteriorate into a hodgepodge of unrelated efforts. Use of unanticipated resources can, if unchecked, become simple opportunism. (Indeed, the Alameda case makes it plain that teachers, especially the School Improvement Plan coordinator and the school site team, were aware that many of their colleagues wanted to use the project in part as a slush fund for field trips and supplies.) Thus, an important part of change management is to create a *post hoc* saga of how various improvement efforts fit together into a reasonable (if slightly untidy) whole. This involves returning to the school's improvement themes, and demonstrating how new plans and activities can potentially contribute to them. The development of a coherent story was particularly in evidence at Agassiz, where the program had so many new components every year that few people in the school could name them all spontaneously. Yet, when prompted about each component, staff could explain how it contributed to the overall school improvement themes.

Revising the Story

Themes are dynamic shorthand descriptions of the change program, and require revision as action and reflection induce creativity in the school. In this case, changes in the story that explains the themes should not be viewed as signs of purposelessness. Instead, the evolution of themes is a normal part of the effort to create and recreate a value consensus in the school. As one eminent management theorist of the 1930s has pointed out, one of the major functions of leadership in organizations is to reinvent and restate organizational purposes regularly, and to invite members of the organization to reaffirm their commitment (Barnard 1938).

Linking the Past and Future

In order for the thematic development-action-reflection pattern to persist in a school, the effort must not only evolve and "fit," it must have a deep meaning to the teachers. One way of creating meaning is to present the story of reform in idealistic terms that appeal to most educators (Louis and Dentler 1988). But idealism is not enough in many schools: the actions and themes must be tied to the staff's collective understanding of their organization.

In the two least successful schools – Chester and Bartholdi – there were strong memories of recent failures in reform. Programs that had only recently captured the imagination of many faculty members – sixty faculty had become involved in Chester – had not yielded significant change, but the failures were not due to resistance or lack of caring on the part of the staff. In both schools stories about the value of the defunct programs' concepts still circulated.

One of the problems that seemed most critical in these schools was that recognition was not given to the good components of these recent programs – the goals that motivated staff, the efforts that, in slightly different circumstances or with more time, might have succeeded, providing a basis for more forward movement. To build on past change efforts, even those that have not been entirely successful, acknowledges the fact that change and improvement are a continuous (and difficult) process. Evolutionary planning must celebrate the energy and hope that still exist, and involve key people who can be counted on for new projects. Throwing out or ignoring previous efforts during the planning process, as we have seen in Chester and Bartholdi, causes doubt and cynicism.

Conclusion

A saga that provides justification for the particular ... mix of actions ... understanding of the past. It thus helps ... meaning of the change effort.

Behind the Classroom Door: The Importance of Shared Planning

As we noted earlier, few urban school reforms today are grappling with issues of instruction and teaching. Teachers, like those in Chester, are often fearful of programs that attempt to open the classroom door and look at teacher behavior – the diagnostic phase of the school's change program was expected to "rip the school apart."

We believe that teacher engagement in planning is crucial. Even the most burned-out staff wants to see good and new things happen; the key is to provide easy working channels where their energy can be mobilized and made most effective. The important point here is that a principal-dominated activity (early planning) needs to become more widely shared. Although the use of cross-role groups may not be essential in the earliest planning phases, it becomes increasingly critical as evolutionary planning proceeds. We will explore the reasons for this in somewhat more detail in the next chapter, where we deal with the importance of sharing ownership of the themes. Here we will show how shared planning may feed the potential for real instructional change.

The depth of the shift to shared planning varies even in the more successful schools. In Alameda, the goal was to design a school that was controlled by the teachers, and the efforts were largely successful. Agassiz, located in a more bureaucratic district that was dedicated to hierarchical control procedures, did not make such a complete transition. Nevertheless, the control structure of the school did become more decentralized. Both department heads and teachers talked about their accountability for improvement.

Changing the focus from principal-dominated to shared control with strong teacher influence over change planning does not ensure impacts on teaching and instruction, but it is a necessary pre-condition. Discussions about instruction, which necessarily include discussions of individual and collective weaknesses, are more likely to occur when effective and successful planning has created an open and trusting environment. We noted the success of the active cadre in Burroughs as implementation proceeded, and the increasing confidence of the cross-role steering group at Bartholdi in dealing with instructional issues that used to be "the domain of the Assistant Principals." In Chester, though the engagement of teachers in curriculum alignment work bore some fruit, the fact that the classroom scanning was to be imposed on them simply led department chairs to walk away quietly from the effort.

Our survey also supports the importance of creating participatory planning rather early in the program. For example, where initial planning is well carried out and effective, it results in a clear understanding of what teachers and administrators should do, and it corresponds with what teachers are able to do. In these circumstances teacher commitment to the change process will be high. Of the schools with high-quality planning, 74 per cent claimed to have high teacher commitment, contrasted with 23 per cent of the schools that had poor planning quality. Teacher commitment seems to promote more active efforts to engage in continued effort to deal with implementation problems: only 38 per cent of the schools where teacher commitment was low had active and successful efforts to cope with later problems, as contrasted with 78 per cent of the schools with high teacher commitment.

Conclusion

Evolutionary planning, particularly in "depressed schools," requires a gradual shift of control from the administrator to department heads and teachers. This later participation is essential to carry out the other elements of evolutionary planning such as the action orientation, a focus on reflection, and the collective development of themes and sagas.

The Enduring Effects of Planning

This chapter has spun out several arguments. First, we claimed that it is not necessary to abandon school-wide planning just because of the messiness of the real world and the lack of rationality that often characterizes educational decision-making. Instead, schools wishing to make major shifts in their operations and effectiveness must recognize that they are embarking on a long journey during which their goals and activities – and the nature of the school itself – will evolve. Major reforms are not planned and then implemented. Nor, as we tried to show from looking at our less successful schools, is a simple modification of this linear model of change – which advocates planning, implementing, testing, and "mutual adaptation" – an appropriate model when large changes are envisioned.

Second, we showed that evolutionary planning departs from most other descriptions of planning in three significant ways. The first premise of evolutionary planning is act – then plan. The second premise is pay less attention to missions and goals and more to inspirational themes to guide the change process. The third premise is that evolutionary change requires reflection on the relationship between action and improvement, including the careful effort to renew staff commitment to both.

Finally, we discussed two key problems in reform-like school improvement efforts – the need to tie what is being proposed to people's images and constructive past change efforts, and the need to increase interaction among staff members in different roles and departments to promote an instructional emphasis.

But the reader may still be left with a "so what" feeling. Does planning really make a difference in most schools, or are these case studies unusual? This chapter has emphasized the process of planning, but if we turn to our survey data we find an answer to this final question. We used multiple regression analysis, a statistical technique that allows us to look at the influence of a wide variety of different factors that may affect whether or not schools actually become more effective.

No matter what we looked at – whether it was the initial emphasis of the program, the implementation problems that the schools encountered, or the pressures and support from the district office and state – consensus and good planning contributed to the movement of schools toward improved teaching effectiveness. The analysis also supports another argument made above: that the process of planning and the way in which it affects commitment are more important than the exact planning steps followed or the "goodness" of the first plan. In the case of our survey data, a factor strongly affecting the school's movement toward improved outcomes – for students, teachers, and the organization – was the level of support for implementation of the change effort.

This finding highlights the centrality of themes for improvement, and suggests that finding the right one(s) and encouraging ownership of them are at the heart of school reform. In the next chapter we will explore this topic in more detail.

Notes

1. This chapter was initially published in K.S. Louis and M.B. Miles (1990) *Improving the Urban High School: What Works and Why.* New York: Teachers College Press.
2. This extract and those that follow are taken from our internal case studies, which were unpublished. They are therefore quoted without a source.

References

Allison, G. (1971) *The Essence of Decision: Explaining the Cuban Missile Crisis.* Boston: Little Brown.

Anderson, S. (1989) *The Management and Implementation of Multiple Changes in Curriculum and Instruction.* Toronto: University of Toronto.

Barnard, C. (1938) *The Functions of the Executive.* Boston: Harvard Business School.

Berman, P. (1981) "Educational change: An implementation paradigm." In R. Lehming and M. Kane (eds), *Improving Schools: Using What we Know.* 253–86. Beverly Hills, CA: Sage.

—— and M. McLaughlin (1974) *Federal Programs Supporting Educational Change, Vol. 1.* Santa Monica: Rand.

Brunsson, N. (1985) *The Irrational Organization.* New York: Wiley.

Clark, D., S. McKibbin, and M. Malkas (1980) *New Perspectives on Planning in Educational Organizations.* San Francisco: Far West Laboratory.

Crandall, D.P., J.W. Eiseman, and K.S. Louis (1986) "Strategic planning issues that bear on the success of school improvement efforts." *Educational Administration Quarterly* 22: 21–53.

Daft, R. and R. Lengel (1984) "Information richness: A new approach to managerial behavior and organizational design." In B. Staw and L. Cummings (eds), *Research in Organizational Behavior,* Vol. 6: 191–223. Greenwich, CT: JAI.

Donaldson, G. and J.W. Lorsch (1983) *Decision Making at the Top: The Shaping of Strategic Direction.* New York: Basic.

Farrar, E., J. DeSanctis, and D. Cohen (1980) "Views from below: Implementation research in education." *Teachers College Record* 82(2): 77–100.

Hopkins, D. (1985) *School-based Review for School Improvement.* Leuven: Acco.

Kanter, R.M. (1983) *The Change Masters.* New York: Simon and Schuster.

Lindblom, C. (1959) "The science of middling through." *Public Administration Review* 19(1): 79–88.

Lotto, L., D. Clark, and M. Carroll (1980) "Understanding planning in educational organizations: generative concepts and key variables." In D. Clark, S. McKibbin, and M. Malkas (eds), *New Perspectives on Planning in Educational Organizations* (p. 20). San Francisco: Far West Laboratory.

Louis, K.S. and R. Dentler (1988) "Knowledge use and school improvement." *Curriculum Inquiry* 18(1): 33–62.

——, S. Rosenblum, and J. Molitor (1981) *Strategies for Knowledge Use and School Improvement.* Washington, DC: National Institute of Education.

March, J.G. and J. Olsen (1986) "Garbage can models of decision making in organizations." In J. March and R. Weissinger-Baylon (eds), *Ambiguity and Command: Organizational Perspectives on Military Decision Making:* 11–52. Marshfield, MA: McCutcheon.

McCune, S.D. (1986) *Guide to Strategic Planning for Educators.* Alexandria, VA: Association for Supervision and Curriculum Development.

Miles, R. and W.A. Randolph (1981) "Influence of organizational learning styles on early development." In J. Kimberly and R. Miles (eds), *The Organizational Life Cycle*. San Francisco: Jossey Bass.

Pava, C. (1986) "New strategies for systems change: Reclaiming non-synoptic methods." *Human Relations* 39(5): 615–33.

Schön, D. (1987) *Educating the Reflective Practitioner*. San Francisco: Jossey Bass.

Snow, C. and L. Hrbiniak (1980) "Strategy, distinctive competence and organizational performance." *Administrative Science Quarterly* 25(4): 315–34.

Steiner, G. (1979) *Strategic Planning: What Every Manager Must Know*. New York: The Free Press.

Tichy, N.M. (1983) *Managing Strategic Change*. New York: Wiley.

Weick, K. (1976) "Educational organizations as loosely coupled systems." *Administrative Science Quarterly* 21(1): 1–19.

4

Professional Cultures in Reforming Schools: Does the Myth of Sisyphus Apply?[1]

Introduction

Sisyphus is one of the best-known minor figures in Greek mythology, remembered because his fate seems so applicable to modern times. Faced daily with the task of pushing a boulder up a mountain only to have it roll down at the moment he reaches the top, Sisyphus is a symbol and touchstone for all committed professionals who believe that we labor long and hard at tasks that, at best, we can only partially or temporarily accomplish. We admire Sisyphus: he perseveres, his will undaunted by impossible circumstances. What educator cannot identify with that?

At the same time, though, we may marvel that he keeps struggling up that mountain without analyzing why he cannot accomplish his task. If evidence repeatedly suggests that a job can't be done, isn't it better to reorganize the activity so that you can at least accomplish something of worth? This essential dilemma – between commitment/perseverance on the one hand, and practicality/compromise on the other – is played out repeatedly in the life of educational reformers who work in schools.

One theme in the current panoply of ideas for improving education rests on the belief that reform may be best stimulated by creating new schools based on new(ish) ideas. These proposals come in varied forms, including, for example, the program of "charter schools" recently passed in Minnesota and supported by the federal administration, and efforts in a number of urban school districts to develop new "schools of choice" that either start from scratch or are substantial overhauls of existing institutions. A modification of this approach is found in efforts to design "schools within schools" that maintain a conventional school structure for many students, but recruit teachers to design alternative programs for students who elect or are assigned to them. Such efforts respond directly to the increasing belief that schools and professional educators who manage them are, like Sisyphus, unable to carry out more effective ways of organizing their work primarily because they are constrained by the structure and culture of public schools. If you free teachers and students from existing bureaucratic chains, the argument goes, the American school will be born again.

New and radically redesigned schools may have an important place in current efforts to genuinely change the pattern of American education. However, we believe that the underlying assumption of many who argue in favor of new schools – that the development of such schools constitutes a relatively straightforward solution to systemic school improvement – is simplistic. In this chapter, we do not intend to argue against the creation of new schools of choice, but focus instead on an empirically based thesis: school reform through the initiation of new schools is no cure-all, but creates instead its own set of challenges.

In particular, many advocates for new schools seem to overlook the fact that starting a new organization creates high levels of strain for adults who work in it and, in the absence of attention to and support for the development of human resources, the demands may prevent teachers from carrying out the goals of reform. Our evidence suggests that such reform will be only partially successful if, idealistic visions notwithstanding, reformers spend all of their time thinking about curriculum and students, and do not pay attention to what happens to the teachers who work there. Dedicated teachers will struggle with the task and the vision but, like Sisyphus, they often face an uphill battle with the possibility that, despite good intentions and back-breaking effort, their work may come to naught.

This chapter will examine the cases of two new middle schools, both located in metropolitan areas with longstanding traditions of educational alternatives. Compared to many urban districts, the districts supporting these schools are relatively resource rich. However, despite positive environments for starting anew, the schools encountered similar problems during their planning phases and early implementation. Our goal in tracing their stresses is not to suggest that the educational strategies used at either were incorrect, but rather to point to common problems that newly created schools are likely to encounter as they design an environment that works for both children and the staff who work with them. In expanding on our thesis, we draw on interviews with teachers, administrators and relevant parents and community members, and documentary data gathered from the fall of 1989 to the winter of 1993. The following topics will be addressed: difficulties in planning; the generic "liabilities of newness" in organizational design; and environmental pressures. In the final section of the chapter, we present implications for practice and policy-making that support the development of new schools of choice.

Student-focused Schools for Early Adolescents

Dewey and Whitehead Middle Schools each speak to the commitment of teachers, parents, and a community to break the mold of traditional schooling. Located on opposite sides of the United States, they share a commitment to innovative education for early adolescents in an urban context. Dewey is an innovative middle grades school (grades 5–7) marking a joint venture of a Northeastern urban school district, business partners, the community, and parents. Following a competition for creative educational programs, organizers slated the winning proposal for immediate implementation in the fall of 1989, and newly hired staff rushed to ready the program. In its first year, the school comprised three separate sites: one in the city's business district; one near an art museum and theatre; and one on a college campus. Groups of students rotated among the sites, moving with one teacher who stayed with the group the entire year. This structure changed after the first year so that students now have a home school base from which they move into the community.

The school exemplifies several innovations. An ongoing curricular focus for student activities is experiential education in an urban environment. Students, approximately 38 per cent of whom are minorities, work at different "learning sites" during the year, working regularly on real-world examples with outside mentors in several subject areas. Professional collaboration is a way of life at Dewey, with teachers working together on a routine basis. As one teacher put it, "The advantage of teaching in this school is working in teams and not by yourself." Site-based, participatory governance takes the form of an overseeing steering committee and several sub-committees representing business, the community, and parents.

The second case, Whitehead Middle School, is located on the west coast. Opened in 1989 as a working model of education for the future, Whitehead is a city-wide middle-grade magnet (grades 4–8) in a large metropolitan district with a 42 per cent minority population and a reputation for "good education." Housed in a renovated building in the center city, the school has become a district showcase and received national attention as an experiment in school restructuring. It has as its primary goal individualized learning in a supportive environment. Each student has an individualized learning plan (ILP) that is reviewed several times a year by the student, parents, and an advisor who remains with the student for five years. Affective outcomes are central to the school's vision.

Visitors to Whitehead are often astonished at the amount of technology available to students. An integrated learning system provides support for math and reading instruction; two computer labs serve as work-sites for word processing and project development; two classrooms are equipped with discourse systems that enable teachers to interact with students during class; and additional computers are available in several classrooms. But staff view technology as a means to an end, not as an end in and of itself. As the founding director of the school notes, Whitehead is "high tech, high-touch, and high-teach" with a student-centered focus that uses technology as one tool in the learning process, not as a substitute for teaching.

Because it is a magnet school, parents choose to send their children and agree to collaborate actively with staff. The student body reflects the diversity of the larger community, including 40 per cent minority and 15 per cent special-education students. A parental site council routinely discusses school matters, and three positions – lead teachers, generalists, and student interns – comprise Whitehead's differentiated staffing pattern.

Planning New Schools: Who's Involved?

At both Dewey and Whitehead, less than a year passed before the schools' doors opened to students. The planning processes occurred in charged political environments, supported in both cases by local school-reform advocates – policy entrepreneurs who serve as innovation gadflies to their respective public-school systems. In the case of Dewey, an external group sponsored a well-advertised design competition with only nominal support of the district superintendent and school board. At Whitehead, the superintendent, aware of an opportunity for national attention, supported a central office visionary to create a magnet school for the future. The superintendent nurtured the board's support.

In both cases, however, the planning process failed to include the actual teachers who would have the very real responsibility for making the new schools succeed. Not surprisingly, the first year at both schools passed in a whirlwind of activity as teachers tried to implement plans that, ultimately, were more conceptual than practical. A Whitehead teacher noted:

> [The planning] was done with the very best of intentions, but absent from contact with the people who were actually involved in the program, both parents and staff. The people who became the school were not … the people who were having these discussions, so there was never really any committee [to work] between the vision that was imagined by those people and the vision that was imagined by the people who actually lived it.

As a Dewey teacher put it, "We need time to sort out roles, expectations, and communication … Options are not always considered, and good decisions aren't made. The staff can't see the forest for the trees." The idealistic visions of the school reform advocates did not translate easily into school practice. At Dewey the lack of internal district support provided little comfort or assistance for the struggling staff. As the creation of an outside group, the school largely faced indifference from other district personnel. Whitehead, viewed by many as the superintendent's favored project in an environment of declining resources, faced annoyance and anger within the district context.

A Whitehead teacher put it this way: "We essentially had to sit down with the people we had and create the school [in less than two months] … We walked in and just said, 'We'll do it.' And we did." In neither case did the year-long planning process – in one case internal, in the other external – provide detailed plans for translating vision to practice. The planners may have thought they pushed the stone up the mountain, but the teachers clearly found their load at the bottom.

The "Liabilities of Newness": Teachers and their Needs

New and restructuring schools often get positive press coverage and massive attention from educators. At least one we are familiar with dedicates nearly a third of a teacher's time to scheduling visitors who wish to have a quick view of the facility and its novel programs; another has allocated a special room to accommodate visitors. However, journalistic and once-over-lightly examinations of these schools have paid little attention to the costs associated with starting from scratch.

Quite a number of years ago, Stinchcomb (1965: 148) identified the "liability of newness." We have known for a long time that new, for-profit organizations are extremely vulnerable; most fail within their first year of incorporation, and the "death rate" during subsequent years is still high. This is true for recently formed organizations that provide a well-understood service or product (for example, fast-food restaurants), and even more true for entrepreneurs who hope to provide a novel service or product. New schools that are founded because of a desire to offer a very different educational program, not, as in the 1950s and 1960s, simply because of increases in the student population, fall into the category of both new and novel. This presents them with a number of potentially difficult problems, including lack of precedent, problems of creating trust within the organization, and environmental pressures. At Dewey and Whitehead, each of these problems took on many dimensions.

Lack of Precedent for Teacher and Administrator Roles

Stinchcomb notes that people create new organizations because of the need for innovative products or procedures. Often, although not always, they involve unprecedented role definitions. In the case of restructured schools the titles remain similar but the expectations of what people will do in the role of teacher, administrator, student, and parent may be quite different. Teachers in new or novel schools have no "old hands" to whom they can turn with a problem and no time-tested set of procedures to follow. Central office administrators and educational experts may have no better grasp of the details of new teacher roles. And not only are teachers' roles poorly defined, but, due to the pressing nature of the workday, they often have little time to discuss their work.

A second related problem Stinchcomb notes is that inventing and learning new roles is inherently inefficient and often fraught with conflict and difficulty: "Bottlenecks which experience will smooth out create situations that can only be solved with a perpetual psychology of crisis" (p. 149). These interrelated problems – the need to learn because of lack of precedent, and the experience of inefficiency and conflict as a consequence of that need – are amply exhibited in the cases of Dewey and Whitehead.

The Press of Schooling

The problems identified above are exacerbated in schools more than other types of organizations because of the custodial functions that schools perform. Students are always present and must at all times be supervised under conditions that ensure safety and reasonably effective learning. During Dewey's and Whitehead's first year, the problem of time and keeping the students occupied with reasonable tasks was clearly the most difficult one facing teachers. In retrospect, a design flaw in both schools was that they were organized to achieve radically different conditions of schooling for *children*, but their schedules made it virtually impossible for *teachers* to meet to develop the new model. Herein lies the applicability of the Sisyphus image: because of the demands of daily work in new schools, the teachers had no time to reflectively (re)consider the task that was given to them. Further thinking about the educational design of the school was impeded by the need to keep pushing the stone up the mountain.

Dewey teachers were located in two-person teams in three separate sites. Although teachers in each team could organize their time to "free up" a teacher for preparation or planning, there was no support system that permitted both teachers on a team to have joint planning time during the school day. Because teachers were committed to a participatory governance model that involved them in a variety of after-school committees, carving out time to reflect and develop the school as a group was simply not possible. During the second year, all the teachers were in the same physical plant, but still had no time during the school day when they were not responsible for supervising students. In the third year, a "prep period" was implemented, but teachers on the same team still did not have overlapping free time.

In Whitehead, the sense of crisis was apparent from the beginning. As one lead teacher put it, "When I first visited the building (two weeks before the school opened) and saw that it was completely empty except for a few tables and chairs, I thought, 'Oh, my God! How are we going to do it?'" During the first year, there were consistent reports that faculty were working sixty or more hours a week just to keep up with the need to develop instructional activities for the students. Like Dewey, the school had "traded" support staff for a low student-teacher ratio, which increased the demands on teachers to supervise students, resulting in few opportunities for collaborative work.

The composition of the student body reinforced the press of the schedule. Middle-grades children are often viewed as requiring more consistent and constant adult supervision because they are neither as compliant as elementary children, nor as responsible as high-school-age children. Both schools were "schools of choice," and one might reasonably expect that this would produce a student body that was more highly motivated than in a non-choice school (Moore and Davenport, 1991). However, because both were also advertised as offering an "alternative environment," many students who applied were viewed by their teachers or parents as intelligent, but unsuccessful in regular classrooms. In other words, many had minor behavior or learning problems. The need to reinforce the open, child-centered focus of the schools' philosophies while maintaining reasonable order in the schools increased teachers' stress. By the middle of the third year, the tension between order and student empowerment remained unresolved in both schools and had intensified frictions among the staff and between staff and parents.

The Curriculum Process

In both schools, teachers who were hired in the summer faced opening day with virtually no curriculum in hand. There were slogans about what the curriculum should look like and, at Whitehead, pieces of curriculum written during the planning year and some clear principles to guide curriculum development. But of explicit content or actual lesson plans there was little, and, in any event, the educational philosophies of both schools demanded constant reconstruction of the curriculum.

At Dewey each teacher team had a mixed age class covering three grades. As a result, any effective curriculum that was developed could only be repeated in a three-year cycle. Thus, each teacher knew that the first three years would involve a new curricular demand for each day. Because teachers were isolated at their three sites, opportunities for working on curriculum together were rare. The initial group of teachers was committed to the concept of experiential education, but had little or no experience in developing experiential curricula: the effort involved in learning and doing at the same time overwhelmed them. By the end of the third year, only two staff members were left from the initial group of seven. Although Dewey could have turned to models of experiential education in pre-existing schools-without-walls, they did not do so until the second year because the teachers and the principal weren't linked into the loosely organized group of school-based educators interested in this topic, and they were consumed with the immediate crises of lurching from day to day.

Whitehead teachers were strongly committed to the belief that the curriculum should be built around student interests and involve student construction of knowledge. Considered "inauthentic," textbooks were not permitted. During each quarter, teachers were obligated to offer new courses that were in part designed to meet student demands. Both the content and pedagogy of many courses changed several times during the year, although it was considered "OK" to repeat a popular course, and some courses (such as writing or foreign languages) changed in focus but not necessarily in instructional strategy. Based on the elective principle, teachers needed to develop the curriculum to some extent before it was even known whether there would be sufficient student interest to sustain the course. For example, one novice language teacher worked with two colleagues to develop a module that integrated music, social studies and foreign language, but so few students signed up for it that it was not offered. In most cases during the first and second year, development occurred in "real time" – syllabi, readings and course outlines were often not available until several weeks into the class, which caused considerable conflict with parents who were anxious to monitor what their children were learning.

The Teachers' Role

As implied in the above discussion, the teachers recruited to Dewey and Whitehead were committed to taking on new roles as well as alternative instructional strategies.

Dewey teachers were expected to participate in a complex set of committee structures that involved them in governance and decision-making outside of the classroom. The design for Dewey was based on the assumption of principal as guide rather than leader. Teachers were also expected to take on roles as counselors. As noted, curriculum development was a major part of the job as well. But there was no additional funding for staff development in any of these areas. Well into the third year we observed that group process and decision-making skills among the teachers were poor, resulting in a great deal of wasted time in staff meetings.

Whitehead teachers encountered a new form of role differentiation. The lead teachers, in particular, were expected to take on responsibilities for staff development, hiring, and most administrative functions. All teachers had the same expanded counseling and curriculum-development roles described previously. In addition, because of the school's emphasis on integrating technology into all aspects of instruction, teachers had to become far more computer literate than most had been, including developing facility in simple programming. Unlike Dewey, there was ample funding and additional time built into the yearly schedule for staff development. However, virtually all of that time went to dealing with the mechanics of the technological component of the school, or for course development by individual teachers. By the third year, less experienced teachers still complained bitterly about the lack of support for learning how to teach in the new ways demanded by the school's philosophy, and many teachers were clearly uncomfortable with all but the simplest aspects of the school's technological resources. A set of interactive video disk players sat locked in a closet because no one knew how to use them.

Summary
The literature on school reform is filled with assertions about the need for collaborative work (Little 1984; Louis 1992), reflection (Schön 1987), and dialogue (Newmann 1991) if teaching is to become more professionalized and reform is to affect the quality of experiences in the classroom. Louis (1992) has argued that schools must become "learning organizations" characterized by dense communication networks and systematic incorporation of new ideas into practice if real restructuring is to persist. Yet, when we look at the experiences of Dewey and Whitehead, we see a paradox. Radical restructuring that focuses on student experiences and does not directly attend to teachers' needs may generate conditions that inhibit collaboration, reflection, and dialogue, which reinforces the tendency to keep pushing the stone up the hill, irrespective of the painful sense of confusion and lack of progress. Unremitting pressures associated with "newness" … do not create a meaningful learning environment, even under conditions of extra resources.

Lack of Trust and Problems of Creating Culture
A third problem Stinchcomb noted is that new organizations are staffed by strangers. Although in modern societies we are used to dealing with strangers on a daily basis, every new organization may face problems in developing a culture of trust and

cooperation. In addition, the lack of previous experience with others in the group often results in simple misunderstandings about who will typically do what with whom and when.

New schools are often staffed through the recruitment of an entirely new volunteer group of teachers and administrators. These individuals begin their work with no knowledge of one another and no history of trust. The same is true of the relationships between the school staff and parents. Because parents have no previous experience with the school, nor any place to turn to establish a sense of expectations about how it will work, there is often anxiety and concern in this important set of relationships as well.

Low Staff Stability

Instability among the staff occurred for different reasons at Dewey and Whitehead, but with similar consequences.

Dewey experienced high teacher turnover during the first two years of operation, largely due to some teachers' belief that the effort required to sustain the school was simply too high. As the school began its third year, only the principal and two teachers remained from the group that had so enthusiastically opened the school. Whitehead opened with three grades in 1989 and added a grade each year for the next two years. During the first year, the school was staffed solely by the four lead teachers (supported by a number of unlicensed staff). During that year the lead teachers developed a high level of value cohesiveness as they struggled to shape the school's philosophy. As "generalist teachers" were added in subsequent years, they reportedly felt shut out of the process of influencing the school's development and unable to raise questions success-fully about school structures and procedures – two left after the second year, and others indicated that they were planning to leave after the third.

In both cases, the stress of starting the school and the constant introduction of new staff who had to adjust to a radically different school setting produced low cohesiveness at best and non-productive conflict at worst. Interviews with new teachers in each school reveal that they perceived trust between the founding teachers and more recent recruits to be a major issue.

The "Community/Parent Relations" Question

Parents did have to choose to send their children to Dewey or Whitehead, and there was, according to parents in both schools, a basis for value congruence with staff. However, parents were also concerned about the lack of structure and the absence of the more obvious characteristics of schooling in both settings. Because the schools were making up their programs as they went along, parents had to "take it on faith" that their children were receiving a high-quality experience. With little formal curriculum, no textbooks to monitor, and unconventional assessment procedures, the parents who were most actively involved in their children's education frequently expressed concern – and even alarm – while trying to remain supportive.

Both schools attempted to keep in touch with parents through more frequent conferences than are typical in a middle school. In Whitehead, for example, parents attend conferences three times per year to help plan their child's individualized program. Nevertheless, complaints about lack of information were prevalent in both schools, and some parents withdrew their children because of their concerns about lack of communication and evidence of growth. Alarmingly, most of the Asian children who initially enrolled in Whitehead because of its technological emphasis withdrew after the first year. The increasing reputation of both schools as having disciplinary problems did little to increase the trust of middle-class parents.

Governance: What's the Right Balance?

Both Dewey and Whitehead aspired to increase trust and cohesiveness by eliminating friction between administrators and teachers and by empowering teachers. In both schools, however, teacher concerns about leadership remained a significant issue.

Dewey exhibited a partial leadership vacuum. The principal was hired after long discussion within the planning group about whether there should be a principal at all. When they finally agreed that it would be more practical to have one (under some pressure from the district), they selected an individual who strongly espoused a commitment to shared leadership. For example, the principal did not run staff meetings; the job rotated among all regular teachers. However, because the school was so small, she was assigned to be the principal of two other experimental schools as well, which took her out of the building. Teachers in the school lacked leadership skills and direction and frequently wasted staff meeting time on trivial issues or failed to come to a decision-point. While Dr Booth was frustrated and wished that she had the resources for staff development in leadership skills, she did not want to deviate from her policy of managing a "teacher run school."

Whitehead, in contrast, rapidly became an oligarchy. The lead teachers provided other staff with limited opportunities to participate in decisions. Meetings had a controlled quality, with agendas pre-set so that efforts by parents or staff to introduce additional topics could often not be accommodated. It was widely believed that "the gang of four" had driven out a generalist teacher who joined the staff in the second year because he disagreed with them on a number of issues. During the third year, a newly appointed half-time principal experienced in assisting troubled schools was appointed to help deal with the increasingly problematic power struggles at Whitehead.

Summary

Developing schools of choice and/or charter schools should increase the chances for developing trust among staff members and between staff and parents (Louis and van Velzen 1990). If both teachers and students select a school rather than being assigned, all stakeholders have more control over the task of finding an environment that reinforces rather than conflicts with personal value systems. Value congruence should, in turn, increase teacher commitment and effort (Metz et al. 1988; Louis 1991). These results may occur in restructured schools that have reached the stage of stabilization. However, in both Dewey and Whitehead, a variety of factors associated with newness interfered with the development of trust and, therefore, contributed to conflict and dissatisfaction.

In both cases initial hopes and enthusiasm about the development of a value-cohesive community focused on children's needs have faded, replaced by frustration, conflict, or a sense of being rudderless. Like Sisyphus, the rocks keep slipping back down the hill.

Environmental Pressures

Stinchcomb's final dilemma for new organizations revolves around the problem of maintaining effective relations with the relevant environment. Existing organizations have stable (if not always productive) relationships with key external constituencies that provide resources, but, as Louis and Miles (1990) and Farrar (1988) have pointed out, schools that attempt to do things differently often find that even overtly supportive districts and boards unwittingly place obstacles in their paths. School boards and school districts may promote alternative schools – but they are then often surprised that the new schools behave differently from traditional models. New schools face a tough job in establishing a legitimate place within a public school system that itself suffers from environmental pressures to conform to popular views of how "real schools" operate from the larger public and the state. Three environmental pressures directly affected the development of Dewey and Whitehead: the districts' accountability needs; the competition for resources in a difficult fiscal environment; and the effects of public visibility.

Accountability – But Little Support

What kind of an accountability process is appropriate for new schools? The two districts in question both adopted a "sunset" posture with regard to Whitehead and Dewey. The districts gave each three years to establish its value, at which time administrators would theoretically decide whether or not to continue to support the school. In addition, each school was expected to participate in an on-going evaluation process.

In both districts, regular school funds supported these radically different models of schooling, and the strings of accountability were unavoidably tied to that money. Central office administrators needed a signal evaluation (King and Pechman 1984) that all was well at these sites. But program evaluation created dilemmas for teachers. At Dewey, while the evaluator's information might have been useful, any time spent on the evaluation was, in an important sense, time taken away from more pressing concerns. The rational assumption that evaluation would somehow help the schools was swallowed up in the press of days. At Whitehead, teachers truly wanted to be open about the problems in their work, but were concerned that to be candid was to potentially threaten the school's existence because of intense scrutiny by the superintendent and the press.

Policy and resource instability

As noted above, Stinchcomb reminds us that new organizations must maintain effective relationships with their external environment. For both schools, that external environment has changed dramatically in three years, placing both, through virtually no fault of their own, in a potentially uncertain status.

Whitehead's history suggests that the support of the superintendent was crucial to its development. He clearly recognized the potential for national visibility, provided support for the project developer and the year-long planning process, and, serving as its political champion, worked to bring the school board along. That superintendent left the district in 1991, to be replaced by a highly respected, long-time district administrator who had risen to the level of deputy superintendent. The new superintendent was well aware of Whitehead's reputation for "favored program status" and, in a year of extreme financial crisis following the failure of a levy referendum, made his position clear: Whitehead was a school like any other in the district. He expected it to operate within district budget constraints and to succeed on the standardized measures the district uses to measure success.

In its third year, Dewey faced even greater instability. The school's concept required instructional resources that, in a time of economic recession, business supporters had never provided. While the district superintendent remained in place, neither he nor the school board had ever been visible proponents of the school. Given its history of limited resources, staff turnover, and perceived disorganization, rumors of Dewey's closing at the end of three years became common-place in the fall of 1991.

Money is only one resource needed in new schools. Human resources in the form of necessary training (for example, on group dynamics and team building) and routine release time for teachers to reflect on their work are important for sustaining change efforts in middle schools (Pechman and Feister 1994). Should new schools receive additional district support to help them establish themselves? The budget crises facing both districts in 1992 made it difficult for administrators to do this, particularly since in neither case did they see the school as their project.

The Effects of Attention: A "Lose-lose" Situation
Early in their development, both Whitehead and Dewey became the darlings of the media, appearing in professional journals, in newspapers, and even on national television as models of innovation. Numerous groups invited teachers to present at local, regional, and national conferences. For the teachers, such professional opportunities were exciting, evidence of their changing role in education. But in retrospect, the old saw "there's no such thing as good news" seems to have found additional support in what has taken place at these schools.

While it is no doubt exciting for a school to appear in the news media and may, at some level, raise national optimism about public-school reform, for Dewey and Whitehead the long-term outcomes of such publicity have not been positive. By using resources that might otherwise have gone to the schools' development, media attention has drained needed energies and created a fish-bowl environment not conducive to growth. To the extent that the publicity was bad, this attention has truly created a lose-lose situation.

Summary
The environmental pressures on new schools point to the realities of their political contexts. The need to produce information for district accountability purposes put teachers in a difficult position, taking time from instructional demands and placing them

in the difficult quandary about whether to withhold potentially damaging information. Political vagaries and the plight of district budgets can inescapably place new schools at risk, and the media attention that creates good press and public support may be costly when the news is bad.

Implications

The stories of Dewey and Whitehead document the ways in which new organizations are vulnerable and subject to stress, conflict, and uncertainty. We do not argue that these schools have failed, but only that they are encountering developmental issues that locate them squarely in the experience reported in other public and private sectors. However, we also believe that at least some of the difficulties that Dewey and Whitehead encountered, if not avoidable, can at least be minimized. As indicated above, we believe that the planning for both schools and, as a consequence, experiences with early implementation were limited by the almost exclusive focus on the education of children. Of course children and learning are the primary justification for efforts to reform, but reform does not occur without the dedication of adults, nor does it occur in the absence of a supportive environment. Thus, reform efforts and the design of new schools must consider issues of organizational design that are broader than those affecting curriculum and instruction.

Creating New Schools: Implications for Practice

Improving Planning?

Dewey and Whitehead were plagued by a common problem of rational managerial thinking: the assumption that planning and implementation are discrete and separable stages in the process of major change. As Louis and Miles (1990) have argued, major changes require evolutionary planning, in which action and development are deliberately intertwined over a relatively long period of time. Some clear recommendations can be drawn using the evolutionary planning assumptions:

- Planning teams should not be distinct from implementation teams. The pattern of having a broad group of stakeholders and experts design a program and then turn it over to a team of administrators and teachers who are to carry it out adds unnecessarily to the pressures of creating a new organization. Political pressures aside, the planning process should include sufficient time for the school's actual teachers to translate visions into implementable plans.
- Policy entrepreneurs and idea champions can be helpful in gaining acceptance for plans and for raising support/funds. However, it should be remembered that policy entrepreneurs are not practitioners and their ideas need to be tempered with the wisdom of recent school- or classroom-based experience.
- Planning should include attention to the needs of teachers as well as to the needs of students. Realistically, the best way to ensure this happens is to have teachers who will be involved in the school involved in planning from the very beginning. In

addition, central office staff must manage the district environment to insure that the
new school is neither ignored nor reviled.

- Planning/implementation should occur over a minimum of a three-year period. The
  focus on short-range planning teams that are distinct from the actors who must flesh
  out and act on the plan adds unnecessarily to the pressures of early implementation.

The Need to Create a Nurturing Environment for Teachers

Ideas for new schools usually focus on students and/or educational philosophies. As
these cases demonstrate, more attention needs to be paid to the needs of adults in the
school if teachers are to be retained and remain committed. Even in traditionally structured schools, teacher engagement has been shown to be associated with student
engagement, which is, in turn, associated with achievement (see, for example, Bryk and
Driscoll 1988). New schools may never be without crisis and conflict, but those that pay
attention to teachers' needs may minimize some of the issues that led to high levels of
turnover and dissatisfaction at Dewey and Whitehead. Program designers should
consider structuring the school to enhance the "quality of work life" factors that have
been shown to be important to teachers' work (Louis 1991):

- A sense of respect from relevant adults both in and outside of the school. The principal and/or lead teachers tend to bear the greatest responsibility for setting a tone of
  respect.
- Influence over decisions that affect teachers' work. In new schools this would mean an
  appropriate balance between teacher empowerment and administrative leadership.
- Opportunities for collaborative work. In new schools this would mean a focus on
  creating time for joint curriculum development, reflection, and problem-solving.
- Opportunities to develop and use new skills. In new schools this would mean a
  serious consideration of what is being asked of teachers and the provision of systematic, developmental training to enhance those skills.
- Feedback on performance. This is particularly critical where teachers are being asked
  to enact teaching roles that are unfamiliar. In the absence of feedback and coaching,
  teachers will not be able to develop these new teaching skills very effectively, may
  feel burned out, and may leave.
- Adequate resources. In the case of new schools, the most critical resources are time
  and staff development money. Without these during the early implementation
  period, the most engaging environment may still result in burnout and turnover.

Overcoming the "Liabilities of Newness"

If the above issues are attended to, it is reasonable to assume that some of the problems
of trust and communication may be significantly reduced. However, in new schools
that may not be enough because they confront additional tensions that make the press of
schooling even more potent. It is not enough to have some release time for teachers to
take them out of the classroom. We would go so far as to assert that unless the designers
of new schools confront the problem of time very directly, the chances are that they will
face the same problems documented here.

While organizers of new schools should insure that the period of school planning includes more explicit attention to curriculum than occurs in many cases, they should at the same time constrain themselves from immediately expecting a full-blown, completely innovative curriculum. During the period of initial organization, it is important to devote energy simultaneously to borrowing and adapting existing curriculum materials and to planning the development over time of the new curriculum. Underlying this recommendation is the assumption that this curriculum should be created, at least in part, by those who will deliver it, given that "real time" curriculum development is often ineffective.

New schools should plan for the socialization of members. The teachers thrown together during the first year usually develop a sense of camaraderie that is profound. But schools typically pay little attention as to how new recruits get to learn the culture and procedures of the school, and assume that, once the locations of the bathrooms and the Xerox machine are pointed out, informal transmission of norms and procedures will be adequate. This omission is not a major issue when schools are operating within a traditional bureaucratic model and are expected to be rather similar to one another. Thus, it is not surprising that these new schools failed to consider that selecting and orienting new members is critical in the early stages of development.

Finally, just as there are few operating models for the pedagogy of the future, designs for new teacher roles are also both incomplete and poorly formulated. If the experiments of today are to pay off in alternative paradigms for effective schooling, teachers should engage in action research and reflective dialogue about their own roles as well as those of students and educational processes (Kemmis and McTaggert 1988). While teachers in both new and restructuring schools are typically rather articulate in delineating the problems that they face in carrying out their jobs, we find that they are less effective in thinking about models for relieving the pressures and problems. Training and support, not just in "stress management" (certainly one of the most popular topics in teacher inservice) but in organizational design could prove helpful.

Creating New Schools: Implications for Policy

What do new schools need to "make it?" The policy implications of the experiences of Dewey and Whitehead speak to the importance of creating a supportive district environment for new schools, acknowledging that they are, in fact, different from existing schools. This special treatment is contained in the following recommendations:

- Openly and willingly provide start-up resources to new schools. To maintain that all schools deserve – or receive – equal treatment flies in the face of the case information presented.
- Control access to new schools during their formative years (1–3). While the value of good publicity cannot be denied, the experiences of Dewey and Whitehead suggest that it comes at a cost. During development, teachers may decide the school is not yet ready for visitors and must be supported in their right to privacy. Once ready, faculty and administrators should decide when the public and the media are welcome to visit and limit access otherwise.

- Exempt new schools from traditional accountability procedures during their formative years (1–3). While a rational model suggests the importance of evaluation from day one, such work must be structured to facilitate the work of teachers, not inhibit it. For this reason, we recommend that new schools engage in internal, in-house studies – whether they go by the name of action research, formative evaluation, or organizational learning – and that staff be assigned to this function. To demand test data prior to that time is more likely to measure where students began than to suggest the effect of the new school.

Conclusion

Does the myth of Sisyphus apply to school reform? Are educators, like Sisyphus, doomed to an endless up-hill challenge, to feel eternally unsuccessful at their tasks? To our minds, the answer is no because, as we noted in our introduction, unlike Sisyphus, we can learn from our experiences. In examining the cases of Dewey and Whitehead, this paper points to potential sticking points in the development of newly created schools and to their resolution. Planning, whether inside or outside a district, must ultimately involve those who will work in the school. The school day must include structured time for teachers to work together, to adapt or develop innovative curriculum, and to make collective sense of their evolving roles.

In addition, members of the school community – teachers, administrators, parents, and students – must consciously come together and work to develop trusting relationships. Finally, to the extent possible, the environmental pressures surrounding a new school must be managed to insure sufficient time for the school's development. Accountability must take internal forms, resources must be identified, and media attention controlled so that teachers may bring to life the vision to which they committed themselves. In the absence of these events, the creation of a new school may sadly reenact Sisyphus' daily struggle.

Notes

1. This appeared originally as K.S. Louis and J.A. King (1993) "Reforming schools: Does the myth of Sisyphus apply?" In J. Murphy and P. Hallinger (eds), *Restructuring Schools: Learning from On-going Efforts*: 216–50. Newbury Park, CA: Corwin.

References

Bryk, A.S. and M.W. Driscoll (1988) *The High School as Community: Contextual Influences and Consequences for Students and Teachers*. Madison, WI: National Center on Effective Secondary Schools, University of Wisconsin-Madison.

Farrar, E. (1988) "Environmental contexts and the implementation of teacher and school-based reforms: Competing interests." Paper presented at the annual meeting of the American Educational Research Association, New Orleans.

Kemmis, S. and R. McTaggert (1988) *Action Research Planner*. Victoria, Australia: Deakin University.

King, J. and E. Pechman (1982) *Improving Evaluation Use in Local Schools*. Washington, DC: National Institute of Education.

Little, J.W. (1984) "Norms of collegiality and experimentation: conditions for school success." *American Educational Research Journal* 19: 325–40.

Louis, K. (1991) "Teacher quality of work life, commitment and sense of efficacy: Results of a survey." Paper presented at the annual meeting of the American Educational Research Association, Chicago.

—— (1992) "Restructuring and the problem of teachers' work." In *The Changing Contexts of Teaching: Yearbook of the National Society for the Study of Education, Vol. 10*, ed. A. Lieberman: 138–57. Chicago: University of Chicago Press.

—— and M.B. Miles (1990) *Improving the Urban High School: What Works and Why*. New York: Teachers College Press.

—— and A.B.M. van Velzen (1990) "A look at choice in the Netherlands." *Educational Leadership* 48: 66–74.

Metz, M., A. Hemmings and A. Tyrie (1988) *Phase I of the Teacher Working Conditions Study: Final Report*. Madison: Center for Effective Secondary Schools.

Moore, D. and S. Davenport (1991) "High school choice and students at risk." *Equity and Choice* 5: 5–10.

Newmann, F. (1991) *Beyond Common Sense in Educational Restructuring: The Issues of Content and Linkage*. Madison, WI: Center for Organization and Restructuring of Schools.

Pechman, E. and L. Feister (1994) *Implementing School-wide Projects: An Ideabook*. Washington, DC: Department of Education.

Schön, D. (1987) *Educating the Reflective Practitioner*. San Francisco: Jossey Bass.

Stinchcomb, A. (1965) "Social structure and organizations." In *Handbook of Organizations*, ed. J.G. March: 142–93. New York: Rand McNally.

Wahlstrom, K. and Louis, K.S. (1993) "Adoption revisited: Decision making and school district politics." In S. Bachrach and R. Ogawa (eds), *Advances in Research and Theory of School Management and Educational Policy*, Vol 1, 61–119. Greenwich, CT: JAI Press

Weick, K., (1976) "Educational organizations as loosely coupled systems." *Administrative Science Quarterly*, 21, 1–19.

5

Beyond "Managed Change": Rethinking How Schools Improve[1]

Introduction

Since the mid-1990s the challenges to educators, both from within and outside the profession, have been numerous and often conflicting. Much of the time the difficulties appear overwhelming, as schools are confronted with seemingly endless challenges such as changing demographics, a sense that student engagement and faith in education is declining, and problems of attracting and retaining high-quality faculty and administrators to work in an embattled professional setting. Yet this is a time when there are serious opportunities for reforming the existing system. Much recent energy has gone into a wide range of commission and research reports that delineate the problems and provide clear images of excellence. There is strong motivation to act on these reports at national, regional and local levels, and many countries are enacting educational reform efforts that require improved performance in return for more autonomy at the school level (Louis *et al.* 1993). Moreover, we are well past the stage of good intentions: there is a substantial batch of tools in the form of well-documented, research-based programs based on the "effective schools" and "effective teaching" programs, as well as other research-based efforts at major reform.

What Do We Know about Changing Schools?

There are many ways to approach the implementation of a reform. If we look at private industry, for example, we see a number of strategies to promote rapid "turnaround," but few are relevant to schools. Schools cannot, for example, engage in massive changes in leadership in order to ensure that changes in policy are carried out, as do many businesses in distress. Even if there were no administrator unions, there are not enough qualified replacements available. Nor can education authorities cut back on unprofitable products to acquire more productive ones: Their line of business is set by law and they must deal with existing constituencies. Thus, the tradition of studying change in schools has tended to fall into a pattern that is more consistent with studies of other public-sector agencies than with private organizations.

Within this tradition Elmore (1978) identifies a number of underlying assumptions from a review of policy research and other literature on educational programs. Change strategies based on a *systems management* perspective make the following assumptions: organizations operate rationally and are goal directed; they are hierarchically structured; subunits can cooperate to maximize overall performance; and some form of management by objectives will enhance goal attainment. This implies that change processes are enhanced by goal setting, monitoring and accountability. Where change is viewed as a *bureaucratic process*, the emphasis shifts to the need to alter the system, in particular the domains of delegated discretion that exist in any formal organization staffed by professionals. Bureaucracies are characterized by nature of their formal and informal routines, and, thus, careful reexamination of the definition of roles, responsibilities, and procedures is key to effective change. The *organizational development* model assumes that interpersonal relationships dominate organizational life and the change process. The model's focus is on individual motivation, the work group as the key unit of change, and the belief that too great a focus on efficiency will undermine effective change processes. Instead the emphasis is placed on developing consensus and commitment to change, cooperation, and interpersonal support. A key premise of a *conflict and bargaining* change model is the centrality of competition for power and scarce resources. Bargaining is the main mode of decision-making, and change is an unstable process of negotiating preferences which rarely results in overall agreement.

Miles and Louis (1987) review the empirical literature on change, and note that it can be classified as focusing on a number of topics: the characteristics of the innovation, the characteristics of schools that are associated with effective implementation of innovations, the characteristics of the environment, and the characteristics of the change process, including how the change manager should operate within the four frames outlined by Elmore.

As these reviews show, most of what we know from research about how to change schools falls into a paradigm that might be best called *managed change*, whether it involves engineering a planning process, an organization chart, people or power. Most critically, the main focus of research is on identifying factors that improve the probability that an innovation will be successfully implemented and maintained, more or less as intended by its initiators. In most cases, organizational change is defined as a small-to-medium scale program, often imported from a source outside the organization, although increasing attention is being paid to larger efforts to "restructure" schools.

Questioning the Image of "Managed Change"

The image of "managed change" as an effective strategy for school improvement has been explicitly challenged by critical theorists such as Giroux (1988), but also by recent empirical research on school improvement that falls outside of a critical-theory framework. In particular, studies of restructuring schools raise questions about the degree to which the traditional ways of thinking about change management apply to efforts to make a major transformation.

Challenges from the Urban High School Study

Louis and Miles (1990) studied change processes in urban high schools that were attempting to implement organization-wide reforms based on the "effective schools" research. They focus on the role of the principal in the change process, but argue that conventional images of leadership in the change process don't apply: Change is largely unmanageable, at least in the sense that is projected in administrative textbooks. It is, rather, messy, uncertain, and circular:

> We have come to think of school improvement as a braid in which a collection of reform programs and plans becomes melded with the exiting political and cultural setting; At best, changes are based on steady and patient efforts to work within the school as it exists, while maintaining a vision that can be ... (Louis and Miles 1990: 15).

The image of change presented is evolutionary and non-synoptic, full of unpredictable "normal crises" and choices that cannot be anticipated ahead of time.

The schools studied were chosen, in part, because they did not have principals with a larger-than-life reputation of being able to turn a nest of vipers into an academy of scholars. Nevertheless, the principal was critical, but the form that leadership of change took was not at all heroic, nor did it play by the book. Among the unanticipated findings are that the most effective schools engaged in:

- *Action before planning.* "In each of the most effective schools major activities, including restructuring and the initiation of significant (and sometimes costly) new programs took place without committee meetings, and with no written plan supporting the decision" (Louis and Miles 1990: 201).
- *Generating vision from activities rather than basing activities on a vision.* "More often, a vision emerges as themes become more linked, successful, and owned by people at all levels in the school ... " (p. 207). "A saga that provides justification for the particular mix of actions evolves as the program themes change, and ... helps to reinforce the meaning of the change effort" (p. 213).

- *Developing a school-specific vision within an externally mandated program.* "… developing a vision in schools typically involves building on … opportunities that come from outside. Leadership involves integrating compatible themes available from different programs" (p. 223).
- *"Minding the store"* or a preoccupation of school-leaders with day-to-day management of change. Change managers engaged in regular scanning for problems, and exhibited "a wide range of coping efforts, matching them to the difficulties of the problem at hand … " (p. 283).

These patterns violate all of the assumptions embedded in the alternative visions of "managed change" outlined above. They are non-linear and non-rational, do not focus on changing the structure of the school, give no clear emphasis to building stronger interpersonal relations in the school except as is necessary in order to get the work done, and are political only in the sense that the school may challenge or confront outside agencies in order to obtain needed resources.

To expand further, classic and more recent writings on school improvement emphasize the need for leaders to maintain at least an oversight role throughout the change process, which involves initiating careful, preferably data-drive problem analysis, a careful choice of solutions, the development of explicit implementation plans, and active monitoring of implementation (Eastwood and Louis 1992). In the United States, many local and state reforms are based on the assumption that this is the process, and that it will be centrally coordinated within the school or the district. In contrast, although Louis and Miles frame their findings in terms of the commonly used concepts of leadership and management, the behaviors of effective leaders that they identify are less familiar. They are:

- *stimulators* – people who get things started, but then turn the action over to others;
- *story-tellers* – people who help others in the schools to discuss and understand the meaning and larger significance of what they are doing as they work on school improvement; the story becomes the "braid" referred to above;
- *networkers* – people who spend their time coordinating and creating opportunities to get people and programs together in ways that contribute to the emerging school effort; and
- *copers* – people who focus daily on problem scavenging, and who develop a wide variety of coping styles to address the unending yet largely unpredictable stream of barriers to change.

The notions of "evolutionary planning" and "coping" presume that large-scale change will be typically unpredictable and disjunctive. In these circumstances, the leaders focus on helping staff to confront, make sense of, and interpret the emerging circumstances in which the school finds itself so that both teachers and administrators can work with each other and those outside the school to reach goals that are never very well defined.

Challenges from the Teacher Quality of Work Life Study

The sense that our understanding of the change process may not be effectively captured by the traditional images of managed change is further tested by another recent study of eight restructured secondary schools (Louis and Smith 1991; Rosenblum *et al.* 1994). The study focused on how teachers' work was altered in schools where significant change efforts had been underway for some time and, again, the data suggested that the roles played by the leaders in the schools did not center on issues that are traditionally emphasized in the "managed change" literature.

Teachers in the study agreed that, no matter how talented the staff, schools with ineffective principals are unlikely to be exciting – and can become exciting quite rapidly after the arrival of a supportive principal. But teachers described the effective principal's role largely as a facilitator, freeing the staff and the school to reach its own potential. In particular, teachers argued that good change leadership consists of (see Rosenblum *et al.* 1994) the following.

- *Providing consistent policies to delegate and empower* – Principals who created healthy environments for teachers made "teachers invent solutions to problems – they aren't the only problem solver." The effective principal, "can leave the building without things falling apart or hitting snags, and has staff empowered to respond to crises."
- *Spending time on the details of life in the school* – Leadership in the eight schools was not efficient. Administrators were proactive, anticipating emerging problems. They hung around, so they "know what's going on in the classrooms, in the lunchroom, etc." They had an open-door policy, and encouraged drop-in visits.
- *Modeling risk-taking* – To stretch professionally, teachers must take risks in the classroom. Over and over again the teachers in these schools claimed that they were willing to do so because their principal was also willing to "bite the bullet when necessary [and] make tough decisions." One aspect of risk-taking was the principal's personal willingness to confront bad teaching, coupled with supportive programs to help less effective teachers improve.
- *Providing leadership about values* – Teachers were clear that the principal set a tone for developing a vision and a value orientation in the school. The principal must understand and reflect the best in community ethical standards and values, and "make clear what is valued – don't keep faculty guessing about what is important."
- *Emphasizing caring for students* – The theme of caring as a significant aspect of teachers' work has been developed elsewhere (Noddings 1984). The high schools all had climates and student-teacher/student-administrator relationships that were more like excellent elementary schools than like traditional secondary schools. Principals reinforced the importance of, as one teacher put it, "... lending your ego for a kid to learn ... you are [not] only teaching a subject and [but] teaching kids ... ".
- *Actively using knowledge and ideas.* In addition to what teachers told us, we also observed that the principals in these schools had another characteristic that differentiated them from principals in traditional schools: they were active and persistent users of "educational knowledge" – not just research reports, but also good ideas emerging from practice. They were themselves linked into local and national networks for

exchanging ideas, and also placed a high emphasis on getting their teachers involved in such networks.

As teachers in the Teacher Quality of Work Life (TQWL) study saw it, effective change management did not involve much oversight of the process (except to ensure that teachers' responsibilities for change were consistently reinforced), or much attention to the specifics of restructuring. Although the good change managers were sensitive to teachers' collective and individual needs (attention to the details of school life), they did not dwell on organization development, nor use any of its accepted techniques. The notion of risk-taking seems to imply elements of a conflict perspective, but there were no well-defined interest groups in most of the schools, and the concept of bargaining was largely absent. Thus, the image of change portrayed is not well captured by any of the four frameworks described by Elmore.

What comes through in these descriptions is the attention to values, both at the grand level ("caring for kids") and at the daily level (reinforcing small behaviors because they are involved in the daily life of the school). Surprisingly, teachers appreciated their principals as intellectuals, and saw this as a major feature of their success in changing the school. Without being overly idealistic, we were surprised to find that teachers in these schools (not all, but a surprising number) also operated as intellectuals to a greater degree than in more typical schools. Engaging in reflective discussions about educational issues and philosophies was not a daily occurrence, but was also not unheard of.

Organizational Learning as an Alternative Perspective

The descriptive findings from the two studies were not anticipated, and did not, therefore, confirm an already established theoretical framework of change. To explain them more fully requires delving into literature that has rarely been applied in educational settings. Theories of organizational learning help us to understand why restructuring may proceed well in some schools, but not in others, and it does so in ways that are overlooked by the "managed change" literature. The organizational learning framework emphasizes the cognitive and behavioral transformations that occur in individuals and groups as part of the emergence of new organizational patterns. Although the frame is poorly developed in educational studies (see Dalin 1978 for an exception), it has potential for helping to think about the problem of how schools change basic assumptions about "what it is we do here" when demands for significant reform are made.

A Definition
Although the concept of the "learning organizations" has recently been popularized by Senge (1990), discussions of organizational learning go back to the cybernetic models of the early 1960s (Cyert and March 1963) and received considerable attention in the 1970s as Argyris and Schön's (1974) psychological model of "single and double loop learning" became well known. However, more recent formulations emphasize that

learning involves the creation of socially constructed interpretations of facts and knowledge that enter the organization from the environment, or are generated from within. This emphasis distinguishes the organizational learning literature reviewed here from studies and theories that are derived from the individual cognition tradition (Sims and Lorenzi 1992).

Some Key Assumptions and their Implications for Reforming Schools

Recent theories also rest on another assumption: the learning that takes place in groups cannot be reduced to the accumulation of the learning of individuals. Organizations cannot learn in the absence of "social processing" of information (Louis and Dentler 1988; Louis *et al.* 1993). Organizations also use information in the same way that individuals do. Hedberg (1981), Senge (1990), and others, for example, point out that learning involves not only psychological adaptation, but also active use of knowledge by the organization to improve its fit with the environment. *Organizational memory* – the conservation of collective experience – as necessary for learning is also important: "Organizations develop and maintain learning systems that not only influence their immediate members, but are then transmitted to others by way of organization histories and norms" (Fiol and Lyles 1985: 804; see also Levitt and March 1988).

Thus, when thinking about schools and restructuring, we are increasingly drawn to the argument that changing education will involve more than improving the credentials and inventiveness of individual teachers, the climate, or the leadership capacities within a school. And it is, perhaps, not an "improvement process" that must be managed, but rather collective norms and procedures for processing and dealing with new ideas that must be addressed.

A second assumption is that organizational learning can range from an *accumulation of random events*, occurring when individuals locate factors that result in a useful statement of cause-and-effect (as implied by Lindblom 1959), to a *systematic search*, where many individuals view the collection and processing of information from both predictable and less predictable sources as part of their daily work. Where organizational learning is more systematic, an interpretive framework is required to simplify the complexity of the world with which the members must collectively deal.

In schools, for example, we would be more interested in cases where the faculty as a whole, or large subgroups of the faculty, engaged in regular efforts to gather information and improve practice (for example, develop a knowledge base), as compared with changes in practice that occurred as a consequence of a one-time contact between a teacher and an "expert," or the chance meeting of two colleagues at a social event (Shrivastava 1983). In both cases learning occurs, but in the latter the chance that school-wide improvement will occur is more remote.

Systematic organizational learning occurs within an *organizational paradigm*, or an elaborate, widely shared theory or frame of reference that guides and organizes actions (Simsek and Louis 1994). But learning is also the source of information about anomalies that may challenge the paradigm and ultimately contribute to its replacement. Organizations and communities of organizations vary widely in the degree to which they are tolerant of anomalies. Schools are widely viewed as being "institutionalized" (Meyer and Rowen 1977), which means that the external characteristics of schools have come to be more important measures of "goodness" than objective information about performance. For example, it is difficult to challenge the existing structure and organization of time in US high schools, even in the face of considerable evidence that it may contribute to poor performance, because people expect that in high schools instruction will take place in a set number of periods between approximately 8 in the morning and 3 in the afternoon. As a number of observers have noted, institutionalized organizations require a "paradigm shift" if they are to begin to do things differently (Mohrman and Lawler 1985; Bartunek and Louis 1988; Simsek and Louis 1994).

Mature organizations such as schools often do not respond to a crisis ("We've weathered this before – just wait and it will go away") or engage in searches for information that will provide evidence that their performance is actually OK. The essence of transformative change is to break these unresponsive reactions to crisis to reshape or reframe members' understanding of mission, identity, and basic operations. The process of transformation is full of conflict and anxiety, and ambiguity, but eventually "groups whose perspectives have been incorporated in the new understanding should experience a sense of comfort and 'rightness' … " (Bartunek and Louis 1988: 121).

Organizational Learning, Change, and Structure

A critical question for school reform is: how are serious anomalies discovered within schools? Organizational learning provides a framework that helps to interpret some of the empirical findings from the two studies discussed above.

Daft and Huber (1987) emphasize the concept of *information richness*, a condition that increasingly characterizes schools in which practitioners and administrators have access to a growing density and variety of information that has implications for their work. Information richness can be handled in traditional ways: Schools can *sift and reduce* the data available to them to an amount that can be easily processed or, alternatively, they can confront the need to *design interpretive systems* to increase the flow of information into and within the organization and to increase opportunities for social interpretation of information.

There are also multiple forms of the organizational learning process, each of which corresponds to a theory of planning. There is the kind of *incremental adaptation* that is based on small-scale adjustments to changing conditions. In this form, learning occurs through largely unanalyzed small changes (Lindblom 1959). In the more *intellectual learning* style, the organization deliberately develops knowledge about the relationship between its actions and outcomes. As Lundberg (1989) points out, this is often related to efforts to significantly improve strategies for goal attainment without challenging their paradigm. A deeper form of learning, however, is *assumption sharing*, which involves changing the pattern of commonly held theories-in-action. We might define this as an opportunity for the development of a consensus about the existence of an anomaly, and a construction of a new reality – that is, a major shift. This type of learning is an integral part of the "evolutionary planning" process identified by Louis and Miles (1990: 201) in urban high schools, and of necessity must incorporate attention to values as noted in the TQWL study.

Daft and Huber (1987) also argue that it is necessary to get away from traditional structural approaches to thinking about learning and information (which often emphasize problems of distorted learning, such as "information overload") and use a more constructivist mode, which emphasizes the role of *organizations as makers of meaning*, and information as meaningless until it is interpreted. This corresponds well to Louis and Miles' (1990: 211–13) emphasis on the need to use stories to help define coherence in programs that are not pre-planned, but emergent. Where environments are relatively richer in information, and where information is more difficult to inter-pret and understand – a situation that increasingly characterizes schools and school districts – the organization must adopt a *self-designing* learning style. This means emphasizing assumption sharing, interpretive approaches, and trial-and-error, and it goes to the heart of why teachers in the TQWL study valued their effective principals as intellectuals and as risk-takers. For organizations exposed to high information rich-ness and equivocality, Daft and Huber also argue that there is a need to develop decentralized communication structures, dense interpersonal networks for sharing and discussing information, and many formal and semi-formal efforts to integrate knowledge across the informal groups (meetings, special integrative roles, and so on). This contrasts markedly with the structures we tend to find in US school districts which, although often loosely linked internally (Weick 1976), nevertheless exercise boundary control over flow of information into the school or district and, in larger systems, emphasize hierarchical flows of information and routine, and regulated data systems (Wahlstrom and Louis 1993).

Conditions for Organizational Learning and School Reform

The discussion above has referred, parenthetically, to a variety of conditions that affect schools' ability to learn and change. Here follows a summary of some of the most important.

Decentralization

Most authors agree that serious organizational learning requires considerable decentral-ization (Daft and Huber 1987; Bartunek and Louis 1988; Senge, 1990):

> … decentralized structure features such as collateral or parallel groups or matrix structures … are more likely than traditional ones to foster the development of alter-native viewpoints in an organization. If new viewpoints and structures that support them are not present … the organization is more likely to enter into decline than a renewing transformation. (Bartunek and Louis 1988: 110)

Decentralization may increase learning but impede transformation because, although decentralized organizations tend to be innovative, changes tend to occur within existing programs or by introducing small-scale projects. The authors emphasize that strong lateral relationships need to be overlaid on the decentralized organization that permit unified action when the circumstances demand it.

Leadership: A Paradox?
Most models of organizational transformation emphasize the need for strong, effective leadership (Bartunek 1984; Tushman and Romanelli 1985). The argument is similar in most cases: the organizational leaders, or the "dominant elite," have the primary influence over the opportunity to reframe the underlying metaphysical assumptions. As Bartunek (1984) points out, they may not initiate the new ideas in all cases, but they clearly determine the receptivity of the organization to alternative interpretations. Although decentralization may be necessary, systemic change also demands more central direction in the form of formal and informal communication and influence, largely because the process is fraught with anxiety and conflict.

Thus, transformational change appears to demand influence from both leaders and subordinates, and frequent adjustments between the degree of decentralization versus coordination and integration. This may account for the dissension, at least in the USA, between advocates of reform based on centralization/national goals, and so on, and those who advocate decentralization/school-based management and choice as the means to improve schools. It also accounts for the finding from the TQWL study suggesting that teachers valued strong leadership on the part of the principal in part because it routinely affirmed their own responsibility and accountability for change.

The organizational-learning literature explores this further, suggesting that decentralized designs demand integration through informal communication networks (Daft and Huber 1987; Senge 1990). Without these, leaders find it difficult to exercise influence, or help units of the organization to coordinate their activities. Handy (1990) argues that leadership in future organizations, including schools, will have to exhibit stronger conceptual skills than in the past, where knowledgeability, decisiveness and "good instincts" may have sufficed. However, they will also have to internalize the fact that they are "post-heroic" in the sense that they neither have sufficient information to lead by themselves, nor will the people who work in "learning organizations" be the type who will function well under authoritative superiors.

These perspectives help to explain the form of leadership identified in the TQWL study, which bears little resemblance to the images of transformative leadership initially proposed by Burns (1978). In contrast, the leadership style described by Handy, and exhibited by the principals in restructured schools involves " ... a mixture of activities, including those of a teacher, a consultant, and a trouble-shooter (Handy 1990: 167; see also Senge 1990: ch. 18). According to the TQWL study, the style may be aptly described as a shift away from leadership behaviors that are traditionally masculine toward those more closely identified as feminine.

The Knowledge Base

March (1991) argues that the tendency of the educational literature to blame the lack of change in education on the "culture of schools" or resistance is misplaced. Rather, teachers' ability to look for new paradigms that might be effective is limited by the absence of "an inventory of prior knowledge that would permit them to use radically new ideas intelligently" (March 1991: 29). The "absorptive capacity" of schools to take in and use new ideas is, according to this view, hindered by the low investment in research and development. (Others might argue that the research knowledge base is adequate, but the development and dissemination systems that would permit teachers to have easy access to needed knowledge are absent in many countries.)

The Environment

Most learning theories suggest that the environment is the major source of information about problems in organizational performance. Furthermore, because existing patterns of schooling are institutionalized, change cannot occur without the environment also accepting not only the existence of anomalies, but also an acceptable alternative to existing practice. Herein lies a genuine dilemma for school reform: although schools are extremely dependent on support from their local setting, changes in the environment are not, by themselves, sufficient to produce real reform in schools. First, the relevant constituencies must accept and agree upon an alternative vision of schooling. This is far more difficult a process than generating a sense of crisis.

Furthermore, an alternative vision of schooling imposed from outside rarely generates learning and real change unless compliance with external constraints is coupled with a shift in interpretive perspective. When compliance occurs without learning, the changed behaviors may disappear as soon as the pressure or other external stimulus subsides (Berman and McLaughlin 1977; Bartunek and Louis 1988). A number of authors argue that there is always a need for sustained pressure and support for change from outside the school (Huberman and Miles 1984; Dalin *et al.* 1993), but one might also argue that a continuing need for pressure and support implies that effective learning has not taken place. High levels of regulation may repress the ability of organizations to respond to new information readily and usually increase centralization within the organization to protect the core functions of the agency/school from interference (Schön 1979).

The impact of the environment is moderated by its degree of complexity. Learning occurs largely through observations of the experience of other similar organizations (Levitt and March 1988): where trial-and-error is confined to experiences within a single unit, it is inefficient and of poor quality. Population ecology theories suggest that organizations that are situated in a competitive environment develop more efficient systems of diffusing major innovations but where, as is the case in education, the environment is non-competitive, learning from others is often reduced.

The Politics of Reform and Restructuring: The Limits of Learning

Incremental learning goes on continuously in effective schools that share the dominant paradigm, but it is typically of the adaptive or intellectual types described above. Second-order learning, which involves challenges to the paradigm and possible paradigm shifts, will not occur without a sense that "business as usual" cannot persist (Schön 1979), and external pressures that make the crisis apparent. Yet the kind of dramatic learning that involves giving up old ways of thinking cannot occur without the emergence of real alternatives (Kuhn 1970; Simsek and Louis 1994).

Schools are becoming increasingly aware of the crisis, both as a result of failures to meet the needs and demands of changing student bodies and of external pressures from constituencies. However, only a few rudimentary new paradigms have emerged, none of which has broad acceptance among teachers, administrators, politicians, and professionals.

The political nature of school restructuring is not avoidable, since schools represent a major public good. Educational systems and schools are expected to be everything to everybody, irrespective of other national or cultural differences, and schools often become the scapegoat for almost every social, cultural, economic, and political problem. Selecting a new vision of schooling that will satisfy all constituencies and meet all of the expressed goals is impossible. What this means is that any school restructuring has to face a particularly difficult challenge of political selection before it is able to settle into a new routine of learning.

The Dark Side of Interpretive Learning

Senge (1990) claims that many organizations suffer from "learning disabilities" because they make false assumptions about how well they know and can control their environment, and the value of their own experience as a learning tool. Levitt and March (1988), however, present a more skeptical view. They point out that the rich and complex interpretive process advocated by Daft and Huber may mitigate against real changes in basic assumptions: the frames that are used for interpretation are often so flexible that they allow a lot of change in practice without disturbing myths and beliefs that have value to organizational members. Also, they point to the problem of "superstitious learning" which occurs where the relationship between action and effect is weak. For example, in periods of externally defined crisis in education public attitudes toward the possibility of reform may be pessimistic. Change in routines, no matter how promising, is unlikely to lead to rapid changes in the public's perception of the quality of education. This is particularly true where efforts to evaluate reforms are premature. Under these circumstances routines will be changed frequently in a fruitless attempt to find some that work. The fact that routines are changed frequently means that they are also less likely to work. The learning that occurs is, therefore, misleading.

This may account for the fact that it is quite typical for schools to respond to environmental pressures by faddish adoption of untested programs that are just as rapidly stored in the closet. The result is the rapid recycling of poor-quality innovations (Nelson and

Sieber 1976). Another common phenomenon is that changes are made so rapidly philo-sophical incompatibilities between them are ignored (at least for short periods) within the same school, causing increased confusion and depressing learning. Ambiguous information about success may have other effects, including "paradigm peddling" and "paradigm politics":

> Ambiguity sustains ... efforts to promote ... favorite frameworks, and the process by which interpretations are developed makes it relatively easy for conflicts of interest within an organization to spawn conflicting interpretations ... disagree-ments over the meaning of history are possible, and different groups develop alter-native stories that interpret the same experience quite differently. (Levitt and March 1988: 324)

Implications for School Restructuring and Reform

The challenge outlined at the beginning of this paper implies a change in basic assump-tions about current educational practice as opposed to tinkering with the system. The question is whether the calls for reform will add up to a period of minor adaptations within the existing vision of schooling, or to a genuine reconsideration of the anomalies and the presentation of a well-formulated alternative. Within this challenge we can turn to the issues outlined above to derive some significant implications for how we should think about, enact, and study restructuring.

Implications for Policy and Practice

Schools currently exist in an environment of high information richness in two senses. First, many ideas or rudimentary paradigms sprout within and outside schools, creating a rich source of new ideas and practices. Second, the educational system has become more receptive to information in and around the school ever since, during what is perceived, at least in many countries, as a crisis in the school's ability to meet the needs of individual students, and the increasing social aspirations about the proportion of students who must "succeed" in school if our societies are to remain robust and adaptive. Teachers and administrators in schools, as well as policy-makers, believe that they *must* change. But, before they are able to do so, some learning issues must be addressed.

School (Re)structuring

An image of schools as learning systems began to emerge from studies such as those discussed in detail at the beginning of this paper, and with it a better understanding of how learning may be related to reform. The image of an effective change process focuses on the ambiguity of practice and knowledge, the need for "doing" and "discussing" as the means to learning, the importance of interpretation in the context of the school's history, and not segregating information or people in ways that impede decentralized sharing. Above all, there is a need to ground thinking about change in a clear value system. It also leads to the conclusion that changing actions (experimenta-tion) may create changes in paradigms, rather than vice versa.

The problem for schools is that this style of processing information is difficult to maintain because it assumes opportunities for information sharing, interpretation and story-telling. This is how universities are organized (to some extent), and most R&D laboratories or scientific research organizations – as well as some industries (Kanter 1983). *This is a serious challenge to current models of schooling, in which teachers work almost exclusively with pupils and rarely with each other. In the absence of opportunities to interact, theo-ries of organizational learning would predict a low capacity for change and development.* In partic-ular, even when schools are decentralized they usually lack the dense communication networks and the easy access to outside ideas that are required for learning. Alternative paradigms may be located and developed, but unless schools can internalize anomalies for themselves, learn about new paradigms and adapt them for experimentation, restructuring will come to nothing.

Reform proposals in many countries focus on the decentralization of authority and accountability from the ministries of education to local schools. However, I would argue that the restructuring of schools is an important *precursor* to real transformational change rather than the focus of change itself, and that decentralization is not by itself a very powerful instrument for reform. If we cannot design schools so that basic assump-tions about teachers' work can be shared on a regular basis, can we expect schools to become self-designing over the long run? If schools are to become learning organiza-tions they will require a profound change in the use of time so that teachers and admin-istrators have the opportunity to work together. Only then can they begin the real restructuring that will affect the paradigms surrounding the central tasks of the school: creating a system that will ensure a higher level of learning for all children.

Changing the Learning Patterns of Schools

The image of educational change embodied in Miles and Louis's book on urban high-school reform is that of a long journey with only a primitive map, and an explorer's will-ingness to alter planned routes as new information becomes available. The goal does not change, but the itinerary does.

In order to achieve this image of evolutionary transformation, schools must address their embedded dysfunctional learning habits. We have referred above to superstitious learning, to the rapid in-and-out of an innovation that prevents real learning, and to the circulation of poor but popular ideas that occur in decentralized systems such as the USA. Different learning problems presumably exist in more centralized systems.

Some of these result from the paucity of the R&D base that is readily available to schools, and the relative isolation of knowledge production units (universities) from the knowledge application units (schools). But some also result from patterns that are unre-lated to the lack of useable information. One example is the emphasis on the teacher as an autonomous professional whose skills at "clinical judgment" demand consultation with peers on rare occasions. This "mental model" of professionalism results in the development of a disjointed shadow curricula within each classroom. Another is the over-dependence of many systems on "quick fix" solutions from outside experts: last year a new instructional model that is touted to fix all reading problems, this year an emphasis on "total quality management," and next year an "outcomes based education" model. Educators accept outside pressure to implement and "show results" in unreasonably short time frames, rather than argue that rapid measurable change in children as a consequence of changes that affect a small percentage of the child's life are unreasonable. Unless schools recognize these bad habits, restructuring to provide more opportunities for learning will be ineffective.

The environment for education is, at this point, highly likely to reinforce superstitious learning and the worst kinds of paradigm peddling. If policy-makers at the district and higher levels do not attend to the need for schools to break the futile cycle of continuous innovation-implementation-discontinuation of many small innovations, which reinforces teachers' sense that "nothing will really change," the promises given in the rhetoric of sweeping transformations of schools are unlikely to occur. Part of this effort to give schools the break that is required to develop serious learning environments must come from efforts of the educational leadership, whether it be located in the central government or in school districts, to challenge the public's hope for instant success.

Retraining Leaders

The expectations that most teachers and principals have about the nature of leadership in schools are inconsistent with the image of leadership presented in the organizational learning literature. In traditionally organized schools (at least in the USA but, presumably, in some other countries as well) principals and teachers both want the former to "be in charge" and to take responsibility for buffering teachers from outside pressures. Most principals insulate themselves from the day-to-day world of the school, and spend their time managing crises to the exclusion of coaching and consulting (Rosenblum *et al.* 1994). Principals also fear that decentralization will bring more responsibilities for guiding and creating visions, which are important functions in the learning organization, but fail to give the school real control over decisions (Alexander 1992). This suggests another arena in which restructuring could founder. Without intervention to improve the abilities and confidence of sitting principals (in addition to redesigning selection and preservice training for school leaders), we will fail to attract the full energies of people who are critical to the organizational learning process.

As noted in the discussion above, the leadership task in a learning organization is both subtle and unstable. On the one hand, one must empower and delegate; but, on the other, one must also become a raconteur who leads through building value consensus and vision, and an intellectual who provides the stimulus for others to seek and interact with new information. The dialectic between strong leadership and delegation is never resolved in the learning organization, at least according to the literature: it requires individuals who are able to operate in the forefront and the background at different points in time. In addition, there is the tricky question of how to encourage teacher leadership without undermining pedagogy and the focus on classroom work. This is not the task that most school leaders aspired to when they decided to apply for the position!

The agenda for helping principals cannot remain decentralized. In most countries, including the USA, which has the highest academic requirements for pre-service administrative training, almost no attention is paid to the needs of the mid-career principal faced with an entirely new set of circumstances and demands. We are dependent on mid-career professionals to create learning organizations, but lack a shared systematic understanding of the conceptual and skill needs of people faced with organizational circumstances that are very different from those that they faced when they became school leaders.

Conclusion

Although the above discussion points to weaknesses in schools, the organizational learning framework shifts the discussion of these weaknesses away from finger-pointing (teachers are lazy and poorly trained; educators resist change because they want to protect their turf) to structural and cultural conditions that make it almost impossible for educators to respond meaningfully to the challenges with which they are presented. On reflection, if we look back at Elmore's different frames, we find that the organizational learning perspective does not contradict any of them – in practice. Teachers and administrators still need to know how to plan and make decisions (albeit in a very different way), to decide how to organize and divide up the work, to interact with each other to maximize both personal and organization objectives, and to manage the inevitable conflict associated with change. However, the focus is very different if one adopts an organizational learning perspective: instead of centering their efforts on any of the above actions, they are treated as a means to a larger goal, which is renewing the capacities of the school to redesign itself to meet student needs.

Implications for Theories of Organizational Change in Education

I have emphasized the implications of the organizational learning concept for policy and practice in restructuring. But the discussion also challenges two major schools of change theory in education, while providing a possible basis for resolving their differences. One stream has viewed educational organizations as anarchic, and change as a random event. These are the theories that label education organizations as "organized anarchies" and change decisions in these organizations as "garbage cans" (March and Olsen 1976). However, the dominant second stream is the "managed change" perspective described above, in which organizations are seen as rational and goal-directed organizations while change is purposeful and by choice. Both view administrators as primary initiators and change agents; their difference lies in the actions to be taken by these change agents.

The first group of theories argue that accumulated unplanned decisions to change made by competent and well-intentioned people will result in a natural (usually beneficial or at least neutral) evolution of practice. The role of administrators is limited. On the other hand, the "managed change" perspective ascribes a more strategic decision-making role to the administrators, but has typically treated the implementation of delimited programs rather than major change. Neither of these streams has dealt with the demands for transformation facing schools in most countries today.

The image of change that emerges in the organizational learning paradigm has elements of both managed change (organizational learning is affected by structures and leadership) and anarchy (the emergence of alternative paradigms and the selection of a new paradigm is a chaotic, largely unpredictable process). This promises the possibility of synthesis, rather than continuing dissension. It is beyond the scope of this article to outline the synthesis, but I would suggest that beginning with the role of change leadership and management, as I have done here, provides a helpful entry point. The application of organizational learning theories may assist in identifying aspects of the change process that are more and less manageable, and may also suggest ways in which the subjective aspects of change may map on to more traditional approaches to directing change, such as strategic planning.

Note

1. This paper, with slight revisions, was published as K.S. Louis (1994) "Beyond 'managed change': Rethinking how schools improve." *School Effectiveness and School Improvement* 5: 1–22.

References

Alexander, G. (1992) "Transformation of an urban principal: Uncertain times, uncertain roles." Paper presented at the annual meetings of the American Educational Research Association, San Francisco.

Argyris, C. and D. Schön (1974) *Organizational Learning: A Theory of Action Perspective.* Reading, MA: Addison Wesley.

Bartunek, J. (1984) "Changing interpretive schemes and organizational restructuring: The example of a religious order." *Administrative Science Quarterly* 29: 355–72.

—— and M.R. Louis (1988) "The interplay of organization development and organizational transformation." *Research in Organizational Change and Development* 2: 97–134.

Berman, P. and M. McLaughlin (1977) *Federal Programs Supporting Educational Change.* Vol. VII, *Factors Affecting Implementation and Continuation.* Santa Monica, CA: Rand Corporation.

Burns, J.M. (1978) *Leadership.* New York: Harper and Row.

Cyert, R. and J.G. March (1963) *A Behavioral Theory of the Firm.* Englewood Cliffs, NJ: Prentice Hall.

Daft, R. and G. Huber (1987) "How organizations learn." In N. DiTomaso and S. Bacharach (eds), *Research in the Sociology of Organizations*, Vol. 5: 1–36. Greenwich, CT: JAI.

Dalin, P. (1978) *Limits to Educational Change.* New York: St Martin's Press.

——, G. Rolff and B. Kleeskamp (1993) *Changing the School Culture.* London: Cassell.

Eastwood, K. and K. Louis (1992) "Lasting school improvement: Exploring the performance dip model." *School Leadership* 2: 212–25.

Elmore, R. (1978) "Organizational models of social programs implementation." In D.
Mann (ed.), *Making Change Happen?* New York: Teachers College Press.

Fiol, C.M. and M.A. Lyles (1985) "Organizational learning." *Academy of Management
Review* 10: 803–13.

Giroux, H. (1988) *Schooling and the Struggle for Public Life: Critical Pedagogy in the Modern
Age.* Minneapolis: University of Minnesota Press.

Handy, C. (1990) *The Age of Unreason.* Boston, MA: Harvard Business School.

Hedberg, B. (1981) "How organizations learn and unlearn." In P.C. Nystrom and
W.H. Starbuck (eds), *Handbook of Organizational Design,* Vol. 1: 3–26. New York:
Oxford University Press.

Huberman, M. and M. Miles (1984) *Innovation up Close: How School Improvement Works.*
New York: Plenum.

Kanter, R. (1983) *The Change Masters.* New York: Simon and Schuster.

Kuhn, T.S. (1970) *The Structure of Scientific Revolutions.* Chicago: University of Chicago
Press.

Levitt, B. and J.G. March (1988) "Organizational learning." *Annual Review of Sociology*
14: 319–40.

Lindblom, C. (1959) "The science of muddling through." *Public Administration Review*
19: 79–83.

Louis, K.S. and R. Dentler (1988) "Knowledge use and school improvement." *Curriculum Inquiry* 18: 33–62.

—— and M. Miles (1990) *Improving the Urban High School: What Works and Why.* New
York: Teachers College Press.

—— and B. Smith (1991) "Restructuring, teacher engagement and school culture:
Perspectives on school reform and the improvement of teachers' work." *School Effectiveness and School Improvement* 2: 34–52.

——, N.J. Lagerweij and J.L. Voogt (1993) "School improvement." In T. Husen and
N. Postlethwaite (eds), *The International Encyclopedia of Education:* 5241–7. London:
Pergamon.

Lundberg, C. (1989) "On organizational learning: Implications and opportunities for
expanding organizational development." *Research in Organizational Change and Development* 3: 61–82.

March, J.G. (1991) "Exploration and exploitation in education." Invited address at the
annual meeting of the American Educational Research Association, Chicago, 4
April.

—— and J. Olsen (1976) *Ambiguity and Organizational Choice.* Bergen: Universitetsforlaget.

Meyer, J. and B. Rowen (1977) "Institutionalized organizations: Formal structure as
myth and ceremony." *American Journal of Sociology* 83: 340–63.

Miles, M. and K.S. Louis (1987) "Research on institutionalization: A reflective
review." In M.B. Miles, M. Ekholm and R. Vandenberghe (eds), *Lasting School
Improvement: Exploring the Process of Institutionalization.* Leuven: Acco.

Mohrman, A.M., Jr. and E.E. Lawler, III (1985) "The diffusion of QWL as a paradigm shift." In W.G. Bennis, K.D. Benne and R. Chin (eds), *The Planning of Change*. New York: Holt, Rinehart and Winston.

Nelson, M. and S. Sieber (1976) "Innovation in urban secondary schools." *School Review* 27: 101–19.

Noddings, N. (1984) *Caring: A Feminine Approach to Ethics and Moral Education*. Berkeley: University of California Press.

Rosenblum, S., K. Seashore Louis and R. Rossmiller (1994) "School leadership and teacher quality of work life in restructuring schools." In J. Murphy and K.S. Louis (eds), *Reshaping the Principalship: Insights from Transformational Reform Efforts*: 110–29. Thousand Oaks, CA: Corwin.

Schön, D. (1979) "Public service organizations and the capacity for public learning." *International Journal of Social Science* 31: 682–95.

Senge, P.M. (1990) *The Fifth Discipline*. New York: Currency/Doubleday.

Shrivastava, P. (1983) "A typology of organizational learning systems." *Journal of Management Studies* 20: 7–28.

Sims, H.P., Jr. and P. Lorenzi (1992) *The Leadership Paradigm: Social Learning and Cognition in Organizations*. Newbury Park, CA: Sage.

Simsek, H. and K.S. Louis (1994) "Organizational change as paradigm shift." *Journal of Higher Education* 65: 670–94.

Tushman, M. and E. Romanelli (1985) "Organizational evolution: A metamorphosis model of convergence and reorientation." In *Research in Organizational Behavior*, 7. Greenwich, CT: JAI Press.

Wahlstrom, K. and K.S. Louis (1993) "Adoption revisited: Decision making and school district politics." In S. Bachrach and R. Ogawa (eds), *Advances in Research and Theory of School Management and Educational Policy*, Vol. 1: 61–119. Greenwich, CT: JAI Press.

Weick, K. (1976) "Educational organizations as loosely coupled systems." *Administrative Science Quarterly* 21: 1–19.

6

Organizational Learning and High-performance Learning Communities[1]

Introduction

My remarks in this chapter are offered in the spirit of theoretical evolution, not revolution. They are stimulated by my own work with the Wisconsin Center for the Organization and Restructuring of Schools (summarized in Newmann 1996) and my familiarity with the school effectiveness and school improvement lines of research in North America, Europe, and Australia. Let me start with two assumptions.

First, it is time to revisit the roots of the effective schools movement, which originated in an effort to show why some schools work for students who had often been viewed as "uneducable." I have devoted much of my research career to the study of schools that reorganize and reform to serve predominantly low-income and minority students. Despite anguish and teeth gnashing of policy analysts over the dismal state of student achievement in these settings, we have made little progress in changing the underlying conditions or the results. Documented success stories (Meier 1994; Raywid 1995) are heartening, but the typical school serving disadvantaged pupils still appears virtually untouched by exhortations for change. As I review this paper, initially written in 1997, I have just returned from yet another international congress where the topic of urban school reform is viewed as more pressing than it was a decade ago.

Second, it is time to integrate organizational learning theory, increasingly popular in business settings, with what we know from the organizational studies of school improvement and school effectiveness. Organizational learning and related concepts can bridge the yawning gulf between what effective schools researchers have found and the problem of extending their good news to low-performing schools on a systematic basis.

Core Organizational Learning Concepts

Organizational learning is a concept borrowed from the business literature, where it began to emerge in the mid-1980s (Simsek and Louis 1994; Tjepkema 1994). To date, most of the publications in education have either been "data free" or based on a few case studies (Wohlstetter *et al.* 1994; Louis and Kruse 1998), although in the past few years more research has begun to emerge (Scribner *et al.* 1999; Leithwood 2000). Only a few studies have been based on larger samples of schools, and these have not been organized around a clear intervention (Leithwood 1994 and 1996; Marks and Louis 1997; Bryk *et al.* 1999). To my knowledge, only one published study ties organizational learning to student learning (Marks *et al.* 2000), although a longitudinal study in Australia (Silins *et al.* 1999) is in the works. The business literature on high-performance or high-reliability organizations is a more useful addition to the educational literature. The high-performance concept is inevitably linked to organizational learning, according to Weick and Sutcliffe's analysis (2001), because both involve "making sense" out of increasingly complex and uncertain settings in order to make more rapid adaptive responses that increase performance.

Proposition: Organizational learning requires a process in which knowledge sources are shared and adapted within the school community. The goal of "social processing" or team learning is that members incrementally agree about "what we know" about performance and what actions might be taken (Louis and Dentler 1988; Huberman 1994). This "information processing" is inherently a collective activity, but in most large urban schools it is only carried out within small, fragmented groups or departments. Hargreaves (2001), however, argues that the former site of learning, the teachers' lounge, has emptied under the increasing pressures: the primary site of sensemaking and adaptation has been replaced by isolated efforts to cope.

Proposition: Organizational learning is accelerated by the cross-fertilization of existing knowledge sources. Teachers' knowledge comes from three main sources: (1) individual knowledge that is brought by both professionals, parents, students, and community members; (2) knowledge that is "imported" from state or national databases, experts and the experiences of other schools; and (3) knowledge that is created by members of the school community to address specific questions or problems (Louis and Kruse 1995; Louis and Raywid 1994). Any effort to improve urban schools must facilitate the conscious integration of knowledge gained from each base, making deliberate what is often haphazard. In the fractured environment of today's urban schools, teachers and administrators must become problem solvers, information seekers, data analysts, and solution designers to produce educated students. The more the members of the (potential) learning community are isolated from each other, the more each individual must invent for him- or herself. This is in direct contradiction to decades of research demonstrating that groups are better at arriving at novel ideas under pressure than are individuals.

Proposition: Organizational learning can only be successful when it is focused on learning about what matters. The goal of knowledge seeking and knowledge integration is to focus the school community on strategies for improving student learning. Elsewhere (Louis and Marks 1998; Marks *et al.* 2000) Helen Marks and I have argued that if teachers talk about new ideas they are more likely to integrate that new knowledge into their teaching practice than if they had only read an article or engaged in a solo action research project. The key, of course, is that the information collectively discussed must be "true" and "useful" (Weiss and Bucuvalas 1980), but when this is the case, organizational learning leads to more intense reflection on teaching practice, which, in turn, leads to adaptation and improved teaching.

Proposition: Without a clear process for organizational learning, no amount of information will help schools improve. Standards and information about effective classroom instructional practices will only make a difference if there are organizational structures, processes, and norms in place that permit faculty to seriously engage with the problem of how to improve performance. Many corporations claiming to be learning organizations are obsessed with information, but don't know how to learn from it (Macdonald 1995). Instead of concentrating on "useable knowledge," they establish vast empires of data, which, through either lack of relevance or accessibility, have little impact on the quality of their core products.

Organizational learning is a tool to help organizations focus on their core objectives and "how to get there." Following the disparate research threads in human relations, cybernetics, management by objectives, and many other trends, the primary barriers to becoming more effective are (1) qualitative and structural aspects of communication systems; (2) information processing; and (3) availability of high-quality, relevant information about performance. These problems are not newly identified, but earlier responses to them have often been directed at shop-floor technical problems of organization – in the common language, how to get factory workers to participate in producing a better widget through minor modifications of existing organizational practices. Alternatively, the problems are defined as "human relations" deficiencies that involve issues of morale and organizational climate. Organizational learning theory recasts these problems, asking how we can get knowledgeable, well-educated professional people to cooperatively obtain, share, and act on information effectively in increasingly uncertain settings.

Proposition: Schools are rarely effective learning organizations. The above is a rather long introduction to my basic assumption: schools often fail to focus on issues of student development and learning because they lack strategies for acquiring relevant information, have weak processes to discriminate good from bad information, and even then fail to support structures to communicate the results of their search processes to the potential learning community.

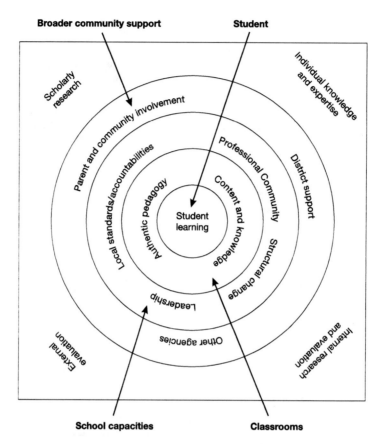

Figure 6.1 Elements of an Organizational Learning Approach to Creating High-performance Learing Communities

Most scholars would agree that barriers to student learning are fundamentally affected by the outside forces such as socio-economic disadvantage, cultural mismatches between school values and family values, and individual predispositions. The "problem of effective schools" reflects larger social dilemmas as well as inefficient organization. What organizational learning theory can do is to create structures and processes of continuous improvement as resolutions to mediate the obstacles to effective teaching and learning that are found and shared throughout the school or even school system.

A High-performance Learning Community Model in Schools

Organizational learning, which emphasizes what schools need to do to obtain or generate knowledge and turn it into action, must be joined with a discussion about what that knowledge should consist of. We need, then, to look at what we know about schools that work for students and teachers. Figure 6.1 summarizes my schema of how the streams of research on organizational learning and effective schooling are related. In this schema, factors closest to the center have the largest direct effect on the student, but indirect factors further out have an equally profound impact. The structures of organizational learning, once in place, interact with all levels in a way that an individual teacher or administrator cannot. I will emphasize seven factors and how the structures of organizational learning can contribute to continuous improvement at all levels.

The main factors that I will emphasize are: (1) authentic pedagogy; (2) professional community; (3) decentralized and expanded leadership; (4) supportive school structures; (5) increased accountability at the school level; (6) increased accountability and support at the LEA and other levels; (7) increased parental and community involvement. The first factor is seen as the best vehicle to create a direct increase in student development and achievement; factors 2–5 are at the school level, while factors 6 and 7 are important, but occur outside of the school.

Classroom Organization and Authentic Pedagogy

Proposition: Urban school students' performance will increase when they experience more "authentic instruction" in their classrooms (Newmann 1996). My model draws on the base of school effectiveness or teaching effectiveness research that has been conducted in the USA and in many other countries since the late 1970s. School and teaching effectiveness research is currently somewhat out of favor among many critical and constructivist theorists in education, who object to the idea that one can identify specific aspects of the school's culture and/or instructional practices that will improve student learning. Theory aside, however, there is a great deal of evidence that change programs emphasizing school effectiveness or teaching effectiveness practices can be successful, even in urban schools (Mortimer *et al.* 1988; Louis and Miles 1990; Stringfield and Teddlie 1991; van de Werf and Weide 1996; Smith *et al.* 2001). From this very large body of research, I focus on selected elements that are applicable to secondary as well as elementary schools.

There are almost as many lists of effectiveness factors as there are research studies. There are, however, consistent themes emerging from this line of research that suggest important areas for school-wide intervention in instruction. These have been recently summarized by Creemers (1994: 119), based on research in the Netherlands, the UK, and by the most comprehensive longitudinal study in the USA (Stringfield and Teddlie 1991). Two features of Creemers' summary that I find very attractive are the inclusion of *opportunity to learn* (the allocation of time to a curriculum that covers critical disciplinary concepts), and the model's emphasis on *different levels of learning* – basic skills, higher order skills and metacognitive skills. Creemers' summary is, however, less useful in identifying *broad patterns of instructional behavior*, as opposed to micro-level techniques of instruction. In addition, Creemers' and Stringfield and Teddlie's synthesis – and virtually all other research with the exception of Stallings (1980) and the more recent work in the UK (Thomas *et al.* 1997) – focuses on elementary-school instruction, which does not address the complexities and disciplinary differences that begin to appear in later grades.

One exception to the generalization that teaching effectiveness research has largely ignored secondary schools is the authentic pedagogy model developed at the Center for the Organization and Restructuring of Schools at the University of Wisconsin, which has been applied in secondary settings and in multiple disciplinary contexts. At the classroom or teaching level, the broad patterns of effective instruction include the elements that the Wisconsin Center (Newmann 1996) summarized in the dimensions of "authentic pedagogy," which incorporates findings from both effective teaching research and models of constructivist teaching:

- Instruction focuses on *higher order thinking*, which involves manipulating information and ideas by synthesizing, generalizing, explaining, hypothesizing, or arriving at conclusions that produce new meaning and understandings for them. (The idea of higher order thinking incorporates Creemers' categories of higher order thinking and metacognitive skills.)
- Instruction focuses on *deep knowledge*, addressing central ideas of a topic or discipline with enough thoroughness to explore connections and produce complex understandings.
- Classrooms are organized to generate *substantive conversation*, or extended exchanges among teachers and students about subject matter in a way that builds improved and shared understanding of these ideas.
- The content of the classroom is *connected to the world beyond the classroom* so that students can make connections between substantive knowledge and either public problems or personal experience.

To these four elements from the Wisconsin Center I would add a fifth from Stallings (1980):
- *Allocated academic time* to support the first four points.

These five points form a basis for instructional improvement that can be adapted to all disciplines; does not rigidly prescribe instructional techniques; can be used for peer observation, research and other assessment of the quality of classroom work; and has prima facie appeal to teachers.

The "authentic teaching" model has been shown, in smaller scale studies and in secondary analyses of US National Assessment of Educational Progress (NAEP) data, to be particularly effective in closing the achievement gap between the more and less advantaged students. It is applicable to disciplinary or interdisciplinary teaching and can be adapted to a wide variety of teaching strategies. When teachers experience success through improved instruction they are also very likely to experience increased commitment and sense of responsibility for student achievement.

Key School Context Factors
While authentic pedagogy is viewed as the most proximate effect on student learning, many studies, especially those using hierarchical modeling, have identified significant school effects that are not based in the classroom (see Scheerens 1992 for a concise review; Stringfield 1995 for a stronger argument). I propose four factors that summarize

the extant research in ways that capture the energies of school practitioners, although researchers often use different terms.

Proposition: School Factor 1: Increasing organizational learning requires stronger professional communities within schools – professional communities that are focused on student learning (Marks and Louis 1997; Bryk *et al.* 1999). In order to obtain a school-wide focus on the core task, *schools must develop the capacity to work toward a consensus about "how to get there."* This school capacity is dependent on a number of factors, including the availability of meaningful local standards for student development and achievement; the availability of research knowledge about practices and structures that will improve student achievement, and the development of stronger professional communities within the school. Developing this school-based capacity demands changes in the human and social resources of the schools, including communication, professional development, and informal accountability mechanisms.

My colleagues and I have subsumed these ideas in the concept of *professional community*. Professional community is a term that encompasses many of the school-level factors that have been shown to be related to student learning. These include: a consistent set of goals for learning with a focus on how the school is expected to meet those goals; opportunities for deep and sustained collaboration; an orientation to problem-solving, which includes an emphasis on peer observations and consultation, and extensive dialogue around issues of pedagogy and learning. Professional community among teachers is a critical component of organized learning (OL), and demands changes in "normal" practice in schools, including increased reflective dialogue, open sharing of classroom practices, the development of a common knowledge base for improvement, collaboration on the development of new materials and curricula, and the development of norms related to good practice and student performance. These factors have been demonstrably related to student learning (Louis and Marks 1996; Marks *et al.* 2000).

Research clearly suggests that socialization and selection of community participants, effective conflict management, the development of sound professional development, an increase in trust and respect, the development of denser informal communication mechanisms and informal accountability or peer pressure contributes significantly both to a school's professional community and its capacity to learn.

Proposition: School Factor 2: Developing a Highp-erformance Learning Community (HPLC) demands different forms of leadership from conventional models (Leithwood 1994; Murphy and Louis 1994; Hallinger 2003). *Leadership* has been identified as a factor in all US studies of effective schools, but these studies generally focus on the principal (Hallinger 2003). Leadership at all levels is important in creating the consensus that characterizes a "high reliability organization" that does not accept failure and is able to cope with unanticipated problems. Most studies linking leadership to effective schools have focused on the principal, but recent research suggests that teacher consensus around and influence over policies that affect the school's learning environment (including disciplinary policies, use of time, and curriculum) are also crucial. Leadership in high-performing, learning organizations is decentralized and facilitative. It requires that learning be exercised fully at different levels in the organization, and that some influence outside of the school be accepted and incorporated. Heifetz's (1994) work on leadership without authority is particularly applicable to public schools. Organizational learning also requires "strong leadership" from school leaders in the articulation of organizational goals in ways that are meaningful and empowering for all participants (Louis 1994). This paradoxical model of strong-but-decentralized leadership is rarely achieved.

Leadership must also address the micro-politics of large, urban schools (Weiss and Bucuvalas 1980; Watkins 1994). Unless the stakes and stands of key constituencies are addressed during the learning process, efforts to focus attention on performance are likely to be ineffective. Changing the internal politics of schools is rarely accomplished through formal governance and participation, but depends on an informal increase in mutual influence and sense of efficacy among groups. In particular, professional educators, students, and parents must be encouraged to exercise "strong democracy" that permits the expression of differences, while realizing the necessity of compromise.

Proposition: *School Factor 3*: *Creating HPLCs requires that school structures be altered* (Louis and Kruse 1995). Recent research has expanded beyond early emphasis on "a safe and orderly climate" to the identification of school characteristics such as a trusting climate, orientation to innovation and problem-solving, adequate professional development, the effective use of time to permit teachers to work in innovative ways both in and outside the classroom, interdependent teaching roles, and so on (see Stringfield 1995; Louis *et al.* 1996). In addition, particularly in secondary schools, there is a need to confront the *structural barriers* to increased classroom performance, including traditional schedules, limited teacher and administrator contact with research and practice knowledge from similar settings and research universities, limited interdependencies in teaching roles, especially between departments, and formal decision-making processes that are perceived as working poorly or even unfairly.

Urban schools – and secondary schools in particular – share structural characteristics that disadvantage them in becoming high-performing organizations. Research on organizational change suggests that the removal of impediments is more critical to the success of a program to improve performance than is the introduction of resources. Among the key impediments are: knowledge isolation and poor professional development practices; limited and fragmented structures to coordinate activities within the school and between school and community; inflexible schedules that prevent teachers and other members of the community from meeting and talking in sustained ways; low interdependence in teaching roles, and between teachers and other key actors in the student's life; and formal decision-making processes that are viewed as "unfair" or arbitrary by many participants. Special attention must be paid to counteracting the effects of school size, which is negatively related to the development of community.

Many secondary schools, like universities, are discipline-based, which can result in professional isolation. Organizational learning requires structural accommodation to make these rigid boundaries permeable to the flow of information and new ideas both within the organization and with constituencies outside the school.

Proposition: *School Factor 4*: *Sustaining a focus on student performance beyond any change intervention means using meaningful local standards* (National Academy of Education Panel on Standards-Based Education Reform 1995; Rothman 1995). Finally, although there is only limited empirical evidence, there is a strong agreement among many improvement scholars that *accountability at the school level* is critical, whether it be an increased sense of collective responsibility for student achievement, collective commitment to student assessment procedures beyond those required by the district and state, or some control over monitoring activities related to school performance (see Stringfield 1995; NEA-KEYS no date). Any effort to improve performance must begin with the development of performance criteria *and* accountability systems that are predictable, and locally meaningful (see National Association of State Boards of Education 1988; National Academy of Education Panel of Standards-Based Education Reform 1995; Rossi and Stringfield 1995). Standards do not necessarily have to be locally initiated to be locally owned. For example, a new set of state standards for high-school performance (the "graduation standards") was established in Minnesota in the late 1990s. Meeting these standards required districts to establish more specific criteria of performance, and to develop effective ways of measuring them. Many schools accepted full responsibility for defining local measures for how well they were doing in relation to the state standards, and were disappointed when this school-focused accountability program was replaced by a more traditional state-wide testing program in 2003.

Factors Outside the School

Fewer studies in the effective schools line of research examine the relationship between factors outside the school and student learning, with the exception of "control variables" such as community demographics, and so forth. At the level of external support outside the school, we will focus on the *district-school* and *parent/community-school relationships* as most critical to creating the environment inside the school that permits teachers to be successful with students in classrooms.

Proposition: Urban students' performance will increase when they experience increased articulation between parents, community, and school (Bryk and Schneider 2001). Although we know this to be true, the involvement of parents and community is often weak in urban schools, particularly at the secondary level. Teachers blame parents who do not show up when they are asked; parents express concerns about lack of responsiveness or difficulty in communicating in a language that is unfamiliar. School-by-school partnerships and programs must build on the characteristics of the student population. For example, Among students, who come from clan-based societies, require different strategies for parent and community involvement from Hispanic students. When communication is opened through existing partnerships and resources, the resulting dialogue can create new locally appropriate solutions.

With the exception of recent research on neighborhood demographic and resource effects, there is an absence of large-scale longitudinal studies that examine district-school and wider community effects on school student performance, particularly in the upper grades. The research and development work of Sandy Christenson, whose carefully designed experimental research demonstrates that where parent involvement is focused on changing how students use their time at home substantial improvements in student retention and performance follow (Adams and Christenson 2000; Godber *et al.* 2000). In particular, Dr Christenson's work demonstrates that parental and school collaboration in "checking" on student behaviors that may put them at risk of school failure, and "connecting" with each other to discuss these, provides a demonstrable way for relatively low-income and poorly educated parents to substantially reduce the probability of their children dropping out.

Proposition: Schools have some capacity to generate knowledge to support an HPLC, but are also dependent on outside agencies to provide knowledge. Learning cannot take place without a knowledge base. Urban schools are largely disconnected from the many sources of information that might help them to improve their performance (Louis 1995). They are remote from the expertise that resides in district offices, and are typically less well connected with institutions of higher education than are more affluent schools. Funding is often tighter, and professional development opportunities that are focused on the school are more limited. Yet, we know that knowledge – pedagogic and subject related, but also knowledge about how students from non-affluent, non-white, non-western cultures learn – is critical for effective teaching (Richardson 2003).

The process of tapping existing knowledge bases to transform an urban school into an HPLC is an ongoing process. Individual knowledge of professionals, parents, students, and community members is communicated and shared as they generate new knowledge to address specific questions or problems. Knowledge from outside experts and the experiences of other schools is imported and channeled into the new structures that have been created to breakdown pre-existing barriers to communication. Outside agencies are also a major source of information about a school's performance and, under the right circumstances, this information can nurture the agenda for improving student performance (Earl and Torrance 2000).

Getting to School Improvement?

Some people think of me as a "school improvement" researcher, and may be surprised that my comments have focused on integrating disparate strands of scholarship that are associated with "school effectiveness." But the school reform research that I have been involved with since the late 1980s has emphasized both. I don't believe in limited "to do" lists for school reformers, and the above discussion is built on a model of change that demands enormous flexibility. Nevertheless, I conclude that to create HPLCs in disadvantaged settings, interventions should:

- promote authentic instruction;
- bolster the social capital and human resources that are already available, and refocus them on student achievement objectives;
- help schools to meet relevant professional, state or national standards as part of becoming a high-performing learning organization;
- identify and share knowledge from each of these three critical sources – individual,

school-based, and external – focusing the learning community's attention on the development of skills that permit members of the school community to become problem-finders, information seekers, and data analysts and solution designers with respect to student performance;

- develop interdisciplinary, cross-role teams and groups, inside and outside the school, that foster knowledge use and performance improvement – these teams should address specific school communities, and involve teachers, students and parents;
- nurture professional communities by altering both the human resource conditions and the structure of the school;
- remove key structural impediments to communication and problem-solving;
- connect schools with the best sources of information about improving schools that is both disciplinary and more generic, and disseminate this information within the school community;
- initiate non-conventional leadership training for teams, not for positions;
- build on performance standards that are currently being implemented, and provide incentives for development based on proximate indicators of increased performance; and
- develop all elements of the HPLC model simultaneously.

My colleagues and I embed these elements in the broader rubric of organizational learning theory to emphasize two elements of our approach:
- First, progress can only be made on this agenda when there is *an increase in information available to the school about what to change and how to change.*
- Second, *knowledge that promotes change must be provided from outside the school, as well as within the school, by using the expertise of the school community.*

Note

1. This chapter is a revised version of an unpublished keynote address delivered at the International Congress for School Effectiveness and School Improvement, Memphis, 1997. The basic outline of the paper has not been changed, and represents my "best thinking" at that time.

References

Adams, K. and S. Christenson (2000) "Trust and the family-school relationship: Examination of parent-teacher differences in elementary and secondary grades." *Journal of School Psychology* 38(5): 477–97.

Avery, P. (1999) "Authentic assessment and instruction." *Social Education* 63(6): 368–73.

Bryk, A. and B. Schneider (2001) *Trust in Schools: A Core Resource for Improvement.* New York: Russell Sage Foundation.

——, E. Camburn, and K.S. Louis, (1999) "Promoting school improvement through professional communities: An analysis of Chicago elementary schools." *Educational Administration Quarterly* 35: 707–50.

Creemers, B. (1994) *The Effective Classroom*. London: Cassell.

Earl, L. and N. Torrance (2000) "Embedding accountability and improvement into large-scale assessment: What difference does it make?" *Peabody Journal of Education* 75(4): 114–41.

Godber, Y., S. Christenson, and A. Esber (2000) *International Journal of Psychology* 35(3–4): 43–53.

Hallinger, P. (2003) "Leading educational change: Reflections on the practice of instructional and transformational leadership." *Cambridge Journal of Education* 33(3): 329–53.

Hargreaves, A. (2001) "Educational change over time? The sustainability and non-sustainability of three decades of secondary school change and continuity." Keynote address at the International Congress of School Effectiveness and School Improvement, Rotterdam, 6–9 January.

Heifetz, R. (1994) *Leadership without Easy Answers*. Cambridge, MA: Belknap Press.

Hoy, W., J. Hannum, and M. Tashannen-Moran (1998) "Organizational climate and student achievement: A parsimonious and longitudinal view." *Journal of School Leadership* 8(4): 336–59.

Huberman, M. (1994) "Research utilization: The state of the art." *Knowledge and Policy* 7(4): 13–33.

Leithwood, K. (1994) "Leadership for school reform." *Educational Administration Quarterly* 4: 498–518.

—— (1996) "Learning in teams." Paper presented at the annual meeting of the American Educational Research Association, New York.

—— (ed.) (2000) *Organizational Learning and School Improvement*. Greenwich, CT: JAI.

Louis, K.S. (1994) "Beyond 'managed change': Rethinking how schools improve." *School Effectiveness and School Improvement* 5: 1–22.

—— (1995) "Improving urban and disadvantaged schools: Dissemination and utilization perspectives." *Knowledge and Policy* 7(4): 13–33.

—— and R.A. Dentler (1988) "Knowledge use and school improvement." *Curriculum Inquiry* 18: 32–62.

—— and S.D. Kruse and associates (1995) *Professionalism and Community: Perspectives on Reforming Urban Schools*. Thousand Oaks, CA: Corwin.

—— and S. Kruse (1998) "Creating community in reform: Images of organizational learning in urban schools." In K. Leithwood and K.S. Louis (eds), *Organizational Learning in Schools*: 17–46. Lisse: Swets and Zeitlinger.

—— and H.M. Marks (1998) "Does professional community affect the classroom? Teachers work and student work in restructuring schools." *American Journal of Education*, 106(4): 532–75.

—— and M. Miles (1990) *Improving the Urban High School: What Works and Why*. New York: Teacher's College Press.

—— and M. Raywid (1994) "A tale of two schools: Knowledge, skill, collaboration and organizational learning." Paper presented at the annual meeting of the American Educational Research Association.

——, H.M. Marks, and S.D. Kruse (1996) "Teachers' professional community and school reform." *American Educational Research Journal* 33(4).

Macdonald, S. (1995) "Learning to change: An information perspective on learning in the organization." *Organization Science* 6: 557–68.

Marks, H. and K.S. Louis (1997) "Does teacher empowerment affect the classroom? The implications of teacher empowerment for instructional practice and student academic performance." *Educational Evaluation and Policy Analysis* 19(3): 245–75.

——, K.S. Louis, and S. Printy (2000) "The capacity for organizational learning: Implications for pedagogy and student achievement." In K. Leithwood (ed.), *Organizational Learning and School Improvement*: 239–66. Greenwich, CT: JAI.

Meier, D. (1994) *The Power of their Ideas*. Boston, MA: Beacon.

Mortimer, P., P. Sammons, L. Stoll, D. Lewis, and R. Ecob (1988) *School Matters: The Junior Years*. Wells: Open Books.

Murphy, J. and K.S. Louis (eds) (1994) *Reshaping the Principalship: Insights from Transformational Reform Efforts*. Thousand Oaks, CA: Corwin.

National Academy of Education Panel on Standards-Based Education Reform (1995) *Improving Education through Standards-based Reform*. Stanford, CA: The National Academy of Education.

National Association of State Boards of Education Accountability Study Group (October, 1988) *Effective Accountability: Improving Schools, Informing the Public*. Alexandria, VA: NASB.

NEA-KEYS (*Your KEYS to school success*). Available online at www.nea.org/schoolquality (last accessed 15 January 2004).

Newmann F. (ed.) (1996) *Authentic Achievement: Restructuring Schools for Intellectual Quality*. San Francisco: Jossey Bass.

Raywid, M. (1995) "Professional community and its yield in Metro Academy." In K.S. Louis and S.D. Kruse and associates, *Professionalism and Community: Perspectives on Reforming Urban Schools*: 29–61. Thousand Oaks, CA: Corwin.

Richardson, V. (2003) "Constructivist pedagogy." *Teachers College Record* 105(9): 1625–40.

Rossi, R. and A. Stringfield (1995) "School reform and students placed at risk: Evidence supporting the need for high reliability organizations and strong school communities." *Phi Delta Kappan* 77: 73–6.

Rothman, R. (1995) *Measuring Up: Standards, Assessment and School Reform*. San Francisco: Jossey Bass.

Scheerens, J. (1992) *Effective Schooling*. London: Cassell.

Scribner, J.P., K. Cockrell, D. Cockrell, and J. Valentine (1999) "Creating professional communities in schools through organizational learning: An evaluation of a school improvement process." *Educational Administration Quarterly* 35(1): 130–60.

Silens, H., B. Mulford, and S. Zarins (1999) "Leadership for organizational learning and student outcomes: The Lolso projects: The first report of an Australian three-year study of international significance." Paper presented at the Annual meeting of the American Educational Research Association, Monteal, 19–23 April.

Simsek, H. and K.S. Louis (1994) "Organizational change as paradigm shift." *Journal of Higher Education* 65(4): 670–95.

Smith, B. (2000) "Quality matters: allocation of instructional time in an urban school system." *Education Administration Quarterly* 36(5): 652–82.

Smith, J., V. Lee, and F. Newmann (2001) *Instruction and Achievement in Chicago Elementary Schools: Improving Chicago's Schools.* Chicago: Consortium on Chicago School Research, University of Chicago.

Spillane, J., R. Halvorson, and J.B. Diamond (2001) "Investigating school leadership practice: A distributed perspective." *Educational Researcher* 30(3): 23–8.

Stallings, J. (1980) "Academic learning time revisited, or beyond time on task." *Educational Researcher* 8: 11–16.

Stringfield, S. (1995) "Attempting to enhance students' learning through innovative programs: The case for schools evolving into high reliability organizations." *School Effectiveness and School Improvement* 6: 67–96.

—— and C. Teddlie (1991) "Observers as predictors of schools' multiyear outlier status on achievement tests." *The Elementary School Journal* 91: 358–76.

Thomas, S., P. Sammons, P. Mortimore, and R. Smees (1997) "Differential secondary school effectiveness: Comparing the performance of different pupil groups." *British Educational Research Journal* 23(4): 451–69.

Tjepkema, S. (1994) *Kenmerken van de lerende organisatie* (Characteristics of the learning organization). Enschede: University of Twente.

Van der Werf, G. and M. Weide (1996) "Differences in quality of instruction and compensating services between effective and ineffective schools for ethnic minorities." *Journal of At-Risk Issues* 3(1): 35–44.

Watkins, J. (1994) "A postmodern critical theory of research use." *Knowledge and Policy* 7(4): 55–77.

Weick, K.E. and K.M. Sutcliffe (2001) *Managing the Unexpected: Assuring High Performance in an Age of Complexity.* San Francisco: Jossey Bass.

Weiss, C. and M. Bucuvalas (1980) *Social Science Research and Decision Making.* New York: Columbia University Press.

Wohlstetter, P., R. Smyer, and S.A. Mohrman (1994) "New boundaries for school-based management: The high involvement model." *Educational Evaluation and Policy Analysis* 16(3) (fall): 268–86.

Section II
Teachers in Changing Schools

Until the mid-1980s I was a research sociologist concentrating on organizational innovation in education. At that time, I joined the research team at the Center for the Study of Secondary Schools (CSSS), a federally funded, multi-disciplinary and multi-university center that was located primarily at the University of Wisconsin. The research program on teachers' work was initially directed by Mary Metz, and she had just completed a two-year investigation of the relationship between local community characteristics and values, and teacher culture. Fred Newmann, the director of the Center, suggested that my work in applying organizational research to evolving urban schools was a natural extension of her work, and I was asked to develop a new project.

This work struck me as a natural fit with the long tradition of studying the (re)organization of existing work groups. At the same time, Mary Metz's research complemented other emerging studies (for example, those conducted by Susan Rosenholtz and Judith Warren Little) that looked more specifically at teachers' work. The blending of personal interests and passions with research can result in our most satisfying endeavors. The third factor in this mix was serendipitous. My father, Stanley E. Seashore, was an active scholar whose career had been devoted to the redesign of work settings, and he had written extensively about issues related to quality of work life. Dad had just retired from the University of Michigan and was available both for father-daughter bonding and as an expert resource around what was clearly developing into an important theme in educational policy and practice.

The first two chapters in this section, "Cultivating Teacher Engagement: Breaking the Iron Law of Social Class" and "The Effects of Teacher Quality of Work Life on Commitment and Sense of Efficacy," are based on the case study and survey work conducted at the CSSS, in six challenging urban school sites that nonetheless had a reputation for being "good places to work." These papers focus on a key concern with revitalizing urban schools: how to keep teachers engaged in their work when the student demographics are changing rapidly.

Based on the study of urban high schools that I had just completed, I knew that most teachers in urban US schools were "well seasoned." This was in the mid-1970s and most teachers had trained before or shortly after the social turmoil of the early part of the decade. Students were now different. Not only did cultural values change (including visible signs such as dress codes), but populations shifted with desegregation, urban riots, white flight, and the northern migration of rural, disenfranchised African-Americans. From the organizational literature, I postulated that if teachers' work was not stimulating and engaging, they would experience frustration as a result of these changes, and consequently be less motivated to invest the time and energy needed to push the edge of their professional knowledge and invent new ways of engaging students. Thus, for theoretical and methodological reasons I focused on organizational characteristics in schools that challenged and facilitated urban teachers to evolve new teaching strategies in environments that were leading to complaints of fatigue and resignation.

As the work at CSSS came to an end in 1990, the federal government requested a proposal for a similar multi-disciplinary or multi-university center to focus on school reform. While our work in the CSSS was limited to secondary schools, as a team we had learned an enormous amount about the school reform movements that were, at that time, emerging from the "bottom up" within individual schools and districts at all grade levels. Our proposal continued to focus on the redesign of teachers' work, which I eagerly helped to organize under the new umbrella of The Center for Restructuring Schools (CORS). At CSSS we had witnessed the characteristics of schools that engaged and challenged their teachers; at CORS we looked more closely at how individual teachers organized their own work to support effective teaching and learning.

Along with my colleagues (Sharon Kruse, Tony Bryk, MaryAnne Raywid, Jean King, and Sharon Rollow) we initiated a grounded research study on how teachers working in "difficult" schools used each other as resources to maintain and improve their own work environment and benefit the lives of the children in their classrooms. Over many tough meetings, using data that we were collecting in our case study sites, we hammered out the idea of *professional community*, which focused on the social values and behavioral underpinnings of teacher engagement, and its connection to real reform. This concept (which research teams in other parts of the country were also bumping into from different angles) became the basis for a book of edited cases, *Professionalism and Community: Perspectives on Reforming Urban Schools*. This book represented a departure from my earlier research, which had focused on how organizational structure and culture constrained or facilitated individual behavior. The professional community concept, on the other hand, put teachers at the core of the reform process. Ultimately, my view of how schools change was deeply affected by this shift, as is evident in Chapter 6 from the previous section. In that chapter, classrooms and classroom practice are at the center of changing education, and the nature of adult relationships behind the scene emerges as the critical and proximate influence on real change.

Moving on from this micro-level qualitative work, Tony Bryk and I convinced the other key actors in the CORS center that we needed to include items in our teacher surveys to measure professional community. The results of these surveys, and the inter-view data collected from teachers in a larger national sample of schools engaged in locally initiated "comprehensive reform," enabled Helen Marks and me to test our emerging understanding. A number of publications emerged from this partnership, including vali-dations of the professional community concept in a larger sample, and investigations of the role of teacher empowerment in reformed practice. I have included one of these publica-tions, "Does Professional Community Affect the Classroom?" in this volume. The central question here is one posed by policy makers: how do we know that paying attention to teachers' work will pay off for students? This chapter, published in 1998, was the first article that I am aware of to use a large sample to demonstrate empirically the impact of the organizational aspects of teachers' work on students' learning.

As my involvement with CORS ended in the late 1990s, I found myself deflated and discouraged. Heartwarming examples of altered conditions for teachers' work in elemen-tary and middle schools contrasted sharply with bleaker conditions in US high schools. Fortuitously for my mental health, in 1997 a national foundation awarded enough money to the school system of my hometown to infuse the fine arts into the regular subject matter in *every* classroom. Coincidentally, the district was pressing forward with another initiative to create a better transition to high school by forming teacher teams that would work closely with smaller groups of students within the school to provide a more cohesive educational experience. My previous work focused on school-wide professional commu-nity, but now, in my own backyard, my colleagues and I were allowed to witness the emergence of smaller learning communities in schools. Chapter 10, "Teacher Teaming and High-school Reform" details how evolving relationships among teachers and a new philosophy of curriculum affected their teaching practice and willingness to innovate. While I continue to believe that organizational culture matters for teachers' work, this research convinced me that we may, paradoxically, need to begin with smaller-scale inter-ventions in schools that are large and complex.

There is a great deal of work to be done on the topic of teachers' work life. In partic-ular, policymakers and scholars in many countries have not satisfactorily addressed how to balance the need for desirable conditions for teachers (which are related, of course, to recruitment and retention) and the press for rapid improvements in student test scores, graduation rates, and preparation for further study or work. The tendency has been to emphasize one or the other without measuring how one affects the other, deflecting attention from the complex interplay among teachers and administrators, and the subse-quently more individual interaction with students in school settings.

7

Cultivating Teacher Engagement: Breaking the Iron Law Of Social Class[1]

Introduction

Facing into the future of public education in the twenty-first century, at least one fact seems inescapably clear: the student population will be increasingly multi-cultural, and from families of lower socio-economic status. This demographic shift poses many problems of adaptation in the educational system, ranging from the need to develop schools that provide on-site social services, to the press to develop more imaginative and effective curricula for students from low socio-economic or otherwise disadvantaged homes.

We deal here with the impact of this shift on teachers' engagement with disadvantaged students and their learning. The research literature suggests a strong association between the socio-economic characteristics of students and teacher satisfaction and engagement with their work. Some have tentatively predicted that as the number of disadvantaged students rises, we may see more difficulty not only engaging students in the classroom, but also in recruiting and retaining teachers who successfully work with these students. The relationships between contemporary demographic shifts and teacher engagement have not been extensively discussed in the recent policy literature but will require attention if effective reforms are to be enacted. In this chapter we will consider the prospects for improving teacher engagement through professional and organizational reform.

Teacher Engagement, Student Engagement and Students' Social Class

Reformers have attributed the problems of student learning to "bad" or "poorly prepared" teachers, but evidence suggests that an equally if not more serious problem is an increasing level of teacher detachment and alienation from their work and students (see NEA 1987; Corcoran *et al.* 1988; Metz 1990). Portraits of unengaged teachers have been at the center of discussions in the recent reform literature (see, for example, Powell *et al.* 1985). In our own study we heard such teachers described as "bored teachers who just go through the text book and aren't thinking," teachers nicknamed "Mrs Ditto," or "Mr Filmstrip," teachers who "taught one year, for thirty years" and teachers "who barely know their student's names."

Because teachers' work and students' work are inextricably intertwined, alienation is a primary stumbling block to improving student engagement. From the student's point of view, teacher engagement is a prerequisite for student engagement; and from the teacher's point of view, student engagement is, in turn, the most important predictor of teacher's interest and effort. In this sense, teacher engagement is a subset of the broader objective of creating effective schools that increase student learning opportunities and improve student achievement.

This assumption has received strong support in recent analyses. For example, Bryk and Thum (1989) show that schools in which teachers exhibit higher levels of engagement and commitment are less likely to have high rates of student absenteeism and drop-outs, while Wehlage *et al.* (1989) provide extensive case studies of programs staffed by engaged teachers which are highly successful in retaining and improving the achievement of students who are at-risk. The "effective schools" research also suggests strong relationships between school-wide teacher engagement with students, and student achievement (Brookover *et al.* 1979; Wilson and Corcoran 1988).

Teacher and student engagement both involve a psychological investment in doing good work, but teacher engagement has its own specific character. It is the teachers' psychological investment in and effort toward teaching the knowledge, skills and crafts they wish their students to master. Engagement can be indicated by a variety of behaviors, such as planning and developing lessons and curriculum, teaching through describing, explaining, helping, listening, reflecting, encouraging and evaluating. And, just as student engagement involves more than indicated behaviors and completing assigned tasks, teacher engagement involves more than meeting the minimum outlines of assigned duties.

Four distinctive types of teacher engagement can be identified, two of which are *affective*, and focus on human relationships in the school, and two of which are *instrumental*, and focus on the goals of teaching and learning (Newmann and Rutter 1987; Bryk and Driscoll 1988; Firestone and Rosenblum 1988; Wehlage *et al.* 1989):

- *Engagement with the school as a social unit.* This form of engagement reflects a sense of community and personal caring among adults within the school and promotes integration between personal life and work life. We see this form of engagement among teachers who "wouldn't want to work at any other school," teachers who refer to peers and students as friends and family, teachers who attend after-hours school events as often as they can, and teachers who are quick to rally together if faced with a troubling event.

- *Engagement with students as unique whole individuals* rather than as "empty vessels to be filled." Teachers demonstrate this type of engagement when they lead classes in ways that acknowledge and respond to students' thoughts and knowledge, listen to their ideas, involve themselves in students' personal as well as school lives, and in general make themselves available to students needing support or assistance. Many types of formal and informal coaching, sponsoring, mentoring, and counseling activities are additional examples of engagement with students.
- *Engagement with academic achievement.* Curriculum writing and development, sharing ideas and experiences about teaching as a craft with other teachers, making good and creative use of class time, expressing high expectations for performance, providing useful feedback to students, and actively considering how students are assessed are all ways teachers can be engaged in their students' achievement.
- *Engagement with one's subject* and the body of knowledge needed to carry out effective teaching. Particularly in secondary schools, teachers need to keep up to date in their content fields and incorporate new subject-related ideas into their classrooms. Expressing one's personal passion for a subject, seeking ways to connect the subject to students' lives, being involved in professional organizations, and pursuing advanced degrees in one's field can be examples of this form of engagement.

Most teachers are engaged with their work along multiple dimensions when they enter the profession. Over time, engagement is almost always affected by the presence and absence of various *demands* on teachers, including the demands teachers place on themselves, demands of their students, their peers, their principal, and students' parents – not to mention the immediate demands of the school environment. While demands may be stressful, they can also energize: students who ask for more and parents who involve themselves in the school create an environment of high expectations for teachers. In order for engagement to be sustained, however, teachers (like students) also need consistent *positive reinforcers* that are *meaningful, relevant, rewarding,* and *enjoyable.* The four types of engagement are distinct, but they are not necessarily reinforced by unique structures or activities. For example, a staff development retreat focusing on cooperative learning can support both the development of a sense of community among adults, and a focus on student achievement.

The "Iron Law of Social Class"

According to some popular case studies, even in the most unpromising contexts – where demands on teachers are low and positive reinforcers limited – some forms of teacher engagement remain high amongst some teachers (Kidder 1989; Freedman 1990). But teacher engagement based only on a few of these dimensions will not necessarily serve students well. A staff may be highly engaged with the social community of adults in their school, but neglect students and achievement. Or they may become so obsessed with achievement that they remain distant from groups of less able students. While each form of engagement may be desirable, all need to be present for teaching to remain vital and effective for all students. There may be no formula to determine, for any specific teacher, what Barnard (1938) referred to as the "balance of inducements" to stay actively involved with teaching. Still, dramatic imbalances can be counterproductive to the functioning of the schools.

As we will argue below, the patterns of demands and positive reinforcement often vary in schools of different socio-economic climates in ways that disadvantage teachers of lower-class students. Thus, redesign of the school organization so teachers working with disadvantaged children enjoy the same opportunities for engagement as those who work with more advantaged children is as fundamental to improving education as altering our conception of authentic school work.

The interconnection between teacher and student engagement, and social class is empirically demonstrated in recent qualitative studies (Firestone and Rosenblum 1988; Metz 1990) and those based on large-scale survey data (Brookover *et al.* 1979; Purkey *et al.* 1986; Dworkin 1987; Bryk *et al.* 1988; see Hurn (1985) for a review of earlier empirical literature). Dworkin (1987), for example, reports that teachers in schools with students from low socio-economic backgrounds are more likely to be burned out and disengaged, while Purkey *et al.* (1986) show that teachers in urban schools (presumably with higher proportions of children from lower socio-economic contexts) are less satisfied with their work. Metz's (1988, 1990) study of eight "ordinary" high schools is particularly pertinent to this chapter. Metz used detailed descriptions of three of the schools to demonstrate the thesis that the socio-economic characteristics of the community affect not only the characteristics of students, but also the behaviors of parents in relation to teachers, the socio-economic and educational characteristics of teachers who are recruited to the schools, the behavior of the principal, and the expectations of the role that education will play in the life expectations of children.

In conclusion, the policy and research literature suggests three sub-hypotheses to "iron law of social class," namely:

1. The higher the socio-economic status of the community, the higher the value placed on education.
2. The higher the value placed on education, the more the system will press teachers to perform.
3. The greater the pressure on teachers to deliver, the higher the performance of the students.

The policy implications of this line of argument are clear: first, low performance of students in lower socio-economic communities is largely the fault of the community itself; and, second, the only way to change this is to pressure teachers to have "high levels of expectation" in opposition to the community (see also Hallinger and Murphy 1986).

An Alternative Perspective

In traditionally organized schools where teachers' lives focus almost exclusively within their classroom, it is not surprising that those who work with the most responsive and quickest students – predominantly those of the middle classes, and the higher tracks – feel most rewarded, since both positive reinforcement and demands are high. Metz's (1988a) argument that teachers are dependent on their students for their professional satisfactions is empirically accurate, but fails to acknowledge how school organization can affect teacher engagement.

Our study began with a different perspective. We realized that *it is not possible to change students' social origins. However, it may be possible to change the relationship between social class and teacher commitment and engagement if we create organizational conditions that make it easier for teachers to experience success with students.* The main point of our research was to study this prospect, that is, to see how to release teachers from an unhealthy "ultimate dependency" on their students by increasing the alternative sources of satisfaction and fulfillment. Thus, rather than viewing teacher engagement solely as a function of student engagement, we sought out the connections between teacher engagement and the organizational conditions of the school. In doing so we acknowledged that success with students is fundamental to teacher satisfaction. We did think it critical to acknowledge the range of professional and organizational conditions that exists in our school system that can provide additional sources of demand and reinforcement.

From 1987 to 1990, we conducted research in eight public, non-selective high schools actively involved in efforts to improve working conditions for teachers. We deliberately chose a diverse sample of community environments. One school was in a predominantly affluent community; three schools – one suburban, one rural, and one urban – were in mixed socio-economic communities of middle-class status overall, and four served communities where over half of the student body came from disadvantaged homes, including students from poor, minority, and immigrant families. In these latter schools, between 55 and 65 per cent of the students were considered disadvantaged by the principal.

In each school, two members of the research staff spent about five to six days observing classrooms, interviewing teachers individually and in groups, interviewing groups of students, "shadowing" the principal, and attending routine meetings and events, ranging from lunch to evening activities. The focus of both interviews and observations was to gather information about the impact of district, and school organization on teachers' work lives (see Louis *et al.* (forthcoming) for a more detailed discussion of methodologies).

A Profile of the Schools and their Communities

In order to illustrate how schools serving the disadvantaged can secure for their teachers working conditions similar to those of schools serving more advantaged students, we focus on three of them, referred to here by pseudonyms. These three schools had the least affluent student bodies of all the eight schools in the study, based both on principal reports and our own observations. However, when we analyzed our survey data and looked at our measures of engagement with teaching, they had reported levels of engagement for the average staff member that were as high or higher than the more affluent schools. Our point is not to argue that teachers prefer the professional conditions of lower SES schools. In fact, according to our survey, teachers in lower SES schools had many complaints about working conditions and acknowledged that their students exhibited behavior patterns that were not always conducive to high achievement. Nevertheless, in these schools they brought effort, energy, and hope to their teaching tasks in excess of what would be predicted by the "iron law."

Particularly striking was the fact that teacher engagement in the three schools was higher than in two other schools where most of the students were from minority and non-English speaking populations, but where more students came from middle-class homes. Thus, in these schools we believe that the effects of the racial composition of the school were not particularly important.

City Park Secondary School

City Park is a small, innovative secondary school located in an impoverished section of a major northeastern city. Surrounded by a public housing project, stores, and other tenements, the community is one where poverty, crime, drugs, and violence touch lives on a daily basis. The school shares a large 1950s-era building with two other small schools – a common practice in the district, which allows parents and students to choose which school to attend. Although the immediate neighborhood is largely Hispanic, the school aims for a diverse enrolment and has largely succeeded: its student body is approximately 45 per cent black, 35 per cent Hispanic, and 20 per cent white, with a broad range of academic ability.

Opened in 1984, the school is rooted in the progressive education tradition of John Dewey and Lillian Weber, and is structured around the following principles: minimization of bureaucracy; a humanistic, open environment characterized by equal respect for staff and students (students do not need passes to go to the bathroom, and students and staff are both addressed by their first name); no tracking; an integrated core curriculum planned and developed by teams of teachers; significant teacher team planning time; instructional and learning strategies oriented around "essential questions" and critical thinking; parent involvement; and an overall sense of family. City Park is also a member of Theodore Sizer's Coalition of Essential Schools. The school enrolls around 600 students. The organization consists of three Divisions (7–8, 9–10 and 11–12), which are further divided into houses of about 80 students. There are no traditional departments, but within each Division there is a Math-Science Team and a Humanities Team, each consisting of about five teachers. Teams meet weekly for two hours and are the primary unit for developing and coordinating curriculum, sharing ideas, and discussing what has and has not worked. Scheduling is non-traditional, with students and teachers meeting for two-hour blocks in cross-grade groups (for example, 9–10). Students stay with the same teachers for two years. There is also a daily one-hour Advisory period, where every teacher assumes guidance responsibility for the academic and personal growth of 12–15 students.

Brigham Alternative High School

Like City Park, Brigham was designed to provide an alternative school experience to any student wishing to enroll. Established four years previously, in a small Southern city, the school sought to emphasize "open education" values, stressing a more interdisciplinary curriculum and student responsibility for learning. For several years Brigham was used as a "dumping ground" by other district schools, and has continued to struggle to shed its image as a place where other schools could send their most troubled and least successful students. Of the student body, 80 per cent is black, and, with the exception of the few students who are children of the school's teachers, most are from working-class or very poor families.

The school's evolving educational philosophy is based on commitment to experiential and cooperative learning, mixed-ability grouping, a humanistic curriculum, and a family-like environment. However, the ability of the school to implement their ideas fully is impeded by the requirement that they follow the rigid outcomes-based district curriculum and testing program, known as CBOK (Common Body of Knowledge), as well as a local culture that still strongly supports "paddling" as a form of student discipline.

The organization of the school has traditional components, with department heads, 50-minute periods, and age grouping. Teachers in some departments allocate teaching by grades, so that a small number of teachers are familiar with all of the students in a grade, thus permitting easier monitoring of student performance and personal problems. The school also uses an Advisory, which is expected to provide an environment for some guidance work, as well as an opportunity for more personal interaction between students and teachers, and has several committees to deal with shared governance.

Hillside High School

Hillside is located only a few miles from a medium-sized "border state" city, but it is located in a hilly, rural setting that appears remarkably bucolic. Although the community is one of the oldest in the state, it never prospered and remains sparsely settled. Most residents used to work at one of several large industrial complexes close by, but layoffs and plant closings have created very high levels of unemployment. The educational level of the community is quite low, and the graduation rate has recently been only about 65 per cent. Of those who graduate, only 30 per cent have gone on to some form of post-secondary education. Three-quarters of the student body are "local rednecks"- a term students and staff use freely; one-quarter are black students bussed in from the nearby city.

Unlike the two previously described schools, Hillside is a long-established and large (over 1,000 students) comprehensive high school with a mostly traditional curriculum delivered by 13 departments in a six-period day. Only five years before this study, Hillside was viewed as one of the worst schools in the district; by the time of this research there was a waiting list of teachers wanting to transfer in. For the previous four years the school had been involved in major reform efforts stimulated by a local professional teacher academy's concern with teacher reform. More recently, the school had become involved with Sizer's Coalition of Essential Schools. Establishing ties with both the local academy and Sizer's Coalition had been approved by a staff vote and were strongly supported by the Principal. The most critical change was the *steering committee*, which is composed of elected faculty members, the principal and assistant principal, a counselor, the athletic director, representatives from the district's teacher center, students, parents, and an elected member of the non-professional support staff. The open meetings of this committee are used to develop directions for program improvement at Hillside, and most of the work is carried out in sub-committees. The steering committee introduced many new programs, such as teacher guided assistance, a daily period which is used for teachers to work with students on specific problems or issues; multi-disciplinary curriculum units; and a "ninth grade bridge," which focuses on the development of an inter-disciplinary curriculum and team teaching of a group of approximately one-third of the incoming freshman class.

Promoting Teacher Engagement in Low-income Schools

The framework for our study is described in more detail elsewhere (Louis and Smith 1990). In studying how these schools promote teacher engagement we considered each of the following five factors.

- *The community and district environment of the school.* A number of researchers have argued that the life inside schools, but particularly in schools in larger districts, is continuously and often negatively affected by local politics and the district office (Farrar 1988). Conversely, Louis (1989) notes that where district and community support is strong, the school "works better," is more easily able to work on improvement issues, and one might logically argue, therefore, that teacher's sense of a "payoff" from making a commitment would be greater. As noted above, many hypothesize that the effects of community socio-economic status are greater than all others – this chapter deals centrally with the question of whether other factors are at least as important, if not more so.

- *School culture, and particularly teacher culture.* Metz argues that school and teacher culture tend to conform to local community norms about education, which are socio-economically based, and that where middle-class staffs teach in lower socio-economic schools, it is especially difficult to generate both high expectations for achievement and sensitivity to students' social backgrounds. We were particularly curious to see whether school and teacher culture in these schools could break this "iron law" and reveal instead norms of high engagement and achievement.

- *The leadership of the principal and others in the school.* Virtually every study of schools that function more effectively for students emphasizes the role of the principal and other leaders in matters such as setting a tone for what is expected, energizing staff, creating an orderly environment, and so on (Brookover *et al.* 1979; Wilson and Corcoran 1988). Louis and Miles (1990) have shown that certain forms of principal leadership and management are associated with improvement in working relations among teachers and general climate. Leadership style would, therefore, also seem to have a major impact on teachers' willingness to engage.

- *The alternative or unusual structures and activities in the school*. This study was initiated in a period where there was a growing assumption that schools could be altered to improve teachers' work. Reports such as those from the Holmes Group (*Tomorrow's Teachers*, 1986) and the Carnegie Forum (*A Nation Prepared: Teachers for the 21st Century*, 1986) have argued that until the organization surrounding the classroom – and even the classroom and curriculum itself – are changed, that we can expect no improvements in our ability to attract and retain the best teachers. The implied problem is that current work is structured so as to be alienating, rather than engaging. We wanted to learn about the extent to which innovative structures contributed to teacher engagement.

In the remainder of this chapter we discuss the choices the three schools made in each of these areas to promote teacher engagement.

Community and District Context

Community and district contexts can be demanding environments for urban schools, and schools that serve lower socio-economic communities. However, these three schools didn't simply react to their contexts, but attempted to mold and create them in a variety of ways.

Stressing Challenge and Respect for the Community

Metz (1990) argues that school norms tended to conform to local community norms about the value and purpose of education, some stressing challenge, others stressing compliance. City Park, Brigham, and Hillside all departed from such mirroring by stressing their own norms about education's importance. Despite the fact that parent and community support for educational achievement has often been very weak, the schools seem to have reconciled two potentially conflicting norms. While being sensitive to community feelings and respecting parents, they also push students toward levels of success that may appear to exceed the parents' own initial expectations.

By reaching out to parents, the schools established the norm that parents care about their children's education and deserve to be listened to. Each of the schools designed conference schedules and locations that were more supportive of explicit and clear communication, even bringing in third-party social workers and counselors to help mediate differences, and providing translators for parents who are not comfortable speaking in English. The schools also set high standards for parent involvement. City Park requires parents to visit the school and to discuss their child with an administrator or teacher before their child will be admitted. They also require parents to come to the school for conferences if the child is not performing well. Similar requirements and relationships are sought by Brigham and Hillside. Also, all three schools involve parents in various school committees, including major governance committees at Hillside.

Negotiating Positive or Minimal District Relations

Recently researchers have argued that life inside schools, but particularly in schools belonging to large school districts, is negatively affected by local politics and the district office (Farrar 1988). Conversely, Louis (1989) noted that where district support is strong, schools are more able to work on improvement issues. More often than not, high schools serving low socio-economic communities operate within large districts, while those serving more advantaged communities operate in much smaller, more supportive, and less regulatory districts. The case studies suggest that schools serving disadvantaged students can support teacher engagement by seeking school-district relationships more like those in high socio-economic communities, where the high school typically enjoys considerable autonomy (as long as graduates continue to be placed in selective colleges). Nevertheless, the difficulty of doing so for many schools should not be underestimated.

In *Brigham*, the district office and other schools were generally viewed as unsupportive and even hostile. Much of this attitude can be traced to the school's beginning, where its "alternative" title was confused with the regional proliferation of "alternative schools" that were intended as last-chance institutions for drop-outs or other students who failed to thrive in a "normal school environment." As one teacher said: "This school has had a lot of negative publicity that was unwarranted, and still today a lot of people will be surprised that if you work at Alternative that we [don't] work in a prison or something."

In addition to the negative image of the school among fellow educators and the community at large, Brigham teachers and administrators worked in a district setting universally perceived to be unfriendly to the goals of the school, and to teachers in general. To support their contentions, Brigham teachers pointed to their extremely low salaries, the efforts of the district to develop a "teacher-proof curriculum" in which teachers had virtually no choice about what to teach or when to teach it, and the lack of money for inservice or professional activities. Surprisingly, despite these conditions, most teachers reported that the environment had brought them together and created an esprit de corps that might not have otherwise existed. Many teachers said that their determination for success increased after a terrible first year during which they were sent "the rejects" from other schools, and shared the building with another school whose staff was antagonistic.

The bureaucratic environment for City Park, despite its location in a school system noted for its massive and insensitive central structure, was in many ways more benign. The district in which the school is located had demonstrated a decade of support for innovative, alternative programming. In addition, because they are designated as an "Alternative School," City Park had the prerogative to request flexibility in rules such as hiring practices, class size, and curriculum issues. City Park also benefited from the national profile of its principal. Considerable media publicity for the school helped to buffer it from district interventions. Thus, although teachers don't see the city school system as an advantage, the district did not figure heavily in their perception of their work setting. In general, teachers viewed the district environment as a "black box" that the principal deals with effectively, and the community as a turbulent environment that poses many hazards for their students.

Finally, district leadership provided Hillside with a powerful catalyst for heightening teachers' morale and commitment. The district loosened its requirements on schools and allowed them more individual flexibility in determining their programs. For example, in order to establish their teacher guided assistance program, the district supported Hillside's request for a schedule that was not in compliance with state mandates. Furthermore, teachers who are working on new projects are provided with both professional and psychological sustenance from the nearby professional academy. During the week that our research team was at Hillside, a 9th grade teaching team spent an entire day at the academy building to plan for several weeks of instruction. There, teachers had access to consultation, working space, and reference materials. In short, the Academy provides both time and resources to create, develop and implement new ideas.

School Site Control

What all three schools sought – and gained to some extent – was control over several key functions, including the ability:

1. to develop an educational mission specific to their school;
2. to hire staff directly;
3. to develop their own curriculum and instruction plans; and
4. to design staff development opportunities accordingly.

Having this sense of organization control improved the sense of membership and ownership among the school staff. Teachers in all three of these schools emphasized how important it was for them to be part of a school that pursued a collective definition of their goals and strategies. Released from predetermined conditions they were freer to develop a school environment and program reflecting the educational values they were most committed to. By being allowed to conduct their own hiring, these schools could employ teachers who were committed to work with the school's vision rather than against it. All of these benefits have helped these schools promote teacher engagement with their schools as a whole, and with its expectations for students' personal and academic development.

Teacher Culture

All three of the schools share norms that make teachers' work life different from conventional schools. We will limit the discussion here to norms that seem to have a significant positive impact on teacher engagement.

"A School with a Mission"

Teachers in all three schools emphasized how important it was to them to be part of a school that had (or was striving for) a collective definition not only of its goals (high achievement) but also its strategies for reaching them. A teacher at Brigham spoke for most of her colleagues when she said: "I was attracted to this school because of the philosophy … I was approached by a faculty member here who knew my philosophy on education, plus I had worked with the principal before … We both had the same ideas about education."

In City Park, where the coherence of the pedagogical approach and the need to develop this approach through team-work was most forcefully articulated, the need both to ascribe to the sense of mission and to draw energy from it was often mentioned: "People know that [the team approach] is … how we are going to work and they know why. If you want to work in this school that is the bottom line … I think [it] makes the job of teaching a creative experience, and creativity feeds on itself."

And at Hillside, where the faculty were still struggling with the precise nature of the "special quality" of the school, there was still a strong sense of being engaged in a risky but exciting joint venture. As one physical education teacher said:

> My personal goals, as far as teaching, go along with this school … I like the changes that have come about … I like it because we are experimenting. We don't know really where we're going … And after 23 years of teaching, to have that freedom to do some things, and the fact that I do not work alone any more, that I work with a group of people – it's made it so much easier.

Developing or being part of a collective vision of education necessitated commitment. As one City Park teacher put it, when asked if they would want to teach somewhere else, "there *is* nowhere else to teach." Teachers in Hillside and Brigham reported that it was hard on teachers who tried to maintain a detachment from the collective commitment:

> One of the things that I have seen happen is that some of the people who were very negative about the whole deal at the beginning, three or four years ago, that I never thought would come on board and work on it, have finally come around and have started working on things because they felt like they've wanted to and they needed to.

In other words, a mission and vision create social pressures for teachers to make commitments to the school as a social unit, and to the version of educational excellence that is embodied in the mission.

An Emphasis on Closeness among Staff Members

At Brigham, this special quality was, in part, a consequence of the fact that the Principal was able to attract and hire the staff that she wanted. One consequence was that the staff often described themselves in terms of family imagery: "Sure, this is what we stress here, this family group, this closeness … We are trying to be close to each other [as teachers], and know each other." In City Park and Hillside there was less use of the family imagery to refer to relationships among adults. However, there was much talk about trust and support. At City Park, one teacher said:

When I came here ... I had to learn a lot. I got a tremendous amount of help. [The principal] helped me; [another teacher] with 14 years of experience became my best friend here ... I used to meet him every morning to talk about what we were going to do and how we were going to do it ... and he would come observe my classes.

An Emphasis on Respect and Caring for Students

The theme of respect and caring as significant aspects of teachers' work in restructured schools has been developed elsewhere (Firestone and Rosenblum 1988). The emphasis on caring for students, and the way in which it is intertwined with teacher and student engagement is probably best summarized by a teacher from City Park: "Part of teaching is lending your ego for a kid to learn ... if you are teaching the kids, you see where each kid is and what their next step is. You have to perceive all of the differences ... you have to handle the resistance so that they may make steps for themselves ... *You have to do that, and that is an engaging process.*"

In Hillside, students talked openly about teachers' caring: "They want you to learn. They will also sit down with you a lot of time, I mean work personally [with you]. It seems like they'll do it all the time, you know, to make sure you understand it."

At Brigham, caring was built into the school's vision, which emphasized the affirmation of individual worth. Brigham teachers saw this as a critical feature of the school, because it gave them a sense of self-worth as well: "And if you can encourage, or you're successful in helping and enabling a person to feel good about themselves and about what they are doing, then the opportunity for that person to be a successful person is enhanced significantly. And that's what we're doing here. We *are* doing that."

Caring is good for students, of course, but it is also good for teachers. Caring makes schools into ethical and moral environments, not just arenas for "getting the job done." Studies of beginning teachers indicate that a significant motivation is the desire to be involved with a profession that has a moral character. This is not simply altruism, but the teacher's need to be engaged with work that has a significance broader than making a better widget.

A Demand for Active Problem-solving among Teachers

This theme arose repeatedly in the three schools. At City Park, one teacher commented about the way in which the problem-solving focus was reflected in student-teacher relationships: "The assumption is that the kids are basically trying to do the best that they can. And that might not be so great at a given point in time, so you try to get everybody together and ... you try to deal with what the problem is ... And that's the way problems are dealt with, even academically." It should be noted that at all of the schools, it was expected that teachers would involve themselves in maintaining constructive human relations, regardless of where they took place: "I used to walk past two kids rolling around on the floor, having a fight. That wasn't my business; that was up to the security guards ... Everything that happens [here] is everybody's business. After all, in your house, if your kids are acting crazy, your husband doesn't wait until you get home!"

The problem-solving focus was also articulated at Hillside, where the emphasis was placed on the responsibility given to teachers to manage their own environment. As one new teacher explained: "If you have an idea [you go to the principal] and usually, if you give her your idea she will say, 'And how do you plan to put this idea into action?'" We observed another new teacher making the following remark to her colleagues in a meeting: "You're all talking about what you want to accomplish at school ... At every other school I've ever been in they would be complaining and whining and griping and saying how bad the administration is. You all are figuring out what you're going to do – that's good, and it's really different."

Problem-solving was also emphasized at Brigham, although teachers also stressed that "if the district says no, then it's no." One teacher pointed out that many of her colleagues "have been in traditional schools where they feel that they're not going to be heard ... so it's just a habit [they have] of complaining to each other and not doing something about their concerns." Still, relative to other schools in the district, Brigham teachers saw themselves as being more active in looking for and solving problems: "... my husband, who teaches in one of the other high schools ... he's surprised that [we] are allowed to make decisions that stick ... you know, about teacher time, teacher responsibility."

For teachers, the sense of being responsible for unearthing and solving problems was the most powerful form of empowerment that they encountered. This sense of influence and responsibility made it difficult for most simply to teach courses and grade papers, but contribute little else to the school and students.

Peer Pressure to Work

Life in the three schools was more demanding than in most schools – but worth it. As one Brigham teacher said: "the teachers [who] have left here and gone to other places in the district ... have said 'gosh, I miss it.' They go to the room and they work. And after school the bell rings and they hit the cars."

City Park teachers talked about being exhausted, feeling that the work of curriculum development and active teaching had no end. But no teacher suggested that the effort made them want to leave. At Hillside, another teacher commented: "I do a lot more work and spend a lot more hours here, and I have to get along with a lot more people but I enjoy it more and so it is worth it."

Why is pressure to work more engaging? Because it is tied to a sense of doing work that addresses the vision of the school, and because it has visible payoff in the impacts on students – kids who are often viewed as dull and uninterested in school. At Hillside, where experienced teachers are working with the same types of students as past years, several spoke with amazement about the differences: "The kids we have as juniors this year were 9th graders when [these changes] first started. They're better behaved, they're more interested, and they're more willing to learn to do the kinds of things that help them learn than kids have been before."

A lesson that we take away is that the demands that are put upon teachers by their peers increase engagement *because they provide valuable professional feedback from peers.* Instead of being isolated in a classroom, and depending on students – many of whom will struggle under the best of circumstances – for feedback, the teacher is able to work with colleagues in ways that make their best work visible. The down-side is that their failures may also be visible, but other norms, especially teachers helping one another, cushion the potentially negative impact of more exposure.

Teacher Engagement and School Leadership

Teacher culture at both Brigham and City Park was dominated by the fact that they were new schools, and that most teachers had chosen to work there. This created a sense of being in a special place, and of working with a special team. At Hillside, on the other hand, most teachers had worked there for more than a decade. Few experienced it as unique until recently, but now, teacher engagement at Hillside is nearly as high as in Brigham and City Park. What the schools have in common, however, is a leadership style that promotes engagement. The "leadership factor" was more important than we expected. There was consensus that a school with an ineffective principal was unlikely to be exciting no matter how talented the staff, and schools became exciting quite rapidly after the arrival of a supportive principal. The role of the effective principal is described by teachers as one that facilitates staff to develop the culture described above, while also taking responsibility for other actions, outlined below.

Buffering Teachers
Studies of conventional schools emphasize the role of the principal in buffering the teacher from unwanted outside interventions by parents (Rossmiller 1990). In these three schools, however, we have already mentioned how these principals emphasize respectful relationships with their communities regardless of parents' social position or history of support for education. While parents and community were often invited in, two of the principals worked hard at buffering their staffs from the demands of district offices. At Brigham and City Park, located in unsupportive district contexts, the principals protected their staff members from distracting external demands and requirements. They recognized teachers' limited energies and struggled to preserve them for students and teaching. Although this was only partially effective at Brigham, teachers recognized the effort that went into trying to create an alternative and more professional work life in a highly centralized and authoritarian district. Having a principal who *cared* deeply about protecting teachers increased engagement.

Spending Time on Daily Routines
Leaders in the eight schools did not conform to the image of the efficient executive who participates only in the highest level of policy and leaves the daily work of the organization to others. Instead, the principals were visible, had open doors, and were available for spontaneous discussion or problem-solving. They spent time with students and tried to be ever-present at school activities, even when informal rewards were given. They were in the lunchroom and around the halls, not to discipline, but to gather information. At City Park and Brigham the principals led student advisory groups. At Hillside, we saw the principal personally praising individual students and teachers every day. This

emphasis on the normal routines of school constantly reminds them of their own importance in the life of their school and students. Obviously, in a big school like Hillside, the principal cannot know everything, but even there faculty commented on her willingness to balance knowledge with empowerment: "There are so many things going on in this building that even she admits that she no longer can keep up with what's going on. But what's really neat about [our principal] is that she trusts our professionalism so much that ... even if she's not aware of every small detail, it's OK."

Delegating and Empowering

Promoting conditions that acknowledge the professional capabilities and judgments of teachers was another shared quality of these principals. Principals who create healthy environments for teachers "make teachers invent solutions to problems – they aren't the only problem solver." The effective principal "can leave the building without things falling apart or hitting snags, and has staff empowered to respond to crises" (Hillside). At City Park, it is important to note that the philosophical conviction was to empower the team rather than the individual teacher. Communal decisions prevailed (even when the administrators were not enthusiastic), and it was up to the individual to implement these collective resolutions, with some autonomy and flexibility. Brigham is the slight exception to the consistent empowerment generalization, since teachers were well aware that the principal's ability to support decisions made by faculty were limited by strong central control.

These leaders also recognize risk-taking as part of problem-solving. To stretch professionally, teachers must take risks in the classroom. For example, they promoted no single formula for maximizing student engagement. Classes that seek to make learning meaningful, appropriate, and fun require new ideas; an atmosphere of risk taking allows teachers to try new approaches.

Confronting Unengaged Teachers

A clear and direct way of emphasizing engagement is to require changes in teachers who do not invest themselves in the four ways outlined at the beginning of this chapter. Teachers are inspired to work hard by those around them, and over and over again the teachers in these schools stressed the positive impact of a principal's personal willingness to confront bad teaching. There were plenty of supportive strategies to help less effective teachers improve, including mentor teachers, an environment that invited teachers to visit one another's classes and help one another, and staff development opportunities. For example, Brigham's principal worked with several teachers who had difficulty changing to a teaching style that deemphasized lecturing and teacher-centered instruction, ultimately encouraging one to leave, but creating a process for others in which they were able to make significant improvements. At City Park, some teachers experienced anxiety about their success with the Advisory classes, but the assistant principal put a great deal of energy into sharing his knowledge about students and his experiences with dealing with more personally. Still, when it was clear that a teacher was unable to develop supportive relationships with his or her students, that person did not return the next year.

Providing Leadership about Values

Teachers agreed that the principal set the tone for developing a vision and a value orientation in the school. It is important for the principal to understand and reflect the best in community ethical standards and values, and to "make clear what is valued – don't keep faculty guessing about what is important." Leadership articulating strong values was most visible in Brigham and City Park, where each principal also founded the school based on a particular educational philosophy. In both cases, that philosophy directly incorporates teacher engagement, since it is premised on eliminating teacher isolation through creating opportunities for collaborative work. In large and well-established Hillside, the influence of leadership values is more subtle, but still acknowledged by all teachers, particularly with regard to increasing parent involvement, a focus on interdisciplinary curriculum development, and on caring for students.

Teacher Engagement and School Organization

These principals encouraged engagement in additional ways, by helping to initiate organizational changes that reinforced (or revived) the staff's commitments to teaching. Their role in the school was not simply one of instructional leadership, however. Instead, teacher needs figured heavily in their administrative priorities.

Creating Structures to Promote Teacher Decision-making

The principals of these schools went beyond informal, open-door discussions and problem-solving. They also built new formal decision-making structures. Although teachers valued informal opportunities to give opinions or make suggestions, formal decision-making bodies were important symbols of their professional position in the school. At Brigham, faculty were involved in electing the assistant principal and set some policies; in City Park most decisions were made by the faculty as a whole or in the teams, while at Hillside the steering-group structure worked well for teachers because it was tied to the curriculum renewal that was at the heart of their interests.

Creating Structures to Promote Collaboration

In all three schools, teachers linked high levels of engagement to school structures that permitted them to spend more time with each other. This not only strengthened personal bonds, but also infused new enthusiasm about instruction. City Park's schedule provides teams with a weekly two-hour meeting in which they develop curriculum, teaching strategies, and student assignments. The schedule reflects the value the school places on teachers' own engagement with their academic program: "In my other school, what I was good at, I stayed good at. What I wasn't good at, I never improved ... I taught a self-contained class, and believe me, self-contained really means self-contained ... I really could have been in the building all by myself."

At Hillside collaborations usually revolve around task-force work. At Brigham, due to lack of resources and the school's inability to change district schedules, collaboration was more informal, and typically involved smaller numbers of teachers, except through the school's strong development work with cooperative learning. Nevertheless, it was expected that teachers would stay after school for collaborative development work. The reduction in isolation was apparent in all settings. A Brigham teacher said:

> I have found … professional collegiality presented here that my husband does not benefit from even though he's been at his school for twenty years … I mean, I have teachers on their off period come by and observe in my classroom that are not even in the English department … I don't know of that ever happening [elsewhere] because in the other schools your room is your domain.

Another Hillside staff member pointed to the collaboration-engagement link: "We work together on so many things (because of the steering committee). And one of the things that has opened up is that if I want to do something within math, there are teachers here that I know I can go to and they will help me teach that in my classroom."

Creating Structures to Promote Professional Development
Collegiality boosts engagement in part because it increases interpersonal knowledge and the "family" feeling. More important, however, is when collegiality is tied directly to the development of professional competence. At Brigham, where the district controlled staff development days, and the school had few resources of its own, the opportunities seemed, on the surface, meager. However, for most of the teachers, simply teaching at Brigham was a learning experience, and teachers hoped for more. Hillside, with its enormous resources and new enthusiasm for change, viewed each day as an occasion to learn from others: "There is tremendous opportunity to develop your skills and knowledge (in part) because of the collegiality that is so very prevalent. I mean, if you want to do it, there are people in this building that will do it with you. If you just want to sit back and be an observer, they'll let you come in and observe."

Both Hillside and City Park viewed their school-wide retreats as critical structures for both personal and collaborative development. Yet, in none of the schools were the days officially dedicated to staff development as important as the provision of more ad hoc or semi-planned development opportunities. The importance of continuing experimentation and skill development to engagement is best summarized by a teacher from City Park: "There's always something new to be thinking about … it encourages you to think about issues, to grapple with important questions."

Creating Structures to Improve Curriculum
Metz (1990) describes inner-city teachers spending their energies on curriculums of questionable benefit to their students. In one case, teachers taught a traditional college preparatory curriculum to students lacking basic skills; in another, teachers were so frustrated by declining student engagement that they often taught nothing but basic skills. Our study suggests that allowing and supporting teachers to write a curriculum specifically for the students they work with can increase many forms of engagement. Some

autonomy over curriculum was a feature in all eight of the schools we studied with the exception of Brigham, which had only recently been released from rigid district controls. Even at Brigham, however, teachers spoke of how they "worked hard to make [the curriculum] ours." For example, a group of history and English teachers found that they could make their assigned curricula more exciting for themselves and their students by merging the two into an interdisciplinary whole.

We have already described how collaborative, group experiences benefit teachers. Beyond that, curriculum writing involves teachers in thinking about fundamental issues relating to knowledge and learning. Furthermore, they can calculate what level of knowledge and what kind of instruction are best for the specific students they teach. That process engages teachers in their students, in the academic program of the school, in the craft of teaching, and in the subject they teach.

Conclusions

A teacher at City Park told us of a visit to her class by a Shakespeare artist: "This guy … transformed my class in a way I could never have done. I was overawed by how good he was with my kids … . He had one of my kids standing on her head!" All of us dream of schools full of such people, but the prospect of transforming schools through exceptional charisma is unrealistic. Such people are rare and, as this teacher said, "you would run out of them pretty quickly!" Also, we have learned that even the most talented teachers can burn out if they are dependent on their individual personal resources as their only support.

It is a mistake to allow teachers to depend only on students as a source of external support and feedback; doing so may put thousands of teachers in frustrating and lonely work environments. At City Park, Brigham, and Hillside we have seen teachers who energetically invest in the personal and academic progress of their students, even though most will not go to college. A variety of collegial, administrative and structural supports help them to remain engaged. Taking these schools as example,s what have we learned about encouraging teacher engagement in all schools?

- Teachers' engagement with the school as a social unit or community is intensified most profoundly when there is a collective sense of vision or purpose about education and the specific students they serve. The importance of individual motivation should not be underestimated, but the cases suggest that a supportive culture within the school can compensate for the lower demands from community and parents that occurred in City Park, Brigham, and Hillside. Knowledgeable leaders play a pivotal role in establishing such a vision, but a range of planning and decision-making opportunities can quickly involve staff in doing the same. Autonomy from district mandates and supportive district relations can facilitate developing vision, but may not be essential where teachers and principals support each other in seeking how best to serve their students.

- Engagement with student achievement is also nourished by opportunities for teachers to collaborate together on school-wide decisions. Too often, collaborative activities converge only on the marginal necessities of school life, such as paperwork, purchasing, or staff parties. At the three schools, teachers participated as a whole and in smaller groups in decisions regarding the fundamental issues of the school: the qualities of individuals to be hired as teachers, the abilities and needs of the students, the nature of teacher-student relationships, the content of the curriculum and the methods of instruction, and the setting or abolishing of policies. Professional dialogue over these tasks builds ownership and empowerment of the classroom in ways that "zoning of decisions" (Johnson 1990), in which teachers make individual decisions about how they teach but defer to administrators about policy matters, does not. Collaboration also contributes to teachers' engagement with achievement because it provides opportunities for teachers to support and give feedback they may not always get from their students. Finally, opportunities to develop curriculum and instructional plans for the students they serve allow teachers to assess an appropriate level of challenge for their students, increasing the likelihood of student engagement in their work.
- Engagement with students as whole individuals is expedited by structures that let teachers interact with students more informally, and in smaller groups. Advisories that emphasize a bond between each student and at least one adult in the building were a feature of each of these schools. At City Park, the block schedule reduced the number of students teachers worked with to around 60. Hillside sought a similar dynamic for some of its students through its own block programs. In addition to structures, we also found a general ethic of care for students. This cultural norm acknowledges the links between students' emotional well-being and their readiness to learn, and emphasizes respect and concern for students' lives as a whole.
- Engagement with subject matter took a somewhat different twist in the three schools, as compared with more typical high schools. The maxim that "elementary teachers teach students, high-school teachers teach subjects" would not reflect the priorities of these schools. Many teachers stayed current with developments in their field through participation in local and national associations, yet it was clear that their engagement with their individual subject was often subordinated to an interest in providing a more interdisciplinary curriculum. Teachers also tried to keep their focus on what worked best for their particular students, even if that meant abandoning a personal passion to lecture on a favorite topic. There is little doubt that making these changes requires teachers to give up a level of self-involvement with subject matter, but the improved opportunities to see students learning made the trade-offs worthwhile.
- The relationship between teacher engagement and organizational leadership, culture and structure is not simple. But the organizational reforms accomplished by these schools demonstrate how schools serving disadvantaged students can sustain levels of teacher engagement comparable to schools in higher socio-economic circumstances. We acknowledge that the success of these three schools is not easy to reproduce. They are, in part, dependent on securing autonomy from district mandates, and on the skills and extraordinary energies of their talented administrators and teachers. But at least we

found that schools serving disadvantaged children can make changes that positively affect teacher engagement. Although communities did not pressure these schools to perform, high demands for teacher performance and engagement were generated from within the schools. Furthermore, the schools we studied successfully freed teachers from an involuntary dependency on students by providing a richer array of feedback and rewards, but also empowered them to make voluntary investments in their success with students. Teachers in these schools gave themselves freely to the task of instruction and student achievement – but had resources to turn to if classroom success was not immediate or as profound as they hoped. This is, perhaps, the balance to which any restructured school must aspire in order to break the "iron law of social class."

Note

1. This chapter is an edited version of K.S. Louis and B. Smith (1992) "Cultivating teacher engagement: Breaking the iron law of social class." In F. Newmann (ed.), *Student Engagement and Achievement in American Secondary Schools*: 119–52. New York: Teachers College Press.

References

Barnard, C. (1938) *The Functions of the Executive*, Cambridge, MA: Harvard Univesity Press.

Brookover, W. et al. (1979) *School Social Systems and Student Achievement: Schools Can Make a Difference*. New York: Praeger.

Bryk, A.S. and M.W. Driscoll (1988) *The High School as Community: Contextual Influences and Consequences for Students and Teachers*. Madison, WI: National Center on Effective Secondary Schools, University of Wisconsin-Madison.

—— and Y.M. Thum (1989) *The Effects of High School Organization on Dropping Out: An Exploratory Investigation*. New Brunswick, NJ: Center for Policy Research in Education, Rutgers, The State University of New Jersey.

——, V. Lee, and J. Smith (1988) "High school organization and its effects on teachers and students: An interpretive summary of the research." In W. Clune and J. Witte (eds), *Choice and Control in Schools*: 135–226. Philadelphia, PA: Falmer.

Carnegie Forum on Education and the Economy (1986) *A Nation Prepared: Teachers for the 21st Century*. New York: Carnegie Forum.

Corcoran, T.B., L.J. Walker, and J.L. White (1988) *Working in Urban Schools*. Washington, DC: Institute for Educational Leadership.

Dworkin, A. (1987) *Teacher Burnout in the Public Schools*. Albany, NY: SUNY Press.

Farrar, E. (1988) "Environmental contexts and the implementation of teacher and school-based reforms: Competing interests." Paper presented at the annual meeting of the American Educational Research Association, New Orleans, LA.

Firestone, W. and S. Rosenblum (1988) "The alienation and commitment of students and teachers in urban high schools: a conceptual framework." *Educational Evaluation and Policy Quarterly* 10: 285–300.

Freedman, S. (1990) *Small Victories: The Real World of a Teacher, Her Students, and Their School.* New York: Harper & Row.

Hallinger, P. and J.F. Murphy (1986) "The social context of effective schools." *American Journal of Education* 3: 328–55.

Holmes Group (1986) *Tomorrow's Teachers.* East Lansing, MI: author.

Hurn, C. (1985) *The Limits and Possibilities of Schooling.* Boston: Allyn and Bacon.

Kidder, Tracy (1989) *Among School Children.* Boston: Houghton Mifflin.

Louis, K.S. (1989) "School district policy for school improvement." In M. Holmes, K. Leithwood, and D. Musella (eds), *Educational Policy for Effective Schools*: 145–67. New York: Teachers College Press.

—— and M.B. Miles (1990) *Improving the Urban High School: What Works and Why.* New York: Teachers College Press.

—— and B.A. Smith (1990) "Teacher working conditions." In P. Reyes (ed.), *Teachers and Their Workplace: Commitment, Performance and Productivity*: 23–47. Newbury Park, CA: Sage.

Metz, M.H. (1988a) "Teachers' ultimate dependence on their students: Implications for teachers' response to student bodies of differing social class." Paper presented at the annual meetings of the American Educational Research Association, New Orleans.

—— and colleagues (1988b) *"Phase I" of the Teacher Working Conditions. Study: Final Report.* Madison: University of Wisconsin, Center for the Study of Effective Secondary Schools.

—— (1990) "How social class differences shape the context of teachers' work." In M. McLaughlin and J. Talbert (eds), *The Secondary School as a Workplace*: 40–107. New York: Teachers College Press.

National Education Association (1987) *Status of the American Public School Teacher: 1985– 85.* Westhaven, CT: NEA Professional Library.

Newmann, F.M. and R.A. Rutter (1987) *Teacher's Sense of Efficacy and Community as Critical Targets for School Improvement.* Madison: University of Wisconsin, Center for the Study of Effective Secondary Schools.

Powell, A., E. Farrar, and D. Cohen (1985) *The Shopping Mall High School.* New York: Houghton Mifflin.

Purkey, S.C., R.A. Rutter, and F.M. Newmann (1986) "United States high school improvement programs: A profile from the high school and beyond supplemental survey." *Metropolitan Education* 3: 59–91.

Rossmiller, R. (1992) "The secondary school principal and teachers' quality of work life." *Educational Management and Administration* 20(3): 132–46.

Wehlage, G.G., R.A. Rutter, N.L. Lesko, and R.R. Fernandez (1989) *Reducing the Risk: Schools as Communities of Support.* Philadelphia, PA: Falmer Press.

Wilson, B. and T. Corcoran (1988) *Successful Secondary Schools: Visions of Excellence in American Public Schools.* East Sussex: Falmer Press.

8

The Effects of Teacher Quality of Work Life on Commitment and Sense of Efficacy[1]

Introduction

There is accumulating evidence that teachers' work in secondary schools is often demoralizing and unprofessional. National commissions have asserted that this is a problem (Carnegie Forum 1986; Holmes Group 1986), and research has affirmed it (Darling Hammond 1984). Opinion polls conducted by the NEA reveal that job satisfaction and indications of a preference to leave the profession have risen rather dramatically (NEA 1987). In addition, some argue that the problem of teacher job satisfaction cannot be easily separated from other evolving characteristics of contemporary schooling: the increase in the number of students from diverse and often lower socio-economic backgrounds, and the increasingly bureaucratic and regulatory structure of schools, which affects the freedom that teachers have to perform their work (Elmore 1988). A major deficiency of analyses and recommendations to date is that they have often been made within a limited framework for analyzing the nature of commitment to work. Because they are poorly grounded in theories of work commitment, the recommended solutions often appear to have been drawn from the hip pocket, rather than being carefully attached to what is known from research.

This paper explores the concept of quality of work life (QWL) as a construct that may identify the characteristics of teachers' work that contribute most to their commitment to teaching, and their sense of efficacy. First, a model that ties organizational characteristics of the work place to important behaviors, attitudes, and psychological characteristics of teachers that affect their teaching effectiveness will be presented. Second, measures of QWL in eight schools will be examined, along with the relationship between the QWL variables and measures of teachers' commitment and sense of efficacy. Finally, the effects of school structure on QWL will be explored. The discussion will focus on the implications of the findings and the model for reform strategies.

Commitment, Sense of Efficacy and Quality of Work Life

Research and commission reports assume that the structure of the school and the profession can be altered, without a radical change in the existing system, to improve the attractiveness of the profession and the probability that teachers will remain excited and involved in their work over a long-term career. However, there is no consensus about how reform proposals that range from merit pay to teacher empowerment will stimulate improved working conditions. The QWL literature defines the outcome of improved job conditions as an increase in general work satisfaction, low absenteeism, and commitment, which is generally defined in the psychological literature as a preference for remaining in the job and a sense of identification with the organization (Hackman and Oldham 1980). These form a base for effective job performance.

The Concept of Teacher Commitment
Recent research on teacher commitment in education (Rosenholz and Simpson 1990) has followed this definition, using attitudinal measures of liking for the job and the school as indicators of commitment. The educational literature, however, suggests that we should also be concerned with a somewhat broader definition of commitment to work in and out of the classroom. Commitment consists of personal and professional investment in a specific workplace and its goals, as indicated by specific *behaviors* that indicate extra effort as well as *attitudes*. The primary reason for emphasizing both attitudes and behaviors is because they may stimulate student engagement (see Newmann 1992). Studies of elementary schools indicate that when students believe that teachers care about them and their performance, they will work harder (Brookover *et al.* 1979). Older adolescents may be less responsive to adult approval than elementary-school students, but there is reason to assume that the "caring" behavior will not disappear (Wehlage *et al.* 1989; Smith *et al.* 1990). In addition, engaged teachers work harder to make classroom activities meaningful – introducing new ways of learning, and altering the presentation of materials so that they are more relevant and of greater intrinsic interest to students (Rosenholz 1989). They are likely to work with students in extra-curricular activities that bind students to the school. This may, in turn, affect achievement, as is shown in Rosenholz's study. Dworkin (1987) shows that the students of

teachers who show lower solidarity and work satisfaction exhibit lower achievement gains and have higher rates of absenteeism, while Bryk and Driscoll (1988) show that teachers' commitment to their work increases students' commitment.

Four distinctive types of commitment can be identified in recent empirical research (Newmann *et al.* 1989; Bryk and Driscoll 1988; Firestone and Rosenblum 1988; Wehlage *et al.* 1989; Rosenholz 1989; Reyes 1990; Louis and Smith 1991):

1. Commitment to the school as a *social unit*. This form of commitment creates a sense of community, affiliation, and personal caring among adults within the schools and facilitates integration between personal life and work life. Teachers who are engaged in this way care about and identify with their specific school, as well as with their profession, and volunteer for extra work that leads to improvements in school climate and general functioning.
2. Commitment to the *academic goals* of the school. Teachers may be socially integrated, yet fail to create an atmosphere of high expectations (Powell *et al.* 1985). Teachers who are engaged with academics spend time working on lesson plans, classroom activities, and constantly think about how to improve students' engagement and performance.
3. Commitment to students *as unique whole individuals* rather than as "empty vessels to be filled." This form of commitment may motivate teachers to deal with students undergoing personal crises, or to be more sensitive and aware of adolescent development. Teachers who care about their students spend time on extra-curricular activities, working with counselors or families, or other activities that help them to understand how to better motivate and support them.
4. Commitment to the *body of knowledge* needed to carry out effective teaching. In schools, particularly within rapidly changing fields (such as science education), teachers must be energized to access and incorporate new ideas in the classroom and curriculum.

Teacher Sense of Efficacy

As Rosenholz and Simpson (1990) note, any model that examines teachers' work cannot ignore sense of efficacy as a critical variable. The recent work of Ashton and Webb (1986) indicates that teachers' sense of efficacy is related to student achievement; thus, improving this social-psychological condition of teaching is an important intervening variable in the improvement of schools. Lee *et al.* (1991) show that in the High School and Beyond data, some aspects of school structure have a strong effect on teacher sense of efficacy.

The research literature on commitment and QWL does not consistently place teacher sense of efficacy in the role of a dependent or independent variable. Rosenholz (1989) and Rosenholz and Simpson (1990) use teacher sense of efficacy as a predictor of teacher commitment, although the latter note that it is "not a characteristic of the workplace, per se" (p. 243). Hackman and Oldham's model (1980) implies that an increased sense of efficacy is an outcome of more effectively designed work environments, and is a predictor of high work effectiveness and job satisfaction (commitment), an assumption that is used in Ashton and Webb's (1986) study of middle schools, and in Lee *et al.* (1991) analysis of High School and Beyond data. On the other hand, it is reasonable to assume an interdependent relationship: an individual is unlikely to become committed unless he or she feels effective at work, but committed people tend to work harder and thus increase their sense of competence (Hackman and Oldham 1980). In this study, sense of efficacy will be viewed as an outcome of objective job conditions, and no assumptions will be made about a causal relationship between sense of efficacy and commitment.

A Quality of Work Life Framework

Although the school reform literature is largely atheoretical, it is often consistent with the conceptual frameworks that have been used to study work life in a variety of other organizational and professional contexts (see, for example, Biderman and Drury 1976; Lawler *et al.* 1980). Most notably, the organizational literature offers a more detailed definition of QWL than does the educational literature, and leads to greater specificity concerning what kinds of restructuring should promote improved working conditions for teachers.

A review of the QWL indicators in the organizational literature cited above identified seven criteria that are consistent with issues expressed in the educational reform literature:

1. *Respect from relevant adults*, such as the administrators in the school and district, parents, and the community at large (Firestone and Rosenblum 1988).
2. *Participation in decision-making* that augments the teachers' influence or control over their work setting (Cohn *et al.* 1987; Firestone and Rosenblum 1988; Sickler 1988).
3. *Frequent and stimulating professional interaction* among peers (such as collaborative work or collegial relationships) within the school (Little 1984; Newmann *et al.* 1989).
4. *Feedback on performance* (for example, structures and procedures that contribute to a high sense of efficacy) (Rosenholz 1985 and 1989).
5. The opportunity to make full *use of existing skills and knowledge*, and to acquire new skills and knowledge (self-development); the opportunity to experiment (Newmann *et al.* 1989; Rosenholz 1989; Sederberg and Clark 1990).
6. *Adequate resources to carry out the job*; a pleasant, orderly physical working environment (Cohn *et al.* 1987; Public School Forum of North Carolina 1987).
7. *Congruence between personal goals and the school's goals* (low alienation) (Cohn *et al.* 1987; Louis and Miles 1990).

Linking Quality of Work Life, and Commitment and Sense of Efficacy

Most studies of the antecedents of commitment emphasize personal characteristics or psychological predispositions rather than the relationship between variables that are similar to those identified as QWL (Reyes 1990). However, research, both inside and outside education, leads to a prediction that QWL variables may affect commitment and efficacy (Stevens *et al.* 1978). The QWL model proposed here is consistent with the "workplace conditions" factors model examined by Rosenholz (1985, 1989) and Rosenholz and Simpson (1990), and the school organization model presented by Lee *et al.*, but focuses attention more narrowly on variables that directly define the nature of teachers' work and which can be affected by organizational policies and practice. Rosenholz's model, for example, emphasizes the importance of personal rewards from teaching, factors that may be products of workplace conditions, but are, in themselves, psychological properties of the individual. Lee *et al.* use hierarchical linear modeling to examine the effects of five organizational characteristics on teachers' sense of efficacy which account for a high proportion of the variance in sense of efficacy. However, several (for example, disorderly behavior on the part of students and school size) do not define the characteristics of teachers' work as much as the environment in which the work is carried out. Ashton and Webb (1986) examined a number of characteristics of schools that related to teachers' sense of efficacy, including school climate, professional role responsibilities, positive collegial relationships, and student conflict. Their teacher interviews indicate that there are strong relationships between work-place characteristics, such as teacher influence in decision-making and positive collegial relationships, that have a marked impact on sense of efficacy, but these relationships are less well measured in their survey data.

School Restructuring as an Intervening Variable

Many schools are making active efforts to change the conditions under which teachers work as part of a response to the calls for school reform, and the premise of this paper is that, in order to improve teachers' work life, we must identify factors that both affect teachers' commitment, and which can also be altered through school, district or state policies, such as those identified in the school reform literature. This assumption has received some support from Rutter's (1986) analysis of the High School and Beyond data, which suggests that schools developing alternative structures, programs, and activities have a correspondingly higher level of teacher commitment. Although the sample of schools in this study is small, we will attempt a preliminary exploration of the question of *how much* restructuring is necessary to improve teachers' work by looking at differences between the eight schools.

The Study and Measures

The research on which this analysis is based was conducted in 1987 and 1988, as part of a larger study on teachers' work life in alternatively structured schools conducted under auspices of the Center for Effective Secondary Schools at the University of Wisconsin. The research involved developing case studies of eight schools that were selected, after a broad, national search, to represent schools that:

1. had been making serious efforts to alter teachers' working situation for at least three years before our research began; and
2. served a high proportion of non-traditional or at-risk students in either rural or urban areas.

In the course of the research we observed 120 classrooms, and interviewed approximately 180 teachers, administrators, and students.

The Survey

In addition, an eleven-page survey of all teachers in each of the eight buildings was conducted. Most questions dealt with working conditions in the schools, teachers' attitudes toward their work, and background characteristics. The instrument was designed to measure the QWL and commitment and sense of efficacy constructs discussed above. Most items were measured on five or six point Likert scales. The surveys were distributed during the site visit, with a request to return them in a sealed envelope with no identification by the end of the site visit period. In most schools, a teacher was designed as a contact point for returning surveys that were not completed during the week. The overall response rate for the survey was 89 per cent.

Clearly the sample of schools that we studied is not representative of typical high schools. Yet during our qualitative data collection we recognized that even within alternatively structured schools there is great variation in the degree to which teachers participate in and experience "alternativeness." Furthermore, although all of the schools had made some efforts to change teachers' work, they varied greatly in the degree to which they might be considered "restructured" in terms of curriculum, use of time, governance, and relationships with the community. Thus, although the variations in perceived QWL may be narrower in these schools simply because the schools were at least attempting to address the problems that have been identified in the reform reports mentioned above, the lack of uniformity suggested that analyzing the model within this set of schools was valuable.

Measures and Scaling[2]

The questionnaire was designed to measure the variables discussed above. Therefore, rather than engaging in exploratory scaling, a confirmatory scaling approach was used. First, correlation matrices of all variables that were intended to tap a particular variable were examined. In a few instances, items were not as highly correlated with other proposed indicators as had been expected; these were eliminated. Then, reliability analyses were conducted for each of the variables. In several cases, where Cronbach's Alpha statistics seemed particularly low, additional variables were eliminated in order to increase internal reliability. A preliminary confirmatory factor analysis indicated that the items that were used as indicators of commitment were too highly correlated to develop four distinct measures and it was decided to compute a single measure of commitment. Teachers' sense of efficacy was measured by three items, one of which taps the individual teacher's sense of efficacy, while the other two address the question of whether

Table 8.1 Stepwise Multiple Regression of Teacher Commitment and Attitudes Toward Students on Quality of Work Life Variables

	Standardized Beta Weights	
	Commitment	Sense of Efficacy
Respect	0.16**	0.41**
Sense of Influence	−0.01	0.10**
Collegial Work	0.07	0.08*
Develop/Use Skills	0.19**	0.22**
Feedback	0.16**	0.01
Resources	0.08	0.06*
Goal Congruence	0.04	0.11**
Multiple R2	0.25	0.62
F	24.99**	119.48**

* Significant at the 0.05 level.

** Significant at the 0.01 level.

teachers in the whole school are able to carry out their educational goals – a measure of collective sense of efficacy. Again, a single measure was computed.

Judgments of the research staff were used to classify the degree to which teachers' work was structured differently from the "typical" high school, in terms both of the content and structure of teaching (curriculum, use of time and space, student assessment, and so on) as well as the structures that were directly intended to improve QWL, such as teacher senates, mentor teacher programs, staff development opportunities, career ladders, and so forth. Three staff members who were familiar with all of the schools independently classified the degree of restructuring that characterized each of the schools. There was unanimity between the three staff about which of three categories – highly restructured, moderately restructured, and minimally restructured – the eight schools fit into. Two schools were in the first category, four in the second, and two in the last.[3]

Findings

A stepwise multiple regression analysis procedure using the SPSS program was used to examine the relationship between the QWL indices, and teacher commitment and sense of efficacy (Table 8.1).

Predicting Teacher Commitment
The variable that shows the strongest relationship to commitment is the ability to "develop and use skills" related to one's work. This suggests that teachers – like most professionals – require sustained stimulation to remain excited about and committed to their work. When teachers feel caught in a daily grind where they are unable to try out new ideas or to receive sustained professional development opportunities, they are less likely to engage with the acts of teaching and working within the school. Because the measure includes indicators of the degree to which the staff development provided in

the district is relevant and useful, this finding also appears to affirm Rosenholz's assertion that providing teachers with effective inservice opportunities increases teacher commitment.

A sense of being respected by peers, students, the principal, and others outside of the school also stands out as having a significant regression coefficient. This finding affirms Firestone and Rosenblum's (1988) qualitative analysis, which suggests that respect is the most critical variable underlying a teacher's willingness to work hard and dedicate themselves to their colleagues and pupils.

Opportunities to receive feedback from colleagues and the school principal is also quite strongly related to commitment in the regression equation. Again, this supports Rosenholz's finding that feedback about performance was an important predictor of teacher commitment. Because the measures of feedback used in this survey focus primarily on opportunities for visiting other's classrooms, and being visited in a non-evaluative context, this suggests that the principle of teacher autonomy in the classroom may be inconsistent with what is needed if we are to increase teachers' willingness to contribute the kind of effort that may be needed to restructure the experiences of children in schools.

The entire equation is significant, and the results indicate that the seven QWL variables explain slightly over 25 per cent of the variance in teacher commitment. However, it is important to point out that the stepwise procedures show that a much reduced model, consisting only of the variables of respect, developing new skills, feedback, and resources, also explains just under 25 per cent of the variance (not tabled).

Predicting Teacher Sense of Efficacy

Turning to sense of efficacy, Table 8.1 shows that the regression model is similar to the previous one in that respect and the development and use of skills are the variables with the largest regression coefficients. In this equation respect is overwhelmingly the most important variable, with a regression coefficient of 0.41, which strongly supports the argument that people must feel valued in order to believe that they are able to have an impact (although, of course, the relationship is likely to be reciprocal: people who are effective in their work are more likely to be respected). The opportunity to develop and use skills, with a regression coefficient of 0.22, also suggests that people need to regenerate their pool of knowledge in order to feel that they can be more effective in their work environments.

However, the model for sense of efficacy is rather different in overall character from the one that included commitment as the dependent variable, because several additional variables have significant regression coefficients, while feedback's coefficient is insignificant.

Goal congruence is significant at the 0.01 level, as is sense of influence. The indicators that make up the goal congruence scale reflect the degree to which the individual respondent works in a setting in which they feel that their values and beliefs are supported and reflected back in the values and beliefs of others. As such, it is a major component of the cohesiveness of the school, and reveals the degree to which there is a sense of implicit or explicit "vision" that people feel attached to. This finding supports the belief that having a strong value base for a school is important not only for students but also for teachers, a contention that has been strongly argued by Bryk and Driscoll (1988) and Bryk et al. (1990).

The moderately large regression coefficient associated with sense of influence (0.10) indicates that the degree to which teachers, as a group, are able to control important decisions of various types contributes to the belief that individual and the group of teachers are potent forces in changing the schools. Again, this both strengthens and extends the findings of Lee et al. (1991). They strengthen in that they are consistent. They extend in that the measure of sense of efficacy used in this study incorporated measures of the perceived potency of teachers *as a group*, as well as individual sense of efficacy.

More modest contributions to the explained variance are made by the opportunities that teachers have to work collegially. This provides limited support for the substantial body of literature that emphasizes the importance of working in groups as a source of rejuvenation and "organizational learning," which leads to more effective performance (and thus, presumably, higher sense of efficacy). Resources, which did not contribute significantly to teacher commitment, do seem to affect teachers' sense of efficacy.

Together the QWL variables explain 62 per cent of the variance in sense of efficacy, which is substantially higher than the measure of individual commitment.

Exploring the Effects of Restructuring

Analysis of variance was used to examine the effects of school restructuring on QWL and teacher commitment (Table 8.2). The results show a significant relationship for all variables, which is also linear in the case of eight of the nine variables tested. This suggests the conclusion, supported by qualitative data reported elsewhere (Louis and Smith 1991), that restructuring supports teacher commitment and sense of efficacy. However, although the tests of linearity are significant, there is a pattern of curvilinearity that is suggestive: for the variables measuring Respect, Collegiality, Develop/Use Skills, Feedback, Resources, Commitment, and Sense of Efficacy, the degree of commitment is highest in the schools that are most and least restructured, and lower in the schools in the middle category.

An examination of the school-by-school means (not shown) indicates that the middle group is composed of two schools that were among the top three in terms of commitment, and two that were at the bottom of the group. The latter two were moderately "alternative" schools that had maintained their "difference" from others in their district over a period of five to ten years. The two high commitment or moderately alternative schools were in the first few years of implementing teacher-designed change programs. This supports the often noted stimulating effect that innovation efforts can have on the individual's feelings about their work – an effect that may not be sustained over time unless the innovation has genuine merit.

Table 8.2 ANOVA: Degree of Restructuring and QWL, Commitment, and Sense of Efficacy

| | Restructuring | | | | | | |
| | Means | | | ANOVA | | Test of linearity | |
	Low	Medium	High	F Ratio	F Prob.	F Ratio	F Prob.
Respect	41.5	39.9	43.2	10.30	0.000	16.90	0.000
Influence	25.5	25.2	28.3	7.46	0.001	6.421	0.0
Collegiality	20.0	19.4	22.5	18.16	0.000	19.19	0.000
Develop Skills	16.6	17.2	17.9	4.73	0.009	4.73	0.009
Feedback	9.7	7.9	10.5	30.28	0.000	57.76	0.000
Resources	13.8	12.7	13.6	5.61	0.004	10.81	0.001
Congruence	15.8	15.8	16.5	3.72	0.025	3.03	0.08
Commitment	49.4	48.1	50.1	5.83	0.003	10.94	0.001
Sense of Efficacy	21.2	18.2	23.8	65.6	0.000	11.99	0.000
(N)	(145)	(252)	(131)				

Discussion and Implications

We must be cautious is drawing final conclusions for theory, policy and practice based on a cross-sectional survey of teachers in schools that are, based on our own observations and those of the teachers who worked in them, better places to work than the typical high school located in similar communities. Nevertheless, despite the survey's limitations, the findings have some implications for both theory and policy that should not be ignored.

Implications for "Practical Theories" of School Improvement and Reform

The writings of the reform movement, although often assertive in pronouncing one or another remedy for current problems as better than others, have failed to generate many theoretically grounded proposals. The weakness of this seat-of-the-pants approach is well articulated by Mahlen et al. (1990) as they analyze why flawed theories lying behind program efforts explain why efforts to introduce school-based management have disappointed their sponsors. More theoretically based arguments, such as are found in the many discussions for and against parental choice as a reform strategy, are confounded on the other side by lack of attention (or one-sided attention) to available data (see Louis and van Velzen 1990).

All too often, those who write about the need to improve teachers' work as part of reform exhibit a similar lack of attention to the need for solidly grounded psychological and sociological frameworks to support a change strategy, and to the availability of data from sources outside education. Research based on large-scale national studies provides excellent insights into the empirical relationships between a variety of measures and teachers' working conditions, but is ultimately flawed by the fact that the measures chosen are dependent on what was included in a particular survey, rather than on a coherent view of teachers' working conditions.

This paper has proposed such a framework, based on a review of literature that comes largely from outside of education (although an increasing number of educational researchers are adopting compatible perspectives). The framework argues that creating effective working conditions for teachers requires paying attention to the multiple dimensions along which individuals experience their work, and which can be potentially affected by changing the social organization of the school. Thus, the model proposed here has excluded attention to psychological predispositions of individuals (such as need for autonomy, or personal preference for specific kinds of rewards) or personal characteristics (such as gender or race) than cannot be effectively altered by administrative or policy intervention.

The regression findings provide strong evidence that a QWL framework is both applicable to the teaching profession and useful in predicting key behaviors and attitudes that have been associated in other studies with effective work performance and higher levels of student achievement. The data suggest that the seven variables identified in the non-educational QWL literature, and verified as reflective of the current school reform literature in the USA, are all important predictors of either commitment or sense of efficacy.

The data suggest that altering teachers' working conditions to directly affect the seven dimensions included here can have a significant, positive effect on teachers' commitment. Thus, although three-quarters of the variance is unexplained by this simple, but theoretically grounded model, there is much to be said for its potential as a means of evaluating alternatively strategies for changing teachers' professional lives.

Implications for Policy

The policy implications of this study must be examined both at a system (outside the school) and school level. From the macro-policy level, a tentative conclusion is that traditionally structured schools that make some efforts to enhance teachers' work, and radically restructured schools *may* provide better work environments for teachers than schools that opt for a middle ground. This finding supports the proposition that it is not always the total amount of change effort but the focus of that effort that is important. A traditional school that hones its performance may be an excellent place to work.

This argument should not be interpreted as "small is beautiful" when it comes to reform. Too much evidence exists to suggest that schools require significant changes rather small adaptations of existing programs. What it does suggest, however, is that the opposite – "more is better" – is also not always true, unless the school is willing to risk designing an environment that is quite dramatically different from the ordinary. And the consequence of the above reasoning is simple: general school restructuring will not necessarily improve teachers' lives at work unless it focuses clearly on the need to create environments that are engaging, not only for students but also for teachers.

Generating micro-policy implications of the above discussion requires a backward mapping process in which we examine the most critical QWL dimensions, and look for the kinds of policy tools that may help to achieve them. These necessarily draw on our qualitative data (see Louis and Smith 1991), but may be briefly summarized.

Increased collegial and collaborative work among teachers was promoted by changes in scheduling that permitted more teacher meetings during the school day. These could be as minor as having a single, longer lunch period, to more major scheduling changes such as those briefly described above in the case of City Park Secondary School. Teachers valued chances to work on curriculum and other types of school development activities. Our data suggest that it is not collegial work per se that is important, but the degree to which collegial work stretches teachers' professional repertoire. Thus, restructuring that placed more emphasis on school-based curriculum work seems important. Even in those districts that had uniform curricula, the schools in our study negotiated exceptions for themselves, or ignored district rules to develop their own approaches.

Enhanced opportunities within the school to use and develop new skills – one of the most important predictors of both efficacy and commitment – was most effectively promoted by all-school, teacher-organized inservice activities, teacher mentoring programs, or programs that provided grants to teachers to develop new programs. Programs that drew upon the talents of teachers within the school, or used "training of trainer" models so that expertise was developed among the staff, were viewed most positively by teachers. More traditional professional development activities – such as attending conferences, district-wide inservice, and taking courses – were less effective, largely because their effects were less likely to spread beyond the individual.

Opportunities for teachers to participate in decisions and take responsibility for them were important. However, the assumption that "empowered teachers" will be more engaged and have a higher sense of efficacy because they have opportunities to influence school policy is less well supported by these data than an alternative interpretation, namely that where teachers are given a visible voice in the school they feel more respected. This accounts for our qualitative findings that teachers were relatively unconcerned about the availability (or lack of availability) of formal participatory groups, such as faculty Senates. When questioned about these structures, few teachers felt that they were critical. Rather, teachers and administrators defined empowerment more broadly as the need to "ensure that teachers have the resources, training and administrative support to become involved and engaged." As one teacher said "It is OK to have a traditionally structured high school. That is no problem [for teacher commitment]. However, I personally believe that what really satisfies a teacher is the opportunity to speak out … we speak out, we're free to critique something, we're free to give advice, to pat each other on the back."

Efforts to "open the classroom door" by encouraging teachers and administrators to observe classes and discuss teaching was expected to lead to improved feedback on performance from colleagues and supervisors, and thus to increased commitment and efficacy. This relationship was confirmed for commitment, but not for sense of efficacy. However, in only two of the schools were frequent class visitations expected. Teachers frequently remarked on how easy it was to ask for help from other teachers; teachers who took advantage of the enhanced opportunities for feedback in the other schools were more committed than those who did not. In all of the schools, however, open discussion about practices of good teaching was more frequent than in more traditionally structured schools.

Resources are important – they are a significant factor in both regressions, and teachers talk about them clearly. However, they are less important than is often believed. The schools in this study ranged from an upper-middle-class resource-rich setting, with all of the amenities of professional life, to bare-bones settings that, to the site visitors, appeared grim and unappealing. The vast differences in actual resources are not reflected in the relatively small differences between the schools (which are, in any case, not consistent with the actual level of resources available).

All of the above opportunities to mix, influence, mingle and engage in self-development appeared to be strongly associated with teachers' perceptions that other professionals in the schools shared their own educational goals and values. In other words, increasing opportunities to communicate and share significantly reduced the alienation that many have observed among both teachers and students in typical high schools.

Teachers and administrators pointed, however, to the need to instititutionalize philosophical commitment to increasing teacher influence by creating steering committees, allocating release time for teachers to become involved in serious ways, having administrative "open door policies," and having decentralized budgets that can support teacher suggestions and ideas. Consistent with the emphasis on collective staff development, there was consistent emphasis on the need to "provide opportunities for teachers to make important instructional decisions" through collaborative decision-making. However, the type of empowerment that was most satisfying fell into the category of broad informal influence over the school, rather than the formal, delegated right to participate in decisions of specific types.

One important practice feature that emerges in these schools is the importance of principal support and leadership. As has been argued elsewhere (Rosenblum *et al.* 1990), leadership styles of the principals in these schools were both distinctively different from those in traditional schools, but also variable within this group. As compared with principals in traditional schools, these principals were more visible in the school, more involved in curriculum and instructional issues, and were more likely to set high standards for teachers. However, effective principal support in the recently changing schools was perceived to be more assertive and challenging, while in the schools that had been restructured for some time, effective principal support was more facilitative and unobtrusive.

Notes

1. This chapter is an edited version of a paper initially published in *School Effectiveness and School Improvement* 9(1): 1–27.
2. This section has been significantly truncated. See original article for more detail.
3. For descriptions of three of the schools in the study, see Chapter 7 in this volume.

References

Ashton, P. and R. Webb (1986) *Making a Difference: Teachers' Sense of Efficacy and Student Achievement*. New York: Longman.

Biderman, A and T. Drury (1976) *Measuring Work Quality for Social Reporting*. New York: Halsted.

Brookover, W. *et al.* (1979) *School Social Systems and Student Achievement: Schools Can Make a Difference*. New York: Praeger.

Bryk, A.S. and M.W. Driscoll (1988) *The High School as Community: Contextual Influences and Consequences for Students and Teachers*. Madison: National Center on Effective Secondary Schools, University of Wisconsin-Madison.

——, V. Lee, and J. Smith (1990) "High school organization and its effects on teachers and students: An interpretive summary of the research." In W. Clune and J. Witte (eds), *Choice and Control in Schools*, vol. 2: 135–226. Philadelphia: Falmer.

Carnegie Forum on Education and the Economy (1986) *A Nation Prepared: Teachers for the 21st Century*. New York: Carnegie Forum.

Cohn, M.M., R.B. Kottkamp, G.N. McCloskey, and E.F. Provenzo (1987) "Teachers' perspective on the problems of their profession: Implications for policymakers and practitioners." Xeroxed paper.

Darling Hammond, L. (1984) *Beyond the Commission Reports: The Coming Crisis in Teaching*. Santa Monica, CA: RAND.

Dworkin, A. (1987) *Teacher Burnout in the Public Schools*. Albany, NY: SUNY Press.

Elmore, R. (1988) "Contested terrain: The next generation of educational reform." Paper prepared for the Commission on Public School Administration and Leadership, Association of California School Administrators.

Firestone, W. and S. Rosenblum (1988) "The alienation and commitment of students and teachers in urban high schools: a conceptual framework." *Educational Evaluation and Policy Quarterly* 10: 285–300.

Hackman, R. and G. Oldham (1980) *Work Redesign*. Reading, MA: Addison Wesley.

Holmes Group (1986) *Tomorrow's Teachers*. East Lansing, MI: author.

Lawler, E., D. Nadler, and P.H. Mirvis (1980) "Organizational change and the conduct of assessment research." In S.E. Seashore *et al.*, *Observing and Measuring Organizational Change: A Guide to Practice*. New York: Wiley Interscience.

Lee, V., R. Dedrick, and J. Smith (1991) "The effect of the social organization of schools on teachers' efficacy and satisfaction." *Sociology of Education* 64: 190–208.

Little, J.W. (1984) "Norms of collegiality and experimentation: conditions for school success." *American Educational Research Journal* 19: 325–40.

Louis, K.S. and M.B. Miles (1990) *Improving the Urban High School: What Works and Why*. New York: Teachers College Press.

—— and B. Smith (1991) "Restructuring, teacher engagement and school culture: Perspectives on school reform and the improvement of teachers' work." *School Effectiveness and School Improvement* 2: 34–52.

——and van Velzen, A.B.M. (1990) "A look at choice in the Netherlands." *Educational Leadership* 48: 66–74.

Mahlen, B., R. Ogawa, and J. Kranz (1990) "What do we know about school-based management? A case study of the literature – A call for research." In W. Clune and J. Witte (eds), *Choice and Control in Schools*, vol. 2: 289–343. Philadelphia, PA: Falmer.

National Education Association (1987) *Status of the American Public School Teacher: 1985–86*. Westhaven, CT: NEA Professional Library.

Newmann, F. (1992) "The significance and sources of student engagement." In F. Newmann (ed.), *Student Engagement and Achievement in American Secondary Schools*. New York: Teachers College Press.

——, R. Rutter, and G. Smith (1989) "Organizational factors that affect school sense of efficacy, community and expectations." *Sociology of Education* 62: 221–38.

Powell, A., D. Cohen, and E. Farrar (1985) *The Shopping Mall High School: Winners and Losers in the Educational Marketplace*. New York: Houghton Mifflin.

Public School Forum of North Carolina (1987) *The Condition of Being a Teacher*. Raleigh: Public School Forum of North Carolina.

Reyes, P. (1990) "Organizational commitment of teachers." In P. Reyes (ed.), *Teachers and their Workplace: Commitment, Performance and Productivity*: 143–62. Newbury Park, CA: Sage.

Rosenblum, S., K.S. Louis, and R. Rossmiller (1994) "School leadership and teacher quality of work life in restructuring schools." In J. Murphy and K.S. Louis (eds), *Reshaping the Principalship: Insights from Transformational Reform Efforts*: 110–29. Thousand Oaks, CA: Corwin.

Rosenholz, S. (1985) "Effective schools: Interpreting the evidence." *American Journal of Education* 93(3): 352–88.

—— (1989) *Teachers' Workplace: The Social Organization of Schools*. New York: Longman.

—— and C. Simpson (1990) "Workplace conditions and the rise and fall of teachers' commitment." *Sociology of Education* 63: 241–57.

Rutter, R. (1986) *Facilitating Teacher Engagement*. Madison: Center for Effective Secondary Schools, University of Wisconsin.

Sederberg, C. and S. Clark (1990) "Motivation, incentives and rewards for high vitality teachers: organizational and administrative considerations." *Journal of Research and Development in Education* 24: 6–13.

Sickler, J.L. (1988) "Teachers in charge: empowering the professionals." *Phi Delta Kappan*, January: 354–6, 375–6.

Smith, B., M. Raywid, and S. Purkey (1990) "Making caring concrete." Paper presented at the annual meetings of the American Educational Research Association, Chicago.

Stevens, J., M. Beyer, and H. Trice (1978) "Assessing personal, role and organizational predictors of managerial commitment." *Academy of Management Journal* 21: 380–96.

Wehlage, G.G., R.A. Rutter, N.L. Lesko, and R.R. Fernandez (1989) *Reducing the Risk: Schools as Communities of Support*. Philadelphia, PA: Falmer Press.

9

Does Professional Community Affect the Classroom? Teachers' Work and Student Experiences in Restructuring Schools[1]

Attention to the development of stimulating workplace environments for teachers has expanded rapidly in the past decade among both researchers and practitioners. Unions and advocates for improved teacher preparation, such as the Holmes Group, have argued that teachers should be regarded as professionals. Accordingly, teachers need to keep abreast of the latest knowledge about their field, and be given the discretionary authority to exercise this knowledge. The teacher-professionalism perspective is not limited to North America, but strikes a powerful chord in other countries as well.

Beginning with the work of Little (1982), Darling-Hammond (1984), Rosenholz (1989), and Bryk and Driscoll (1988), researchers studying the organization of effective schools have regarded the development of professionally enriching workgroups as a major facilitator of commitment and effort with the potential to improve student learning. Augmenting these early investigations of teachers' work life within schools, recent studies have emphasized the multiple, embedded ways in which teachers seek and use professional networks to increase their knowledge and skills (McLaughlin 1994).

Professionalizing the work environment of teachers has become a centerpiece of many proposals for restructuring the "common school" (Lieberman 1992). Little (1993), for example, explores in detail the variety of ways in which policies and practices support (or prevent) teachers in comprehensive high schools from seeking and using professional networks to support their classroom practice and intellectual development; Siskin (1994) suggests that subject-matter departments are a locus for revitalization; while Louis and Kruse (1995) articulate a model of school-wide professional community that focuses teachers' attention on student learning.

Whether such efforts to develop schools as sites for professional networks and/or communities will succeed in affecting school performance is uncertain. Huberman (1993) and Little (1995) suggest the difficulties of achieving closer cooperation even within schools enmeshed in reform. Recent sociometric studies of Dutch primary schools, where engagement with the demands for school-level curriculum development and reform is longstanding, also indicate that many teachers remain isolated or situated within isolated groups in schools that are very small by US standards (Bakkenes et al. 1993). Norms of autonomy and isolation tend to persist and can easily interfere with reform efforts intended to focus a whole staff's attention on specific student learning outcomes.

Another key strain in the literature is the locus of community. Authors who agree on the importance of community as a factor in school reform differ in how and where it is best achieved. Louis and Kruse (1995) focus on the school as the primary unit of analysis, while McLaughlin (1994) and Lieberman (1996) emphasize the importance of professional networks in multiple contexts, and on choosing communities of like-minded people. One of the differences between their work is that Louis and Kruse focus primarily on elementary and middles schools, and smaller high schools, while McLaughlin's research was conducted primarily in larger comprehensive high schools. School type and level remains, however, an under-explored variable.

Research linking teacher networks or professional communities to student experiences is sparse. Nonetheless, it is reasonable to expect that teachers who extend themselves professionally and work in concert with others to improve their practice will become "better teachers" – in the sense of being more effective with pupils (Louis and Kruse 1995). Based on this hypothesis, we investigate whether the development of school-wide professional community among teachers positively affects classroom organization and, subsequently, the performance of students on authentic assessments. Authentic assessment tasks require students to produce work reflecting higher-order thinking, conceptual understanding, and elaborated communication (Newmann et al. 1995).

Our analyses draw on survey data collected in 24 nationally selected, restructuring elementary, middle, and high schools; classroom observational data collected on students and teachers in 144 mathematics and social studies classrooms; 235 assessment tasks collected at two time points from these same teachers; 5,100 samples of student work in response to these assessment tasks; and in-depth case studies of each of the 24 schools.

We focus primarily on professionally supportive relationships among teachers *within* their schools, rather than on external networks. The analysis builds on a previous study (Louis et al. 1996a) in which the development of strong *professional communities* within schools was associated with an increased sense of *collective responsibility for student learning*, a school attribute shown to be related to gains in student achievement on standardized tests in comprehensive high schools (Lee and Smith 1996). Extending the previous research in two ways, this study examines:

1. the impact of school professional community on the intellectual quality of student performance (authentic achievement); and
2. the relationship of professional community to the technical and social organization of the classroom, including the mediating relationship of these classroom organizational features on authentic achievement.

Theoretical Perspective

As part of their efforts to improve student achievement, schools often attempt to restructure the learning environment, that is, to make significant departures from their conventional practice (Newmann and associates 1996). By embarking on structural changes such as block scheduling, teaching teams, interdisciplinary curricula, advisories, or "looping," these schools expect their programs to become more conducive to student learning. But if restructuring fails to go beyond structural innovation, according to researchers on the School Restructuring Study (SRS) who investigated the restructuring movement nationally, student performance is not likely to improve significantly (Newmann and Wehlage 1995). When restructuring does achieve its intended goals of improving student achievement, the SRS researchers found that, schools typically developed an intellectually-oriented school culture in addition to making educationally useful structural and programmatic innovations (Newmann and Associates, 1996).

Through a combination of supportive structural conditions (such as shared decision-making and time to meet and plan) and human and social resources (such as facilitative leadership, feedback on performance, and focused professional development), teachers can coalesce around a shared vision of what counts for high-quality teaching and learning and begin to take collective responsibility for the students they teach (Little 1990; Lee and Smith 1995; Louis et al. 1996a). Refining the vision over time through ongoing collaborative activity and reflective dialogue about their teaching and students' learning, teachers learn to function as professional communities. Formerly routine practice then becomes responsive to the needs of students and to the standards they and their colleagues have set for teaching and learning. When teaching practice is nonroutine, teachers tend to resolve the issues and problems they encounter with help from each other, thus reinforcing communitarian relationships with their colleagues (Rowan et al. 1993).

Authentic Student Achievement

Research on the relationship between the organization of schools and/or classrooms and student achievement has typically relied on standardized tests, often state or district mandated. Because they fail to assess students' ability to think critically and to solve challenging real-world problems, standardized tests have limited ability to measure what students actually know and can do (Berlak et al. 1992; Gardner 1993; Wiggins 1993).

To assess authentic student achievement, researchers at the Center on Organization and Restructuring of Schools (CORS) at the University of Wisconsin developed a set of standards for intellectual quality that could be applied across grade levels and disciplines in both practice and research settings (Newmann and Wehlage 1995; Newmann *et al.* 1995). The underlying conceptual framework for these measures argues that the standards for judging the intellectual quality of student achievement should correspond to the hallmarks of authentic human achievement in any arena. To measure up to the standards for authentic performance, students must demonstrate an ability to *analyze and interpret knowledge*, and to *engage disciplinary concepts* (for example, from social studies, mathematics, science) *in depth*, using *elaborated written communication*. The concept of authenticity can be equally well applied to a content-oriented curriculum or to one that is highly contructivist. Because the concept assumes no particular instructional style, a teacher-centered classroom might score as well on these standards as a student-centered classroom. CORS research has indicated that these standards can be applied reliably to student work at elementary-, middle- and high-school levels.

Classroom Organization and its Impact on Student Achievement

If the organization of classrooms is not conducive to intellectually rigorous work, students are unlikely to learn much. A continuous stream of research in the "effective schools" tradition published since the late 1980s in several countries supports this contention (Creemers 1994). We focus on two dimensions of classroom organization, the technical (authentic pedagogy) and the social (social support for learning). Reflecting findings of previous research, we posit a relationship between these dimensions (Oakes 1985; Newmann 1989). Authentic pedagogy and social support operate in tandem, according to our theory.

Authentic Pedagogy as Improved Core Technology

The *"technical" view of effective organizational functioning* is well grounded in sociological research both in schools and in other organizational settings. Teaching and learning constitute the core work technology of classrooms. Factors that affect the core technology – such as "time on task" and "opportunity to learn" – are often considered technical approaches to improving student achievement. Authentic pedagogy, however, because it encompasses teachers' instructional and assessment practices, is more than a technical approach: Pedagogy is *constitutive* of the core technology of the classroom. In describing pedagogy as "authentic," we wish to differentiate it from instructional and assessment practices that fail to demonstrate and call forth high levels of intellectual quality.

Because authentic pedagogy has been described extensively elsewhere (Newmann *et al.* 1995, 1996; Newmann and associates 1996), we summarize its fundamental features. Authentic pedagogy reflects the hallmarks of authentic human achievement referred to above – *construction of meaning, disciplined inquiry*, and *value beyond the classroom*.

Social Support for Achievement

The core technology of the classroom – authentic pedagogy – is not the only component of a successful classroom. Because the classroom is a social system, its efficacy and improvement depend on mobilizing the efforts of its members toward group ends. Social relationships in schools and classrooms profoundly affect students' ability to learn (Cohen 1986; Natriello 1994). Where teacher strategies make it difficult for students to "label" some children as smarter or less smart than others, students engage in more cooperative, helping relationships. The structuring of student-peer relations creates incentives and disincentives for learning (Ogbu 1987; Bennett and LeCompte 1990).

We focus on one aspect of the affective environment of schools and classrooms – social support directed toward authentic achievement (Marks *et al.* 1996). Social support for authentic achievement, as we operationalize it, is distinguished by three principal characteristics – the learning environment is orderly and the discipline is fair; teachers set high expectations for student achievement; and students can count on the help of their teacher and peers in achieving ambitious learning goals (Marks *et al.* 1996).

School-wide Professional Community

Professional community is a school organizational structure with an intellectually directed culture. Admittedly, teachers may experience professionally supportive community in multiple contexts (see, for example, Little and McLaughlin 1993; Siskin 1994), but our focus here is on professional community as a defining element of school organizational culture. Five elements of practice typify school-wide professional community – shared values, focus on student learning, collaboration, deprivatized practice, and reflective dialogue (Louis and Kruse 1995). These elements are not a hierarchy, but their presence distinguishes professional community that is school-wide from other forms of school cultures.

Fundamental to any community are *shared values* and expectations. Among a school professional community, teachers affirm, through language and action, common beliefs and values underlying assumptions about children, learning, teaching and teacher's roles; the nature of human needs, human activity, and human relationships; and the organization's extended societal role and its relationship with the surrounding environment (Schein 1985; Giroux 1990; Newmann 1991).

A *collective focus on student learning* is central to school professional community, leading its members to construct their work to benefit students' opportunity to learn (Little 1990; Abbott 1991; Darling-Hammond and Snyder 1992) and to provide instruction that promotes students' intellectual growth and development. To hone their skills for instructing effectively, teachers share expertise through collaboration, a process that increases teachers' sense of affiliation with each other and with the school (Louis 1992).

Where professional community exists, teachers share and trade off the roles of mentor, advisor, or specialist (Little 1990). Peer coaching, team teaching, and structured classroom observations entail *deprivatized practice* to improve pedagogy and collegial relationships. By engaging in *reflective dialogue* about teaching and learning, teachers can examine the assumptions basic to quality practice (Newmann 1991). Reflection upon practice leads to deepened understandings of the process of instruction and the products of teaching and learning.

The Importance of Statistical Controls

Because student background can influence achievement independently of school or classroom features, it is important to take it into account when evaluating organizational effects on achievement. Thus, our analyses control for students' prior achievement, gender, race-ethnicity and socio-economic status. Similarly, at the classroom level where we examine the relationship of technical and social support to achievement, we control for subject matter. Given documented differences between mathematics and social studies classrooms (Stodolsky 1988; Stodolsky *et al.* 1991), we control for class-room subject matter. Because school professional community and social support for achievement, variables of particular interest here, are most characteristic of the elementary schools in the sample, we also control for elementary school.

Research Questions

Our analysis flows from the theory we have proposed, positing the interrelationships between school professional community, classroom technical and social organization. and authentic student achievement. Aspects of classroom technical and social organization – specifically, authentic pedagogy and social support for achievement – are intermediate outcomes, which we hypothesize to influence authentic achievement positively. According to our hypothesis, professional community will have a positive relationship to both classroom organization and student achievement. To evaluate these relationships, we investigate two research questions:

1. To what extent does professional community influence the social and technical organization of the classroom?
2. What is the relative effect of school professional community and classroom social and technical organization on student achievement?

Method

Sample and Data

Data for this study were collected between 1991 and 1994 as part of the School Restructuring Study (SRS) of the Center on Organization and Restructuring of Schools (CORS). Eight elementary, eight middle, and eight high schools were selected through a national search for public schools that had made substantial progress in organizational restructuring in the areas of student experiences; the professional life of teachers; school governance, management, and leadership; and the coordination of community resources (see Newmann 1991; Berends and King 1994).

All teachers were asked to complete a questionnaire on their instructional practices, professional activities, personal and professional background, as well as their perceptions of the school culture and the effects of school restructuring. The subject response rate, with 910 teachers completing surveys, ranged from 69 per cent to 100 per cent across schools. The item response rate for completed teacher surveys averaged 95 per cent. All students in the observed classes, along with other classmates in the same grade, were asked to complete a survey asking about their experiences in the class and the school. The overall response rate for students was 82 per cent.

Teams of three SRS researchers visited the participating schools in the fall and spring of each year for the purpose of observing instruction; conducting interviews with between 25 and 35 teachers, administrators, and other school stakeholders; and experiencing the "life" of school, including such regular activities as meetings of the faculty, governance councils, and other groups.

The instructional practice of 144 core class teachers (three mathematics and three social studies teachers from each of the 24 schools) received extensive scrutiny according to the view of authentic pedagogy discussed above. Approximately a quarter of the observed classes were rated by two SRS researchers, and their rate of agreement for the four dimensions of authenticity is estimated as a correlation of 0.78. In addition, all 144 core teachers were asked to provide two written assessment tasks that they assigned to students in the fall and the spring: these tasks were selected by the teacher as typical. Subject matter specialists from the SRS staff in collaboration with teacher practitioners from the Madison, Wisconsin area rated the authenticity of the tasks. The teachers also submitted student work completed in response to the assessment tasks. The collected materials – over 5,000 student papers – were rated by trained researchers and practitioners using the criteria for authentic student achievement. (For more information about the instruments and procedures for observing teachers, and collecting and rating assessment tasks and student work, see Newmann et al. 1995, 1996; Newmann and associates 1996).

Each core class teacher was also interviewed twice during the year about his or her work life. In addition, other representative teachers were interviewed twice, and teachers nominated by their peers as influential in the school, or exceptional teachers, were interviewed and observed at least once. The interview, observation and documentary material were summarized in school case studies, which followed a common topic outline. We use the case studies to develop our model and to assist in interpreting the results of the quantitative analyses; more data from the case study component of the study is available in Louis et al. (1996b).

Measures[2]

Authentic Academic Achievement
The achievement measure sums student scores in mathematics and social studies on three dimensions of performance – analysis, disciplinary concepts, and elaborated written communication. Student work was scored on each standard, using a scale of 1–4.

Authentic Pedagogy
Authentic pedagogy is a composite measure combining teachers' scores on observed classroom instruction and assessment tasks. The standards for instruction and assessment tasks were described earlier during our discussion of the conceptual model. The instruction standards are on a scale of 1–5, while standards for assessment tasks are on a 1–3 or

1–4 scale. The score for authentic pedagogy is the sum of a teacher's instruction score on each standard (averaged over four observations) and assessment task score (averaged over two tasks).

Social support for achievement

Construction of this measure entailed the use of classroom observational data and student responses to survey items pertaining to their school as a learning environment generally conducive to learning and to their mathematics and social studies classrooms. The observational measure of support is on a 1–5 scale. Students characterized their school environment for learning by responding to six survey items on a 1–4 scale: strongly disagree to strongly agree (such as "Discipline is fair" and "Students make friends with students of other racial and social groups). Students also rated the learning environment of their mathematics and social studies classrooms by responding to eight items on a 1–4 scale (for example, "If I have trouble with my work, my teacher gives me help"). The composite measure of social support for achievement is the sum of the three standardized measures – observed social support in the classroom, students' reports of the school environment for learning, and students' reports of the classroom learning environment (Cronbach's alpha = 0.79).

Teachers' Professional Community

We operationalize professional community as a characteristic of both teachers and schools through an index that represents the sum of five components (Cronbach's alpha = 0.69). For the school measure of professional community, each of the factors (shared sense of purpose, collaborative activity, a collective focus on students' learning, deprivatized practice, and reflective dialogue) was aggregated to the school level.

Analytic Approach

Because schools vary considerably in their organization by grade level (elementary, middle, or high school), we introduce the analyses with a comparison of observed grade level differences. Employing one-way analysis of variance (ANOVA) for this comparison, we consider the complete set of study variables – that is, those measured on schools (professional community), classrooms (social support for achievement, authentic pedagogy, and subject area of the core class), and students (authentic performance, gender, race-ethnicity, socio-economic status, and prior [National Assessment of Educational Progress – NAEP] achievement).

To address the first research question, evaluating the relationship of school professional community to the technical and social organization of the classroom – authentic pedagogy and social support for achievement – we use a multilevel analytic technique, hierarchical linear modeling (HLM) (Bryk and Raudenbush 1992; Bryk et al. 1994). To learn how much of the variation in the school average level of authentic pedagogy and social support for achievement can be explained as a function of school professional community, we use a means-as-outcome HLM model. We take into account classroom compositional features that could influence these dimensions of classroom organization, incorporating statistical adjustments for the proportion of students who are female,

African-American, or Hispanic, the average socio-economic status of the students, and the students' NAEP achievement.

To evaluate the influence of school professional community and classroom technical and social organization on student achievement, our second research question, we take into account the increased nesting of our data – students nested within classrooms which are also nested in schools. Accordingly, we use the HLM three-level program. Addressing the school and classroom organizational dimensions of our second research question sequentially, we conduct this set of analyses by evaluating our model in three stages, focusing in the following order on:

1. the social organization of the school – school professional community;
2. classroom social organization – social support for achievement; and
3. the technical organization of the classroom – authentic pedagogy.

Taking the social and academic background of students into account but including no predictors at the classroom level, we estimate the effect of school professional community on student achievement (stage one). We expand the model to examine the contribution of classroom social organization to authentic achievement (stage two). In the fully developed model, we incorporate authentic pedagogy – the measure of classroom technical organization (stage three). Based on the implications of subject matter for classroom organization, in the second and third analyses we adjust for whether the class is in mathematics or social studies.

Results

Observed Differences

Comparing the SRS schools by grade level on the set of organizational properties discussed above, we found school professional community to be most characteristic of elementary schools and – separated by more than a standard deviation – least characteristic of high schools ($P \le 0.01$) (Table 9.1). Classroom social organization varies by grade level, with social support for achievement strongest in elementary schools and, again a standard deviation apart, weakest in high schools ($P \le 0.001$). Classroom technical organization, as measured by authentic pedagogy, is constant across grade levels. While the ratio of mathematics to social studies classes is relatively even, the slight differences that occur are attributable to the patterns of missing data for student work. (Only classrooms with authentic achievement data for a representative number of students are included in the analyses.)

Among the students within SRS classrooms, the ratio of girls to boys is even. More African-American students (32 per cent) are represented in SRS high-school classrooms than at the lower grade levels ($P \le 0.001$); and, conversely, more Hispanic students (37 per cent) occupy the elementary-school classrooms ($P \le 0.001$). Student performance on the SRS authentic measures is lowest in elementary schools and highest in middle

Table 9.1   Observed Differences on Study Variables by Grade Level

	Elementary	Middle	High
Schools	(*N*=8)	(*N*=8)	(*N*=8)
Professional Community†	0.61	−0.11	−0.50
Classrooms	(*N*=46)	(*N*=41)	(*N*=44)
Support for Achievement†	0.64★★★	−0.13	−0.40
Authentic Pedagogy†	0.11	−0.05	−0.06
% Mathematics Classes	47.8	51.2	47.7
Students	(*N*=1340)	(*N*=1119)	(*N*=1131)
% Female	50.6	52.3	51.7
% African–American	14.9	10.1	31.7★★★
% Hispanic	36.8★★★	11.8	15.7
SRS Achievement†	−0.17	0.18★★★	0.04
Socio-economic Status†	−0.01	0.16★★★	−0.15
NAEP Achievement†	0.27★★	−0.08	−0.29

†Variable is standardized, M = 0, SD = 1.0.

★★ $P \leq 0.01$ ★★★ $P \leq 0.001$

schools ($P \leq 0.001$). Conversely, NAEP achievement scores are highest in SRS elementary classrooms and lowest in middle schools ($P \leq 0.001$).

School Professional Community and Classroom Organization

To what extent does professional community contribute to the social and technical organization of classrooms? Adjusting for school grade level (because of the substantial variation in professional community and social support for achievement occurring among schools according to level) and classroom social and academic composition, we found that, to the extent that school professional community is present, social support for achievement will be higher in the classroom (0.31, $P \leq 0.01$) (Table 9.2). The model accounts for over 90 per cent of the variance in support for achievement occurring among schools. Similarly, where schools achieve professional community, the quality of classroom pedagogy is considerably higher (0.36, $P \leq 0.01$). The model accounts for 36 per cent of the variation among schools in authentic pedagogy.

Among the control variables included in this analysis, elementary level strongly influences the level of social support for learning found in schools (0.57, $P \leq 0.01$), but its negative relationship to authentic pedagogy is not significant. The variation among schools in social support for learning is not attributable to measured classroom compositional characteristics, but the school level of authentic pedagogy is significantly higher when the classroom level of NAEP achievement is higher.

Pathways to Student Achievement: A Comparison of Models

To what extent is the variation in student achievement that occurs among schools associated with their organization as professional communities? Adjusting for grade level and student background – with no classroom-level predictors (Model 1), we found that

Table 9.2 The Effect of School Professional Community on Social Support for Achievement and Authentic Pedagogy

	Dependent Variables	
	Social Support for Achievement	Authentic Pedagogy
Intercept	−0.37	0.08
School professional community	−0.31★	0.36★
Elementary school	−0.57★	−0.33
% Female	0.00	−0.01
% African-American	−0.02	0.08
% Hispanic	−0.03	0.09
Average SES	−0.05	0.06
Average NAEP achievement	−0.13	0.25★
Percentage of between-school variance explained	91.4%	36.2%

★P=.01

the achievement level is significantly higher to the extent that schools are strong professional communities (0.26, $P \leq 0.001$) (Table 9.3). The model accounts for 85 per cent of the variation in authentic achievement. Since the pattern of effects for the control variables is similar across the three models, we will reserve discussion of these relationships to our presentation of Model 3.

Examining school professional community and classroom social organization simultaneously (Model 2) – adjusting for grade level, classroom subject area, and student background – we note that classroom social support for authentic achievement further lifts school authentic achievement levels (0.19, $P \leq 0.01$) in addition to the boost to the school provided by professional community (0.20, $P \leq 0.01$). Adding classroom social organization to the model results in some diminishment of the school organizational effect exerted by the professional community. The result suggests, therefore, that the effect of professional community on school levels of authentic achievement is partially explained by classroom social organization of those schools. Social support for authentic achievement tends to correspond to school professional community as our earlier analysis (Table 9.2) suggested.

Investigating the impact of classroom technical organization on school average level of authentic achievement – while simultaneously examining school and classroom social organizational influences – we find a striking result. Authentic pedagogy subsumes the social organizational effects (school and classroom) previously found to contribute to authentic student performance (0.36, $P \leq 0.001$). Drawing on our earlier finding that school professional community strongly predicts the school's level of teaching quality as measured by authentic pedagogy (Table 9.2), we suggest professional community boosts achievement because it tends toward authentic pedagogy. That is, the focus on the intellectual quality of student learning at the core of professional community suggests that teachers will adopt pedagogical approaches reflecting standards of intellectual quality.

Table 9.3   Pathways to Authentic Student Achievement: Professional Community and Classroom Organization – A Comparison of Models

	Dependent Variable Authentic Student Achievement		
	Model 1	Model 2	Model 3
Intercept	0.13	0.31**	0.22**
School	0.26***	0.20**	0.09
Professional Community Elementary Level	−0.63***	−0.77***	−0.60***
Classroom	—	0.19**	0.04
Social Support for Achievement Authentic Pedagogy	—	—	0.36***
Mathematics	—	−0.26**	−0.15
Students	0.14***	0.13***	0.13***
Female African-American	−0.17**	−0.17**	−0.17**
Hispanic	−0.10*	−0.09*	−0.09
Socioeconomic Status	0.06**	0.06**	0.06**
NAEP Achievement	0.27***	0.27***	0.26***
Percentage of Between-School Variance Explained	85.0%	78.2%	99.8%
Percentage of Between-Class Variance Explained	11.4%	10.9%	65.4%

* $P \leq 0.05$ ** $P \leq 0.01$ *** $P \leq 0.001$

Authentic pedagogy also eliminates the effect of classroom social organization on achievement. Authentic pedagogy and social support for achievement are correlated in classrooms (0.50, $P \leq 0.05$).

The final model explains virtually all of the variation in authentic achievement occurring among schools and 65 per cent of the variation occurring among the classrooms in these schools.

Although we return to these findings in the discussion section, we wish to make two points here. First, authentic pedagogy and authentic student achievement, as is pointed out elsewhere (Newmann *et al.* 1996), are closely linked; that is, the measure of achievement is linked to an assessment task prepared by a teacher whose score on the quality of that task is a component of the authentic pedagogy construct. Second, as results of the analyses suggest, the major constructs in these analyses are strongly interrelated. Other SRS studies explicate the interrelationship between professional community, authentic pedagogy, and social support for authentic achievement (Marks *et al.* 1996). Put very briefly, these studies demonstrate how professional community creates a school culture where support for authentic learning is strong and authentic pedagogy is the means for bringing it about. Moreover, the challenging intellectual work that, by definition, constitutes authentic pedagogy tends to encourage social support in the classroom.

To conclude the presentation of the quantitative analyses, we discuss briefly the relationship of the control variables to authentic achievement (Model 3). Authentic achievement in the SRS elementary schools proves significantly lower than in the secondary (middle and high) schools (−0.60, $P \leq 0.001$). Girls and students with higher prior achievement (NAEP) scores tend to rank higher on the authentic achievement measure; the positive effect of social class is very small. African-American students score significantly lower than their classmates on the authentic achievement measure.

Scatterplot analyses provide a useful way of depicting relationships between two variables – such as between school professional community and authentic pedagogy and between school professional community and social support for achievement. Our qualitative analysis focuses on three of these schools – Cibola High School, Lamar Elementary, and Huron High School.

Professional Community and the Classroom: Snapshots of Three Schools

The case study data regarding professional community help to illuminate the processes by which some of the above findings occur, and some of the differences between elementary and secondary schools. Here we offer some examples of how professional community enhances classroom practice in schools that scored very highly on both professional community and authentic pedagogy: Lamar, an elementary school on the west coast, and Cibola, a small high school on the east coast. In addition, we will examine a high school that scored more-or-less in the middle of the sample in terms of professional community and authentic pedagogy. All are located in large, metropolitan districts, and serve relatively low-performing and disadvantaged populations. Lamar and Cibola are both well-established schools of choice (that is, in operation for six years or more at the time of our site visit), while Huron is a new school, designed to reflect restructuring principles, which had been in operation for six years when we collected our data. We hasten to add that the characteristics of newness and choice, while indicative of school autonomy that fosters professional community (Louis and Kruse 1995; Newmann and Wehlage 1995), are not the primary cause of their high levels of professional community: other schools that were not district-wide choice schools for all students also scored very highly on both of these variables. We examine two ways in which aspects of Lamar's and Cibola's professional community – shared norms and values, and deprivatized practice – fostered both strong support for achievement in the classroom and authentic pedagogy. Because Cibola is an outlier among the secondary schools in the sample on many dimensions, we then contrast it with Huron, a "regular comprehensive high school."

Shared Norms and Values

Cibola and Lamar placed less value on the individual teacher's passion for subject matter than did many other of the SRS schools, and more value on the common commitment to a particular set of educational goals for students. Such school values were core operating principles at Cibola and Lamar, but they permitted a great deal of flexibility for individual and team choices about specific elements of the curriculum.

Cibola's shared values were reflected in two educational goals demonstrated by faculty and administration:

1. to help all students learn to use their minds well; and
2. to prepare all students for college.

The commitment to fostering students' "habits of mind" is connected, quite explicitly, to authentic pedagogy. To foster the core educational goals, Cibola sought to maintain a democratic community of staff and students.

Lamar's strong set of espoused values supported authentic pedagogy. These values included:

1. the worth of creating self-motivated, independent learners who could think for themselves and take responsibility for asking the questions and doing the work required to learn;
2. a regard for depth of understanding that fostered insight into relationships rather than learning of facts; and
3. the need for students to make connections between subject matter knowledge and real life issues and questions, especially those related to human relations and the environment.

Despite the very high levels of cohesiveness around values exhibited by Cibola and Lamar, professional community did not result in uniformity of opinion about pedagogy or student needs within the school. In fact, the opportunity to share alternative perspectives within a context of shared values sustains the intellectual culture of professional communities. Such discussions can challenge teachers' deeply held beliefs or can contest teachers' assumptions, while at the same time pushing forward teachers' thinking about intellectual quality. As one teacher from Cibola noted,

> Given the fact that everybody came here and that everybody is a thinking educator, I don't know how you can expect them [to agree on everything] – and also in an atmosphere to encourage people to come with different cultural backgrounds and different beliefs – and to encourage and welcome that.

In discussions around pedagogy and student needs, teachers have the opportunity to consider and change their practice. The perspectives of colleagues and new information can influence practice. For genuine dialogue to occur, where differences can be freely aired, requires a context of trust and respect for each other's professional skills and contributions to the school community. Another teacher from Cibola added:

> I think that in as much as everybody who works here came because they wanted to, because of the nature of the work, everybody who works here is a thoughtful, thinking person about education. There's nobody here that doesn't like kids, who's

just putting in their time until they retire, or who doesn't at some level think about teaching and learning.

Deprivatization of Practice

Both Cibola and Lamar have organizational supports for deprivatization of practice. Both schools use the same primary vehicle – a teamed pair of teachers. Other strategies for deprivatization existed among the 24 schools, but teacher teaming, in the context of professional community, continually focused teachers' attention on improving practice and creating sustained, supportive relationships with students.

At Lamar, all teachers were assigned to a two-person team, which provided the opportunity for teachers to directly observe one another's teaching on a regular basis. Teacher teams regularly plan units and lessons, discussing fine points of curriculum development and student's reactions to previous lessons. Overwhelmingly teachers support this arrangement:

> I wouldn't give my partner up for the lottery. We really have it [teaching together] down and really complement and supplement one another. I couldn't ever imagine teaching without a partner again. It's just so nice having another adult in there.

Another teacher underscores her colleague's feelings by adding, "That's what makes it work; the give and take of sharing, and having a stake in this place. This is our school, not just a place that we come and work." The deprivatization afforded by teaming reinforced teachers' sense of responsibility for student inclusion in their classrooms, with each student being followed by one team for at least two of their years in the school. For Lamar teachers, the opportunity to work with other teachers in an open and public relationship enhanced both the quality of their work life and their feelings of success with students on both the academic and social level.

Because Cibola is a high school, the commitment to deprivatized practice – while similar to Lamar's – functions somewhat differently. Teams also form the basic unit for collaborative work, with a pair of teachers taking on responsibility for the full curriculum and 40 pupils. Students remain with their team for two years. Team organization at Cibola requires intense collaboration, because teachers expect to remediate the many deficiencies in social skills that students often bring to class with them and to instruct students in the full range of high-school subject matter. Team partners need to agree on what knowledge is essential for each unit and to negotiate practices with their colleagues who share the students. At Cibola, teachers' social relationships with students were more like those of an elementary school than a typical high school. As one teacher said, "If a kid sneezes on the fourth floor, we say gesundheit on the third. They resent it, but they love it … What kid wouldn't like that kind of attention?" Students clearly recognize the difference, noting that "you are a name and a face, in other words, a person. In some other schools you're just an ID."

Teaming also results in substantive discussion about pedagogy, at the daily and most intimate level. Although team members typically do not co-teach classes, one teacher reports that:

When I get frustrated with a kid [and] I don't know what to do ... I go to [my team-mate]. "What do you do that works with this kid?" We sit down and brainstorm ... I'd say every other afternoon we talk to each other. We're always in each other's rooms.

While other groups of teachers share experiences and work on curriculum (especially on projects or units that all students in a two-grade level cohort will experience), it is the close relationship with a highly respected partner that sustains Cibola's commitment to high achievement goals (and college) for what is a largely poor population.

Professional Community and Classroom Practice in a Comprehensive High School

Although Cibola and Huron had approximately the same life-span as new schools, the path toward restructuring and professional community in Huron was less direct. Never-theless, it is an example of a comprehensive high school that exhibits a culture that is distinctively different from more traditional high schools and which, despite its size, has maintained commitments to school-wide professional community.

Core Values

The school was committed to a program of interdisciplinary studies for the 10th grade students, and to heterogeneous grouping (at least in the 10th and 11th grades). Even a former teacher in a high track expressed his colleagues' commitment to "less is more" and equity in program content and instructional strategies: "The good stuff is good stuff for everyone ... Why [shouldn't] everyone get to learn that? Why [shouldn't] everyone get to learn about their creativity and take it to whatever level they want?" Teachers also agree that "territorialism" is bad for their commitments to interdisciplinary core curric-ulum, and have chosen to create a sense of community by rotating their class and committee assignments every third year: "After two years on a committee ... [you] have a different vision of where we're going ... you continue to expand [your] vision of what a total school program is for kids, as opposed to what French means for kids."

A school-wide curriculum committee has considerable influence on both content and pedagogy, and has final responsibility for what is taught in the disciplinary depart-ments (which have no chairs). They often go well beyond content in their discussions and negotiations with teachers who have proposals: in one case, for example, they accepted a department's proposal for a new course, but only on the condition that the teachers change their instructional style away from traditional lecture and drill. The entire department, on the recommendation of the committee, received advanced training from staff in another school.

Deprivatized Practice

Although the alternating block schedule used by the school has been problematic at Huron, as in many other places, staff professional development in the school frequently focuses on how to use the block and to change instruction and assessment. The professional development committee, which plans four school-based inservice days per year, has chosen topics such as a "Block Party" to share ideas for better teaching in a longer class period, and new assessment techniques, which will also be led by teachers from the school. Teachers from other high schools in the district are invited, and attend. However, in general staff development occurs outside of the school and is discipline based.

Most deeper discussions of instruction and practice do not, occur at the school level. Rather, for teachers in the 11th and 12th grades, they tend to occur in the departments, while teachers in 10th grade are teamed to teach an interdisciplinary core program, and the teams tend to provide most support. There is little sustained discussion about teaching outside of these two contexts. However, since teachers rotate their assignments every two years, these supportive units are somewhat fragile.

In summary, Huron High teachers are committed to restructuring and to improved classroom practice. They have ceded personal and department control over content and instruction to interdisciplinary committees, and are accustomed to discussing teaching and instruction across disciplinary boundaries. However, in part due to size, to their constant struggles with the block schedule, and to the frequently changing nature of their collaborative teams, they have not developed a strong tradition of deprivatized practice. In addition, like many of the other community high schools in our sample (and in contrast to most of the elementary schools), Huron was frequently distracted by community concerns, in this case from strong right-wing and fundamentalist coalitions.

Conclusion and Discussion

Our findings suggest that the organization of teachers' work in ways that promote professional community has a positive relationship with the organization of classrooms for learning and the academic performance of students. Professional community among teachers proved to be associated with both authentic pedagogy and social support for achievement among students. In schools with professional communities, students achieved at high levels. Social support for achievement in the classroom also boosted school authentic achievement levels. Ultimately, however, the beneficial influence of both professional community and support for achievement on school average authentic performance proved to be explained by authentic pedagogy at the technical core of the classrooms within these schools.

SRS Schools: A Distinctive Sample

These results are derived from a nonrepresentative sample of 24 schools, most of them located in bureaucratized urban environments, selected for study because they were engaged in an ambitious effort at reform. Compared to their counterparts nationally, the students enrolled in these schools were more likely to be economically disadvantaged and from a minority. Although the uniqueness of the sample limits our findings' general applicability, we also suspect that the constrained variation in all of the major variables has attenuated our findings.

As we demonstrated in the study on which the present investigation builds, the context for professional community varied considerably among the SRS elementary, middle, and high schools (Louis *et al.* 1996a). In the previous study, we examined the distribution of facilitative conditions for professional community (that is, human and social resources and supportive structural conditions) by grade level. Elementary schools were less organizationally complex than middle and high schools, and their teaching staffs reported greater respect from the community, more participation in decision-making, and more openness to innovation than their peers at other grade levels. These factors all contributed to professional community, but other important influences – such as a supportive principal, feedback from parents and colleagues, and focused professional development – did not differ significantly by grade level among the schools. Elementary schools also differed from the other schools in the gender composition of the teaching staff (mostly female). However, while elementary schools' gender composition influenced teachers' collective responsibility for student learning (that attribute of school culture was our focus in the analysis), professional community exerted an independent and more powerful effect on the outcome.

Our measures of authentic pedagogy and authentic student achievement are also unique. Although we recommend further research to evaluate our model on a representative sample of schools, we find support for our findings in an SRS study using data from the National Education Longitudinal Study of 1988 (NELS:88) (Lee and Smith 1995). Our colleagues found that more organic forms of school management and more authentic pedagogy are associated with increased student learning as measured by conventional tests in a large national sample of 850 high schools (Lee and Smith 1995).

Beyond the immediate findings, our data have some implications for both theories of school organization and practical issues of school reform. We will address each of these in turn.

Implications for School Organization Theory

Since the beginning of the "effective schools" debate, scholars studying classroom organization and their counterparts studying school organization have rarely found common ground in accounting for organizational effects on student achievement. Classroom-oriented researchers, arguing that gains in student achievement occur in classrooms, have attended to such diverse topics as the effects of cooperative learning, creating an inclusive classroom climate, the development of peer groups in the classroom, and the use of action research strategies to improve classroom performance. Extant research in the classroom organizational stream incorporates both the technological and social support frameworks articulated in our model.

School organization scholars, many of them buoyed by the initial effective schools findings, have also continued to focus primarily on a single unit of analysis – the school. Undaunted by findings that *within*-school variance in student performance exceeds that *between*-schools, these scholars continued to model themselves after organizational sociologists and management theorists who were primarily interested in how to predict which kinds of units would function better. Increasingly refined data sets and better analytic techniques, such as HLM, have permitted researchers to examine school and classroom effects on student outcomes simultaneously, while controlling for individual differences. The availability of better research tools has increased the theoretical interest in this line of research.

Our model and analysis suggest the usefulness of theories that better connect school to classroom-level organization. Despite the limitations of a relatively small and rarified sample of schools, the strength of the predictive results between school and classroom organizational variables suggests a need for further analysis and development. SRS researchers have demonstrated that when teachers focus their efforts at establishing a learning environment where intellectual quality is normative, students clearly perceive attention to their learning as the central activity of their schools and classrooms (Marks *et al.* 1996). Higher-order intellectual work in the classroom required these students to work together and to help each other learn. Moreover, as teachers developed authentic pedagogy in practice, their efforts furthered mutual reflection and collaboration around practice, thus sustaining and strengthening professional community.

A second implication is the recognition that both the technical and social organization of schools and classrooms foster students' success. This theme was clearly outlined in Bryk *et al.* (1990), but is rarely fully integrated into theories about how schools work in practice. Descriptions of the technology of teaching and the social conditions surrounding instruction are, nonetheless, embedded in most qualitative studies of teaching and classrooms. Public policy discourse has acknowledged that both the technical and social issues of schools and classrooms need critical attention. But few *new* models of schools as organizations – reflecting a socio-technical integration – have developed. By noting this lack of development, we do not recommend elaborating existing socio-technical models. Such models, often embedded in old language (and dichotomies, such as "Theory X and Theory Y"), do not reflect newer streams of thinking about schools. Rather, we suggest that the significant accumulation of research evidence since the late 1980s about what makes schools work better or less well be reexamined for important theoretical lessons (for example, Little 1982, 1990; Bryk *et al.* 1993; Little and McLaughlin 1993; Lee and Smith 1995,1996; Louis *et al.* 1996a).

A third implication is that the tension discussed in our introduction between the "school-wide community" and "intentional" or "disciplinary community" as stimuli to improved instructions may have avoided the core question: what can be done to create vibrant within- and between-schools professional community in "regular high schools?" Our data suggest that, with the exception of Cibola, high schools and departmentalized middle schools find it difficult to develop professional community, and are less likely to exhibit authentic pedagogy and social support for student achievement. While the evidence from qualitative data are only suggestive, they indicate that a "restructured high school" such as Huron can take steps toward both intentional and school-wide community, and that both are viewed as valued contributors toward improved classroom practice.

Implications for School Reform

The tensions in the arena of school reform are formidable. We point to three of them. Policy-makers at state and national levels want "systemic reform" very quickly, which often includes focusing more on the development of standards and accountability systems than on teacher and school development. Others, representing virtually every political persuasion, argue that because the key site for improving education is the school, control over educational practice ought to be decentralized to groups of committed teachers and administrators (Chubb and Moe 1988; Meier 1995). A major trend in colleges of education, in contrast, is to reexamine the role of individual teachers as intellectuals and as critical actors both within and outside the classroom (Giroux 1990). The focus on action research and intervention to increase the ability of individual teachers to be more reflective as a strategy for changing education is a concomitant approach.

These debates will not be resolved by a study of 24 restructuring schools. However, the data presented here do suggest a great potential for joining the three perspectives: to develop policies to support schools and teachers in building forms of school organization to promote student learning suited to the economic and social uncertainties of the future. All three levels may be important: schools and teachers will need help from outside in learning new forms of pedagogy, and in how to assess the development of classroom qualities that foster learning. The problem goes beyond better training or more solid implementation plans, however. The significance of professional community as a variable influencing classroom organization demands attention to the development of school workplace relationships that promote openness, genuine reflection, and collaboration focused on student learning, as contrasted to the "contrived collaboration" that so frequently emerges when standardized efforts to promote community are imposed on the school from without. Our data suggest that individual teacher performance in classrooms is critical, but that both immediate collegial support and extensive external support may be necessary to get there.

Notes

1. A longer version of this chapter was published as K.S. Louis and H.M. Marks (1998) "Does professional community affect the classroom? Teachers' work and student work in restructuring schools." *American Journal of Education* 106(4): 532–75. This version eliminates most of the technical appendices and footnotes, and some tables and figures.
2. For more details, see the original article.

References

Abbott, A. (1991) "The order of professionalization: An empirical analysis." *Work and Occupations* 18(4): 355–84.

Bakkenes, I., C. de Brabander, and J. Imants (1999) "Teacher isolation and communication network analysis in primary schools." *Educational Administration Quarterly* 35(2): 166–202.

Bennett, K. and M. LeCompte (1990) *The Way Schools Work: A Sociological Analysis of Education.* New York: Longman.

Berends, M. and M.B. King (1994) "A description of restructuring in nationally nominated schools: Legacy of the iron cage?" *Educational Policy* 8(1): 28–50.

Berlak, H., F. Newmann, E. Adams, D. Archbald, T. Burgess, J. Raven, and T. Romberg (1992) *Toward a New Science of Educational Testing and Assessment.* Albany, NY: SUNY Press.

Bryk, A. and M. Driscoll (1988) *The School as Community: Theoretical Foundations, Contextual Influences, and Consequences for Students and Teachers.* Madison: Center for Effective Secondary Schools, University of Wisconsin.

—— and S.W. Raudenbush (1992) *Hierarchical Linear Models: Applications and Data Analysis Methods.* Newbury Park, CA: Sage.

——, V. Lee, and J. Smith (1990) "High school organization and its effects on teachers and students: An interpretive summary of the research." In W.T. Clune and J.F. Witte (eds), *Choice and Control in American Education*, Vol. 1: 135–226. Philadelphia, PA: Falmer.

——, V. Lee, and P. Holland (1993) *The Catholic School and the Common Good.* Cambridge, MA: Harvard University Press.

——, S.W. Raudenbush, and R.T. Congdon (1994) *Hierarchical Linear Modeling with the HLM/2L and HLM/3L Programs.* Newbury Park, CA: Sage.

Chubb, J. and T. Moe (1988) "Politics, markets and the organization of schools." *American Political Science Review* 82: 1065–87.

Cohen, E.G. (1986) "On the sociology of the classroom." In J. Hannaway and M.E. Lockheed (eds), *The Contributions of the Social Sciences to Educational Policy and Practice: 1965–1985*: 127–62. Berkeley, CA: McCutchan.

Creemers, B. (1994) *The Effective Classroom.* London: Cassell.

Darling-Hammond, L. (1984) *Beyond the Commission Reports: The Coming Crisis in Teaching.* Santa Monica, CA: RAND Corporation.

—— and J. Snyder (1992) "Framing accountability: Creating learner-centered schools." In A Lieberman (ed.), *The Changing Contexts of Teaching* (Ninety-first Yearbook of the National Society for the Study of Education): 11–36. Chicago: University of Chicago Press.

Gardner, H. (1993) *Multiple Intelligences: The Theory in Practice.* New York: Basic Books.

Giroux, H. (1990) *Teacher as Intellectual.* Minneapolis, MN: University of Minnesota Press.

Huberman, M. (1993) "The model of the independent artisan in teachers? Professional relations." In J.W. Little and M.W. McLaughlin (eds), *Teachers? Work: Individuals, Colleagues and Contexts.* New York: Teachers College Press.

Lee, V.E. and J.B. Smith (1995) "Effects of high school restructuring and size on gains in student achievement and engagement for early secondary students." *Sociology of Education* 68: 241–70.

—— and J.B. Smith (1996) "Collective responsibility for learning and its effects on gains in achievement for early secondary school students." *American Journal of Education* 104(2): 103–47.

Lieberman, A. (1992) *The Changing Contexts of Teaching* (Ninety-first Yearbook of the National Society for the Study of Education). Chicago: University of Chicago Press.

—— (1996) "Creating intentional learning communities." *Educational Leadership* 54(3): 51–5.

Little, J. (1982) "Norms of collegiality and experimentation: Workplace conditions of school success." *American Educational Research Journal* 19: 325–40.

—— (1990) "The persistence of privacy: Autonomy and initiative in teachers' professional relations." *Teachers College Record* 91(4): 509–36.

—— (1993) "Teachers' professional development in a climate of educational reform." *Educational Evaluation and Policy Analysis* 15: 129–51.

—— (1995) "Contested ground: The basis of teacher leadership in high schools that restructure." *Elementary School Journal* 96: 47–63.

—— and M.W. McLaughlin (1993) *Teachers' Work: Individuals, Colleagues and Contexts.* New York: Teachers College Press.

Louis, K.S. (1992) "Restructuring and the problem of teachers' work." In A. Lieberman (ed.), *The Changing Contexts of Teaching: Yearbook of the National Society for the Study of Education, Vol. 10*: 138–57. Chicago: University of Chicago Press.

—— and S.D. Kruse (1995) *Professionalism and Community: Perspectives on Reforming Urban Schools.* Thousand Oaks, CA: Corwin.

——, H.M. Marks, and S.D. Kruse (1996a) Teachers' professional community in restructuring schools." *American Education Research Journal,* 33(4): 757–98.

——, S.D. Kruse, and H.M. Marks (1996b) "Schoolwide professional community." In F.M. Newmann and associates, *Authentic Achievement: Restructuring Schools for Intellectual Quality*: 179–203. San Francisco: Jossey Bass.

Marks, H.M., K. Doane, and W.G. Secada (1996) "Support for student achievement." In F.M. Newmann and associates, *Authentic Achievement: Restructuring Schools for Intellectual Quality*: 209–27. San Francisco: Jossey Bass.

McLaughlin, M. (1994) "Strategic sites for teachers' professional development." In P.O. Grimmett and J.P. Neufeld (eds), *Teacher Development and the Struggle for Authenticity*: 31–51. San Francisco: Jossey Bass.

Meier, D. (1995) *The Power of their Ideas: Lessons from a Small School in Harlem.* Boston: Beacon.

Natriello, G. (1994) "Coming together and breaking apart: Unifying and differentiating processes in schools and classrooms." In *Research in Sociology of Education and Socialization,* Vol. 10: 111–45. Westport, CT: JAI Press.

Newmann, F. M. (1989) "Student engagement and high school reform." *Educational Leadership* 46: 34–6.

—— (1991) "What is a restructured school? A framework to clarify means and ends." In K. Prager (ed.), *A Framework for School Restructuring. Issues in restructuring schools, I.* Madison, WI: Center on Organization and Restructuring of Schools.

—— and G.G. Wehlage (1995) *Successful School Restructuring*. Madison, WI: Center on Organization and Restructuring of Schools.

—— and associates (1996) *Authentic Achievement: Restructuring Schools for Intellectual Quality*. San Francisco: Jossey Bass.

——, W.G. Secada, and G.G. Wehlage (1995) *A Guide to Authentic Instruction and Assessment: Vision, Standards and Scoring*. Madison: Wisconsin Center for Educational Research.

——, H.M. Marks, and A. Gamoran (1996) "Authentic pedagogy and student performance." *American Journal of Education* 104(4): 280–312.

Oakes, J. (1985) *Keeping Track: How Schools Structure Inequality*. New Haven, CT: Yale University Press.

Ogbu, J. (1987) "Variability in minority school performance." *Anthropology and Education Quarterly* 25: 312–34.

Rosenholz, S. (1989) *Teachers? Workplace: The Social Organization of Schools*. New York: Longman.

Rowan, B., S.W. Raudenbush, and Y.F. Cheong (1993) "Teaching as a nonroutine task: Implications for the management of schools." *Educational Administration Quarterly* 29(4): 479–500.

Schein, E. (1992) *Organizational Culture and Leadership*. San Francisco: Jossey Bass.

Siskin, L.S. (1994) *Realms of Knowledge: Academic Departments in Secondary Schools*. Washington, DC: Falmer.

Stodolsky, S.S. (1988) *The Subject Matters: Classroom Activity in Math and Social Studies*. Chicago: The University of Chicago Press.

——, S. Salk, and B. Glaessner (1991) "Student views about learning math and social studies." *American Education Research Journal* 28(1): 89–116.

Wiggins, G. (1993) *Assessing Student Performance*. San Francisco: Jossey Bass.

10

Teacher Teaming and High-school Reform[1]

Introduction: The Problem of High Schools

Ask any urban superintendent about their school reform initiatives. They will typically point to improvements in their elementary schools – increased reading and math scores, new professional development programs, and supplementary programs focusing on enriched learning experiences. Ask the same superintendents about high schools, and they will describe some planning efforts, but their voices trail off as they admit that they are perplexed about what to do.

The evidence from many sources is overwhelming: US elementary schools look pretty good in comparison with those of other countries (as reported in the Trends in International Mathematics and Science Study), but student achievement begins to fall behind slightly in middle school. By high school, on the other hand, the USA ranks in the bottom half in science, and the bottom third in math (Gonzales *et al.* 2000). Our graduation rates are relatively flat, while they have been climbing in most other countries (OECD 2000), and dropout rates are skewed by race (Kaufman 2000). The results of the trend data from the National Assessment of Educational Progress indicate that the reform efforts, many of which have been in place since the mid-1980s, have had only limited effect, especially when compared to improvements in elementary and middle schools (Braswell *et al.* 2001; Wirt *et al.* 2001). Perhaps most exasperating is the finding that many students actually learn almost nothing in the latter years of high school, at least as measured by conventional math and science tests, largely because of a bloated and unchallenging curriculum (Lee and Smith 1997).

Teaming as a Reform Strategy

There is evidence that the design of the large comprehensive high school may be part of the problem (Lee and Smith 1997; Lee *et al.* 2000). In an effort to reach disadvantaged students, and prevent early drop-outs, many urban schools have considered ways of reducing size by creating schools-within-schools, where a smaller group of students works closely with a team of teachers (Raywid 1995). Some view the creation of small, self-contained 9th-grade teams as a particularly promising approach to ease struggling students' often-difficult transition to high school (McPartland 1996). The goal here is to build on emerging research about learning that emphasizes the importance of social learning and "communities of learners" as contrasted to individualistic knowledge consumption (JohnSteiner and Mahn 1996; Brown 1997; Crawford *et al.* 1999).

Teaming is also viewed as a powerful mechanism for enhancing teachers' work life, particularly in schools where students' out-of-school disadvantages pose daily challenges and uncertainties (Kruse and Louis 1997; Pounder 1999). Pounder, for example, found that teamed teachers reported higher skill levels, more knowledge of their students, more satisfaction and professional commitment, and higher work motivation than teachers who were not teamed. Team members tend to view their work as interdependent, but also have a stronger sense of collective responsibility for the outcomes of their individual tasks. The psychological benefits of teaming are significant where work is highly complex and unpredictable (Van Der Vegt *et al.* 2000). Teams may be particularly important where invention and innovation – the generation of new ideas – is critical to success (Paulus 2000). All of these conditions pertain to teaching as a profession.

Introducing interdisciplinary teams into high schools is hardly a simple change, however. The culture of high schools is, traditionally, individualistic (Lortie 1975). High schools have, in general, considerably lower levels of professional community than do elementary and middle schools (Louis *et al.* 1996). Furthermore, the high-school curriculum is discipline-based, which increases fragmentation. Insofar as teachers seek out collegial support for their work, they tend to do so among those who teach in similar subjects (Siskin and Little 1995). In addition, the organization of the work day in high schools mitigates against teaming: complex "master schedules" often mean that it is difficult to schedule a group of teachers to have the same planning period, and even when they do, the brief time available may not permit in-depth conversation around complex topics – like an interdisciplinary curriculum, new teaching methods, or strategies for increasing student engagement. Yet until these topics are addressed, the daily routines of high-school classrooms are likely to remain unchanged (Newman and associates 1996)

Teams may provide social support for students, but research indicates that social support is, by itself, insufficient to create student learning (Lee and Smith 1999). Urban high-school teachers are hard-pressed to develop new curriculum models that provide the kind of "authentic pedagogy" that will keep students engaged (Newmann and associates 1996; Smith 1997; Cross and Applebaum 1998). One of the challenges is to stimulate and stretch students without watering down the curriculum (Cross and Applebaum 1998). Increasing the pressure on high-school teachers – who are laboring under increasing demands to cover disciplinary standards, and who typically feel the brunt of the school system's responsibility for making sure that students pass high-stakes state tests – mitigates against curriculum innovation.

Investigating Curriculum Change and Teaming

Our research was conducted in conjunction with a large-scale curriculum initiative program in Minneapolis. Funded by the Annenberg Foundation, the initiative's overall goal was to increase arts integration in all Minneapolis schools in ways that would take advantage of the local "arts-rich" community, and would be sustainable after the initial funding period. The Annenberg Challenge in Minneapolis was to transform teaching and learning through partnerships between schools, artists, and arts organizations. The theory of action underlying the initiative was that when teachers and artists collaboratively develop instruction that integrates arts and non-arts disciplines, instruction in non-arts disciplines, such as reading and science, becomes more effective and student achievement increases.

The Annenberg Initiative, as it was locally known, was a "bottom-up" change effort in which a team of interested teachers within a school designed a program of arts integration and arts partnerships that reflects the unique context of its school and community. Teams, which operated in 44 of the 60 Minneapolis schools, were required to link their program goals to school and district improvement plans, but the project did not specify a curriculum framework or model for teacher-artist collaboration, nor did it stipulate which arts and non-arts disciplines should be included in the plan. Teams were required to conduct an annual action research project assessing the relationship between arts integration and student achievement.

The data for this analysis were culled from a larger project evaluating the Annenberg Initiative, and come from the personal interviews, group interviews, and observations of teachers and classes in a variety of schools. Elementary and high schools were included, as well as both traditional schools and non-traditional "opportunity centers." The Annenberg Initiative applied to all schools in Minneapolis, and some sites were already arts magnet schools, while others had no music or visual arts specialists on staff. Lakeside was one of six schools selected for more intensive case studies over a three-year period. As part of this case study, one of the authors of this chapter attended most team meetings, many of the arts activities, and conducted informal interviews on a regular basis. She was also given access to information collected by the teams as part of their action research activities.

All group and individual interviews were recorded and transcribed. The data were then entered into a qualitative software program (NUD★IST) and coded to appropriate categories (for example, teacher interaction with students, conceptions about what a classroom looks like or is run, delivery of instruction, reflection about teaching, use of standards, collaboration with other teachers, use of professional development, and other practice changes). Emergent patterns and themes were then analyzed and trends from year one to year two were identified. This approach facilitated checking reliability among the three coders and assured accuracy in findings.

This paper does not analyze the success or impacts of arts integration (Ingram and Louis 2003), but looks instead at what happened in two 9th-grade teams located in a single high school. Our focus is on how teams evolved, and the effects of team structures and processes on how teachers interpret their work and their students' success. In other words, while we cannot ignore curriculum change as the driver of the initiative, we emphasize teacher teams as the vehicle for making curriculum change happen.

Lakeside High School as a Site

Lakeside High School is a grade 9–12 comprehensive high school. It draws its student body of about 1,900 students from across the city (as do all Minneapolis high schools). The high school is a popular school of choice in the city because of its two magnet programs. The third program in the school, drawing students who have not selected a specific high school magnet curriculum, is called the General Program. The majority of Lakeside's students are white (63 per cent), with 18 per cent African-American, 9 per cent Asian, and 6 per cent Native American students. The proportion of students eligible for free or reduced lunch is 31 per cent. There are approximately 100 certified teachers on staff.

The teachers who worked with 9th-grade General Program students wrote the following rationale for the goals they set for the 9th-grade Annenberg Initiative project at Lakeside:

> Only one-third of Lakeside's student body is part of the General Program, [but] many General students feel inferior and disenfranchised because of the selective Open and Liberal Arts programs which encompass the rest of school. General freshmen quickly became aware of the stigma attached to their program, and some freely say they are embarrassed to admit what program they are in to other students. Coupled with the fact that many General students are "at-risk" because of low achievement in junior high, poor attendance, behavioral problems, and lack of support at home, Lakeside continues to face the challenge of finding ways to encourage General Program students to succeed.

In its 1998 application for Annenberg funds, Lakeside High School teachers described themselves as "committed and moving into full partnership" with arts partners. Lakeside already had arts-rich opportunities for students who were enrolled in one of the magnet programs, and had strong collaborative relationships with major museums, theaters, and artists' groups in the city. Even with all these activities, few arts activities were available to the 9th-grade teachers and students in the General Program, and it was here that the full force of the Annenberg Initiative was targeted.

Ninth-grade Teams

The Lakeside High General Program included two 9th-grade teams of teachers and students. One team, called the Inclusive Team, had four teachers (math, science, English, and social studies) and about 100 students. The second team, new in 1998–99, called the Diversity Team, also included a full-time special-education teacher. Many of its 100 students were Native American. Each team met daily during a common preparation period. Both teams were born of the efforts of teachers concerned about students who came into Lakeside as 9th-graders, who had not applied to a magnet program, and who were statistically at risk for dropping out. The teachers were committed to creating a feeling of community within each team with the aim of helping students to feel connected to Lakeside and to finish their high-school degree. Annenberg Initiative goals dovetailed neatly with this team building approach by encouraging students to interact with each other while participating in various art forms in their classes.

During the first year of the Annenberg Initiative, the 9th-grade teachers had their plates full. The math and science curricula were new, and the English and social studies teachers were implementing state performance assessments (student projects required for graduation) for the first time. To top it off, the teams had new members who had not previously worked together.

Images of Effective Interdisciplinary Teaching: Making Masks

In order to understand the kind of changes that were demanded of both teachers and students by the Annenberg Initiative, it is necessary to describe what goes into an arts-integrated lesson in a high-school setting. We present one lesson – an activity that covered several months during the second year of the Annenberg Initiative project – to illustrate what arts integration looks like in practice. This is not the only exemplary activity that we observed but it is one that we followed over several years. The mask-making unit involved a partnership among the Diversity Team's English, reading, and special-education teachers and an experimental repertory theater. All students assigned to the team participated through their English or reading classes.

Early Planning and Evolving Teacher Goals

The Diversity Team teachers reported that they spent about two hours preparing with the theater company ahead of time. The special-education teacher facilitated the contacts:

> Nancy (math) and I talked with them at the Urban Retreat, and then we set up a time … in August when Katia (English) and I met with them. We talked about what

we wanted. They told us more about what exactly they did – we kind of selected the particular type of masks that we wanted to make and then we talked about what we were building around that … I had several other conversations with them about the materials they gave us. They sent us a list of supplies that we needed to have here, and some of the things I wasn't familiar with so I had to talk with them.

All of the teachers remarked that their artist partners were very easy to work with, particularly noting that they were responsive to the teachers' desires to incorporate (or at least foreshadow) particular disciplinary concepts into the artistic event. They tied the mask-making activity to their opening of the school year team-building activities and to their writing curriculum. The special-education teacher articulated the primary goal: giving this student population "a way for the kids, in a more informal setting, to share who they are with one another … a chance to talk about their own identity in a way that was not particularly threatening." The goals quickly evolved as the team discovered that the year's students were "far less mature than last year's group – far, far less mature. These students are still, still in the middle-school mentality." Teachers agreed that "We didn't feel like the mask-making wasn't useful, or that it wasn't a good thing to do because it was such a different group, but it did turn out to be different than we anticipated."

Setting the Scene and Making the Masks

Theater artists helped the English, reading, and special-education teachers plan activities that would prepare the students for making their masks. Their contributions were not specific, but adaptable suggestions that were intended as warm-ups. The teachers, in turn, used the suggestions as a framework to develop other skills. One artist suggested that students work with the integration of emotions, color, and writing in their English class:

The first day, we did an examination of emotions. First, we brainstormed about 50 different kinds of emotions that they would just throw out there. Then I would have them pick one and write about it – how they felt or how they think they would feel, and then I had them associate a color with it. Some of them were really good, very creative, so I was very pleased with that. The second day, I brought in six different pieces of music … I turned the lights down really low … and then had them write about what the music made them feel or any images that they would associate with music. Some of the kids were dead on … One of the pieces … was a very violent piece, and they picked up on that right away. The next day there was a visualization piece. They didn't quite get that. It is something that I think I would need to set up differently in the future because they weren't quite into visualization. I'm not sure why. The last day, I showed a slide show that the [theater partner] had provided. [That was a] really, really great collection of masks. And the kids really enjoyed it.

Teachers and students participated together in making masks. The special-education teacher, who was nervous about the potential for acting out on the part of her students, was impressed:

(The artists) really worked at engaging the kids. It wasn't like, "Oh, we're here now and it's up to you. If these kids aren't engaged, it's your fault." I felt that they really went the extra mile, because some of the kids are difficult to engage, and I thought that they really personalized things and made contacts with kids in such a good way.

The mask-making activity was a multi-day process in which students learned what the creative structure of the activity was like:

It was so effective. They had a little stage … and a little puppet show to show what needed to be done that day … . The first day, they had a little piece of paper dancing around and pretty soon, that little piece of paper got mushed into a ball. And then the kids knew the step without somebody standing up there and saying, "Do this, do that." It was great. And the next day, I know my kids were all ready … That was so much better than putting a list on the board or talking to the kids.

Teachers were also amazed by the effect of low-level music on the behavior of their students even though some of them didn't like the unfamiliar world sound.

Follow-up and Results

After the mask building, the teachers led the students into related writing activities. The special-education teacher led a writing activity using an excerpt from the Jim Carrey movie *The Mask*; the English teacher used a different stimulus, but with a similar goal. Later, the teachers created an exhibit of the masks and the writing in the school library, where families could view them during the parent-teacher conferences evening. Every teacher involved in the project believed that the academic results were greater than they had anticipated: "Effort wise, it was way superior to any other written project we've done." Motivation and success were also part of the student experience. The special-education teacher noted that some of her students said "I never did anything like that before. I didn't know I could do anything like that," while the English teacher found that some students were motivated to work outside of class to finish the project. The special-education teacher, whose students were usually segregated from the regular English classes, was thrilled to observe that they were able to work alongside of, and perform as well as, their peers.

How Did this Happen? A Tale of Two Teams

One may conclude from this example that arts integration has the potential of creating social and academic opportunity for at-risk students. Teachers learned from the experience, and were able to generalize about how to motivate and challenge students who were immature and behaviorally challenging. For all its success, arts integration did not just happen. It required enormous planning and efforts within the teams.

Year One: "Messing Around with the Arts"

None of the teachers who were involved with the Annenberg Initiative at Lakeside had significant experience in using the arts, or in interdisciplinary teaching. How, then, was it possible that the Masks Project came to fruition in a relatively short period of time, with such a profound effect? The experience of the first year at Lakeside did not easily foreshadow the success of the Masks Project in the second year. Rather, it provided a window into the teachers' efforts to grapple with new ways of thinking about curriculum and instruction.

Team 1: The Diversity Team

The Diversity Team learned of the Annenberg Initiative grant just after their team was formed in the spring of 1998. They had much to do before the next school year. One member said:

> I think our summer was really consumed with just figuring out what the team was going to be … and we just tried to figure out what we were going to be doing – how we were going to function as a team … We were really starting at zero. We saw [the Annenberg Initiative] as a supplementary, wonderful benefit that we needed to learn how to use.

The Diversity Team articulated an informal goal – or a hope – for their first year:

> by being able to offer some of these different opportunities to the kids, hopefully, we were going to hook a few more kids in. We see it as a way for some kids to connect. To say that we're more elevated than that would not be particularly truthful. Our main goal was to have these kids go on to be sophomores.

True to their goal, the Diversity Team used their Annenberg funding to increase school attendance through sponsored events, of which there were seven – some were judged by teachers and students as exciting, while others were less than successful. Three examples illustrate one hit and two of the near misses:

- Seventeen students who attained a C+ grade point average were rewarded with a field trip to see a group of Japanese drummers at a major theater. Students had mixed evaluations about the activity. They did not know what to expect and thought they should have known more about it before going; a few reported (shamefully) that some students laughed because they did not understand it. Students talked about what they learned about another culture, and Native American students noted that the Japanese treat the drum quite differently from Native Americans.
- Native American actors, some known to the students, performed a play called *Ni Nokomis Zagayug*. The play dealt with issues faced by teenagers today, including family relationships, drugs, sex, AIDS, and attending school. The students enjoyed the performance and appreciated the messages of the play. They were particularly respectful during the performance because they knew the actors.

- Math and English teachers planned an activity around Edgar Allen Poe's "The Pit and the Pendulum." An actor came in to set the mood with costuming, recitation, and discussion of the poem. The math teacher taught the math concepts related to pendulums, a major unit in the math curriculum. Though the students had been prepared by reading the story in class the actor did not know how to engage the students. One teacher said that "It was even difficult for me to figure out what the story was saying," while the math teacher expressed similar disappointment because the concept of a pendulum was not well explained.

Team 2: The Inclusive Team

The Inclusive Team's specific purposes and experiences also evolved through the first year. Although the Inclusive Team was well established in the school, in 1998 three of the four teachers were new to the team and had not worked in a team setting before. Like the Diversity Team, they began by selecting activities they hoped would help students "feel like a team." A first field trip/arts effort was viewed as unsuccessful by teachers because of student behavior, and by students because it was boring. They searched for other activities that would engage their students, and attended the *Ni Nokomis Zagayug* event arranged by the Diversity Team. Their students' reactions were equally positive.

Using Annenberg Initiative resources, individual teachers planned activities they could infuse into their curriculum. The science teacher invited an artist to teach drawing skills, and used the lesson to work on the relationship of shadowing, perspective, and angles to scientific concepts. The students then practiced drawing skills once a week, visually reinforcing what they learned. The math teacher joined with the problematic "Pit and the Pendulum" performance, and later explored the idea that an oral history storyteller "might help with their vocabulary and just understanding the whole picture" but that activity did not occur. In social studies, an artist taught the students how to make a book, and students used this art product when writing a new ending to Animal Farm.

By the second half of the year, the Inclusive Team felt more positive about the cohesiveness of their team, but not comfortable enough to have all-team events. However, they planned after-school field trips to an African-American theater for self-selected students. Students who were interviewed indicated that they enjoyed the plays and interacting with other students in a new way. However, teachers felt that the self-selection drew from a group that was already more positive about school. Another 25 students went to a workshop where they were led through listening, discussion, and creation exercises. The students complained that there was too much lecture, while teachers were unhappy about student behavior. The most successful activity was an African drumming event, which drew half the Inclusive Team students. A teacher reported that "They really enjoyed it … It kept their attention the whole time."

End of the Year Reflections

At the end of the first year teachers felt optimism and frustration in equal measures. No one yet realized that a major change in teaching practice was around the corner. Even the tentative beginnings of the first year, however, would not have been possible without the full-time arts coach, who coordinated outside activities and suggested visiting artists. One team member summed it up: "I was happy that we built some relationships. Our goal was to help us to build relationships this year that we can carry through to next year, so we are not trying to start over from scratch again." But the teachers on the two teams also felt intimidated and unprepared (compared with teachers in other schools) for infusing the arts into their teaching. One said: "We felt like a bunch of losers ... We talked about whether we were all supposed to be artists and if we were supposed to have some heavy-duty arts background, because none of us felt like we did."

Meeting with teachers from other schools didn't allay these misgivings. One teacher came away from district-wide Annenberg Initiative workshops saying "They seem so far advanced in their ideas and interdisciplinary curriculum and involving the arts with that. We're mostly concerned right now about getting the kids to school, to class." The vagueness of the goals and the demands for interdisciplinary curriculum were also intimidating. Both teams agreed, however, that the arts activities changed the way they thought about teaching. One teacher spoke for several when she said:

> I know I look at things differently. As a teacher, most of the time I hear or read about things and immediately block them out as not being possible, because that would cost money. It is changing my attitude toward that – we can consider some of the possibilities out there ... I'm getting better at that in that I don't reject things right away as easily.

Nevertheless, teachers continued to think of the program as a "reward" rather than the real stuff of learning:

> There was an article put in our mailboxes about three weeks ago ... talking about the fears we create and how we basically personify them ... I had the kids read it, and then I handed them drawing paper, and I told them they had to personify (draw) their monsters ... *they had been working on a paper all week, so I wanted to reward them with not writing.*

Years Two and Three: Continuity vs. Distraction

At the beginning of the second year of the project, both 9th-grade teams felt that the goal from the school's Improvement Plan to which the Annenberg Initiative most closely connected was "creating a respectful environment." Their primary concern continued to be keeping the students connected to the school. While this goal may seem very basic, one arts partner said "Getting them to connect with school seems like a simple goal, but I think it's a tough thing to do." In spite of their commonalities, conditions outside of the teams' control pushed them in different directions.

The Diversity Team and Steady Work

The Diversity Team experienced a growing sophistication in thinking about the curriculum. Their primary goal of keeping students, particularly Native Americans, in school was met. One teacher summarized the team's sense of satisfaction:

We had 64 10th-grade Native Americans this year [that is, students who completed 9th-grade and enrolled again at Lakeside]. I guess that was enough for me to think we needed to do it again, it's that connectedness and creating a sense of community.

One particularly problematic curriculum dilemma was the need for the 9th-grade students to complete a state-required unit on career planning, which involved a "show what you know" demonstration as well as written tests. This particular unit was dreaded by the teachers because of the difficulty of getting students, many of whom came from unemployed or under-employed families, to engage with the concept of career planning. However, in the second year of the Annenberg Initiative, the team decided to tie the unit into a local stage production of Studs Terkel's *Working*. Several of the actors came to meet with the students, while a playwright and an actor worked with them afterwards to write Terkel-like monologues on their future employment. The special-education teacher, who had collaborated closely with the English teacher around this project, reflected: "[The actor] clearly knows the kinds of things that a school [like ours] needs ... [he has] a really good sense of 'well, you know, you can't just get up in front of a group of kids and expect them to do everything you suggest,' and he has a million things in his back pocket that he is ready to pull off." Artists and teachers came away from the project satisfied with the result, even while reflecting on how they could have done even more.

In the third year, the Diversity Team picked up a new teacher member, and continued to evaluate the role of the arts in their core curriculum and learning goals. At the beginning of the year, the team reflected that:

Our plan sort of grew out of last year's problems. We had so many behaviour issues last year that we decided that our focus ... this year would be on values and ethical behaviors ... What we did was we talked to these Seven Ojibwa teachings; they are values like honesty and truth and respect, wisdom, love, humility, courage ... That was really our whole idea ... that we would have this platform that we could use all year long ... It's not to suggest that everything is going just perfectly, behavior wise now, but it's nice that we all have this common language that we use ... [Even the mask-making] was different this year ... Last year it was more a representation of you; this time, more to the theme.

The Seven Ojibwa Virtues were thematically tied into many curriculum units in addition to art, according to all of the teachers. The social-studies teacher made the connection between ethical behavior and accountability in government and among citizens. The math teacher tied ethics to a unit on statistics and probability, showing how important it is to use numbers for the purposes of truth rather than personal gain, while the English teacher reported that "In my classroom we're doing short stories and poetry based on the seven teachings." Teachers and students talked most about their efforts to work thematically and to deliver the same messages through the arts. At the end of the third year, all four teachers predicted that they would be back in the fall to continue their common efforts.

The Inclusive Team: Turnover and Continued "Messing Around"

In contrast to the Diversity Team, the Inclusive Team had a complete turnover of personnel. Work on team spirit started from scratch as the team continued to struggle with how best to use the Annenberg Initiative funds. An intern English teacher was assigned primary responsibility for the coordination and implementation of the Annenberg activities. Early in the year, the team designated each Friday at 2:30 as the time to talk about the Annenberg Project, but the special-education and reading teachers were not included due to scheduling problems. But in fact their Friday meetings were rarely spent on joint curriculum planning. One teacher commented "It's difficult to talk about how to integrate the arts into the curriculum since the team was new. [School] Policy and procedures [have] been a main topic." The group of novice teachers, whose main goal was understandably daily survival, did not gel into a smoothly functioning team with common expectations. In this void, student behavior problems returned – if indeed they had ever left. The English teacher said, "The eternal thing is behavior of students, and it's like we're acting as social workers at times and meeting with parents … things just come up which disrupt our focus and concentration on the curriculum."

Because of the distractions and lack of experience, the members didn't know how to use their "arts broker" and, in fact, did not meet with her until after they had committed all of their Annenberg Initiative funds. Over the year, teachers began to understand the potential of using arts in the curriculum, but only the English teacher thought deeply about how to incorporate planned arts events. Although he attended as many district and arts-partner-sponsored professional development activities as possible, as a novice teacher he was hard pressed to engage in anything deeper. For the rest of the team, arts activities were viewed positively, but were not incorporated. For example, the team attended a play dealing with differences of sexuality and gender early in the year, but, as a teacher noted, "I don't even remember it that clearly." Teachers were somewhat more prepared for integrating later art experiences, but again the effects were mixed because of limited collaboration with the participating artists. One teacher reflected that "I should have asked them even more questions, even more specific … Since we're all new to this it was difficult," while another reinforced the fact that students were not adequately prepared: "[The arts partner] told us about some of the themes present in the show, but the thing that the students weren't ready for, as well as the teachers, was the lack of dialogue … It was a bit more abstract than we were expecting."

The regularities of life in high schools also impinged on the effectiveness of the arts experiences. Four 9th-grade regular classes were observed on 10 December before the day of a performance. Students were cooperative in all the classes, but engagement varied a great deal, interrupted by a fire drill, journal writing with low participation, and a test.

Early in the spring, team members admitted that morale was low, and three teachers decided to transfer to other positions in the district. The returning teacher coordinated the team's arts integration work the third year, but the same pattern of episodic incorporation and low levels of teacher involvement, made more difficult by the team's discontinuous membership, permeated the third year of the project. Only two teachers were involved, and even these two held low expectations for what the arts could do for their students. The social studies teacher stated that "The one thing that I'm probably proudest of … is their awareness of what it means to be an audience member." As the third year of the Annenberg Initiative project drew to a close, it appeared that none of the members of the team would be back for the fourth year of the project.

Explaining the Team's Different Trajectories

Clearly a major difference between the two teams was membership stability. However, it is too simple to suggest that mandating stability would solve the problems that plagued the Inclusive Team, or ensure the progress of the Diversity Team. Rather, stability engendered other social responses that fostered the goal of arts integration.

Creating Team Commitments

The Diversity Team took advantage of stability by developing a stronger and deeper sense of commitment to particular learning goals and strategies to reach their students. As it turned out, this commitment saw them through an extremely difficult year in which they were faced with an exceptionally challenging group of students. When they met over the summer to reexamine their team goals, they sharpened their focus on using the arts to create student connections to their peers and to the curriculum. Teachers pointed out that requiring a clear goal statement "provid[ed] an opportunity that otherwise would not have been there for us to have dialogue, as teachers who support students." In a sense, the teachers realized early on that the grant was an opportunity to build community not only among the students, but also among themselves.

Continuity also increased the stake that the teachers had in the project – even those who were initially less involved. The teachers were learning together, and sharing their learning; their colleagues, even when they were a bit bemused about how it would fit in to their courses, wanted to celebrate that growth. One teacher summarized this: "They may not all be interdisciplinary activities, but it's something everybody has a stake in … I know our expectations were higher [this year] … We expect to end up feeling like we have more when we get done with something now."

Teachers began to develop a new understanding of what an interdisciplinary curriculum could do for their teaching, and moved away from the idea that the arts were an "add on" to engage students. This became apparent during the third year's successful focus on the Seven Ojibwa Virtues. Working together around themes also made it easier to carry out the much advocated (but rarely practiced) strategy of teaching writing across the curriculum. But all of this required a different mind-set from what they were used to. The teachers talked openly about the need to make rapid adjustments within their classes in order to accommodate the thematic work and the emergence of fresh understanding of student needs, and they attributed this to their increasing experience of team work and joint planning: "An idea will come up and Tracy will say, 'well, I have a book that will tie in so well' so we'll [all] do that … it just seems easier for us to do [this flexible planning] this year."

In summary, teachers returned to the team because the team – and the collaboration provided by arts infused work – became important to them.

Meeting the Needs of Students as a Group

Increased cohesiveness occurred at the same time that both teams faced challenges to effective teaching due to increasingly poor student behavior. The new teachers on the Inclusive Team all left after the second year, in large measure because of the problems. In contrast, the Diversity Team continued to work hard to maintain a sense of hope and progress, and to address collectively the needs of what they termed "immature students." One clear example was the Masks Project, which was expanded in scope and importance as teachers realized the difficulty their students had in expressing themselves. They shared stories about student success (sometimes measured in tiny steps), and refused to give up on taking the students to events outside of the school, although their first experiences with "audience behavior" were painful. Rather than eliminating outside activities, they worked on figuring out how they could use creativity to find the best in their students:

> We really push safety and respect. [Art] really gives them an arena to say who they are and let themselves get out there. They really start to make friends and get to know each other and care about each other ... they really respect each other for what they create.

The difficult second year led to a cohesive plan to incorporate civility and virtue as key curriculum themes for the third year.

Learning from Students – Even Difficult Students

The Diversity Team also committed themselves to making databased decisions to improve their interdisciplinary teaching. The team required each student to complete an individual, open-ended evaluation after every type of event that they were engaged in. They viewed this as a teaching tool, as well as learning for themselves: "We ... feel that it's really important for the kids to learn how to critique things and to give us input on their likes, their dislikes, whether they felt they learned anything." Of course not all student comments were thoughtful, but asking for and incorporating their responses was done respectfully. In the Inclusive Team, in contrast, survey data from students, gathered at the end of the year, did not encourage students to write about their own views or experiences. Due to teacher turnover, the data were not collectively analyzed.

Learning from Artists – Thinking about Teaching

As part of the increasing team dialogue, the Diversity Team began to see their artist collaborators as their most important source of professional development: "It's a whole different way to plan." Learning from other teachers in the district was also important. First, the teachers were shocked by their naiveté when they were exposed to what other teachers were doing as part of the Annenberg Initiative ("we really felt like a ditsy bunch last year") but then they began to soak up information from other teachers and schools. Their exposure to other school activities (including initiatives in elementary and middle schools) was reflected in how they experimented with teaching:

> I know that teachers on our team are doing things that they didn't do a year ago ... I remember when I discovered that [a theater] was doing *Working* and we had been tossing around this whole thing about this careers unit ... I thought, 'My gosh! We could do something with this' ... And I think that we all do that ... we think about [interdisciplinary teaching] differently now.

Student Learning

The Diversity Team members believe that they are on the right course to improve their goals – retention and engagement. The way in which the Annenberg Initiative was implemented in high schools precludes easy answers to questions about its effects on student achievement, although we have demonstrated effects in elementary schools (Ingram and Louis 2003). Teachers, however, are deeply concerned with the answers, and have developed multiple measures to track their students' progress over time, as well as multiple classroom assessments. Even so, it is not possible to show a definitive casual link between arts integration and student outcomes due to the number of changes at the schools and the variability of students in this period. This led the Diversity Team to track progress through quantitative measure that mirrored their original goals – continued enrolment, reduced suspensions, and improved attendance. Notwithstanding the lack of achievement indicators, there is little question that these learning experiences – whether they dealt with civil behavior, understanding the beauty of a concert hall, or learning how to express an idea or an emotion in multiple ways – may have positive effects on low-income students whose previous experiences with school are largely negative. Teachers at Lakeside believe that they are providing the grounding for student success, by increasing attendance, engagement, and an understanding of the connection between school and self, and they believe that the arts integration is central to their goals.

Reflections on Changing High Schools

The team focus of Lakeside meshed a growing national emphasis on the transition to high school for "at risk" students with the Annenberg Initiative's financial incentives. Teachers and artists in this project agreed that their discussions about what to teach and how to teach it were a profound learning experience even before students became involved. This type of interaction did not occur in the past when individual teachers planned occasional events. Although our analysis was limited to one school and one team, data from other schools reinforce these findings (see Freeman and Louis 2003).

The results from Lakeside High School suggest a number of findings that are worthy of investigation and action research in other settings:

- First, we conclude that teaming is not, per se, a solution to the problems of urban high schools. Teams can work to effect change; but without the appropriate support systems they may provide little more than a "safe place" for incoming high-school students. Teachers who are assigned to groups of students for a single year may also, like the teachers in Lakeside's Inclusive Team, believe that they are thwarted in their desire to have an impact on the destiny of inner-city students.

- Second, although Lakeside High School provided additional support for teamed teachers, such as common prep time and some additional funds, these limited conditions do not necessarily create professional community that can facilitate a change in teaching and learning. What was not present, even in a "good high school" such as Lakeside, was systematic support for developing the team as a strategy for reform of teaching.

- Third, improving urban high schools requires continuity – in administration (not discussed directly in this analysis), in staffing, and in policies. The inspiring results that we observed occurred only in the team with teachers who made a commitment to each other over time.

- Fourth, a novel stimulus – in this case the idea of interdisciplinary arts-infused lessons – may, within a stable team of teachers, engender reflective discussions about teaching and subject matter comprehension that will lead to significant improvement in urban high schools. Teacher discussions focused on learning and increased cognitive and life-skills outcomes. In this case, reflective discussion was more important than prior arts expertise. The arts focus energized teachers in their disciplinary practice, encouraging them to work on both state standards and in-depth learning appropriate to their student population. We chose to highlight Lakeside High School's Diversity Team in part because we found that all teachers – social studies, math, English, special education, and science – benefited from discussions around arts integration.

In sum, our research supports the contention that altering the conditions of teaching and learning in urban high schools requires combining structural (teaming) and curricular (arts integration) changes to encourage professional community. However, our case study also suggests that the path between the formation of teams and changed classroom practices requires deeper attention to the development of policies and administrative practices that can sustain the human side of change and support teachers in their efforts to do their best for students in challenging situations.

Note

1. This chapter is co-authored with Carol J. Freeman. An earlier version was web-published at www.carei.education.umn.edu. The names of the school, the teams, and teachers have been changed.

References

Braswell, J.S., A.D. Lutkus, W.S. Grigg, S.L. Santapau, B. Tay-Lim, and M. Johnson (2001) *The Nation's Report Card: Mathematics 2000*. Washington, DC: National Center for Educational Statistics.

Brown, A.L. (1997) "Transforming schools into communities of thinking and learning about serious matters." *American Psychologist* 52(4): 399–413.

Crawford, B.A., J.S. Krajcik, and R.W. Marx (1999) "Elements of a community of learners in a middle school science classroom." *Science Education* 83(6): 701–23.

Cross, C.T. and K. Applebaum (1998) "Stretching students' minds is basic education." *Educational Leadership* 55(6): 74-+.

Freeman, C. and K.S. Louis (2003) "Models of Arts Integrated Teaching" (online research report). University of Minnesota: http://education.umn.edu/CAREI/Reports/Annenberg/Integrating_UrbanHS.html (last accessed 16 August 2005).

Gonzales, P., C. Calsyn, L. Jocelyn, K. Mak, D. Kastberg, S. Arafeh, T. Williams, and W. Tsen (2000) *Highlights from TIMMS-R*. Washington, DC: National Center for Educational Statistics.

Ingram, D. and K.S. Louis (2003) "Summative Evaluation Report" (online report). Minneapolis, MN: University of Minnesota: http://education.umn.edu/CAREI/Reports/Annenberg/reports.html (last accessed 16 August 2005).

JohnSteiner, V. and H. Mahn (1996) "Sociocultural approaches to learning and development: A Vygotskian framework." *Educational Psychologist* 31(3–4): 191–206.

Kaufman, P., J. Kwon, S. Klein, and C. Chapman (2000) *Dropout Rates in the United States: 1999*. Washington, DC: National Center for Educational Statistics.

Kruse, S.D. and K.S. Louis (1997) "Teacher teaming in middle schools: Dilemmas for a schoolwide community." *Educational Administration Quarterly* 33(3): 261–89.

Lee, V.E. and J. Smith (1997) "High school size: Which works best and for whom?" *Educational Evaluation and Policy Analysis* 19(3): 205–27.

—— and J. Smith (1999) "Social support and achievement for young adolescents in Chicago: The role of school academic press." *American Educational Research Journal* 36(4): 907–35.

——, B.A. Smerdon, C. Alfeld-Liro, and S.L. Brown (2000) "Inside large and small high schools: Curriculum and social relations." *Educational Evaluation and Policy Analysis* 22(2): 147–71.

Lortie, D. (1975) *Schoolteacher*. Chicago: University of Chicago Press.

Louis, K.S., H. Marks, and S. Kruse (1996) "Teachers' professional community in restructuring schools." *American Educational Research Journal* 33(4): 757–98.

McPartland, J. (1996) *The Talent Development High School: Early Evidence of Impact on School Climate, Attendance, and Student Promotion. Report No. 2*. College Park, MD: Johns Hopkins' Center for Research on the Education of Students Placed At Risk.

Newmann, F. and associates (1996) *Authentic Achievement: Restructuring Schools for Intellectual Quality*. San Francisco: Jossey Bass.

OECD (2000) *Education at a Glance*. Paris: Organization for Economic Cooperation and Development.

Paulus, P.B. (2000) "Groups, teams, and creativity: The creative potential of idea-generating groups." *Applied Psychology: An International Review – Psychologie Appliquée: Revue Internationale* 49(2): 237–62.

Pounder, D.G. (1999) "Teacher teams: Exploring job characteristics and work-related outcomes of work group enhancement." *Education Administration Quarterly* 35(3): 317–48.

Raywid, M. (1995) *The Subschools/Small Schools Movement – Taking Stock*. Madison: Wisconsin Center for Educational Research.

Siskin, L.S. and J.W. Little (eds) (1995) *The Subjects in Question: Departmental Organization and the High School*. New York: Teachers College Press.

Smith, L.A.H. (1997) "'Open education' revisited: Promise and problems in American educational reform (1967–1976)." *Teachers College Record* 99(2): 371–415.

Van Der Vegt, G., B. Emans, and E. Van De Vliert (2000) "Team members' affective responses to patterns of intragroup interdependence and job complexity." *Journal of Management* 26(4): 633–55.

Wirt, J., S. Choy, D. Gerald, S. Provasnik, P. Rooney, S. Watanabe, R. Tobin, and M. Glander (2001) "The Condition of Education: 2001." Washington, DC: National Center for Educational Statistics.

Section III
Organizational
Perspectives on
Innovation and Change

In my introduction to Section I, I emphasized that organizational theorists were the well from which I have drawn most of my thinking about the process of educational change. There is a fine line between articles that concentrate on innovation processes and those that emphasize organizational theory, but in arranging and categorizing my work I wanted to draw attention to my efforts to contribute to theories about schools and districts as exemplars of modern bureaucracies.

When I began my graduate training in the late 1960s, British and American organizational theory was focused on structure. From scholars such as Charles Perrow and Paul Lawrence (who generated a line of inquiry into how an organization's "technology" affects structure) to those such as Marshall Meyer and Jerald Hage (who are associated with research that looked at the effects of size and complexity), quantitative studies of structure were all the rage. Counterpoints quickly emerged from other scholars, who argued that people and culture were at least equally important. These theorists, ranging from Seymour Sarason's (1971) classic work on the *Culture of Schools and the Problem of Change* to Burton Clark's study in the early 1970s of the cultures and "organizational sagas" of distinctive colleges, fueled an equally influential parallel line of qualitative research that looked at variables such as values, power relationships, and social integration. I was deeply influenced by these debates and, in the early period of my research career culminating in the late 1970s with my work on the Rural Experimental Schools project (mentioned in the introduction to Section I), I consistently looked for evidence of both structure and culture as factors in the organizational change process.

My reliance on organizational theory is evident in the chapters included in the previous two sections but by the late 1980s some of the studies that I was working on focused less on the change process and more on general organizational behavior. My reenergized interest in organizational theory was stimulated by Kyla Wahlstrom, the first author of Chapter 11, "Adoption Revisited." As Kyla and I worked to develop a framework for her case studies, we discussed how theories of organizations that focused on the role of key actors and agencies were related to those that emphasized decision processes, and how both of these intersected with organizational structures and communication systems. My partiality for the framework used in this paper stems from the introduction of the theme of raw politics and power into the more benign images of school organization that I used previously. The four case studies presented here allowed us to conclude that both organizational culture and structure *and* the highly politicized roles of "idea champion" and "gatekeeper" were critical to understanding the evolution of decisions affecting innovation in school districts. Political and organizational theories of change are also combined in Chapter 17 in Section IV, but with a greater emphasis on knowledge use.

The next chapter in this section, "Creating Community in Reform," was a byproduct of conversations that my colleagues and I had as we were working on the topic of teachers' professional community. It struck us that professional community provided a useful explanation of how a school's social structure facilitated the incorporation of new practices, but that it ignored how new ideas got into professional discourse in the first place, and how individual reflection influences broader school improvement. In seeking a solution we turned to the emerging thinking about organizational learning that was popularized by Peter Senge's 1990 book, *The Fifth Discipline*. My earlier work on knowledge use (see Chapter 1) came into play as well, as we incorporated the often-identified problem of the weak transfer of research-based ideas from universities to practitioners into considering how schools process and use knowledge. This was an "a-ha!" moment for me: knowledge use and organizational theory could be viewed as intersecting and complementary perspectives for studying school change rather than as alternative approaches. The chapter lays out the model of organizational learning that Sharon Kruse and I developed at that time, and applies it to two urban schools that were identified from a larger set of cases as strong generators and consumers of knowledge (see Chapter 9 for more on the range of cases). The features of the model that are associated with strong organizational learning capacities were later verified in a quantitative analysis conducted by Tony Bryk, Eric Camburn, and myself. I continue to be fascinated with the relationship between individual and collective reflection and development.

During the 1990s, my commitment to research on school improvement was challenged by educational policy initiatives that proposed the need for comprehensive or systemic reform, often brought in as a "New American School" model. While I am not opposed to developing and disseminating models for school-wide improvement, I felt that the dialogue of the day focused too heavily on pre-designed *deus ex machina* solutions to the complex problems faced by schools. The assumptions behind systemic improvement initiatives also contrasted starkly with the dominant theories in the general organizational literature, which have not supported the effectiveness of total redesign. In this state of awareness I was open to accidental exposure to the work of a management school colleague, Roger Schroeder, who invited me to kibitz on his research program looking at quality management in schools. Out of this informal relationship we developed a common interest in thinking about what quality cultures (as contrasted with continuous improvement behaviors on the part of individual professionals) would look like in schools. One intriguing aspect of this work was the possibility of translating Roger's business-related language into the context of schools, which we have done in Chapter 13, "A Culture Framework for Education." I continue to explore this framework in an ongoing project that is examining school cultures in the context of the accountability movement.

Chapter 14, "The Impact of Mental Models, Professional Community, and Interdisciplinary Teaming on Classroom Practice," integrates some themes that were separate in earlier work. The mental-models concept is drawn from the organizational learning literature, while professional community and teaming come from my own research on teachers' work. While the paper is far from an inclusive cultural model of organizational change, it does represent a new direction for me. Until very recently my sociological roots have been visible with my emphasis on the organization as the primary unit of analysis. More recently, as part of my qualitative work on professional community and organizational learning, I have become more attuned to interpretive approaches to studying schools. The introduction of the concept of mental models is also influenced by my former doctoral student, Jim Toole, whose dissertation looked at how teachers' thinking about their craft influenced their willingness to incorporate service learning into the core of their work. The results presented in this chapter were unexpected, which is one of the reasons I chose to include it in this volume. My implicit theory of change will continue to develop, paying closer attention to the interaction of individually held ideas, collective social structures, and external stimuli than they have in the past.

At this stage of my career I am convinced that until educational researchers and policy-makers find the levers for change that already exist within schools and district as organizations, school improvement will continue to be a haphazard affair. It will take grounded and evolving theories pointing the way to these levers to move beyond only tinkering about the edges of classroom practice to reverse Sarason's 40-year-old contention that the essential impediment to change lies in the culture of the school.

11

Adoption Revisited: Decision-making and School District Policy[1]

Introduction

Understanding effective change strategies requires an examination of the earliest phases of a change process. Rosenblum and Louis (1981), for example, found that the institutionalization of major changes in rural school districts was well predicted by early characteristics of the program's design, while Louis *et al.* (1981) found that planning processes during adoption predicted effective implementation. Both Rogers and Agarwala-Rogers (1976) and Fullan (1991), however, note that there has been a lack of research about innovation adoption (as opposed to implementation) since the mid-1960s. This has persisted, in part, because educational policy research in the 1980s focused its attention more on the effects of implemented educational reforms.

This chapter attempts to redress this gap. Rather than using a traditional diffusion of innovations model, however, we adopt a framework that is based in research on decision-making and organizational politics. Our research examines a single substantial innovation that has received increasing attention in recent years: the expansion of public education through the addition of classes to accommodate children who are age-eligible for Kindergarten, but are developmentally "immature." While this innovation affects a small number of students in any district, it poses interesting problems because it is central to issues of curriculum and instruction at the primary level and represents a change in a district's definitions of their responsibilities for educating pre-school children. In the remainder of this chapter, we will outline a theoretical framework for investigating the process of adoption, briefly present the four cases, investigate common and divergent findings across the cases, and draw conclusions related to both theory and policy.

Review of the Literature

Our choice of theoretical frameworks is based on what we believe to be a realistic assumption, namely that policy-making in school districts is a politically sensitive activity. In developing our framework, we draw on research on decision-making behaviors, politics and power in organizational settings and organizational communication. This section is structured around these basic themes.

The Politics of Decision-making: Random or Predictable?

The decision-making models proposed by Cohen et al. (1972) and March and Olsen (1976) (the garbage can model), and Allison's (1962) Model III (the bureaucratic politics model) appear to be rather distinct, except for a common interest in organizational behavior. Although both assume that politics is a fact of life in organizations, Allison's perspective emphasizes the predictable patterning of the use of power, while Cohen et al. focus on the difficulty of determining ahead of time how influence will be exercised.

Cohen et al. (1972) examine decision-making behaviors in settings that are characterized by problematic preferences, unclear technology, and fluid participation. "Organized anarchies" experience uncertainty about goals, and confront poorly defined and inconsistent choice alternatives. The authors consider educational institutions as exemplars of organized anarchies (see also Sproull et al. 1978). The dilemma posed by March and his colleagues is that decision opportunities usually present themselves ambiguously. Thus, an organization becomes "a collection of choices looking for problems, issues and feelings looking for decision situations in which they might be aired, [and] solutions looking for issues to which they might be the answer" (Cohen and March 1972: 2). There are four streams that interrelate in the decision-making process. The first is *problems*, which can be defined by members or outside groups; the second is *solutions*, which consist of an independent stream of preferences for various organizational actions; the third is *participants*, whose variations in organizational activity stem from unclear role requirements and the many other demands on their time; and the fourth is *choice opportunities*, or the occasions when the behavior of the organization normally produces an outcome that would be labeled as a "decision." The most important implication of the garbage can framework for this study is that "the garbage can process does not resolve problems well. But it does enable choices to be made ... even when the organization is plagued with goal ambiguity and conflict, with poorly understood problems that wander in and out of the system, with a variable environment, and with decision makers who may have other things on their minds" (Cohen and March 1972: 16).

An alternative framework is found in Allison's (1971) model of decision-making in political contexts, which emphasizes the dynamics of competing interests within groups: "The name of the game is politics: bargaining along regularized circuits among players positioned hierarchically within the [organization, and whose] behavior can be thus understood ... not as organizational outputs but as results of these bargaining games" (p. 144). Allison's view of the centrality of politics is affirmed by many recent writers, such as Bacharach and Lawler (1980) and Pfeffer (1981). Politics are not necessarily negative in Allison's view. Like Cohen and March, he assumes that leadership is diffused, and this encourages differences about both goals and means. Allison, like Pfeffer (1981) and Fullan (1991), views misperception as the "grease" of change. The mixture of conflicting preferences and the unequal power will often lead to a result that is distinct from what any person or group intended – and may ultimately be a better outcome (p. 145). This game of politics, unlike Cohen and March's, is not random. "Rather, certain processes structure the play. Processes are regularized channels for bringing issues to the point of choice" (149). Bargaining, persuasion, and accommodation are significant components of the decision process.

Allison's political model is organized around four questions. The first is *Who plays?*, or whose actions and interests have an important effect upon decisions? The second question is *What determines each player's stand?*, or what are the perceptions and interests leading to that stand? Allison makes an important distinction here by distinguishing between issue identification and the third question, *What determines each player's impact?* Players are viewed as able to gain bargaining advantages from many different sources such as formal authority, control over the information, personal persuasiveness and charisma, and access to other powerful players. The fourth question is *What is the game?* Formal or informal rules establish positions and power channels for action; but also constrict the range of decisions and actions that are acceptable and sanction the behaviors of the individuals within the game itself (p. 171). Allison's model is expanded and largely affirmed in Pfeffer's (1981) comprehensive review of politics in organizations.

Politics and Power

The concepts of power, authority, and influence are considered to be political attributes of organizations by many theorists (Cyert and March 1963; Allison 1971; Pfeffer and Salancik 1974; Kanter 1977; Bacharach and Lawler 1980; Pfeffer 1981; and others). For purposes of this study, politics is defined as the distribution and use of power, and the capacity to accomplish a task or to effect a change. Finally, power is considered to be comprised of authority (positional power) and influence (power based on personal characteristics) (Bacharach and Lawler 1980).

Pfeffer (1981) points out that power is not a fixed attribute of an individual or group, but is context- or relationship-specific. He also argues that power can be horizontally as well as vertically distributed. Pfeffer and Salancik (1977), for example, found that the distribution of power among university departments is predictable based on structural features, and affects the budgetary process. Depending on the task or decision at hand, power in educational settings may shift among the various individual subunits (Warren

1968). Pfeffer (1981) follows Pettigrew (1973) and Kanter (1977) in identifying the importance of the structure of the organization's communication network as a predictor of individual power, because it permits control over information.

Roles and Decision Processes

Other theorists provide insights into the intermediate steps that occur before a final decision is reached. New ideas may be received differently, depending upon the role that one has within the organization. Common (1983) proposes an explanation of why change in schools has often been ineffective, asserting that the different perspectives that teachers and school administrators have about one another's role in the change process is at the base of the problem. Administrators and central policy-makers tend to take a top-down approach to school reform, but "teachers see themselves as one of the main sources of curriculum stability ... As a result, they have a tenacious hold on the status quo" (p. 206). The presence of a gatekeeper within the network (Pettigrew 1973; Rogers and Agarwala-Rogers 1976) is pivotal, since this is the juncture at which a new idea is either allowed to move between the levels or to die quietly.

Daft and Becker's (1978) study of innovative behavior in thirteen school districts (one of the last major studies of the adoption of innovations in school districts) demonstrates the importance of role and decision processes. The authors argue that three factors enable an organization to innovate:

1. incentives or pressure to change;
2. mechanisms to communicate the innovation idea; and
3. an absence of organizational barriers.

Educational innovations tend to flow upward from teachers to administrators, while administrative innovations tend to originate near the top of the hierarchy and trickle down. They also found a positive correlation between the presence of district curriculum coordinators and the number of innovations adopted. Daft and Becker conclude that there must be an "individual [who wants] the innovation badly enough to do the groundwork necessary to carry the innovation forward to adoption. We are going to call the individual ... the idea champion" (p. 178). Pettigrew (1973) identifies another role: the person with the information is often considered to be an expert. "The position the expert occupies in the structure ... will affect his ability to control ... the actions of others, as will his position in the communication structure" (p. 29). Pettigrew asserts that the concentration of knowledge among a few individuals increases uncertainty and political behavior surrounding a decision to innovate (p. 30).

Organizational Structure and Communication

There is a considerable body of research that examines the relationship between organizational structure and communication. The authors cited here were selected for their theoretical work concerning decision-making as it relates to the consideration of new ideas. Weick (1976) asserts that educational systems are characterized by a variety of linked and overlapping subunits that are "loosely coupled," and argues that "Loosely coupled systems preserve many independent sensing elements, and therefore 'know' their environments better than is true for more tightly coupled systems which have fewer externally constrained, independent elements" (p. 6). Another advantage is that "in a loosely coupled system there is more room available for self-determination by the actors" because they have a better sense of their own efficacy and their sense of discretion is not overly limited and organizationally defined (p. 8). These two characteristics suggest that loosely coupled organizations are more likely to be innovative. Perrow (1970) argues that uncertainty (for example about the environment and the efficacy of organizational procedures) demands a looser form of organizational structure in situations where knowledge is very certain.

This theme is picked up by writers such as Daft and Huber (1987), who are concerned with the rates at which organizations "learn" by processing and changing to accommodate new information. These authors also argue that organizations that exist in environments in which information is equivocal and subject to interpretation require decentralized, interpersonally based communication systems if they are to effectively adapt. Attempts to decentralize and democratize school districts through school-based management and shared decision-making are symptomatic of such a view. This contrasts with a traditional bureaucratic perspective, in which adhering to prescribed vertical communication lines reduces delays in decision-making and eliminates irrelevant stimuli (Perrow 1970).

Rogers and Agarwala-Rogers (1976) focus on innovation as a communication-dependent process. They note that formal structures "lend a certain degree of predictability" (p. 80), but also note that "one of the most important functions of organizational structure is to restrict communication flows, and thus decrease problems of information overload" (p. 91). But informal communication structures are often important during non-routine situations – such as innovation – and are multidirectional (horizontal and/or vertical). This notion is also explored in Louis and Dentler's (1988) study of information flow and knowledge use in school systems. They show that in educational settings, new information is rarely used in the absence of significant "social processing" of knowledge, which involves the original recipient (often an idea champion) and others in the school or district. In addition, both Rogers and Agarwala-Rogers, and Louis and Dentler note that interaction is necessary in order for people to reach an agreement that an innovation has the potential for solving a problem. Usually organizations do not adopt a single blueprint as the innovation, but rather adopt a more "general concept whose operational meaning gradually unfolds [over time]" (Rogers and Agarwala-Rogers 1976: 160; see also Louis and Miles 1990).

Summary

The study presented below emphasizes a number of the concepts reviewed above. First, we assume that the process of decision-making has both elements of apparent randomness (non-predictability) as argued by March and his colleagues, but is also modestly predictable, based on knowledge about the power and routine political patterns in the organizational setting, as argued by Allison. Second, we emphasize the importance of specific roles that are played in the process of change, notably the roles of idea champion and gatekeeper. Third, we believe that the details of the process of decision-making that concern an innovation must be examined very closely for the way in which power is used and various constituencies and coalitions organized, drawing largely on the work of Bacharach and Lawler, and Pfeffer. Here we are concerned with individual goals and interests, parochial priorities, individual and organizational resources, rules of the game, and the way in which authority and influence evolve. Finally, we pay considerable attention to the patterned communication – and to the deviations from normal communication rules in the districts.

Methodology[2]

The basic unit of analysis in this study was the school district. Four school districts were selected as the representative sites in order to examine the questions being proposed. They were purposely selected for the fact that they each had recently considered a district-wide adoption of the same innovation. Systematic variation was introduced on two variables: two districts are considered to be rural, and the other two are considered to be suburban; three finally adopted Junior Kindergarten, while one did not. Variation was minimized on three other variables that might contribute to effective change: in each case the district was relatively stable (the superintendents had been in place for 5–19 years), and none was experiencing serious fiscal constraints. All of the districts were middle or upper-middle class.

In-depth personal interviews using a semi-structured protocol were conducted with 44 respondents. Decisions about who to interview were made using a triangulation method. The initial person approached to be interviewed as part of this study was the "idea champion" in each of the districts, and he or she provided additional suggestions about further appropriate respondents. In each district the superintendent, district administrators, principals, teachers, school psychologists, parents, and school board members were interviewed, whether they were nominated or not. In each case at least one person who was opposed to adopting Junior Kindergarten was sought out.

The transcribed interview narratives were the primary source of data being analyzed. A within-site analysis was conducted for each of the four school districts studied. The outcome of the within-site analyses revealed a well-grounded sense of the local reality as viewed within a particular setting or context. An analysis across all four of the school districts, or sites, was used to ensure "that the events and processes in one well-described setting are not wholly idiosyncratic" (Louis 1982: 12). "By comparing sites or cases, one can establish the range of generality of a finding or explanation, and, at the same time, pin down the conditions under which that finding will occur" (Miles and Huberman 1984: 151). Data displays used in the cross-case analysis summarized the activities and impressions of all respondents.

Four Cases of Political Decision-making

Riverwell District (Rural)

> It all went through very quickly, from something that was discussed in the summer and passed in August ... if they were going to get it going [in the fall], they had to pass it [right away].
>
> (School Board Member)

The Idea Champion

The arrival of a new elementary principal was greeted by the town with hopeful anticipation. When the new principal heard of the widely expressed concerns of the parents and the teachers about the unmet needs of some Kindergarten children, he knew he had a satisfactory solution in his pocket. However, he moved cautiously, waiting nearly a year:

> Ideally I had wanted to bring ... [it] in right away, but I just sat back and watched. I planted the seeds and talked a little bit about it ... it ended up coming from the parents when they said 'What can we do?' ... That was my cue ... [I] went back and I put some stuff together and I presented the idea to the superintendent. I just gave him a little nutshell of what it was, and said "I'll get back to you when I know more." I plant a lot of seeds, so I don't spring anything on him.

Clearly, he had an adoption plan fully in mind before ever attempting to put forth the idea. He carefully selected the best possible group to advocate for his innovation; in this case it was the parents. Finally, he knew precisely when he wanted to step in and present the solution to the welcome relief of all who had been concerned. As he concluded, "This was an alternative that fit. It fit really well."

The Gatekeeper

The role of a gatekeeper may be specific to a particular situation or specific to a particular group of people. In the case of Riverwell, the superintendent functions as a gatekeeper of information going to and from the school board. He actively monitors the type and the timing of items in bringing them to the school board: "I've got some control in what goes on the agenda; and superintendents ... are real politicians ... You know your board and you know what they want and you know what your community wants."

The superintendent was eager to embrace an innovation that would not only solve a problem, but also would reflect positively on him as being a concerned educator. Therefore, the potential success of the Junior Kindergarten initiative would address not only the needs of the parents and the teachers, but would ascribe a certain amount of competent risk-taking behavior to him as well. The teacher of the Junior Kindergarten was direct in her appraisal of his motives, saying "Oh ... his name's on all the papers ... he's never asked me what I do ... yet he sings our praises to the board."

The more critical gatekeeping role was performed by the elementary principal, who has the power to control the flow of concerns and ideas before they ever reach the level of the superintendent. When one teacher was asked about how she would bring a new idea forward, she said, "There is a ladder of responsibility that we feel we should always bounce it off our principal first." As for the flow from the top down, the principal explained, "I control what goes out to the staff and what doesn't." Being both the gate-keeper and the idea champion enables the elementary principal to have immediate access to all levels of the decision-making and adoption structure.

Other Actors

The idea champion did not choose to rely on formal input from teachers to bolster the case for the innovation being adopted. A Kindergarten teacher explained, "Well, we kind of discussed it … but not to a great extent … Mainly, I think the parents got involved." The elementary principal understood their concerns but was also well aware that, in Riverwell, administrative advocacy for a particular position when backed by a parent group is the surest route for board approval. One of the teachers who supported the adoption of the innovation said that "The staff didn't bother to talk to [the principal] about it because they just said, 'Oh, he knows what he's doing.'" This case was typical of Riverwell, where, as the teachers quietly do their job, the administration generally gives them a fair amount of latitude. Remaining neutral and out of the local spotlight serves, in their view, to perpetuate teacher autonomy.

Rules of the Game

Even though the administrative structure seems reactive, there are clear expectations of behavior that are centered on the basic rule of maintaining a public face of harmony. If ideas have the slightest hint of controversy – which would include all innovations – it is expected that the concerned individual will initially take it to his or her most immediate superior. Circumventing appropriate channels in a public forum typically results in being ignored. When the Junior Kindergarten first came up for discussion at a board meeting, a newly elected member's initial response was to ask for a specific course plan, which had not yet been prepared. The other board members ignored her question and did not ask for a response.

One of the strongest rules is the strict adherence to the pre-set agenda for a school board meeting. The chair of the board meets with the superintendent a week prior to the board meeting to set the agenda. Once that is set, "we publish it in the paper … so the public has more than enough time to read [it] … And if there's a concern, they'll be there … very, very seldom are there any surprises." The reasoning behind the closely followed communication rules was noted by both the superintendent and the board members. Said the board chair, "I don't feel that he should surprise the board, and he doesn't. I think we've got a good relationship like that … " while he noted "I think you've got to look all the time to make your board look good." The principle of a harmonious public face is acknowledged by the elementary principal as well: "I'll know going into a board meeting where things stand. But he (the superintendent) is also very good in that if he can't support me, he won't come out [publicly] in opposition."

Communication Channels

The informal communication structure of this small town conditions how issues make it to the table. A teacher explained that "[i]n a small town like this, you know who the board members are and they're your neighbors. So you just mention in passing, 'Hey. my kids got to walk to school' or 'The furnace is breaking down every month.'" Another teacher echoed a similar view "You really have a feeling of accessibility to people." Likewise, the parents expressed a feeling that the communication access points were many and very receptive: "I feel it's real fluid here. You can express it to the superintendent, principal, and the board members." This means that individuals have great influence, which helps to account for the extremely powerful role assumed by the idea champion.

The new elementary principal brought a grasp of educational and curricular issues that had previously been missing from Riverwell for some time. His apparent strengths increasingly contrasted with those of both the secondary principal and the superintendent. As a result, his influence is on a steady rise, and according to several, has surpassed that of the superintendent. A parent noted that " ... I feel that the elementary principal has more control and more input than the superintendent does. I think he's the added link that makes the school work." A board member said, "The superintendent is a [more] powerful position, [but] it is the [elementary] principal who really runs the show." Several of the board members explained his influence in terms of his fit in the community: "As a family man, and his wife and everything, they're active in the community. You like to see that in a small town. [He's] at a level that you can meet him on." Parenthetically, the superintendent accepts his limited role as the district's financial manager.

The principal's influence has also been enhanced by his ability to work with a coalition of activist elementary parents, which had a history of violating the norm of low controversy. Said one board member. "I think our elementary principal has got them eating out of his hand." The elementary principal candidly described his role vis-à-vis the parent group with the following comment: "It is totally a parent group and teachers hate the group ... So I kind of work as a liaison between them [the teachers and the parents]." The principal used this influence when he assumed the role of the idea champion for the Junior Kindergarten. He was asked if the parent group was part of the support he garnered to push for the adoption of the idea. Without hesitation, his response was, "Absolutely."

Perspectives on the Process and Outcomes

Perceived expertise, which has been discussed above, was viewed as a major reason for the rapid and uncontroversial decision process. A board member recalled that there was very little debate about the merits of the idea because the board felt that the elementary principal as the idea champion was giving them very accurate information. "He had good facts, good figures." This board member was concerned that the new program would not be a financial drain on the district and was assured that it would be nearly self-supporting.

The swiftness of the decision-making process clearly had an effect on the interplay among the actors. With the idea champion having already negotiated support for the idea before it was presented to the school board, he was able to defuse potential political problems as well as keeping to the "no surprises" code. Therefore, it is not a surprise that the perceived level of controversy from all respondents was very low. One of the teachers felt that the lack of community debate about the program was due to the speed of the decision. "It was done so rapidly, that's probably why." She also agreed that the decision "wasn't a big controversial thing because the money (funding) was not controversial."

The lack of community awareness of the proposal was substantiated by both a school board member and parents. This low profile was affirmed by one board member, saying that a school district should not "make a big splash out of a new idea" but rather focus on it while identifying and "quietly breaking the power blocks" that potentially could have a negative impact upon a district's pursuit of educational change.

The positive notoriety that the adoption of the Junior Kindergarten has had among neighboring school districts is cited as one of the reasons that it has a secure future even with its low profile among the citizenry. A parent reported that "We get asked constantly about Riverwell's Junior Kindergarten. You know, that's a new buzz word." One of the school board members echoed those sentiments when she explained her vote to go forward with adopting the program, "I thought it was a great opportunity for our area. So, it was progress, it was good."

Beachwood District (Suburban)

> We survive on our short-term visions ... But the district survives on the long-term planning, and if you're really sincere about what you're doing, you will look long term to see the effect of your decisions today.
>
> (Beachwood Superintendent)

After more than a year's deliberation, Beachwood's Kindergarten Committee recommended that the adoption of a Junior Kindergarten program be put on hold. In the interim, the committee intended to refine a philosophy for Kindergarten education. In so doing, the members may revisit this innovation, or look to curricular revision and improved parent education as possible means of eliminating the need for a Junior Kindergarten.

The Idea Champion

The idea champion, the director of curriculum, was unanimously viewed as a knowledgeable administrator. His credibility was enhanced during the eighteen months that he had occupied his position by his regular classroom visits, his understanding of primary education, and his history as a source of new ideas. He was not, however, viewed as a neutral source of information during the first year's deliberations in the Kindergarten committee. A teacher noted that "Last year I kind of felt that he always leaned more toward the pro-side of a pre-k program." This situation changed significantly when he appointed a new principal as the committee chairperson during the second year of discussion and abruptly left the committee without explanation.

The Gatekeeper

In Beachwood, principals actively filter information flows upward and downward. A principal candidly noted, "You know, I can pretty much kill ... or sidetrack [any idea]." The key gatekeeper was the principal on the committee, but his actions reflected the opinions of his committee colleagues.

The Superintendent

The superintendent of Beachwood Schools is careful to be associated with success, but to share the credit: "The reason [we are] successful is not me as much as our ability as a team to get together." Her staff concurred, indicating that "She is a very open, involved individual, so fairness is just going to come naturally there." But, she also sees herself as playing a critical quality-control function: "If a concept didn't work, I'd dump it ... the staff knows: We don't go with losers." The superintendent took no strong position for or against the Junior Kindergarten.

The School Board

In a similar vein, the stands of the school board members are well known. As one school board member candidly put it, "Really, we are politicians and salesmen ... Public relations, first and foremost ... is what makes the district either go or stand still." Trust and participation help to make school board work amicable, and largely low key. A board member explained that "If you have effective communication ... and the facts ... reasonable people come to a reasonable solution."

Teachers

The Kindergarten teachers were individually worried about what to do with immature students, but had not discussed the issue collectively. So, when the District's curriculum director mentioned the idea for a Junior Kindergarten, which he had picked up from a colleague in another district at a regularly scheduled meeting, they were immediately interested. One teacher emotionally recalled, "It was a moment of excitement ... 'There's finally a place for those kids.'" Yet Beachwood teachers did not generally view themselves as major actors in decision-making: "You tended to listen to what they (the administrators on the committee) had to say. And if you didn't agree with it, I kind of felt like, 'Gee, I'd better not say anything because my vote's not going to count.'"

Parents

Parents in this affluent suburb are included on all committees. Yet, the parents' role is not clear: "That's a little bit about my discomfort of serving on this committee ... [the principal] caught me at conferences or something and asked if I wanted to be on it ... Then I showed up and I was the only parent. It was like, 'Well, who's the other parent?' and there was never anything said."

Rules of the Game

Despite the principals' power, the district's conventions did not give them full discretion. One principal succinctly laid out the real organizational scenario: "She (the superintendent) wants it to come from down below, and some of it does come up. But a lot comes from the board, from her, and we've got to play that finesse game like it came from us." Another principal noted that "She runs this district and that board, and she knows them very, very well, and … she does get her way." As one board member put it, "I'm not trying to sell (the superintendent), but she seems to be one step ahead, just a beat ahead, of what things could possibly transpire." The director of curriculum believes that the clear rules in this district help to develop a sense of trust, and another administrator noted that "There are no surprises. You know what you can expect." The rules for getting an item on any meeting agenda ostensibly allow for anything to be discussed but as one teacher explained, "it's [the convener's] agenda … Yeah, definitely, that happens every committee meeting I've ever been on." Parents are usually hand-chosen to serve on committees, and one noted that "I don't know how much real input they have … that's kind of protecting themselves to [be able to] say, down the line, 'Wait a minute … parents served on the committee.'"

Communication Channels

Beachwood is administered "through the structure." The use of informal communication channels is associated with position, being most often used within the upper administrative ranks, more rarely by principals and board members (with the exception of informal communications coming to them from constituents), and hardly at all by teachers. The superintendent is not the type to merely sit in her office at the District Administration Building. She is frequently out in the schools, observing classrooms and informally conversing with teachers and principals. This works to her advantage because people tend to believe that her decisions were made based upon accurate knowledge. The director of curriculum uses informal channels similarly. With regard to Junior Kindergarten, for example, he said "If I had gone into all the buildings and they had given me a negative, I sure wouldn't have gone to the [school) board." Another communication channel utilized by the curriculum director is the informal lunch he holds each month with the principals. "We meet away from the building, … and we sit down and talk about … anything that might come up that doesn't need to be brought [in the formal meetings]." This is a forum for him to test the waters. Informal upward communication channels are occasionally used by a principal, but work less well because reaching one district administrator does not necessarily mean that all will get the message.

Perspectives on the Process and Outcomes

Other than school board members, who had limited involvement in the discussions, all respondents have some kind of personal opinion about why the decision was made to table the adoption. Yet, overall the story is one of confusion and even surprise at the outcome. The idea champion believes that adoption is on hold because the group is still wrestling with developing a philosophy of Kindergarten education. Ever since his departure as the chairperson of the Kindergarten committee, he has divorced himself from responsibility for the decision. The principal who stepped in to become the new chair of the committee was as surprised as anyone about the outcome. "I started out thinking 'we're having it,' that there wasn't any question. But as we started digging into things ... we just started questioning it more and more." For him "The biggest dilemma that made us recommend not going with it yet is that there is not enough [research]," but he also pointed to lack of demand in the community. Another principal believed that the process was disorganized, and commented that the elementary principals "haven't been given an update ... I've just picked up bits and pieces, more by accident than on purpose." He also remarked that the decision to postpone probably rested with the curriculum director.

The departure of the idea champion was noted by teachers as having a significant effect, but for different reasons. Two were not convinced from the beginning that a Junior Kindergarten program was the best solution to the problem. A third teacher was in favor of adoption, but the strength of her conviction diminished during the second year as the committee confronted ambiguous evidence. She saw fear of failure as an important issue: "I guess we didn't feel real secure ... We didn't want to ... take a chance on it and have it not work out, and then make a bad name for [the program]." These fears of failure arose only when the idea champion left the committee. The psychologist also welcomed the departure of the idea champion, because it increased the freedom to closely examine the negatives.

The sole parent committee member felt that, as the discussion evolved, a solution which was initially embraced as ideal began to be seen as a stop-gap: "I think what came out of the committee is that maybe Kindergarten needs to change." While the commitment towards making a good decision increased, the commitment towards the innovation itself became secondary.

When the superintendent was asked why the decision to adopt the Junior Kindergarten program was tabled, she affirmed the sense of disorganization, but attributed the influence to herself: "The reason I've held it up this year is basically because I don't think they've got their act together." She also pointed to an unresolved facility problem that would have located the program in a building without other Kindergarten students.

None of the other respondents who were part of the actual committee deliberations ever mentioned the influence that the superintendent might have had upon the outcome of the decision, although an uninvolved principal speculated that the superintendent may have or suggested to the idea champion "Hey, let's knock it off. Let's get on to other things."

Martin-Mason District (Suburban)

> Ideas originate with individuals ... We have never used a strong committee process ... The planting of the seed is done individually ... Then the stakeholding aspect evolves at that stage.
>
> (Martin-Mason Superintendent)

Unlike Beachwood, with its diverse set of key actors, there was no broadly based committee to address the Junior Kindergarten issue in the suburban Martin-Mason district, and there was little controversy during the development of the proposal. The Junior Kindergarten committee had prepared their board presentation thoroughly. Two teachers described the key meeting: "I remember we went ... kind of thinking, 'Oh, they're going to ... put us on the spot.'" To their amazement, it was rapid and uncontroversial: "It went through without any questions at all. We didn't even have to speak to the issue!"

The Idea Champion
The curriculum director was recently promoted to her position, but has already made a big impact. She is, in the words of the superintendent, "a leader [who is] willing to do [her] homework well, stand at the gap when the partisan flak comes through, and defend [her] points of view." Others also referred to her tenacity and the general trust in her competence. She had come from another state where developmental readiness issues were being discussed. As one teacher explained, "She was the first principal [I've known] who really seemed committed to Kindergarten and knew what it was about." Teachers and other administrators have little difficulty accepting both her role and the power.

The Gatekeeper
An elementary principal aptly described the traditional gatekeeper role: "In the past, we [principals] could stop things, even if the proposal came out of the central office." Another characterized the principal's role as "the constrictor in this district. That's because there's really no one else who is dealing with communication." This powerful role was confirmed by both teachers and central-office respondents. The flow from the bottom up can also be controlled by the principal. A teacher spoke of her experiences, saying, "We can voice concerns to our building principal ... [The problem is] as staff, we don't know how far it gets."

Other Committee Members
The first few meetings of the Junior Kindergarten Committee were not formally convened, but consisted of two teachers from the faculty-teacher communications council and the director of curriculum. The committee grew when the director of basic skills was brought in, along with an elementary principal, but they "only showed up at a couple of meetings." The other significant person in the process was the school psychologist, who was added, according to an elementary principal because, "the director of curriculum had a high regard for ... her expertise, ... and so do I." Another principal echoed that view saying, "I would say that it was her work in terms of looking around, identifying facts, that the director of curriculum [as the idea champion] could rely on."

The Superintendent
Although supportive, the superintendent's involvement was limited to periodically receiving information from the director of curriculum. His view of leadership supported his rather remote role, as he emphasized "empowerment, or mutual respect

in one another's professional capability, integrity and motives ... In this district I have been blessed with outstanding elementary leaders ... they became questers and venturers and riskers." He knew that the idea champion had frequent contact with teachers and believed that "the closer you can get to the point of where the rubber meets the road ... the more effectively programs can be developed."

The School Board
The school board is viewed as powerful by nearly all persons interviewed. As one teacher put it, "I mean, let's face it ... They have the power to cut any program or any administrator if they want to." Within the board, the chair is central: "No agendas are presented to other board members unless the chairman of the board has approved them, and added or deleted [items]." Nevertheless, the board was excluded from the consultative process prior to the presentation of the proposal for Junior Kindergarten, a normal practice in the district.

Parents
There were no parents involved in this Junior Kindergarten Committee. One of the teachers recalled, "We ... never thought of it at that time."

Rules of the Game
The presence of a new idea does not necessarily generate a response in Martin-Mason. The idea may not get out of a committee or receive approval from a building principal. However, if an idea moves forward, according to the superintendent, it is the result of a "great person." Others concur. In this case, there was neither a strong leader nor a receptive ear within the administration until the director of curriculum stepped into her new position. A board member notes that, "It was a situation where the buildings saw the need ... But [it had] to come ... from the district office."

The primary operating rules in Martin-Mason are to know whose support you need to make a change, and then to be sure that your information and support are clearly lined up. An elementary principal described the flow of events in the case of Junior Kindergarten: "The director of curriculum was head of [the state-mandated improvement planning] committee. The plan [for Junior Kindergarten] was quasi-approved by the principals. It was supported by [the improvement planning committee]. It went from there to the superintendent, and from there to the board of education." When asked about the need for the idea to go through all of those steps, he went on to note that there is a tacit agreement that acting by these rules is the way to avoid a "divide and conquer mentality" on the part of some school board members.

The involvement of the principals was therefore politically important, but the superintendent described their role as one which "validated the idea ... [The curriculum director] empowered [them] with knowledge ... took their input ... and looked at it objectively." A principal commented that "I think she did a pretty good job of involving ... us ... so we knew what direction it was going." The amount of attention given to details is a rule which is understood by teachers, but which annoys them as well. One of the task force teachers explained, "Our director of curriculum was very thorough ... She wanted everything in detail ... [At times] I just shook my head because we had so many other major decisions to make."

Communication Channels

The teachers' access points are either through the various curriculum committees or through a "meet and confer" process with the principals. The power of the principals to stop ideas from progressing out of the building level appears to be accepted by the teaching staff, in part because it is reinforced by the district office. Similarly, access to the system for administrators is expected to follow the route of involving the principals and the superintendent before proceeding to the board for their action and approval.

Despite efforts to control the school board, the sense that its agenda is unpredictable is prevalent. The director of curriculum reported that the board would "vote on something out of the middle of nowhere." The school psychologist explained that issues "will come up overnight ... there may not be anybody present to be an advocate." Long-range planning requires that an organization have a formalized process for input. Several respondents, such as the school psychologist, noted, "I don't see that kind of planning happening here ... That's how programs get started around here, they kind of come up." Informal communications in Martin-Mason schools are often issue-specific: "You might be able to get a new program started faster in our district than you could someplace else. If it's popular with four out of seven board members, and if you can get it on the agenda, you could maybe get it through in one month." Unlike teachers and building administrators, parents have few formalized ways in which they can provide input, but feel free to circumvent the hierarchical channels. The school psychologist said, "It's not unusual for a parent to call the superintendent directly and say, 'I need this or want this.' And usually that gets them what they want – action of some kind."

The use of informal communication channels is a breeding ground for the formation of coalitions in Martin-Mason. The elementary principals find that by maintaining their solidarity, they are less vulnerable to the whims of the school board: "that's what has made us somewhat successful ... the central office and school board members see us as being a pretty effective group ... You can't get one elementary principal pitted against another." The curriculum director's notes that "it was just something that through their own intuitive sense of self-defense that the [principals] coalition arose." The basic-skills director corroborated the role of the principal's solidarity in the adoption of the Junior Kindergarten. Initially, not all of them were sold on the idea. However, "once they decided that something [had] to be done, they were content [to go ahead]."

Perspectives on the Process and its Outcomes

The basic-skills coordinator gave the fullest response to a question about why the proposal was adopted so quickly and without board controversy:

I was aware of a pervasive sense that … they would block [the innovation]. That all had to be carefully managed and handled in such a way that they wouldn't have the opportunity to do that. So, much energy was devoted to making the proposal bullet-proof.

The director of curriculum agreed that the program was adopted so readily "because it was so well-planned. It was all laid out." In the words of the superintendent, she had "done extremely good homework." The smoothness of the deliberations process and the board presentation was characterized by one of the principals within a political framework when he said, "The curriculum director just picked it up and moved it through, and she didn't take no for an answer anywhere. It was a marvelous piece of work on her part." Her administrative access and political acuity enabled her to move forward without raising the ire of her colleagues. This was important in order to be able to reach the level of the school board for a vote of adoption.

The school board members cited the completeness of the information given to the board and the presence of school district funds as reasons why the board action was positive and rapid. One of the members explained that the presentation was made "by a group of people who were really supportive … And we were not as financially stressed as we are now." Another board member spontaneously mentioned district finances too, when he said, "I think that's one of the peak times when we had money." The lack of structured committee processes was another reason that the deliberation period was relatively short. The school psychologist noted that "Junior Kindergarten got off the ground faster here than it probably would have in most other school districts because we didn't have to go through a lot of other committees to get approval." The curriculum director commented that "Having much involvement by many people takes more time."

Dorchester Unified District (Exurban-Rural)

The idea was greased, so, unlike anything in the recent past, it went "Bang, Bang."
(School Psychologist)

Unlike the previous two cases, which occurred in stable communities, the Dorchester Unified Schools faced some difficult choices in the last five years before the study. A new high school was built that brought students together from the three communities that make up the district, a new superintendent was hired, and the administrative structure was reorganized. The district's rural lifestyle has confronted suburban expansion and new perspectives on educational priorities and procedures. Despite the more uncertain environment, the planning process for Junior Kindergarten was relatively uneventful.

The first meeting that brought together the Dorchester area Kindergarten and 1st-grade teachers from the three elementary schools occurred in the late fall. Mutual concern over Kindergarten retention was discovered and discussed. The number of actors involved was limited although, in a departure from usual district practice, parents were brought into the picture at the last moment. A subcommittee visited several school districts that were operating a Junior Kindergarten classroom. Once the visits and the information gathering had been completed, the planning proceeded rapidly. Much to everyone's surprise the board chose to act at the first meeting at which the idea was presented, giving unanimous approval to the proposal to add an additional Kindergarten year for immature students.

The Idea Champion

The surfacing of the issue of Kindergarten retention coincided with a teacher's attendance at a workshop. She brought information back to discuss with her colleagues, all of whom identified her as the initial champion of the Junior Kindergarten idea. This individual sought support from her building principal, who considered the innovation to be well worth sponsoring. He initially chaired the task force and pushed for the addition of a grade prior to Kindergarten. The superintendent clearly viewed him as the champion: "[He was] a real kid advocate ... He was, I think, more of the spirit behind this than was ever evident."

When the idea was in its final stages of development, the idea champion's baton was passed to a third individual. This was necessary because, as the superintendent explained, "The principal in charge of the task force knew that the idea ... would have a much better chance if the director of curriculum were the vehicle through which this came forward [to the school board]." The director of curriculum saw himself as a facilitator rather than as an advocate but once he joined the committee he began to prepare the board presentation. Few outside the committee remember any person other than the director of curriculum in the role of idea champion.

The Gatekeeper

Not all school districts have a clearly defined gatekeeper. Respondents noted that the administrative structure previously gave tremendous power to the building principal, but current policies also emphasize teacher empowerment. Not all were comfortable with the change. One school board member, for example, stated that having the principal in the formal role of gatekeeper engendered trust in the information that reached the school board level: "[If] it comes from there, I know that the principal knows and has worked with this group ... and that they think it's feasible in that building." In the case of the Junior Kindergarten decision, the support of the elementary principal was clearly viewed as critical.

Parents

The Kindergarten teachers' goals were shared by parents. One teacher stated that: "[The board] still might have gone for the program, but it was definitely more persuasive to see the parents'point of view." The director of curriculum echoed that view, saying "The message [of parent groups] is listened to [by the board] very closely, and therefore that makes them effective."

The Superintendent

The previous administration in Dorchester viewed the district's size and diverse community opinions as obstacles to effective problem-solving, a perception that was immediately challenged by the new superintendent. Nevertheless, she did not view herself as a source of "expert knowledge" about educational problems and solutions:

> I don't have time to read my mail, much less to do information searches on anything. It's more gut level ... [it's] sensing a need, sensing a major theme or major question and going after it, rather than any kind of flow chart or strategic plan.

The superintendent's policy to openly consider most new ideas, irrespective of where they come from, is acknowledged as current district practice.

The School Board

The school board was very supportive of the superintendent, and also responded to the influence of the director of curriculum and a program coordinator. As the coordinator put it, "I think they (the school board) ... were trusting us to have done our homework and to have come up with what we thought was the best option at that point in time."

Rules of the Game

The rules are changing in Dorchester. One of the elementary principals explained that the main difference between the old patterns and the new is that both formal and informal influence is more widely diffused: "I'm not sure there's really any *one* person that can get any one idea through right now, especially in the framework that we've designed these last couple of years in terms of [shared] decision-making."

She emphasized the importance of having an established process for input and having defined "goals and objectives that give you some sense of future orientation." This has dramatically affected the role of the school board. Said one board member, "I cannot give any person in the district an order ... But people have a hard time hearing that, because they perceive it as how [it used to be]." This board member believed that the new focus of board behavior was on setting policy as opposed to administering the schools. Also, there was a clarification and a reaffirmation sought by the administration that, among the individual members, each of them must separate their personal concerns and personal agenda from what is necessary to operate a well-run school district.

Communication Channels

Until five years before the study, the use of formal communication channels in Dorchester was rather infrequent. The formal channels were basically those established by the principal, who was a sort of clearing-house for building-level concerns, the teachers' union for general teacher-rights concerns, and the formal relationship between the former superintendent and the school board. Each of these subunits had their own system of access and internal regulations, but there were no interconnections between or among them. A school district that has three distinct town centers faces an inherent communication dilemma, in that issues being informally discussed in one location are not necessarily those engaging the citizens and educators in another. Poor management of this problem led to the resignation of the previous superintendent.

The current superintendent moved quickly to establish procedures to formalize communications. The strategy most frequently mentioned was the widespread use of committees, a practice which had begun five years before. A teacher recalled the move towards a participatory structure saying, "Since we've had a new superintendent I've seen a big change in the amount of input asked for by the administration in making decisions. And I think people feel much better about how those things happen." School board members and parents concurred. Yet assumptions about communication were still predicated on the old system. The director of curriculum openly declared, "There is a ton of communication going on ... and yet there's [still] not enough ... We're really struggling with how to structure it ..." The rules for formal vs. informal access are ambiguous. A district office staff member noted that the superintendent was comfortable with citizens directly contacting him, a position that was also held by the superintendent for herself. Previously, teachers bypassed the authority structure to avoid gatekeeping or to increase their personal influence, but the new rules also allowed for and even encouraged direct contact with the superintendent. When a teacher was asked if the new superintendent was unapproachable, she declared, "Oh, no, no, no. I've called her personally at home ... so I feel like it's very open."

Perspectives on the Process and Outcomes

Strong support for adopting the innovation came from the superintendent. For her, all of the elements of a sound decision were present to allow her to act in the affirmative. She believed she had good information from respected teachers, she trusted the support being given by the idea champion, and the board and the parents were supportive as well. One school board member recalls that many different reasons entered into the picture as to why this innovation was necessary, but summed them all up when she said, "I think certainly all of those things were a part of the decision, but the bottom line was, it was perceived at that point to be a better program for those kids." A parent was asked whether the consideration of the proposal by the school board was controversial: "I mean, who would object? ... If those kids need two years to get ready for 1st grade, then let's do it ... Let's make it a positive instead of a failure ... who could argue with that?"

The perception that moving forward was better than doing nothing seems to be a critical piece of information explaining why the innovation was so quickly adopted. But another subtext was the perceived difficulty in attempting real change in Kindergarten teachers or their closely held curricula:

This [innovation] was simply putting in a program that took some of those kinds of issues away from [the Kindergarten] teachers, and put them in the laps of two people who wanted to deal with them. That's not hard, you can do that easily.

In addition, a parent noted that sometimes the decision-making process is facilitated by a lack of knowledge. This may be particularly the case when the innovation is so new that there isn't a broad research base either to support or criticize it. Certainly in the case of the Junior Kindergarten program, information that the Dorchester staff and school board had to work with was primarily experiential in nature, and they made little use of empirically based research information. The fact that the innovation was introduced in a era of trust also made a difference. The school board was relieved to have a competent, well-liked superintendent, teachers were pleased to be more centrally involved in decision-making, and parents were more comfortable with the school system's directions.

The only negative opinions about the decision came from the two school psychologists, one of whom expressed the concern that the plan was not well formulated or studied, and did not follow normally careful district procedures. He saw the potential adoption become "a political thing, [with a] 'Can you top this?' mentality." However, the committee process was in place, and a minority voice did not make much of a difference.

Discussion of Findings

Our interpretation of the four cases will be organized around five main findings:

1. A clearly defined process was found whereby an innovation is discovered, discussed, and decided upon by a school district. Elements of both the garbage can model and the bureaucratic politics model are present at different points in that process.
2. There must be an idea champion associated with the proposed innovation in order to permit the idea to receive any formal organizational attention.
3. A gatekeeper of the flow of information is a verified reality in a school district and is likely to be a principal. During the process of problem definition, this person has significant control over which innovative ideas move beyond the local building level.
4. For school district actors in the decision process, power is derived from having both a high degree of authority and a high degree of influence. In the case of parents, their power is based on influence alone. The variability in the locus of influence in districts is substantial.
5. Careful attention to the political context, particularly to the way in which communication channels are used during all stages of the decision-making process, is essential for the idea champion. Understanding, managing, and using these effectively will help to determine whether to proceed to the school board for a decision or to abandon the quest.

Garbage Can or Bureaucratic Politics?

Garbage Can Elements

Elements of the model proposed by March and his colleagues clearly characterize the problem identification process in school districts. The presence of a garbage can, which tended to contain diverse and unsolved problems, was a salient feature of the school district environment in all four locations, despite the many differences in local context. There was agreement by district administrators, principals, and school board members that there was a continuous stream of often-unrelated issues for which there was no apparent solution.

The degree of volatility in the garbage can differed among the cases, however. Several respondents in each of the two rural districts made a comment about the ease – and unpredictability – with which new ideas emerge for district-wide adoption. Said the Riverwell elementary principal, "When new ideas come back [to the district], we're willing to consider just about anything." Similarly, a Dorchester Unified program coordinator stated, "This particular district embraces new ideas, maybe sometimes too much." Conversely, bureaucratic politics was somewhat more apparent in both of the suburban districts, where hierarchy was bolstered by clear rules about who had the right to bring forward a potential solution. For example, in Beachwood, it was quite clear that, while ideas could circulate freely among teachers, only those ideas that were thoroughly considered by district administrators would make it on to a public agenda. We speculate that suburban districts may feel that it is necessary to be able to apply greater control mechanisms because the likelihood that the staff will encounter solutions is greater than in more isolated rural settings. In addition, because suburban schools have more district administrators, there are simply more decision-makers at this level who can attend to the management of the problem and solution-selection process.

In each case, however, the "problem" of Junior Kindergarten stayed in the garbage can until a coalition had formed over concern about the issue, or unless the problem was of particular interest to one of the administrators or board members. Thus, a "sense of urgency" emerges as a consequence of either public pressure or individual interest among powerful individuals. The garbage can also emerged as a prominent explanation for the adoption process at the stage when a policy decision was made. In three of the four cases, the vote of the school board was viewed as unpredictable by participants, who, in each case, expressed surprise that there was so little controversy. Actors in some districts – particularly Riverwell – also considered this later stage of the process to be as ambiguous and unpredictable as the emergence stage. In the two suburban districts, and in rural Dorchester Unified, actors believed that they had more control over the political process. Only in Beachwood was there a sense that the outcomes of board meetings were genuinely manageable.

Bureaucratic Politics

While the garbage can model explains the process by which a problem and a potential solution get on the agenda and are finally adopted, it was equally clear that political regularities that were well known by participants governed the activities associated with internal decision-making. Some of the regularities include the following.

- The emergence of an idea champion, or a person who is able to "place a requirement on the formal organizational system for a decision to innovate" (Daft and Becker 1978: 179). While the idea champions in these cases had the necessary political clout to ask for a decision, they were required to do a great deal of groundwork, most of which involved knowledge acquisition and the consideration of the innovation for local application.

- The presence of significant gatekeepers, whose involvement needed to be effectively managed in order to smooth the adoption process.
- A key role played by the superintendent and/or the school board in authorizing the work, and endorsing it.
- The perceived need to "play by the rules" (which differed between districts), which covered issues such as who should be involved and at what stages, how open the process should be, how much evidence should be collected and considered, and how to manage the process of getting the innovation onto the board's agenda.
- The perceived need to manage the district's informal and formal communication channels, which constituted the routes by which known powerful actors and coalitions could affect the process.
- The perceived need to use politically relevant knowledge as part of managing the process. In these cases we have identified two types of important knowledge: intimate knowledge of the local context – its problems and its "rules" – and competent knowledge of the content of the idea being proposed. Taken together, these two forms of knowledge provided the idea champion with the influence necessary to bring about organizational change.

In each case – even in Riverwell, where the sense of powerlessness on the part of professional educators was relatively high – the actors perceived that these components of the process were understandable and generally operated in much the same way, irrespective of the specific curriculum or instructional decision.

The Idea Champion

The idea champion's role was, as indicated above, part of the regularity of bureaucratic politics, and also a key role in the decision process. A number of characteristics of successful idea champions in school district politics can be derived from the cases.

In a Position of Authority

The idea champion in each of the cases was a person from within the organization. Unlike the concept of a "change agent" found in business management literature where one brings in changes or ideas for organizational change from the outside, these idea champions were bound into the upper levels of the organizational structure. They tended to know of many unmet organizational needs by virtue of their position as a member of the district's executive administrative council. In addition, they also had representational membership on the district's administrative council or served as chair for a number of other district committees.

Because of their informal interactions with top decision-makers, idea champions were also able to relate to them on a more personal level. Dealing with ambiguous and unsolved problems is a frequent experience for persons in positions of authority, and it often creates a sense of frustration and isolation among school administrators and decision-makers. In these cases the idea champion's position of authority provided him or her with a very subtle sense of this negative organizational connectedness among the decision-makers. Thus, the idea champion was generally perceived as "one of the gang" within the upper echelon, and a recipient of their trust as a result. Engaging in frequent and informal discussions with the decision-makers also permitted the idea champion to be viewed as someone who is up-to-date and involved with the same concerns that they themselves face. In sum, the idea champion comes to have intimate knowledge of the problem and of the context in which the problem exists.

A Boundary Spanner

People who become aware of a possible solution to a known, but unsolved, problem are often persons who cross over an organizational boundary into another educational environment. There they discover the possibility that the problem might be able to be addressed in their home district. Teachers seem to encounter such solutions while attending a professional workshop or when visiting other school districts. Central office administrators and principals tend to learn of possible solutions by talking with their peers at regional collegial meetings.

The one legitimized boundary-spanning role that was similarly defined in all four of the districts was that of the curriculum director. This person was expected and, in fact, encouraged to be an initiator. News of changes and discussions about proposals coming from the individual in the position of curriculum director were considered by all of the respondents in this study as usual behavior for the person in that role. In each of the four cases, it was the director of curriculum who served as the idea champion when bringing the idea before the school board. It is as though the position is organizationally sanctioned to be the accepted "boat rocker." Another critical feature of the role is that its occupant generally enjoys unrestricted communication access to players above and below within the hierarchical structure. The benefit of the access was that reaction to new ideas could be gathered from superiors as well as from selected teaching staff. Essentially, a natural feedback loop was available to the person occupying the position of curriculum director because "testing the waters" was assumed to be part of the role description. Potential changes to the status quo somehow seem less threatening and less for personal gain when they emanate from the curriculum director's position.

Has Competent Knowledge of Classrooms and the Innovation

There was agreement among all respondents in this study that the person championing the idea had competent knowledge of all aspects of the issue. In schools, unlike many other organizations, a person almost never rises to a position of leadership and authority (for example, principal, or curriculum director) without having had hands-on experience working directly with the product (student). Because of this, teachers perceive that the principal probably knows how difficult or intractable some of the problems are that confront them. Automatic credibility is generally accorded to school leaders initially, and remains in place until the leader does or says something that shatters this assumption. If a school leader regularly meets with teachers to discuss ideas and concerns, the teachers will assume that this leader is knowledgeable about those issues. Thus, when a leader steps into the role of an idea champion, explaining the various aspects of new idea or suggested change, the view by teachers seemed to be that this person has connected his or her knowledge of the classroom and instructional issues with knowledge of the innovation being proposed. A perception of competent knowledge is the result. The degree to which their opinion or stand carried weight with decision-makers was the most salient characteristic of their organizational influence, and this was bolstered, according to virtually all respondents, by the presence of competent knowledge.

Has Intimate Knowledge of Local Context

Understanding the local political milieu is vitally important for any individual attempting to bring about organizational change. Three out of the four idea champions in this study had been hired or promoted into their district-wide administrative positions within a year of initiating the idea of the Junior Kindergarten innovation. Both the Riverwell and the Beachwood idea champions knew of the innovation at the time that they were hired. Each, however, chose to wait about a year to become better acquainted with the local needs (and constraints) before bringing up the idea with the teachers. The Martin-Mason idea champion had risen through the ranks in his district and knew of the needs in Kindergarten before he was appointed to become an administrator. Because he was already highly knowledgeable about the local context, he chose to move on the idea right away.

In all four cases, the idea champion understood the importance of dealing with and managing the local political context. Since the idea champion was an "insider" by definition, the amount of influence that he or she was able to exert in decision situations appeared to be directly related to his or her ability to "read" the interest in and the intensity of concern about a local problem. Much of what an idea champion learned about the local context came from experiences that required him or her to observe the organization in action. It was during committee meetings with fellow administrators or with teachers, or during informal conversations with principals, parents, or district support staff, or other encounters that a sense of the local environment developed. Getting a feel for what occurs at the interface between an organizational structure and the individuals in the organization is what gaining political knowledge is all about.

Consistent Level of Involvement

The cases suggest that an idea champion must be involved at all stages of the adoption process, although the champion's baton may be passed. In Martin-Mason and in Riverwell, the idea champion was the same individual from start to finish. In Dorchester, the role was transferred up the ladder of hierarchical authority as the idea gained momentum. In all three school districts that eventually did vote to adopt the innovation of the Junior Kindergarten, there was an intensive involvement of the individual functioning as the idea champion throughout the decision-making process. The case of Beachwood demonstrates what happens when this rule is breached. When the district administrator dropped out of the process after about nine months of direct involvement in the committee deliberations, the principal who stepped in as committee chair had less positional authority and interest. The "problem" of "what to do with those kids" did not go away, but the framework in which the problem was being discussed irrevocably changed.

Is Perceived as Trustworthy by Powerful Coalitions

If a recommendation for a change is factually based, then those seeking to influence a decision with facts understand that they must be perceived by the decision-makers as being trustworthy as well as knowledgeable. A group that takes a stand about an issue still needs to rely upon at least one or more individuals in the group to be the spokesperson to the decision-makers. Being represented by an individual regarded as both knowledgeable and trustworthy is what gives influence to the stand taken by the group.

In each of the cases, the idea champion had to identify the critical groups within the organization. Furthermore, the idea champion then had to be certain that the groups' membership perceived his or her knowledge about the proposed change to be complete and in concert with the needs of the local school district. In the three school districts where a decision was made to adopt the Junior Kindergarten innovation, the idea champions were perceived as being knowledgeable and trustworthy by those critical groups. In addition to the superintendent, the group approached by each idea champion during the discussion phase was the Kindergarten and 1st-grade teachers. In addition, the elementary principals were consulted in Martin-Mason. In Riverwell, it was the parents' group that was approached as the third critical group.

Another aspect of trustworthiness is associated with a perceived lack of personal gain with the outcome of the decision process. The idea champion was not necessarily a critical stakeholder who would experience direct impact as a result of the proposed innovation. In fact, being viewed as a stakeholder has the potential of jeopardizing the ability of the idea champion to keep the idea moving forward if he or she is seen as promoting the idea merely for professional gain, as was the case, to some extent, in Beachwood. A person who is successful in being an idea champion determines early in the change process the amount of identifiable connection he or she can have with a stakeholder role. Sensitivity to the local political context becomes the crucial variable in perceiving or knowing the acceptable stance. In districts where the trust level was generally high between the school board and the idea champion who had organizational access to them, serving as an advocate was acceptable. In districts where the trust level between the board and the administration was relatively low, efforts were made to distance the idea champion from advocates and stakeholders. The difference was not a suburban versus rural issue, but more clearly perceived to be tied to the presence or absence of trust among the organization's members.

The Gatekeepers

Another actor in the structure of an organization who also takes on a political character is the gatekeeper. Organizations are often concerned with the amount and flow of information into and out of its structure, and communication flows are often restricted in order to decrease problems of information overload. The person within the structure of the organization through whom information passes as it goes to units where it is most needed and who restricts it from those where it is not needed is the gatekeeper. Such a person prevents an overload of messages coming from lower levels and the outside from reaching the upper echelons of hierarchical responsibility (Rogers and Agarwala-Rogers 1976: 92).

Bypassing a Hierarchical Constrictor

The role of organizational gatekeeper in each of the districts surveyed was within the purview of the role of building principal. One of the Beachwood principals explained that her job was to "sift out the good from the bad, and the bandwagon jumping from what's really worthwhile." In Martin-Mason, one of the principals declared that his responsibility was to determine whether the innovation "fit in within … the direction or goals of the [school] committee." The principal has the power to stop the idea from receiving any further organizational consideration in both suburban districts. While the gatekeeper role belongs to the principal in the rural districts as well, the ability of individuals to use informal access to higher administrators limits this power to some extent. In three out of the four cases, the idea champion was hierarchically on par with or above the principal. This allowed the entry level of the innovation to be such that it was automatically guaranteed at least minimal consideration by the highest level of the organization's decision-makers. It also meant that in three out of four districts, an innovation having district-wide impact did not have to go through the narrow, personalized filter of information gatekeeping, a function that principals normally served within the organization. In the fourth district, Dorchester Unified, the sequential involvement of three persons in the role of idea champion appears to substantiate the premise that an innovation generally needs to be affirmed by the gatekeeper (a principal) before it can be organizationally addressed, but needs to be handed off to someone who has direct access up and down the hierarchy.

In addition to the limited access that a principal has to directly interact with the school board, school districts generally do not seem to look favorably upon a principal who takes on the role of an idea champion for a district-wide innovation. Rather, principals are expected, and in most cases limited, to being an idea champion only in his or her own building. Changes being sought by a principal that have district-wide impact are usually viewed with much skepticism and, in Riverwell, the principal-gatekeeper-idea champion had to be replaced with the curriculum director during the preparations of a proposal to the board. An assumption of strong parochial priorities often overwhelms and can discredit a suggestion or idea coming from a principal for a district-wide change. Principals who enjoy long-term survival with their peers somehow learn of this "rule of the game" early on.

A Coalition of Gatekeepers

The gatekeeper role was initially circumvented in the Martin-Mason School District because the idea champion was directly involved with the teachers' group who was already confronting various Kindergarten issues. The curriculum director, as the idea champion, knew that she had to gain the approval of the principals' group before she could proceed to present the idea to the school board for approval. This was because the principals had been, as a group, organizationally vested with the role of filtering new ideas before they could be considered by district administration. Although in private the group opinion was not unanimous regarding the Junior Kindergarten, a majority of principals agreed to support the adoption of that innovation. Consequently, the public display of support among the gatekeepers appeared unanimous, which gave notice to the school board that the idea had been thoroughly considered.

The gatekeeper in Riverwell, the principal, was also the initial idea champion. This permitted the idea to be considered and brought forward in rapid succession. Within six months, the innovation was discovered, briefly discussed, and adopted. This quick action was in sharp contrast to the deliberations of more than two years in the Beachwood School District about whether or not to adopt the Junior Kindergarten idea. The difference can be found in the immediate access that the Riverwell idea champion/gatekeeper had to the decision arena. As a contrast, in Beachwood, the idea champion stepped away from that role after one year of committee discussions. The person taking his place as the committee chair, a principal (in other words, a gate-keeper), was not convinced that the innovation was the best possible solution to the issue. As a result, he was able to effectively stall the progress and the move towards its adoption. The role of the Beachwood gatekeeper served to keep the deliberations going to a point where a decision was never reached; the idea was tabled indefinitely.

Power and Influence

Most decision situations involve multiple key decision-makers, each with a different basis of control and information sources. It has already been noted that role definition is highly context-specific. This view was confirmed by this study, which found that nearly any role had the potential of being defined differently in the four districts, and also by different individuals within each district. For example, within a district teachers rarely hold the same expectations for the superintendent, and the same is true for teachers' view of the role they expected parents or school board members to play in decision-making. Somewhere between the personal expectations of the role occupant and the expectations that the other participants in the organization have for that position lies the ambiguous definition of each key actor's role.

The defined parameters of each role also shifted as the organizational membership changed. The concept of the role as defined by the organization appeared to be not only context-specific but also time-specific within the district. This was because ongoing changes in district personnel served to continually reshape and redefine organizational roles. Thus, for example, the role of the superintendent and the school board changed substantially in Dorchester Unified with the coming of the new superintendent, while the new elementary principal's high level of competent curriculum and classroom knowledge permitted the Riverwell actors to redefine the role of the superintendent as "a keeper of the budget." Despite this ambiguity, respondents in this study had no difficulty identifying positions that were perceived to be vested with positional authority. The superintendent, the director of curriculum, the principals, and the school board as a group were all identified as having organizationally sanctioned authority.

The Role of the Superintendent

There are two critical features to understand in the role of the superintendent. The first view involves the static dimensions of the role itself. Simply by virtue of the hierarchical structure of education, the superintendent is the one person with the most direct link to the school board as a unit. Such positional authority, however, did not necessarily mean that this person was also the most powerful player in the arena when a curricular or instructional policy change is indicated. In fact, the power of both the idea champion and the gatekeeper, as discussed earlier, must be considered when viewing the triad of "power brokers" in the change process framework.

Whatever the locale, the role itself of the superintendent is critical to understanding and analyzing educational decision-making. The positional authority vested in the superintendent's position required the idea champion to have the superintendent agree with the perception that a problem existed and that a change was indicated. This did not mean that the superintendent had to initially endorse the idea champion's proposed solution, but only to tacitly acknowledge that a problem and a possible solution were before him or her. If the superintendent did not acknowledge or agree that the problem existed, then the idea champion had to overtly or covertly orchestrate the formation of a coalition to voice common concerns about the problem and broad support of the proposed solution. All four of the superintendents in this study agreed with the concerns expressed by the idea champion about the gap in services for some Kindergarten children. However, they were generally not aware of the scope of the problem – that is, that it was dormant in the garbage can – until open discussions began where they heard from teachers and parents as well. The fact that a single innovation addressed the concerns of so many different constituent groups made support of the innovation by the superintendent uncontroversial. The decision to advocate, however, for the innovation's adoption was left by the superintendent in each case to the discretion and leadership capabilities of the idea champion.

Each of the superintendents made it clear that if teachers and parents are united in seeking the same change, then almost any idea will be likely to receive administrative support, unless a shortage of resources stands in the way. In the two districts where the superintendent was considered effective by all parties – Beachwood and Dorchester – the prevailing view was supportive of a superintendent-led organization, and the "rule of utilizing appropriate channels" to bring an idea or concern forward was clearer to all participants. In the districts where the superintendent's role was weaker – Riverwell and Martin-Mason – informal communication channels were more often used to gain access to the "real" decision-makers. In a sense, not following the hierarchical rules for school district communication became the new rule. This is a specific case of the general point that roles in school districts are subject to frequent modification, depending on historical circumstances and the characteristics of individual occupants. The roles of the critical actors must be reexamined (albeit not always with great consciousness or care) each time a new problem and solution enter the decision process.

Power = Authority + Influence for District Actors

Positional authority constitutes only half of the perception of who was viewed to be powerful within the organization. Most respondents also believed that the degree of influence that one had was the other critical half. Bringing positional authority and personal influence together resulted in the perception that an individual had power within the organization. There were groups and individuals who were identified by many respondents as influential. Those named were often individual teachers and teachers as a group. However, in no school district did these individuals or groups possess positional authority from which to exercise their influence with ease. School administrators confirmed this as fact, noting that individual teachers possessed influence primarily or only at the building level. Thus, our study modifies Daft and Becker's (1978) finding that curricular innovations tend to be introduced by teachers. This may be the case where the innovations are confined to a specific building, but is not true for district-wide innovations, where teachers and parents are largely disenfranchised.

All school district leaders in this study unquestioningly viewed parents as having a significant amount of power, although few parents concurred due to their lack of a positional base. However, the power of parents in the rural districts was far greater than in the suburban districts, where the "rules of the game" prohibited direct access to the superintendent and school board. In suburban districts, parent roles were largely confined to committee work, where they had less opportunity to exercise influence. But, if influence does not make individuals or groups powerful in the decision process, neither does positional authority alone. Riverwell and Martin-Mason, where the superintendents did not have a high degree of personal influence over curricular change, are cases in point. On the other hand, the director of curriculum in each of these districts was perceived as having prominent influence in curricular matters. Consequently, they had greater power within the organizational process to effect the adoption of the Junior Kindergarten innovation.

The superintendents of Beachwood and Dorchester Unified districts were believed to have a high degree of both authority and influence. Yet, in those districts, as in the other two, the superintendent's use of power in the decision to adopt or not adopt the Junior Kindergarten was indirect. Their power was important, but it was exercised behind the scenes and was not well understood by most of the actors who were not intimately involved.

The Intersection of Power and Decision-making: The School Board

Of the four school boards, those in Riverwell and Martin-Mason exerted the most active influence, and these were also the districts where the superintendent was perceived to have less power in certain situations. Attempts to exercise influence by individual board members was most visible when they increased the perceived uncertainty about the outcome by asking a lot of questions. Thus, reducing unanticipated questions is seen as a key to controlling the board, as is evidence that powerful coalitions support a recommended decision. Mustering substantiation of good process and the involvement of multiple constituents also increases trust in the recommendation. This feature was prevalent in all four of the districts studied. However, in all four of the districts in this study, the school board appeared to be as concerned as the administrators to maintain at least a veneer of cordiality and cohesiveness.

The Primacy of Context

Our data suggest that any theory of organizational decision-making must have, at its core, the understanding that change is context-specific. This is true from the very first moment that an idea champion encounters a possible solution to a problem residing in the local garbage can of unsolved problems to the moment when the proposed change is brought before the school board for a vote. The events that happen between those two endpoints are inextricably tied into the local fabric.

Woven together to form the local context are two dimensions. In one direction there are the structural dimensions of the local school district as an organization. Intersecting those lines is the broad array of individuals who play a role in the delivery of local educational services. Taken together they form the context in which decisions are made about the education of the children living and growing in the local environment. In the cases that we have presented above, this context-dominant feature is possibly best exemplified by the way in which it influenced the communication linkages that were established, and how they were used.

Formal Communication Channels

Because a school district is a formal organization, all persons who come into contact with it assume that there are prescribed communication channels. Part of that assumption is based upon our experiences with the organizational expectations and characteristics of schools as we progressed through the system. Typically, we are socialized to believe in positional authority, and to expect that negative sanctions were entirely possible and acceptable within the realm of control that the organization is permitted to have over its members.

Teachers seemed to experience anxiety about circumventing the formal communication process. However, differences in the willingness of rural and suburban teachers to seek a forum in which to voice their concerns were apparent. Rural teachers indicated that they were more likely to bypass the middle levels of the communication hierarchy and go directly to the top if they felt that they were not being heard. Teachers in suburban districts viewed the prescribed formal communication channels much more deferentially: teachers and psychologists considered the act of going around their building principal as taking a risk. The potential negative sanctions that the principal could bring to bear upon the work relationship between the principal and the teacher were stronger than the possible benefit to be gained with voicing a particular concern at a higher level.

In all four districts, parents and community members expressed a belief in the importance of formal communication channels within any organization. Parents further explained that if a problem or a concern existed, they would go either to the building principal or to the top of the administrative ladder. None of them mentioned that they would initially seek the director of curriculum, for instance, as an arbiter of their concerns. Perhaps their childhood experiences with positional authority have led them to the assumption that only persons in the top roles have the power to resolve their problem. It is perceived that using formal channels and seeking the persons at the highest possible endpoint of a channel will at least generate a formal response in most cases. Formal communication systems were significantly more important in the suburban districts of Beachwood and Martin-Mason, where control over agendas appeared, at times, to be almost an obsession.

The use of informal channels in all of the districts studied was instrumental in garnering public support for an idea. Most parents and community members noted (in the same breath as they expressed confidence in the formal channels) that they felt comfortable making direct contact with the superintendent or members of the school board. The basis for that feeling of access had to do with one's rights as a parent and a taxpayer.

Informal Communication: Rural/Suburban Differences
There was a clear difference between rural and suburban school districts in the use and impact of informal channels of communication. The smaller the district size, the more frequently were informal channels used to convey concerns and ideas. In Riverwell, the smallest district, informal conversations with decision-makers at all levels was the dominant form of organizational communication. In Beachwood, the largest district, informal conversations did not generally lead to any formal organizational response unless a committee was officially convened to discuss the concern or idea.

In a small town, daily contact was a frequent occurrence among the teachers and the decision-makers. It seemed that a strong sense of obligation to the wishes and concerns of the community was a dominant feature in both Riverwell and Dorchester. Meeting the needs of the local constituency appeared to take precedence over the need to follow a prescribed approach to focus organizational attention on a problem. Larger and more administratively complex districts, such as Martin-Mason and Beachwood, required the use of formal channels for both professionals and community members. The prime filter for those concerns was the building principal, and the only other way to have a concern addressed was to form a committee (in other words, a coalition) to force a particular level of the district structure to respond.

The more extensive informal channels of communication in rural districts increase the potential number of powerful actors in a decision, and permit more political behavior to occur among the individual participants in the change process. A more complex hierarchical structure such as is found in larger suburban school districts, by its design, limits the potential impact of the behavior of individuals. Thus, a rural school district operates more often in a "garbage can" mode. Perhaps a successful rural school administrator is consciously or subconsciously aware of this tendency and adjusts his or her management of the local political context accordingly.

In rural districts informal communication often involved spanning the boundary between the community of professionals and the community of parents, and occurred in face-to-face or telephone contact between teachers and parents, or between parents and administrators. In suburban districts, boundary-spanning at lower levels was infrequent, and the most prevalent informal linkages occurred when teachers talked among themselves and then informally approached a principal for an initial response. Suburban parents might informally approach an administrator or a school board member first, but would almost always be told that they must go through regularized channels to have their concerns addressed in any way.

Prevalent informal communication led, in the two rural cases, to quick action on the decision about Junior Kindergarten. However, in neither Riverwell nor Dorchester Unified did the implications of the decision appear to have been fully considered. On the one hand, having a more complex structure responding to informal pressure may result in an apparent lack of responsiveness, but may then allow for a more complete examination of the idea or concern. On the other hand, the heavy reliance on formal communication channels in Beachwood and Martin-Mason meant that at times the right questions were not being asked because insufficient informal exploration of the meaning and value of the solution had not taken place.

The research literature devotes a great deal of attention to the purported benefits of strong informal channels or a strong hierarchical structure. Still, such discussion may be moot because the characteristic use of informal communication is essentially an attribute of the community, and not an easily controllable feature of school district administrative style. Rather, administrators must understand how communication characteristically operates in their community, and how it will affect the policy process.

Informal Communication and the Management of Coalitions

There appears to be a natural fit between the formal roles of the curriculum director and the informal role of the idea champion. The idea champion carried the message of the educational problem and the proposed solution among the various sectors. He or she was able to articulate from one segment to another the questions and the concerns that each segment felt. As a result, strategies emerged that were then used to answer or counteract any negative reaction. The outcome of the shuttle activity was to develop a base of knowledge and trust among the stakeholders and constituents. This translated into formal influence at the time that the school board met to consider the innovation's adoption. The shuttle activity also permitted the idea champion to sense any positive or negative coalitions that were beginning to emerge. The shuttle activity thus allowed the Riverwell idea champion to slowly "feed" the influential parent coalition information he possessed about the innovation, and then to gauge their response to his suggestions at each measured step. The Martin-Mason idea champion, likewise, knew that the principals' group was the primary coalition in the district to have the crucial voice in that which is approved and goes forward, and that which has a quiet, internal demise. With coalitions evident, quietly working out the details and answering their questions privately was the only means by which a public vote of confidence in the proposed district-wide change would occur. It was the understanding and utilization of this political knowledge that enabled the idea champion to be successful in having the idea be adopted in the three cases where it finally reached the school board and the decision arena.

Implications

The findings from this study of the process of school district decision-making led us inevitably to the intersection of school management issues and educational policy concerns. We will not attempt to draw an exhaustive set of conclusions in this last section, but to highlight those that we believe to be most important.

In the preceding section we argued that, to make sense of school change efforts, it is absolutely imperative that all initiatives for change be viewed as a reflection of persons and local conditions interacting within a given period of time about a single issue and its attending concerns. Yet innovation and change are not entirely idiosyncratic and singularly specific as has sometimes been argued by theorists of "non-rationality" in organizations. District-wide change, indeed, can be better managed when the context is understood and when local policies address that context.

The management of decision-making and change must consider the three elements that were found to be at the heart of the policy adoption process:

1. knowing and playing by the local "rules of the game";
2. understanding and using the local communication channels to best advantage; and
3. acknowledging the roles of the key actors – the idea champion, the gatekeeper, and the superintendent – the discussion and decision stages, with a view to the sense of trust within the organization regarding their knowledge and their motives.

There are two related problems that superintendents encounter when "managing" policy decisions and innovation. The first is the need to have only good-quality ideas put before the school board for a policy decision, while the second is to appear careful as well as fiscally cautious when promoting change. However, we saw differences between the superintendents in terms of their comfort level with the management of the turbulent garbage can of problems and solutions. For instance, an authoritarian superintendent generally manages the garbage can with an iron hand in an attempt to prevent any "public surprises." A weak superintendent, however, will generally allow the other political actors in the district to supervise the garbage can, which generates the perception that decisions are often out of administrative control and subject to local whims. An effective superintendent, on the other hand, manages the garbage can with a balanced and realistic view of the job as well as of him- or herself. As a policy formulator, apart from the policy-maker role of the school board, an effective superintendent is able to anticipate and work within the garbage can while still being able to meet his or her own needs to maintain a strong professional face in the district.

This leads us to a second, related problem facing superintendents, which is one that they apparently handle less well: encouraging good ideas to percolate up to the decision-makers for discussion and possible adoption. Without incentives on the part of teachers, parents, and middle-level administrators to bring forward new ideas, the chances for maintaining a vital, adaptive educational system are much diminished according to many organizational theorists (Weick 1976; Daft and Huber 1987; Chubb and Moe 1990). Yet school district decision processes are structured such that commu-nication upward is highly constrained.

Policy-makers need to acknowledge the critical importance of the principal as the organizational gatekeeper of potential change. As a middle manager and a constrictor in the flow of information, a principal has power over both sides of the hierarchical struc-ture – that is, the superintendent as lead policy formulator on one side and the teachers as practitioners on the other. Otherwise effective superintendents, especially in larger districts, have little access to teachers' ideas for change. To stimulate more sources of ideas for change and improvement in curriculum and instruction, school administrators should expand the number of individuals who are legitimated boundary-spanners. Increasing the number of persons who are sanctioned and encouraged to serve in a boundary-spanning capacity will broaden the range and perspective of ideas brought into the district to be given at least some form of local consideration. With the limited array of boundary-spanners, principals are equally constricted in the adoption of inno-vation. The search for answers to local building needs and concerns is as hampered as the search process for district-wide change.

Political behavior is regularly used as a means by which policy-makers, and others, reduce the true uncertainty found in the management of garbage cans. Finding an answer to a problem can be expected to be difficult; discussing and implementing a possible solution can be even worse. This is because the local "rules of the game" are, unless in transition, embedded in the local context and consequently difficult to change. Therefore, political behavior is often necessary and helpful in understanding and managing the rules and the local context. To manage the garbage can is to manage the attending risks and the range of possible information associated with the change. Policy-makers who have a clear sense of the goals and direction of the school district will likely have an equally clear sense of where the risks lie when a proposed change is put before them. This study showed that the more abstract the risk concerns became, as was the case in Beachwood, the slower the decision process became. Conversely, the presence of clear-cut, definable risks such as resource issues were much more easily addressed and solved in the other three districts.

Research knowledge was not used to make a decision in any of the successful adop-tion efforts, but the lack of it was used as one of many *post hoc* justifications for not adopting the innovation. Policy-makers need to become more aware of the part and place that research information has during the discussion phases prior to the moment of decision. In this discussion, we are not advocating any position that policy-makers should take with regard to the existence or non-existence of research information being available before a decision to change is made. Rather, what is important is the need to be aware of who, if anyone, is using research information during the decision discussions.

Well-considered policy management is inextricably tied to successful school adminis-tration, and successful administration is highly dependent upon understanding and managing the local context. Successful educational administrators successfully manage change. Those who don't seek to control and manage the process won't have long to wait before the process begins to control them. Being proactive and aware of the dynamics of change will enhance the work lives of the individuals involved in school administration. It will also serve to enhance the health of the school district as a viable organization.

Notes

1. Originally published as K. Wahlstrom and K.S. Louis (1993) "Adoption revisited: Decision-making and school district policy." In S. Bacharach and R. Ogawa (eds), *Advances in Research and Theories of School Management and Educational Policy, Vol. 1*: 61–119. Greenwich, CT: JAI. This version has been edited to reduce its length.
2. This section has been heavily edited, and technical appendices have been eliminated.

References

Allison, G.T. (1971) *Essence of Decision*. Boston: Little, Brown and Company.

Bacharach, S.B. and E.J. Lawler (1980) *Power and Policies in Organizations*. San Francisco: Jossey Bass.

Chubb, J. and T. Moe (1990) *Politics, Markets, and America's Schools*. Washington, DC: Brookings Institution.

Cohen, M. and J. March (1972) "A garbage can model of organizational choice." *Administrative Science Quarterly* 17(1): 1–25.

——, J.G. March, and J.P. Olsen (1972) "A garbage can model of organizational choice." *Administrative Science Quarterly* 17: 1–25.

Common, D. L. (1983) "Power: The missing concept in the dominant model of school change." *Theory Into Practice* 22(3): 203–10.

Cyert, R.M. and J.G. March (1963) *A Behavioral Theory of the Firm*. Englewood Cliffs, NJ: Prentice-Hall.

Daft, R.L. and S.W. Becker (1978) *The Innovative Organization: Innovation Adoption in School Organizations*. New York: Elsevier North-Holland, Inc.

—— and G.P. Huber (1987) "How organizations learn: A communication framework." In S.B. Bacharach and N. DiTomaso (eds), *Research in the Sociology of Organizations* Vol. 5: 1–36. Greenwich, CT: JAI.

Fullan, M. with S. Stiegelbauer (1991) *The New Meaning of Educational Change*. New York: Teachers College Press.

Kanter, R.M. (1977) *Men and Women of the Corporation*. New York, NY: Basic Books, Inc.

Louis, K.S. (1982) "Multi site/multi method studies: An overview." *American Behavioral Scientist* 26(6): 6–22.

—— and R.A. Dentler (1988) "Knowledge use and school improvement." *Curriculum Inquiry* 18: 32–62.

—— and M.B. Miles (1990) *Improving Urban High Schools: What Works and Why*. New York: Teachers College Press.

——, S. Rosenblum, and J. Molitor (1981) *Strategies for School Improvement*. Washington, DC: National Institute of Education.

Miles, M.B. and A.M. Huberman (1984) *Qualitative Data Analysis: A Sourcebook of New Methods*. Beverly Hills, CA: Sage.

Perrow, C.B. (1970) *Organizational Analysis: A Sociological View*. Belmont, CA: Brooks/Cole Publishing Company.

Pettigrew, A.M. (1973) *The Politics of Organizational Decision-making*. London: Tavistock.

Pfeffer, J. (1981) *Power in Organizations*. Marshfield, MA: Pitman Publishing Inc.

—— and G. Salancik (1974) "Organizational decision making as a political process: The case of a University budget." *Administrative Science Quarterly* 19: 135–51.

Rogers, E.M. and R. Agarwala-Rogers (1976) *Communication in Organizations*. New York: The Free Press.

Rosenblum, S. and K.S. Louis (1981) *Stability and Change: Innovation in an Educational Context*. New York: Plenum Press.

Sproull, L., S. Weiner, and D. Wolf (1978) *Organizing an Anarchy: Belief Bureaucracy and Politics in the National Institute of Education*. Chicago: University of Chicago Press.

Warren, D.L. (1968) "Power, visibility, and conformity in formal organizations." *American Sociological Review* 33: 951–69.

Weick, K.E. (1976) "Educational organizations as loosely coupled systems." *Administrative Science Quarterly* 21: 1–19.

12

Creating Community in Reform: Images of Organizational Learning in Inner-city Schools[1]

Introduction

The current school reform movement focuses on *structural changes* (block scheduling, teacher teaming, and multi-age classrooms) and *curricular changes* (cooperative learning, inquiry method, problem-based science and mathematics) as the main features of effective schools. Less attention has been paid in the reform literature on altering the culture of the school. We argue that organizational learning theory provides teachers and principals a useful model to begin the re-design of school cultures to address student needs better, and we document this claim with case studies from recent research.

Building an organization's ability to learn has been a key element in discussions of innovation in both restructured schools and businesses (see, for example, Hedberg 1981; Daft and Huber 1987; Senge 1990). Organizational learning as a model for school reform suggests that people working within school organizations are part of a shared, social construction of meaning *common* to all members of the school organization. Images of the learning organization evoke assumptions about the members of the school organization as more participative, more intrinsically motivated, and engaged in learning with greater personal effort than the other organizational models. The model assumes that learning takes place in groups and cannot be reduced to a random accumulation of individuals' knowledge (Louis 1994), and that learning occurs within a framework of systematic collection and focus on information.

In a learning school teachers work together to gather more information about their teaching and their content areas and then discuss, share, and critique the new ideas so that all members understand and can use – when they feel appropriate – the new information. An organizational learning perspective emphasizes the benefits that accrue as a consequence of collective, regular processes in which teachers and administrators work together around issues of practice rather than more radical change models that emphasize "reengineering" or "restructuring."

A Model of Organizational Learning

Organizational learning is marked by a variety of processes that enhance the school's capacity to gain, use, and retrieve necessary information. These processes are organizational memory, the development of a shared knowledge base, and the ability to store and access needed information.

Organizational Memory

Collective memory is an essential feature of culture that influences the ability of the school organization to learn. Our research suggests three possible consequences of varied forms of organizational memory on school culture. When *positive memories* from previous learning situations are attached to current situations, change efforts are enhanced. Conversely, negative *memories* can act as barriers to new learning efforts. In our work in new schools, we have also observed that the *absence of memory* can inhibit change. Without an adequate base of experience from which to draw, teachers can be reticent to begin new learning activities. As a new school works to shake out the forces that will influence their embryonic culture, learning may be set aside as too risky an activity to be attempted. Presumably, some level of both social and structural support is needed before schools can begin the difficult task of organizational learning.

Our successful cases of organizational learning suggest that once acquired, knowledge then must be stored and retrieved to be of use to the organization. Information that is held within an individual department or by an individual faculty member or administrator is of little use to the organization as a whole. Information must be stored and understood at numerous sites around the organization and organizational memory must be shared with new employees in order for it to have an impact on change processes. It is this process of storage and retrieval of information and the emotional tenor which accompanies learning that contribute to the accumulation of organizational memories.

Knowledge Base and Development

Traditionally, individual learning has been defined by the notions of acquisition, storage, and retrieval (Lave 1984). Organizational learning differs in that it requires that knowledge have a shared, social construction common to all members of the school organization. It is in the social construction and development of the knowledge base that organizational learning differs from individual learning. However, knowledge may come from many sources.

Individually held knowledge

Teachers, through pre-service and in-service experiences, enter schools equipped with large, often disparate, foundations of information related to both content and pedagogy. Such individually held knowledge is often difficult for colleagues to access and utilize. Although some new structures, such as teaching-teams or peer-coaching relationships, hold the promise of becoming effective structures in which individually held knowledge may be accessed by other staff members (Kruse and Louis 1997), they often fail to meet this objective (Hargreaves 1994). Isolating teachers in individual classrooms, departments and grade-level configurations militates against the efficient or effective sharing of individually held knowledge. Further, the endemic uncertainty of the teaching profession exacerbates the problem. Teachers, many of whom work in schools characterized by low levels of trust and respect, and a lack of effective communication structures, rarely participate in conversations that require sharing professional knowledge (Louis and Kruse 1995).

Knowledge Generated by Self-appraisal

New information is generated as the result of district or state-level accountability policies, as well as internal action research and evaluation. These sources of data can be turned into commonly held knowledge when they provide teachers and administrators with a common vocabulary and incentives to discuss "findings." However, this will not occur in the absence of structures and routines that support learning. Shared planning periods, regular faculty meetings devoted to discussion, and frequent lateral communication networks, provide an organizational design for acquiring information (Cohen 1991). In the absence of supporting structures, discussion of evaluative information is often viewed as threatening or shameful.

Knowledge gained by organized search efforts

Finally, we suggest that schools can enter into organized search efforts to gain new information. As schools search for solutions to identified problems, knowledge is generated that both further defines the problem and suggests alternative actions. Search efforts vary depending on the absorptive capacity of the organization to take in and use new ideas to create alternative organizational structures and ideas (Louis 1994). Our case studies suggest that relying on only one search procedure or source of outside knowledge can be detrimental to the overall health and longevity of the school culture. We submit that the activity of knowledge base development is tightly linked to that of a third characteristic of organizational learning: information distribution and interpretation.

Information Distribution and Interpretation

Information distribution is a process by which knowledge from different sources is shared, while information interpretation is a process in which organizationally distributed information is assigned one or more commonly understood interpretations (Huber 1991). Within a school, multiple opportunities for information distribution and interpretation exist. They may be associated with the belief structures, frames of reference and organizationally based social constructions; the cues and feedback related to organizational symbols and shared understandings; or the process of unlearning old, now replaced, practices and beliefs. Information distribution involves more than placing photocopied articles in teacher mailboxes, nor is it one-way transfer of information from one who knows to one who doesn't. Instead, we think of it as the construction of meaningful contexts and conditions under which new routines are practiced. Individual effort is expended in the learning and understanding of the new curriculum or instructional methodology. Organizationally, however, learners are also acquiring the embodied understanding of how to act collectively on the knowledge. It is this common interpretation of the "good practice" implications of new knowledge that permits individual teachers to apply it in their classrooms in ways that are mutually supportive and consistent.

Organization Learning in Agassiz Elementary School

Agassiz Elementary School is located at the edges of a sprawling school district in a Southern district. From 1981 to 1988, the city's school system suffered from the chaotic effects of court-ordered desegregation imposed without significant assertive efforts by local educational and political leaders effort to make it work. In 1988, after six years of "white flight," a new superintendent began a major effort to revitalize the system using a combination of open-enrolment magnet programs, school-based management, and selective relief from prescriptive state curricula, personnel, and testing regulations. According to one district administrator, Agassiz was one of the most enthusiastic participants in the revitalization effort: "To me [it] is really a showplace of true entrepreneurship, site-based management, parent involvement, locational budgeting, children's involvement."

Agassiz, which is located in an all-white neighborhood, has been successful in attracting African-American children from other parts of the city because of its reputation as innovative but caring, and at the cutting edge, particularly in the arts and technology. Both white and African-American teachers and parents view it as a school that provides an excellent education for children of all races, and the quality of instruction, particularly in mathematics and reading, is high. For an elementary school, Agassiz is relatively large, enrolling approximately 650 students and employing 39 full-time teachers, two full-time administrators, a guidance counselor and a part-time librarian. All but one of the professional staff is female; 75 per cent are white. One-third of the students are poor, receiving federally subsidized lunch.

Key Features of Agassiz: Learning from Each Other
Agassiz, like many forward-looking schools, has a broad array of innovative efforts, ranging from an active Advisory Council composed of teachers and parents, to special programs designed to increase student learning, particularly among students who are less

well prepared. But perhaps one of the most obvious features of Agassiz is the level of enthusiasm expressed by teachers about their work, and the degree to which they view the school as more demanding than what would be required in other schools in the district. The principal, Mrs Cole, said: "I think our pressures are internal ... we could do half of what we're doing and be successful ... but it's not enough for us." Other teachers voice the sense of pressure and support that is felt from peers: "There is a 'healthy competitiveness' in the school ... [but] here we are all involved ... growing as a unit ... it takes a team effort" and "Nobody is just pulling a paycheck ... teachers ... believe [that you should] do your best ... learn new ideas ... and seek outside views." Many teachers also mentioned that the sense of being constantly driven to improve meant that not all of their peers would be happy at Agassiz.

In addition, teachers pointed to other more subtle features that differentiate Aggasiz from more typical schools. Teachers spend a lot of time talking to each other, and helping each other to interpret both ideas and their own instructional practice. Much of this occurs on Saturdays or after school because the schedule does not allow for extensive meeting time during the regular day. One teacher reported how powerful these interpretive experiences could be:

What you're talking about is meeting that starts at 4.15 and finishes at 7.15, so it's a long meeting ... [we observe each other teaching through a one-way mirror]. I remember the first time it went [poorly], because everybody was afraid to hurt everybody's feelings ... I'll never forget when Greta came out of there and said, "All right, pan me. Tell me so I can grow." She was the one who turned the tide ... we're all at a level where we come out of there saying, "help me, how can I help this child."

Teachers also comment on the school's focus on mutual planning for improvement:

[We have a faculty study group] for grades K–2. There are a variety of opinions among those in the group. This discussion provides [us with] growth and exposure to other people's ideas ... It pushes [us] to think that [our own] way is not the only way to approach things.

One teacher emphasized that Agassiz's environment is totally different from a previous school that she had been in, in which differences of opinion were viewed as signs of hostility. Dialogue among teachers has recently moved beyond discussions of coordinated planning for curriculum, to more fundamental topics related to assumptions about teaching and learning. As one teacher noted "Dialoguing [has been] going on at grade level meetings etc. ... The reading is all [we] need to get started [on more fundamental discussions]."

Intellectual Leadership from the Principal
Everyone both inside and outside of the school agrees that much of the credit for Agassiz's steady devotion to the improvement of education for all students is the result of the

principal's efforts. According to Mrs Cole herself, a key to her work is to provide opportunities for open discussion in "safe" conditions where people feel free to take risks: "Our trust level has grown ... we used to say no to new ideas ... We've gotten comfortable with sharing things that don't work ... that have not been successful." Teachers concur with this observation: "our principal wants us to succeed. If I make a mistake she would never fuss, she would just say let's see [if] we can make it better."

In addition, Cole keeps up-to-date on current issues in education, although she admits that she has learned a lot from teachers in the building. Her expertise is readily available to teachers, largely through informal communication. By promoting teacher reading, Cole reminds teachers that the improvement process is a permanent feature of good schools, and that "essential questions" are more important than trivial ones; she guides teachers to critical discussion: "[At one meeting we asked] 'how long will this take?' Cole stated 'how long do we have? What are we doing, why are we doing, what can we do to make it better?'"

Part of Cole's style, which she describes as facilitative, is to express her own opinion but not to impose it on others, and teachers describe their sense that the school fosters the norm of continuous discussion, but does not demand closure or conformity: "I think in some schools the principal might say 'this [is] what we're gonna do' ... We have the freedom and trust from the principal that allow you to do whichever you choose."

Of course there are limits to this freedom. Although there is a strong belief that teachers are empowered and have an active voice in the school, Cole is ultimately in charge. All but one of the teachers views her exercise of the decision-making prerogative as fair.

Intellectual Leadership from Teachers

While the principal is behind the scenes stimulating discussion, the teachers view themselves as the intellectual leaders of the school. Every teacher points to some leadership role that they play in promoting discussion about critical educational ideas, either internally or with teachers outside the school. Teachers are used to sharing ideas, and see themselves as having a common base of knowledge. For example, curriculum decisions are often made informally, but informal information is shared. Teachers know or find out about new ideas and then try them in the classroom, and they keep the school's Curriculum Committee and the Advisory Committee informed. Sometimes the Curriculum Committee will poll teachers and get input about new efforts. Teachers emphasize that their norms lead to high levels of participation and learning: "It's reflective, it's significant ... It gives me courage to try ... It makes me curious and whets my appetite about 'hey, if they're doing it, then I should be doing it.'"

An experienced teacher, accustomed to using her own reflection as a key to improved practice, remarks on how different her experience is at Agassiz: "For a long time, the strongest professional development was a dialogue between myself and the literature, and refining it as I shared it with others ... That's changed totally." She describes a K–2 staff meeting, where two teachers were new and the others were less experienced than she:

One of the teachers there presented a lesson plan ... and I said, let's take 5 minutes and reflect on this. And they took off; it wasn't me any more, it wasn't me imparting information ... As we played around with different ideas, I felt I was indeed just as much a learner as anything else.

Perhaps as significant as the openness to learning from each other is the shift in Agassiz's teachers' collective sense of themselves as producers of knowledge. This is particularly apparent in their 'Restructuring Roundup' program, which provides a weekend conference environment for other teachers:

All the teachers perform mini sessions ... on whatever topic they want to do. We have reading, math, and science. Teachers come in from about four or five states. They pay $40 a day to attend sessions. They go to three or four a day ... That was our decision to do that ... If you prefer [to] not do a mini session, then you usually help ... Every single teacher has done one.

In fact, Restructuring Roundup, according to the Assistant Principal, has become a major focus for the professional development of individual teachers in Agassiz, turning the school into a producer rather than a consumer of knowledge. Teachers themselves recognize the magnitude of their accomplishments in terms of how the teacher role is played out: "Through Restructuring Roundup teachers are building a relationship among each other across the district, state, and region. There is also sharing of ideas among the teachers." While the required preparation is significant, usually involving most preparation periods and weekends during the spring, the sense of reward for individual Agassiz teachers exceeds the effort: "It was giving me confidence about what I've done ... it was personally rewarding [because] others were interested in what we had done ... the experience makes you more open to what others are doing."

While Restructuring Roundup is the clearest example of how teachers view themselves as educators, there are others as well. For example, a growing number of teachers have expanded their role to include teaching lower-income parents how to teach their own children:

When Agassiz had parent workshops at the school they would not get these parents. So they decided to go into the communities ... to do a parent workshop on a Saturday morning ... Parents were encouraged to bring children to help demonstrate the learning activities parents can do with their children.

For the teachers who have become involved, this effort demands an expanded repertoire of skills, which they have largely acquired from a dedicated colleague.

What Makes it Work?
The intellectual vibrancy and collective commitment to learning and improving at Agassiz are no accident. Agassiz has a dense informal network that encourages sharing and

collaboration between pairs of teachers, but most teachers point to structured settings that foster collegial stimulation. Particularly important are weekly grade-level meetings. According to one teacher the grade-level meetings have been "wonderful because we've [decided to integrate] the gifted classrooms with the regular classrooms. We're actually mixing up the kids", while another commented that "we all bring in our ideas ... and I think that's what helps us to grow. It's from the feedback from other teachers." In addition, 'faculty study' brings K–3 and 4–6 teachers together once a month to think more broadly about school needs. Each of the study groups was asked to develop a plan for professional development that reflects on the concerns of the group. The primary function of both groups is to provide safe settings for deeper reflection, with application to the here-and-now:

> It's something different for us because basically we're taking one topic and we're carrying it through ... I guess we're reflecting on ... what kinds of things we find important to us as a teacher, what kinds of things do we want our children to leave us with, what kinds of things do we want our kids to have when they come to us. So I think it's been really important, productive, more so than any of the others things because it applies so much to me here and now.

Equally important is the emergence of interdependent teaching roles, all of which are voluntary. Every teacher is expected to observe another teacher – on any grade level – for thirty minutes a month. Teachers agree that this is useful, as are the observations that the principal and assistant principal do of them, because they stimulate discussion with others that they do not always know well. In addition to peer observation, teachers have, at their own initiative, developed other ways of sharing information in their class-rooms. Both of the special-education teachers, for example, work with some teachers collaboratively, an approach that they initiated after attending a conference on inclusion several years ago; a "Teach for America" faculty member team-taught with one of the school's master teachers for her first year; and several teachers identified themselves as classroom mentors or were identified as such by others.

Although the district was strapped for funds, virtually all Agassiz teachers say that they spend their own money to go to conferences and workshops that can hone their skills. As the principal explained, all of the activity in the school has "made us stronger, ravenous for knowledge ... to have knowledge before we start changing things."

Organizational Learning in Okanagon Middle School

In 1981, the Okanagon Community School, a 6th–8th grade middle school located in a poor residential section of a large district, closed its doors after rumors of its ineffectiveness caused its enrolment to plummet. To the community's consternation, "their school" was replaced by a performing arts magnet, which attracted few students. In 1990, the school reopened as a non-selective "neighborhood magnet" after a year of planning by a team consisting of several teachers, the principal, representatives of social service agencies, citizen groups and local business. The school enrolls nearly 1,500 students from very diverse ethnic backgrounds (largely minority and immigrant). Over half receive free lunch.

"The Dream"

Okanagon was founded on the assumption that dedicated professionals could outwit a system that had failed to create a "level playing field." According to Bill Stone, the principal, the school's vision is both educational and political: "One advanced curriculum for all children in three years, so they can go to any high school in America and not get tracked out of the power class."

A significant part of the curriculum centers on interdisciplinary units, which are collaboratively developed to meet student learning needs. In addition to the focus on content relevance, the school has established "The Okanagon Standard," which consists of required student performance "challenges" ranging from community service to a research project. Although the faculty remains attuned to the state's curriculum standards and assessment procedures, local goals drive the teachers' passion: "We try to honor those things but I think that [our measures of performance are] more important. What ... they get here and what they do while they are here. And also what they do once they get into high school."

In addition to the emphasis on academics, teachers and administrators argue that their students need social and emotional support, both because of their age and because many of them come from a community context that does not provide enough security and certainty. To "make big, small," the school is divided into nine "Families" that form the basis of both teacher and student life, and are the primary unit for day-to-day work and decision-making. All core academic teachers (social studies, math, language, arts, and science) are assigned to a family; the remaining specialist teachers (special education, band, languages, and so on) are part of the "Discovery Family": "Basically, we say there are two levels of decision-making at this school: the Family and the Community Council. And it's sacred, that all decisions that have to do with teaching and learning are made only by Families ... ."

During the planning year, teachers decided that they would take on roles normally carried out by administrators and specialists in return for more teachers and smaller class sizes. In practice, this means that each Family has discretion over staffing, schedules, use of paraprofessionals and special-education resources, and, to some extent, curriculum. Family Leaders play a central role in the life of the school:

> as Family Leader, I am the representative on the [Community] Council ... I am a Mentor teacher, and I work with new teachers, student teachers, teaching assistants ... It's a key role in that I can keep a handle on the heartbeat of the school and the morale of what's going on.

It is not just Family Leaders who see a difference. The expanded teacher roles also have significance in working with students, creating closer ties with students that reinforce "The Dream" that the school will have a family-like character:

At our school we [teachers] are also counselors and administrators ... My complaint early in my teaching was that as a math teacher I didn't have an "in" [because students didn't write about themselves in my classes] ... At this school, since I'm a counselor, I get to see inside the children and ... I understand them more.

Teacher Intellectual Leadership and Teacher Learning
An unspoken aspect of "The Dream" is that faculty must take responsibility for the quality of professional work in the school. According to most, this is a never-ending task that requires that all faculty read, attend conferences, reflect, and share ideas. The faculty uniformly point to the ways in which the school is connected to ideas and reform networks outside the school that provide stimulation for their own evolution. Teachers point out that the opportunities for involvement outside the school are so numerous that they must place limits on them or risk cutting into important time with colleagues and even time to develop the curriculum. The school has also developed norms ensuring that most teachers are involved in external activities, and that no teacher becomes a "star": "Those corporations that we're involved with will say to us, 'Oh, send Barb again,' and we will say to them 'No ... The Okanagon Way is to allow every-body to have an opportunity [to go to national meetings]' because we believe that when we talk about what's important to us then it helps *us* remember what's important." And they are careful to make the national trips a responsibility to colleagues: "What we have done is [use time in faculty meetings] as another means of being accountable for those of us who go places. There is a responsibility to give [information] back, which helps us to professionally grow too."

As this implies, although teachers value the important connections with groups outside of the school, they also learn a great deal from each other through planned and sustained interactions. The staff view each other as expert resources, and often provide both formal and informal professional development opportunities to their colleagues:

> I've been doing training in Socratic seminars ... It's incredible to work with [other] teachers. I love that. People can have new ideas, pick your brains, and you learn back from their giving you a scenario and it makes me think ... and in that way I feel like I grow too because I can't say, 'Oh I have all the answers.'

Okanagon also has ongoing self-study activities in a number of school-wide commit-tees. For example, there is an Evaluation Committee, whose responsibility is to collect longitudinal data about the school's performance. The district cannot meet the needs of data-hungry Okanagon staff and, in response, the school has begun to initiate its own research and assessment, and to develop its own standards of performance:

> The other method of assessment that we are working on is [our own] school-wide assessment, where everyone writes on the same topic for language arts and everyone received the same math problem. The whole staff sat down to determine what a 1 looked like and a 2 and a 3 and a 4.

The teachers developed these standards for assessing performance in interdisciplinary groups – it was considered important development for teachers to understand and contribute to what constituted a high or low level of performance in mathematics, even if the individual was not a math teacher: "We are counselors to these students, and we keep the results of those tests for our students … By doing this, I think we set an example to the kids that all teachers are on one accord [about performance standards]."

After the students were tested, teachers graded the papers of students from other teams, and the results were shared with the entire school. Teachers seemed unconcerned about this public insight into the performance of their own students: "Well, it could [cause concern], but I think that we all look at it like a training thing for us. I mean, if for some reason all of your kids didn't do too well, then we can help each other" and "The [school-wide assessment] is a pain … but I like it. It gives you a sense of where the kids are relative to the whole school. It gets the whole school involved in where the strengths and weaknesses are."

Time for informal discussion is allocated to the Families, which are scheduled during the school day. Not all meetings focus on educational issues, but most teachers pointed to the value of the time for refining curriculum and instruction:

> Our Family spends some … planning time dealing with children and discipline, and some amount of time scheduling parent conferences, but I would say 75 per cent of our time is spent on the kinds of issues that we set up this time for.

Even within school-wide activities Families have the discretion to dapt projects to fit their students' learning styles. For example, in one meeting the Dragon Family teachers talked about the criteria to judge the research papers that the students are required to write to earn the Okanagon Standard. The meeting didn't resolve the issue, but they ended by deciding which team members were going to develop rubrics to score the papers.

The principal's comments about the teachers summarize the conditions that most believe they work with:

> There's a passion here for teaching, an excitement … Different people are emerging as leaders, and … are taking their gifts and making them go and other people are learning from them, and there's collegiality and co-teaching and peer evaluation.

Making Okanagon Work: The Challenge of Autonomy and Coordination

Okanagon is a large school, and the initially simple structure – Families and a Community Council – worked well only during the initial year of operation, when the school had one-third of its full enrolment, and most of the teachers had been involved in the initial planning process. Now, teachers and other key observers agree that coordination and communication are barriers to achieving "The Dream." Some of the issues are temporary and related to the school's rapid growth, such as the problem of socializing new teachers. Others, however, are more permanent. One of the key features of the "Okanagon Way" is that Families are responsible for making decisions about their own organization and functioning. While most of the Families appear to function effectively, the accumulation of independent decisions has fragmented teachers' understanding of the school's mission: "I think that the school as a whole is trying to bring children to high academic levels. I am not sure that we all agree on what that is. And I am not sure that we agree on how to do that."

The need to develop new ways of approaching the education of poor, inner-city children also strains teacher resources and increases differences between Families: "So the curriculum is kind of picking and pulling pieces and putting them together, which is really exciting on the one hand but it's all on my shoulders or my team mates'."A district office supporter commented succinctly that:

> one of the big issues is communication, and making sure everybody has common understandings and access to information ... What I would wish for Okanagon is ... to make sure that teachers could have more time to meet and make sure they really are on track with each other.

Teachers noted that the informal system of sharing between Families was bolstered during the first three years by foundation-funded retreats. In their absence, the school's committee structure has begun to serve a more formal coordinating function. The Curriculum Committee, which consists of members from each of the Families and the principal, was initially intended to propose school-wide projects. More recently, however, it has taken on an important policy-making role, such as initiating the school-wide assessment activities. The Committee and its subcommittees (such as the Portfolio Assessment Committee) are widely viewed among the staff as more influential than the Community Council, in large measure because they meet more often and discuss more substantive educational issues. Family representatives to these committees report back to their Family unit and the Families are expected to collaborate on how to facilitate the school-wide projects. Teachers agreed that this line of communication is essential to school coordination, but there is a lingering sense that the lack of direct participation in making important school-wide decisions may be undermining a sense of common purpose and has added a new layer of work.

The growing role of school-wide coordination of curriculum and assessment is not the only conflict between school-wide versus within-Family concerns. Okanagon faculty have intense debates over where "The Dream" should go. Among the issues are whether there should be cross-age grouping, whether students who are severely learning disabled should be fully mainstreamed, and whether Families should have complete freedom to determine their schedules, even when these create problems for the cross-Family "Discovery Team." Other teachers express concerns that even though the teachers are all striving toward "The Dream," layers of innovation and multiple roles may distract from the central task of teaching children who have many needs and few resources outside of school:

[Because teachers do the administrative work] it's sometimes difficult to run around and get information because it's spread over the whole school. Sometimes one job depends on another person's job, so it becomes a monumental task just to get everybody together … Even things like arranging for me to attend a conference might involve me seeing three people as opposed to one.

Others worry that the school has yet to demonstrate that it can raise the performance of the school's disadvantaged children on any of the state's external assessments, and, although they believe that their students are doing better in high school, there is still feedback that they are not fully prepared for the higher levels of academic work.

Teachers at Okanagon debate these issues fiercely, and in open forums, including retreats, staff meetings and school-wide committees. Teachers agree that the school belongs to them, and that all of the constraints on their freedom are those that they collectively choose. Nevertheless, there is ambivalence about whether the ongoing learning experiences are a stimulus (as most agree) or a constraint (as most also agree):

I think that we do have a lot more freedom to do things in our classroom but it is harder sometimes [when you are not involved in making the decision] … It sounds and feels a lot like what happens in our old schools like "You have to do it like this." You know what people's reaction is to that!

But, as faculty noted, at Okanagon there is no certainty except that things will be changing for the foreseeable future. Teachers who are not willing to live with that may leave (as several have done); those that stay express a certain resignation about the ever-unfolding nature of the school:

I just have to trust. I have got to trust that they (members of other committees) are about the same issue as I am – educating children and that maybe this is the best … and then the opportunity is always given to say, "What do you still have a problem with?" … And if there is no resolution … a subcommittee is assigned to see if we can resolve those issues.

Comparing Agassiz and Okanagon

We regard both Agassiz and Okanagon as schools that have, in many ways, demonstrated conformity to the definition of a learning organization that we posed above. However, there are also some differences between the image of organizational learning presented by these schools, and what one would expect based on theory alone.

Organizational Memory

Unlearning as a Key Process

Attention is paid in the literature to the importance of collective memory, and the ability of the organizational members to draw upon it both to define issues or problems that need to be addressed and to look for promising solutions (or to reject proposed solutions) based on previous experience. These cases show limited importance associated with memory. Okanagon was a relatively new school with only a little history to draw on. But lack of interest or reference to the past also characterizes Agassiz, which is a school with a continuous history in a district whose history is both dramatic and contains important discontinuities associated with desegregation and changes in the district office and state.

The cases give us some clues. Teachers in both schools are preoccupied with "unlearning" the past, rather than drawing on it. Most, when referring to the past, cite experiences in other schools or at other times that they believe exemplify poor practice, structure or values. What they point to is the fact that they are on the cutting edge: they create new models through constantly reexamining their own behavior for pernicious evidence of "traditional thinking" rather than looking to previous experience as a guide. In education, this may be a condition that most learning schools will confront in the next decade or so: learning must occur, but there are few images that teachers can draw on in either their own or their school's experiences that will help them to move forward. Where unlearning is more important than memory, the process of using the past to guide the future is significantly different.

"Organizational Newness" as a Stimulus to Short-term Memory

Although neither school exhibited a significant attention to using collective memory, staff in Okanagon, which was a new school (albeit with a prehistory), refer to its past more than at Agassiz, where change has evolved gradually. In particular, many people at Okanagon refer to the planning year (in which six of the teachers and the principal were key actors), "The Dream" that stimulated the school's founding, and key events, such as the hiring and socializing of many new teachers. One explanation for this finding is that new schools may be more dependent on past reference points that exemplify "what we are about" precisely because the teachers must rapidly develop common understandings. The case studies do not suggest that Okanagon was more cohesive than Agassiz – on the contrary, teachers were open about the fact that reaching consensus is an arduous and uncompleted task. Having a common past and a dream is a mechanism for building "we-ness" in sentiment.

The Knowledge Base: Using External and Internal Sources of Knowledge

Both schools are creating a knowledge base fed by both internal and external sources. Individuals and small groups are actively involved in external networks, ranging from local groups (Agassiz's work with other schools on Reading Recovery) to multiple national organizations (such as the Coalition of Essential Schools). Teachers *read* in these schools: they do not just attend courses. This is most clearly exemplified by the Faculty

Study Committee at Agassiz, which formalized the teachers' hope of directly connecting with big ideas, but is also evident less formally at Okanagon. Both schools share the assumption that teachers are responsible for distributing externally acquired ideas to peers by demonstrating, running seminars, and other ways of increasing teacher-to-teacher communication. Okanagon, in particular, is deeply committed to getting information about its performance: from parents, from the high schools that its students attend, and even from the state's standardized tests. Teachers also explicitly see themselves as a collection of experts whose knowledge is available to others. Teachers are not jealous of each other's expertise because they do not assume that they are equal in all ways. Rather, they talk about special skills or knowledge of others as additional evidence of their school's professional character.

Learning Processes

Assumption Sharing and Interpretation

Okanagon and Agassiz staff rarely assume that they know what other teachers believe and are doing. Rather, they view the development of a common set of assumptions as problematic and in need of constant reinforcement. A significant example from Okanagon is the concern over maintaining shared beliefs about the meaning of the "Okanagon Standard" (required demonstrations of competence that students must carry out before they graduate) between Families. At Agassiz, continuing discussions about the role and importance of standardized testing demonstrate teachers' commitment to collective wrestling with difficult issues.

But teachers in both schools do more than share assumptions. They also spend time on the more mundane task of making sure that they agree. In Okanagon, for example, teachers work hard to develop consensus about scoring their school-wide assessments, and spend a lot of time discussing the meaning of the results. Agassiz teachers regularly brainstorm about indicators of success at each grade level, as well as for the school as a whole, and struggle to interpret and deal with the troubling absence of minority children in the state-mandated gifted program.

Systematic versus Incremental Learning

Research from the private sector suggests that all organizations learn incrementally. What distinguishes organizations that *only* learn slowly and informally from more dynamic learning environments is the emphasis on regularized strategies to promote learning. Both schools have teacher-developed structures that encourage systematic study. At Agassiz, grade-level meetings focus on specific learning related to the curriculum, while the Faculty Study Committees struggle toward a school-wide learning process. The Restructuring Roundup also presents an important opportunity to reinforce pulling together "craft knowledge" in ways that make it more visible and accessible to colleagues. At Okanagon, the emphasis on systematic learning is more structured, with many powerful committees that attack different aspects of self-examination and decision-making.

Paradigm Shifts

There is evidence that these teachers think about their work quite differently from typical teachers. One example is the emphasis on their role as professional developers as well as classroom teachers. In Agassiz, teachers are increasingly involved in parent education, while at Okanagon recent efforts to design and score school-wide assessments reflect a sea-change in their sense of collective responsibility for student learning. These self-concious shifts increase teachers' excitement about their own learning: they see themselves challenging what others think and believe about teachers and inner-city schools.

Some Additional Differences Between the Two Schools

Although both Agassiz and Okanagon share important characteristics of organizational learning, the brief case studies also reveal some profound differences between them that suggest that there will be many models for what a "learning school" may look like.

Leadership Styles: Internal Mentoring versus External Sponsorship

Leaders were acknowledged as powerful forces in the intellectual development of both schools. The enactment of the principal's role was strikingly different, however. In Agassiz, the principal and the assistant principal were viewed by teachers (and viewed themselves) as the source of intellectual leadership on a daily basis. Teachers are grateful that leaders retain a constant focus on the identification and resolution of educational dilemmas; they refer to the principal often in their interviews as the source of ideas to resolve issues that are perplexing and difficult. In addition, they view their own empowerment as contingent: it is still "granted" rather than something to which they are entitled.

In Okanagon, in contrast, the power of the principal's intellectual vision is acknowledged, but he was not seen as an involved problem-solver. Ideas that were too far out of line with "The Dream" (for example, when a few teachers wanted a substantially separate program for severely learning-disabled children) stimulated conditional warnings that a particular line of thinking was inappropriate. Yet, although he was the "Keeper of The Dream" (a title that he used in lieu of his formal position), most teachers viewed him as a distant influence on day-to-day work. They saw his role as a publicist and as an astute politician who could keep their efforts simultaneously visible and protected. When asked what would happen if he left, most teachers felt that they could find another leader from within their own group who could carry on with the job.

Size and its Consequences

Although Agassiz is a large elementary school, it is less than half the size of Okanagon. Both schools have found it necessary to create communication structures that involve subunits of the faculty, but the additional consultation problems induced by size and its associated complexity are striking. In Agassiz, smaller and more intimate grade-level meetings (approximately six teachers in each of six grades) and the division into two Faculty Study Groups of approximately twenty teachers each, served to keep conversations flowing: there is a strong sense of the whole that is expressed by most teachers.

In Okanagon, a structure that includes ten Families and eighty-four teachers creates more significant problems of communication, particularly related to issues of sharing assumptions and interpretations. Okanagon's solution was to develop a complex system of committees that have overlapping responsibilities, and which represent Families. However, because the school's smaller committees often make critical decisions, the issue of how to gain ownership and ensure quality consultation with others is at the top of many people's minds. In large measure, emerging frustration with the apparently endless committee work among some teachers is a consequence of trying to create a unitary democracy in an organization that is too large to function as a whole.

Managing Conflict in a Learning School

All schools have conflicts, whether they are interpersonal, intellectual, or concern power and its consequences. In both Okanagon and Agassiz, the controversial issues revolved around educational ideas, providing strong support for the assertion that these are learning communities. In addition, in both schools there was agreement among teachers about the content of contentious issues: teachers in Agassiz, for example, tended to agree that the issue of low African-American representation in the gifted program was of concern, while in Okanagon, teachers pointed to the tension between the desirability of school-wide coordination, and the demands that it made on teachers. On the surface Agassiz appears to be more serene, while Okanagon teachers are more forthright about conflicts. We attribute this in part to "norms of politeness" in the Deep South as compared to the West, but more importantly to the relative ease of resolving many disputes in Agassiz as contrasted to Okanagon. In Agassiz, all teachers agreed that the principal would adjudicate disputes that could not be addressed within the staff. In Okanagon, they were forced to forge their own resolutions because the principal refused to do so unless "The Dream" was at stake. Even some of the most influential teachers longed for an impartial judge.

Some Additional Structural Similarities

While there are clear differences between the two schools in terms of what organizational learning looks like, there are also some critical similarities in how the schools are structured, and how human resources are used to support this.

Time, Time, Time

The structure of the school day, week, and year is organized in both schools to make sure that teachers have time to work together. The amount of time spent in meetings is substantial, and varied in terms of length, purpose, and focus. Short meetings of teams or grade levels occur several times a week, and often cover logistics (how to teach a unit that they have decided on in common). Longer meetings occur in committees or in specialized professional development contexts, often after school. Both schools have more extended all-day professional development experiences where the whole staff engages in activities that focus on learning, especially on examining assumptions and generating consensus. Teachers also talk about informal interactions, but these play a small role compared to the formal contexts – including agendas and expectations of action – that have been developed.

Multiple Structures and Strategies for Creating Interdependence
In spite of the emphasis on consensus, teachers believe that they have room for individuality in their classrooms. Yet, in both cases there are also both opportunities and arrangements that encourage interdependent teaching, including peer observation, voluntary teaming for short or long periods, and coordination of teaching strategies and materials. These opportunities are used by teachers when they suit, and ignored when they do not. In Agassiz, teachers are encouraged to observe each other's classrooms on a monthly basis, and cooperative learning also takes place in preparing for the Restructuring Roundup. Grade-level teams occasionally organize common student experiences, but do not feel pressured to do so all the time. In Okanagon, the Family structure provided easy chances for collaboration and "safe" interdependence: several teachers reported that the ease of working with each other in more intimate ways was growing over time. In addition, special projects, such as the school-wide assessment, are used to create interdependence. Again, however, interdependence is voluntary.

Some Additional Human Resources Similarities
The above discussion highlights some of the changes in structures, role definitions and distribution of power and authority that are associated with organizational learning in the schools. In addition, teachers in both schools noted other key features that are more associated with changing the culture of the teaching environment.

Recruiting and Socializing Teachers
Although the opportunity to interview and hire teachers is often associated with teacher empowerment, these teachers speak of it as an opportunity to ensure that their colleagues share the same values, and are willing to work within a framework that they have designed. At both schools, teachers discuss recruitment as an occasion to present the school, to explain its philosophy, and to be clear about peer expectations. The goal in both settings (where schools are obligated to take teachers whose jobs had been eliminated in other schools) is to ensure that those who would not fit in choose to go elsewhere. For the most part they believe that they are successful in providing mentorship and support to new teachers to help them fit in (and, for the most part, newer teachers agreed that they are supported). In both schools, teachers who did not fit in or were not willing to work to the expectations of the school left voluntarily. As this implies, both schools exhibited significant peer pressure. When teachers were asked who they felt accountable to, a number reported that they worked to the expectations of their peers – to meet the norms of the group, and not to let people down.

Effort and its Consequences
Much has been made of the problems of "burnout" among teachers in urban schools: too much work, too much pressure, and too little support. No teacher in these schools reported being burned out. Several indicated that they had felt overextended in the

past, and had responded by leaving one committee, or resigning as head of a task force. Other teachers were in line to take their place as they achieved a different balance. Teachers worked very hard in these schools; far more than the contract required, and far more than many professionals in other fields. While we have no hard data, it seems clear that the average teacher that was interviewed in this study was working more than 50 hours per week, and often worked in the summer. Yet, despite the fact that many of them had been putting in the kind of extra effort necessary to create a learning organization environment, most seemed energized rather than tired. We believe that this is because the additional effort was voluntary, intellectually stimulating, and associative – that is, connected with other people. Under these conditions, the amount of work was rarely considered, except in passing: it was part of the enjoyment of life. The old adage about people, when dying, never saying that they wished they had spent more time in the office would not apply to this group: most would say that the time that they spent at work was both professional time and time in service of a higher goal.

Note

1. This chapter is an edited version of K.S. Louis and S. Kruse (1998) "Creating community in reform: Images of organizational learning in urban schools". In K. Leithwood and K.S. Louis (eds), *Organizational Learning in Schools*: 17–46. Lisse: Swets and Zeitlinger. A brief discussion of the data-collection methods may be found in Chapter 9.

References

Cohen, M.D. (1991) "Individual learning and organizational routine: Emerging connections." *Organizational Science* 2(1): 135–9.

Daft, R. and G. Huber (1987) "How organizations learn." In N. DiTomaso and S. Bacharach (eds), *Research in Sociology of Organizations*, Vol. 5: 1–36. Greenwich: JAI.

Hargreaves, A. (1994) *Changing Teachers, Changing Times: Teachers Work and Culture in the Postmodern Age*. New York: Teachers College Press.

Hedberg, B. (1981) "How organizations learn and unlearn." In P.C. Nystrom and W.H. Starbuck (eds), *The Handbook of Organizational Design*, Vol. 1. New York: Oxford University Press.

Huber, G.P. (1991) "Organizational learning: The contributing processes and the literatures." *Organization Science* 2(1): 88–115.

Kruse, S.D. and K.S. Louis (1997) "Teacher teaming in middle schools: Dilemmas for a school wide community." *Educational Administration Quarterly* 33(3): 261–89.

Lave, J. (1984) *Everyday Cognition: Its Development in Social Context*. Cambridge, MA: Harvard University Press.

Louis, K.S. (1994) "Beyond managed change." *School Effectiveness and School Improvement* 5(1): 1–22.

—— and S.D. Kruse (1995) *Professionalism and Community: Perspectives from Urban Schools*. Thousand Oaks, CA: Corwin.

Senge, P. (1990) *The Fifth Discipline*. New York: Doubleday.

13

A Culture Framework for Education: Defining Quality Values and their Impact[1]

Introduction

One of the most highly touted improvement programs in for-profit organizations in the 1980s was Quality Management (QM), the set of philosophies, principles, and practices credited for the phenomenal growth and success of Japanese companies in the period following the Second World War. By the late 1990s, the main tenets of quality management (in other words, customer-focus, continuous improvement, teamwork) are the *sine qua non* of many successful corporations. While the 1980s was the decade for introducing QM in US industry, the 1990s and beyond appear to be the decades for QM (or its close cousins) in educational institutions. With its focus on the study and improvement of processes, data-driven decision-making, and shared purpose and responsibility for meeting and exceeding client expectations, QM has great appeal to schools under increasing pressure to be more efficient, more accountable, and more focused on meeting the needs of students and communities.

Despite this appeal to school administrators, QM has engendered controversies in its transition to an educational context. Both in higher education and K–12 settings, the language of "customers" and the apparent emphasis on efficiency has been problematic. Critics such as Prawat (1996) and Kohn (1993) argued that the idea of "quality management" implies the antithesis of liberal education, which involves the expansion of meaning in individual lives and a focus on relationships rather than production.

In spite of these criticisms, however, QM in various guises has invaded the educational world. "QM" has been replaced in many educators' language with terms such as "continuous improvement," "quality assurance," or "knowledge work supervision" (Duffy 1997) to avoid the impression that it is an attempt to deny agency to teachers and students; Stringfield (1995) prefers the term "high reliability schools." Whatever it is called, the elements of QM as espoused by Deming, Juran, and others map well on to the current context of school policy (Deming 1986; Juran 1988). For example, the notion that schools must be responsive to "customer satisfaction" (Rinehart 1993; Davies and Ellison 1995; Peck and Carr 1997; Salisbury et al., 1997) is supported by attempts in most states and countries to make individual schools' learning results public. Initiatives for vouchers and charter schools remind educators on a daily basis that pleasing their constituents is a critical task.

On the other hand, efforts to translate QM processes into educational programs appear, based on written materials, incomplete. Many emphasize only one aspect of the broader quality model espoused by Deming: for example, a focus on data-based decision-making is prominent in many states with detailed testing programs. The emphasis is on teacher teaming, cooperation, and professional development in other contexts (Wilson 1994; Weller and Weller 1997), while still others focus on creating vision and collaboration in the administrative team (Manley 1996). Some districts misinterpret QM entirely, fitting the funding of individual teachers or change agents under the generous umbrella of QM (Rist 1993). More importantly, QM is often sidelined to support financial efficiency in the business office, the transportation department, or the food service program – without any direct focus on the "core technology" of teaching and learning. An additional problem is institutionalization of QM. Sarason (1996) argues that, because the principles and language associated with QM often collide with the traditional culture of schools, deep changes in the way in which administrators and teachers work are difficult to come by (Sarason 1996).

This chapter makes two contributions to the discussion of QM practices and culture in schools. First, it presents a framework of QM values and beliefs that, we argue, represents the cultural backbone of successful QM adoption in school settings. We argue that the explicit mapping of the ideal culture for QM implementation is a necessary starting point for empirical work investigating the relationship between QM and organizational culture in schools. Thus, the organization of the paper flows from general to specific and from descriptive to normative. Second, we present a series of theoretical propositions for future testing aimed at understanding QM culture in schools. These propositions are related to the systemic nature of cultural values, the gaps one may find between existing cultural values and ideal QM values, and the problems created by subcultures.

The culture theory and framework of QM values presented herein is aimed at assisting in school reform, since by their nature all systemic reforms contain an implicit or explicit set of cultural assumptions. The specific focus of our research has been on secondary schools because the educational literature in general speaks of the failure of school innovations to produce long-term changes in high-school practices or cultures (Firestone and Herriott 1982; Rossman *et al.* 1988; Louis and Miles 1990; Sarason 1996; Firestone and Louis 1999; Louis and Marks 1999). In the USA, but also in other countries, more concerns are expressed about the effectiveness of secondary schools in preparing students both cognitively, and for adult social roles, than about primary schools. Nevertheless, while our empirical concerns have been specific, this paper is intended to set a theoretical framework that is generally applicable to all educational settings.

Culture and Organizations

Clearly QM is no "quick fix" for school problems. We should not be surprised: as the research in industry suggests, many QM initiatives were *not* institutionalized as "the way we do things around here." In *post hoc* analyses, organizational culture was often blamed (for example, Becker 1993; Rago 1993). Yet the claim that an organization's culture is a key predictor of QM's successful (or unsuccessful) implementation has little empirical basis. Indeed, the use of organizational culture as a useful research construct in education has, in general, been stunted by limited empirical work and theoretical development (Firestone and Louis 1999). Researchers in both profit and non-profit settings have argued that interest in organizational culture as a driver of organizational innovation and performance is likely to fade unless this dearth of research is addressed (Pettigrew 1990; Smart and St John 1996).

The long history of studying culture, whether in small or large social units, has attracted many perspectives (Kroeber and Kluckhohn 1952), although most empirical research in organizations agrees with a view of culture as an enduring, independent phenomenon that consists of some combination of values, beliefs, and/or assumptions that organizational members *share* about appropriate behavior (Rossman *et al.* 1988; Schein 1992). The idea that these shared conceptions act in a normative fashion to guide behavior has resulted in culture being termed the "social glue" that binds the organization (Smircich 1983). But, in order to define and measure QM culture in secondary schools we need to examine the multiple levels at which culture exists and is manifest in organizations (Hofstede *et al.* 1990; Pettigrew 1990; Schein 1992). These levels or manifestations are often described as a tripartite of *artifacts, (espoused) values,* and *basic assumptions.* At one level, cultural artifacts are revealed by the tangibles that one sees, hears, and feels when entering an organization. Artifacts include the unique symbols, heroes, rites and rituals, myths, ceremonies, and sagas of an organization (Masland 1985; Trice 1985; Hofstede 1991). These manifestations of culture are easiest to observe but arguably the most difficult to interpret (Schein 1992).

Values – enduring beliefs or tendencies to prefer certain modes of conduct or states of affairs over others – are, perhaps, the most commonly articulated component of culture (Rokeach 1973; O'Reilly *et al.* 1991). Values provide meaning for social actions and standards for social behavior; they represent the "shoulds" and "oughts" of organizational culture. Often taken for granted, they provide strong communal guidelines for how to act that provide continuity in rapidly shifting circumstances. Most educational researchers also treat shared values (Deal and Peterson 1991; Hoy and Miskel 1996) or tacit knowledge about what "should be" (Erickson 1987; Wilson 1971: 90) as a defining aspect of school culture.

According to Schein (1992) and others, one must look deeper than values to find the essence of a culture. This view is based on evidence that values are often "espoused" as opposed to "in-use" – that is, what people say should or ought to be is often quite inconsistent with their actual behavior (Argyris and Schon 1974). Thus, according to Schein, culture is:

> A pattern of shared basic assumptions that the group learned as it solved its problems of external adaptation and internal integration, that has worked well enough to be considered valid and, therefore to be taught to new members as the correct way to perceive, think, and feel in relation to those problems.

Basic assumptions, the real drivers of behavior in Schein's view, can be uncovered by asking people to explain the observed inconsistencies between their espoused values and actual behaviors. However, there is limited empirical evidence to support his view that basic assumptions are the most important aspect of culture or to explain how basic assumptions are different from (or a deeper level of culture than) values-in-use. Therefore, in this paper, we focus on the values, beliefs, and underlying assumptions of QM without making a technical distinction of how these terms may be slightly different from one another. The important point, we argue, is to move beyond the usual tendency of both would-be implementers and researchers of systemic improvement initiatives such as QM to concentrate solely on the visible practices (artifacts) of new programs. An exclusive focus on the artifacts of new programs ignores the more fundamental task of changing the deep-seated cultural values and beliefs that are inconsistent with new practices or structures.

Toward a QM Culture Framework for Schools

We scanned the QM literature to determine what normative dimensions have been used to define the ideal culture of a QM organization. While many authors recognize the importance of values or culture in QM implementation, the *specific* values underlying QM practices (artifacts) have been explicitly investigated in only a few studies that fall into two general categories. The first claim to be exploring QM and its culture, yet deal almost exclusively in the realm of QM practices (Reynolds 1986; Flynn *et al.* 1994; Snyder and Acker-Hocevar 1995). These studies are helpful in pointing out the artifacts that one would expect to find in a QM organization, but say little about the underlying values or assumptions in such organizations. The second type focus exclusively on the measurement of culture and its relationship to QM implementation. These studies use existing instruments for measuring culture such as the Competing Values Framework (Cameron and Freeman 1991; Zammuto and Krakower 1991; Chang 1996), and the School Work Culture Profile (Rigsby 1994). These studies provide useful information about some aspects of culture and QM implementation, but are limited because the instruments were not designed to specifically measure *QM* values. For example, values and beliefs about the importance of customers are clearly a key aspect of QM, but they are not covered by most existing culture instruments.

Given the limitations of these strands of research, our approach was to focus explicitly on defining the cultural values underlying QM in educational organizations, specifically US secondary schools. As shown throughout this section, our approach yielded a set of values that align well with generic organizational culture dimensions.

Methods

The starting point for this task was the US-based Malcolm Baldrige National Quality Award's 1999 Education Criteria for Performance Excellence which explicitly provides a list of "concepts and values" that should be adopted by Quality schools (National Institute of Standards and Technology, 1999). While a useful starting point in identifying values related to QM, the Baldrige values criteria have not been empirically studied and thus served only as a guideline as we searched the rest of the Quality literature for implied or explicit cultural values.

To sharpen the results of our literature review we convened an expert panel of fifteen educators and business executives to discuss QM values in education. The educators included at least one person from each of the following classifications: teacher, principal, central administration, and superintendent. The work roles of the businesspersons present included quality consultant, executive director, and vice-president. All participants have been involved with QM as practitioners, consultants, or researchers. Several have or are currently serving as state or national judges for Baldrige-based Quality awards. A modified nominal group technique (NGT) (Van de Ven and Delbecq 1972) focused the group on the discussion and clarification of Quality-related artifacts and values they had recorded before attending the panel meeting. The panel discussion helped clarify the difference between Quality practices (which are cultural artifacts) and underlying Quality values and put QM "concepts and values" into a language more consistent with the organizational and school culture literature.

Based on the Baldrige values, the empirical literature, and input from the expert panel, we generated nine cultural values for QM. Each of these values is stated succinctly in Table 13.1. For each value dimension listed in the table, several additional sentences further clarify the meaning of the Quality value. These statements provide a useful starting point for the next step in this work – operationalizing these values into measurement instruments. For each dimension in the table we have also articulated an opposite/alternative value and a set of additional statements clarifying the opposite value state. Stating clearly what something "is not" is an important step in achieving construct clarity (Osigweh 1989).

Table 13.1 A Proposed Model of QM Values and Beliefs for Schools

QM Culture in Schools
Values and Beliefs of Teachers and Administrators Essential for Quality

Value 1: *A shared vision and shared goals among faculty, staff, and administrators is critical for school success.*
A "constancy of purpose" must be agreed upon and shared by all staff members. Individuals should be willing to sacrifice some autonomy for the sake of organization-wide goals. Successful schools are those in which staff agree on what's most important and pursue those areas jointly.

Opposite: *Successful schools respect the right of individuals to establish their own vision and goals without regard for higher levels of goals, which are often ambiguous and difficult to interpret.*

As professionals, teachers should choose their own classroom goals and practices. As long as effective teachers meets their classroom goals, they are contributing to school effectiveness. Innovative and high-quality teaching is inhibited by excessive emphasis on common goals and practices.

Value 2: *Educational needs should be determined primarily by parents, community groups, students, and other stakeholders.*
Learning-centered education focuses on learning and meeting the real needs of students. These needs are derived from the "marketplace," the requirements of citizenship, and the need to develop every student to his or her full potential. In learning-centered education, students, teachers, parents, and community groups should have a substantial voice in the curriculum and programs offered by the school.

Opposite: *Educational experts should make the important educational decisions.*
Parents and community members don't know what their children really need when it comes to curriculum. Teacher expertise should be the basis of decision-making about curriculum, assessment, and so on. The goals of a school should be determined primarily by the faculty and principal.

Value 3: *Improving education requires a long-term commitment.*
The school should be driven by long-term stable improvement goals. Short-term sacrifices – especially in teacher's effort and time – may be necessary.

Opposite: *Present pressures – the students in a school and the immediate external demands – are most important; the future is too uncertain to plan for or worry about.*
Things are so bad now, anything we can do to get results quickly is worthwhile. Goals and programs should be changed if results can't be demonstrated quickly.

Value 4: *A school should strive to make continuous changes to improve education.*
Teachers and others in the school should devote time and energy to make things better. This is a never-ending process. People should be willing to take risks associated with making change.

Opposite: *Schools should be conservative about making changes.*
It is better to stick with what we know than risk failure, given the significant consequence of schooling for individual children. Change does not always mean improvement.

Table 13.1 A Proposed Model of QM Values and Beliefs for Schools (cont.)

QM Culture in Schools
Values and Beliefs of Teachers and Administrators Essential for Quality

Value 5: *Teachers should be active in improving the overall school operation.*

Teachers' judgment about the educational process is valuable and needed to improve quality. Decisions should be decentralized to involve teachers in key school decisions.

Opposite: *Overall school operations should be left to administrators and a few teacher-leaders.*

Decisions should be made by a few individuals in a school. Shared decision-making is too slow and inconsistent. Teachers should rarely be taken out of the classroom for team meetings, committee work, or administrative tasks. The principal (not teachers) is paid to make school-wide decisions.

Value 6: *Collaboration is necessary for an effective school.*

The entire organization must work together for a quality education to occur. Teachers should not be left to do their own work. Collaboration leads to better decisions, higher quality, and more satisfied employees. Departments should engage in cooperative behavior.

Opposite: *Professional autonomy with a minimum of cooperation is key to school effectiveness.*

Teachers are most effective when left to make classroom decisions by themselves. Working alone is usually more productive than working in teams and attending endless committee meetings.

Value 7: *Decision-making should rely on factual information.*

A school runs best on facts, not opinion. The best decisions are driven by data and analysis. It is better to be open about data than to be defensive. Data feedback to teachers and students should be objective and oriented toward process improvement.

Opposite: *Decision-making should rely on personal, professional experience.*

The best decisions are based on applying personal experience and judgments made by education professionals. Data about school performance is difficult to interpret. The most important schooling processes and outcomes can't be measured accurately. Unlike other fields such as medicine or business, there are few data that are comparable across organizations.

Value 8: *Quality problems are caused by poor systems and processes, not by teachers.*

Quality should be improved by using better processes and more customer input, rather than imploring teachers to work harder. Most people are competent and motivated to do a good job.

Opposite: *The cause of most problems is human error.*

When something goes wrong, it is usually because someone made a mistake. Our system is pretty good. Supervising people's actions and taking disciplinary measures when something goes wrong are a necessary part of motivating people to improve quality. School outcomes would improve substantially if some teachers made fewer mistakes.

Value 9: *Quality can be improved with the existing resources.*

By improving processes and preventing problems, schools can improve the quality of education with little or no additional resources. This requires doing things in a different way and fixing some of the processes and methods that waste resources.

Opposite: *We are doing the best we can with existing resources.*

There is little waste or inefficiency in our system. We cannot improve the results of this school significantly without more money.

Quality Management Values: Empirical and Theoretical Support

The nine QM values are discussed below. Where helpful, examples are provided of artifacts or practices that make these values visible within an organization. Each QM value is also related to the general organizational culture literature.

QM Value 1

"A shared vision and shared goals among faculty, staff and administrators are critical for school success."

This value refers to a belief in the power of coordinated action. According to this value, individuals should be willing to sacrifice some autonomy for the sake of organization-wide goals because doing so will lead to superior outcomes. A shared vision and shared goals requires that all staff members know and understand the organization's vision and are willing to align their behavior accordingly.

The most common statement of this value within the QM literature comes from Deming, who argued that his first point, "adopt a constancy of purpose," formed the core of his thinking about Total Quality (Deming 1986). The Baldrige education criteria do not explicitly state shared vision and goals as a key Quality value, which is puzzling given the idea's prevalence in the literature (Anderson et al. 1994; Leithwood et al. 1995) and its clear articulation by the expert panel we assembled.

In the organizational culture literature, this value represents a normative judgment about the value of collaboration over isolated behavior and about the responsibility of individual employees to align their practice with organization-wide priorities (Reynolds 1986; Louis and Kruse 1995; Heck and Marcoulides 1996; Leonard 1997). Note that while the organizational culture literature makes no claim whether collaboration is preferred to isolation, the QM literature is clear that collaboration is preferred.

QM Value 2

"Educational needs should be determined primarily by parents, community groups, students, and other stakeholders."

This value focuses on the nexus of decision-making input and authority concerning students and their learning needs. These needs are derived from the marketplace, the requirements of citizenship, and the need to develop every student to his or her full potential. According to this value, for example, the professional knowledge held by teachers is not the sole basis for decisions about curriculum. Instead, the professional knowledge of teachers is combined with input from parents, the community, and other stakeholders to determine what is most appropriate for students. This value (called "learning-centered education" in the Baldrige education criteria) replaces "customer-driven quality" in the business language and is the education equivalent of meeting the customer's or society's needs.

The idea of "customer-driven quality" has been endorsed explicitly in the QM literature and was clearly articulated by our expert panel. Both learning-centered education and customer-driven quality stress the idea that the needs and requirements of various stakeholders must be the primary determinant of organizational actions. This value is a manifestation of the "orientation and focus" dimension described in the organizational and school culture literature; specifically, it advocates a primary focus on the wants and needs of various external stakeholders (Coleman and Hoffer 1987; Leithwood and Aitken 1995; Snyder and Acker-Hocevar 1995; Leonard 1997). In education, this perspective is controversial among those who advocate more teacher and professional control over the content and processes of school practice.

QM Value 3

"Improving education requires a long-term commitment."

This value places a premium on long-term commitment to improved performance – including the belief that short-term sacrifices may be necessary to enhance quality. Furthermore, a long-term commitment includes the idea that schools or districts should make investments that support the school's long-range mission. For example, schools should invest in learning programs and assessment systems that support and document progress on long-range goals, rather than focusing primarily on year-to-year fluctuations in standardized test scores, as may be the consequence of poorly thought through educational accountability standards.

The long-term commitment value is endorsed by only some of the QM literature. Most assume that a long-range view is incorporated into visionary leadership, which implies that only top management needs a long-range view (Anderson *et al.* 1994; Dean and Bowen 1994). However, our QM expert panel supported this value as an important part of the QM philosophy for schools, which are "flat" organizations staffed by professionals. This value is consistent with the "ideas about the nature of time and time horizon" from the organizational culture literature (Lortie 1975; Quinn and Rohrbaugh 1981; Sashkin and Sashkin 1993). In particular, this value advocates a longer time horizon than is typical in many school organizations, which articulate the pressure to show short-term improvements to meet state or national "league tables" or accountability schemes.

QM Value 4

"A school should strive to make continuous changes to improve education."

This value represents a mind-set in which things are never viewed as "good enough" and is found in organizations where processes and products are continuously studied for improvement. For example, this idea is reflected in Deming's fourteen points, paraphrased as "improve constantly and forever, systems of production to improve quality and productivity" (Deming 1986). According to the Baldrige education criteria, continuous improvement in a school should be oriented around a collective learning style, with students, teachers, and parents involved in assessing progress and actively seeking to improve both the content of and rate at which learning occurs. Continuous improvement is (implicitly or explicitly) endorsed as a core value in state and district efforts to encourage schools to set rate-of-improvement standards around important school productivity outcomes that do not fall into the annual "high stakes" category, such as attendance, increasing equity of student achievement, or decreasing disciplinary actions. Such programs differ fundamentally from the "league tables" or school-rating programs based not on improvement but on annual measures of objective performance (Cuttance 1994; Wilson 1994; Manley 1996). The importance of (positive) experiences with many improvement initiatives was identified as central to the ability of schools to achieve improvement goals (Louis and Miles 1990) and replicated by other studies of reforming schools in North America (Marks and Louis 1997).

This fundamental QM value is most closely linked to the "stability versus innovation/personal growth" described in the general culture literature (Quinn and Rohrbaugh 1981; Reynolds 1986; O'Reilly et al. 1991; Denison and Mishra 1995; Heck and Marcoulides 1996; Louis et al. 1999), with the QM value clearly aligned with the change end of this dimension.

QM Value 5

"Teachers should be active in improving the overall school operation."

This value reflects the QM belief in the importance and involvement of all employees in decision-making. As applied to educational institutions, this value states that faculty and staff involvement in planning and decision-making is a critical determinant of school quality. According to this value, decision-making should not be left to a few individuals at the top.

The QM literature stresses the importance of employees, but in somewhat inconsistent ways. The Deming theory (Anderson et al. 1994) represents valuing employees through cooperation, learning opportunities, and employee fulfilment, while the Baldrige education criteria call for the acceptance of teacher and staff input on curriculum and educational matters, supported by appropriate levels of teacher development, not only in content areas, but in assessment and learning approaches. Teamwork is often mentioned (Dean and Bowen 1994), as is professional development (Barth 1990; Beck 1994).

The underlying value of teacher development – as contrasted to accountability schemes based only on student performance standards – emphasizes the fundamental belief that schools will not improve unless teachers are supported in efforts to take risks and to make changes. Valuing faculty and staff is supported by the general organizational culture literature. First, the idea of providing appropriate development opportunities for people is consistent with the notion of change/innovation/personal growth. Innovative organizations, it seems, encourage their employees to experiment, to reach out to the knowledge bases, and to upgrade their professional knowledge through formal or informal education (Saphier and King 1985; Leonard 1997; Leithwood and Louis 1998). Second, the idea that valuing faculty and staff includes the acceptance of their input into key decisions is consistent with ideas about "control, coordination, and responsibility, namely, that control and responsibility should be shared widely within an organization" (Louis et al. 1999). Increasing empowerment does not necessarily increase productivity (Sashkin 1990), but evidence from schools suggests that teacher influence over school policies is associated with improved classroom outcomes (Marks and Louis 1997).

QM Value 6

"Collaboration is necessary for an effective school."

This value explicitly focuses on the importance of interdependency for achieving maximum effectiveness. Specifically, this value is centered on the belief that collaboration leads to better decisions, higher quality, and higher morale. Most QM articles represent this value as taking form through partnerships with "suppliers" and "customers" (for example Flynn *et al.* 1994; Hackman and Wageman 1995) or through internal cooperation within the organization (Anderson *et al.* 1994; Flynn *et al.* 1994). These ideas are based on the belief that the organization will benefit from partnerships and cooperative arrangements in the pursuit of quality.

The Baldrige education criteria refer to both internal and external partnerships as something a school should value. This criterion is stated explicitly as a value – that is, the word "should" is used to describe a school's partnership-building efforts. Internally, these partnerships might be evidenced by a cooperative rather than competitive relationship with teacher unions (Kerchner *et al.* 1997) and by the existence of cross-departmental teams (Louis and Kruse 1995). Externally, a school valuing cooperation could form partnerships with the community, other schools, and businesses. The importance of internal and external networking to support school-initiated reforms is also strongly supported by Newmann and associates (1996). There is also increasing evidence that partnerships with parents that value joint responsibility for the individual student can be very effective in improving school outcomes (Christensen 1992; Keith 1993). These QM-focused parent-teacher practices differ significantly from the more traditional "back to school night" or parent conference because they incorporate a belief that the role that parents play in their children's development is important to school work.

This value is also consistent with the general organizational culture literature. In collaborative environments, people are more likely to understand the impact of their actions on others within the organization. In contrast, in individualistic organizations collegial competition (Quinn and Rohrbaugh 1981; Tucker and McCoy 1988; Smart and St John 1996), and failure to resolve basic differences in values (Rossman *et al.* 1988; Little 1990) is the norm. A belief in the importance of external cooperation is a clear statement about an organization's beliefs regarding the importance of gaining information from those outside the school (Quinn and Rohrbaugh 1981; Reynolds 1986; Smart and St John 1996).

QM Value 7

"Decision-making should rely on factual information."

This value is typically called "management by fact" and is a central value in the QM literature. The idea that facts and data should form the backbone of decision-making is seen as enabling individuals to make decisions (Dyer 1985; Saphier and King 1985; Reynolds 1986; Tucker and McCoy 1988). An artifact of this criterion would be a comprehensive, integrated information system. In schools this could take the form of measurement of input data, environmental data, and learning progress and analysis which indicates what changes would enhance the learning process. Central to this criterion is the belief that trends, cause and effect, and interrelations among variables are too complex to be evident without such data collection and analysis. For our expert panel, this value was stated as "use of data, rather than intuition, leads to better decisions."

As noted above, improved teacher professional development practices are advocated as a critical component of quality management (Wilson 1994; Hord and Boyd 1995). However, the QM literature insists that a specific form of rationality – cause-and-effect analysis – be endorsed. While this is consistent with most perspectives on teacher-as-researcher, where data are not limited to tests or to quantitative information (Hopkins 1996), it conflicts with some views of postmodernist, constructivist practice in education. The belief that not all important data for decision-making in schools can be reduced to "simple numbers" is a further source of resistance to QM principles in schools. In addition, the relatively low investment in professional development to increase the data collection and analysis capacities of teachers and administrators suggests a low premium is placed on the value of fact-based decision-making, which stands in sharp contrast to state or national policies (artifacts) that ask schools to use test information to locate problems of practice and student learning, and to make incremental progress in student achievement.

QM Value 8
"Quality problems are caused by poor systems and processes, not by teachers."

This Quality value represents the belief that people want to do a good job, but are often thwarted by the system in which they work. For example, poor systems can lead to erroneous or incomplete information upon which to act. As a result, failures to improve that appear to be due to human effort are actually due to inadequate systems. In education, this phenomenon was first examined empirically by Gross et al. (1969). This value is strongly supported by the general literature (for example, Amundson et al. 1997). Deming (1986), for example, stated this value in his fourteen points as, "Drive out fear" – don't blame employees for systems problems. Recent research in schools suggests that the promotion by school leaders of risk-taking to improve the system without fear of incrimination is central to organizational learning (Leithwood et al. 1995).

Still, in most organizations it is commonplace to blame individuals for errors: if high-school students don't write well enough it is because teachers are lazy and not because they must grade assignments for 150 students each week. In education, this belief is supported by popular sentiments that teacher unions and tenure protect large numbers of incompetent educators; according to some critics, eliminating life-long job security would automatically increase quality (Lieberman 1993). This pessimistic view of the teaching profession is contrasted with the more optimistic perspective that argues that current teachers, if given appropriate support, can easily become "knowledge workers" (Kerchner et al. 1997).

QM Value 9
"Quality can be improved within existing resources."

This value stresses that quality can be improved without adding resources to a system. Instead, improving internal processes, focusing on customers' needs, and preventing quality problems from occurring in the first place can achieve improvements. This idea is related to the general QM value, reframed in the Baldrige education criteria, advocating the importance of effective design of educational programs, curricula, and learning environments focused on prevention (see also Scheerens 1992).

Such design requires the early identification of whether learning is occurring and an effective means of corrective action (Stringfield 1995; Wilson 1994). The underlying belief is that preventing student failure is less costly (in terms of time, money, and negative affect) than detecting and "fixing" failure late in the educational process. In particular, the consequence of not meeting students' needs is that they become high-cost recipients of welfare, prison, or other social services. Thus, it is reasoned, quality should cost the same or less, particularly if the long-term costs are considered. The redirection of funding to early intervention programs in schools clearly reflects this value. However, the dominant view among educators seems to be that higher quality will cost more. This assertion is based on the belief that there is little waste and ineffi-ciency in the present system, and that there are no "slack resosurces" to cover innova-tion. As such, this value provides a major point of difference between the beliefs of educators and business managers, as most managers have seen how quality has been increased in business over the past decade while holding steady or reducing costs (Juran 1988).

This Quality value falls within the idea of the fundamental importance of organiza-tional attitudes about stability versus changing/learning/innovating in the general orga-nizational culture literature. When schools as a whole try to promote risk-taking, conceptions of "innovation" take center stage (Quinn and Rohrbaugh 1981; Reynolds 1986; O'Reilly et al. 1991; Denison and Mishra 1995; Heck and Marcoulides 1996). In contrast, risk-averse schools focus on "not rocking the boat" and conceptions about being "good enough" abound. Put simply, if one does not believe that quality can be improved with the same or fewer resources then status quo behavior is the result when resources remain the same.

Summary

In this section we have articulated a set of nine Quality values/beliefs, which we argue represent the underlying core of the QM philosophy as applied to an education context. These values were inferred and synthesized from the Baldrige framework, the QM liter-ature, the general organizational culture literature, and the recommendations of a panel of QM experts. They represent a system of values, or value framework, regarding Total Quality. Thus, while the nine values represent distinct concepts we would not expect them to be orthogonal to one another when measured in organizations. In the final section of this chapter we present five propositions regarding the relationships among cultural values, the implementation of systemic improvement initiatives such as Quality Management, and key organizational and individual outcomes such as student achieve-ment and employee satisfaction.

Propositions Regarding QM and Culture in Schools

Proposition 1: The nine QM values in Table 13.1 represent a system of values, all of which are important to the implementation and maintenance of quality practices in schools.

If our assertion that the nine Quality values outlined in Table 13.1 are "essential" is accurate, then, by definition, some minimum support for each of these values must be present within a school organization to support total QM practice. We believe the values are mutually reinforcing and that inconsistencies within this value system undermine the overall quality effort. For example, an organizational culture in which teachers share a long-term orientation toward a shared vision that is based on staff involvement and a belief in the goodness of employees will not lead to success with QM if this culture also supports decision-making about educational processes that is based primarily on teachers' personal experience and intuition rather than stakeholder input and data analysis.

Rokeach (1973) was among the first to explain the importance of a system of values. He argued that a value system is an enduring organization of beliefs concerning preferable modes of conduct or end-states of existence along a continuum of relative importance. The idea that culture is an interrelated set or web of signs or beliefs is an agreed-upon premise among distinguished scholars (Geertz 1973; Schein 1992). It is somewhat puzzling, therefore, to find that the majority of culture research since the early 1980s has focused on only one or two dimensions of culture. Thus, Proposition 1 is offered in response to Trice and Beyer's accurate portrayal of previous organizational culture work as often focused "on single, discrete elements of culture, while ignoring the multidimensional nature of culture, that is, a construct composed of several intimately interrelated variables" (Trice and Beyer 1984: 653).

Value Gaps and the Role of Culture Fit

Nadler and Tushman formally suggested that various fits, such as between individual and task, between task and the organization, and between formal and informal organization, are potentially useful explanations of micro- and macro-level behaviors and outcomes (Nadler and Tushman 1980). Since then, "fit" research has been extended to the area of value congruence, which seems to us to be a promising approach to the study of culture and its impacts. We offer two propositions regarding the congruence or fit of organizational culture (values), improvement initiatives, and outcomes.

Proposition 2a: Value gaps between the values-in-use in a school and the underlying values of a reform/improvement initiative are related to the degree of implementation and institutionalization of the initiative.

Proposition 2a focuses on the link between values-in-use in an organization and initiative implementation. As we have argued, we believe that the appropriate type of culture is a critical prerequisite to the implementation and continued use of QM practices or other systemic improvement programs. This proposition suggests a link between value gaps and program implementation, mediated by the use of various quality tools and collaborative analysis of the school's situation. If this proposition is true, it would follow that educational leaders should focus on cultural value gaps along with the implementation of the new practices and procedures of an initiative. Failure to address inconsistent belief systems would result in limited success instituting and maintaining new behaviors. As Reger and her colleagues (1994) have noted, value gaps (which they refer to as dissonance between actions or evidence and personal bi-polar constructs) may lead individuals to adopt the new behaviors of the program and change their cognitive schema in ways that reduce the level of dissonance. However, the reverse is also true. Groups that sense a lack of fit between their values and newly requested behaviors can simply resort back to their old behaviors to reduce cognitive dissonance. Thus, in schools the lack of fit may more often lead to the rejection of new behaviors than the alteration of existing value systems. This tendency may be reinforced in an environment characterized by high autonomy and low control over employee behavior, and where frequent leadership changes allow employees to "wait it out" rather than change either their behavior or values (Sarason 1996).

Proposition 2b: The sizes of the gaps between what "is" (values-in-use) and what "should be" (espoused) in employees' minds regarding the values in the general culture framework are correlated with key individual-level affective and behavioral outcomes.

Whereas proposition 2a focuses on value fit and outcomes at an aggregate level, proposition 2b focuses on the importance of individual value fit. This proposition is based on the idea that employees must be able to align their own philosophy of work with the dominant values of their organization if they are to be satisfied and productive (Nadler and Tushman 1980). For example, a large discrepancy between how a teacher feels that his or her school should function and the way it actually functions may lead to negative work behaviors, such as withdrawal from active participation, negativism, and, in the extreme, transfer to another setting. These value gaps are different from those described in 2a in that these gaps refer to incongruity between actual and desired culture (both in the minds of employees), whether or not the actual culture is consistent with the ideal culture of any specific improvement initiative.

We assert that there are likely to be gaps between desired and actual cultural values in all schools because all employees have their own mental picture of an ideal culture that is unlikely to be completely aligned with the actual culture of their school. These value gaps between what is and what is desired could result from external or structural constraints and demands, technical problems, or power imbalances. This proposition is consistent with previous work that has identified fit between teachers' values and those of the principal and district leadership as critical to employee and school effectiveness (Sashkin and Sashkin 1993; Heck and Marcoulides 1996). Proposition 2b suggests that it is important, therefore, to deal not only with the aggregate of employees' values in relation to an existing culture (whether they are based on the cultural artifacts of new initiatives such as QM or OL or simply long-standing leadership-based behaviors) but also with individual employees, how their values are aligned (or not) with the dominant values of their school, and how incongruities affect their emotional well-being.

Acknowledging and Focusing on Teacher Subcultures

One of the reasons organizational culture research has so far added little to discussions of the implementation and impact of systemic initiatives (such as QM) concerns the level of analysis at which cultural discussions generally occur in this context. Despite the large body of empirical evidence suggesting that the idea of a single, dominant culture in large or complex organizations is largely a myth (Van Maanen and Barley 1984; Pettigrew 1990; Martin 1992; Denison and Mishra 1995), most discussions of cultural impediments to organizational change have treated culture as unitary. In fact, most organizations seem to have two or more subcultures operating at any given point in time (Riley 1983). Subcultures in schools may be comprised of educators in different roles, departments, or grade levels. Firestone and Louis (1999), for example, explained the reasons for the existence and perpetuation of departmental subcultures in secondary schools, while Rossman *et al.* (1988) documented four outcome-based subcultures within the schools they studied – academic focus, balanced focus, vocational focus, and psychological development focus.

> Proposition 3: The adoption of collective values aligned with an improvement initiative (that is, lower value gaps within teacher subcultures) leads to sustained implementation and improvement in organizational outcomes; adoption of key values in non-core subcultures does not.

Not all roles or tasks have the same impact on the achievement of key student outcomes. Teaching represents the "core technology" or "core competence" of schools, with other functions and roles supporting this core. This, by default, makes the subculture(s) of teachers most critical to the sustained implementation and effectiveness of an improvement initiative. Thus, we propose in Proposition 3 that value alignment within teacher subculture(s) (the core of schooling) will lead to sustained implementation and improvement in key outcomes, whereas alignment of values within non-core areas will not. If true, one key role for school administrators is actively uncovering the cultural beliefs of teachers regarding specific innovations and working to align teachers' values with those of the proposed initiative (Sweeney 1986).

Conclusion

In this paper we attempted to address existing ambiguities about the concept of culture and its relationship to QM initiatives. We did so by reviewing the organizational culture and quality literature and by presenting a framework of "Quality values" that we argued will facilitate the implementation of QM in educational settings. Admittedly, this is but one possible framework; one that must be verified and refined with qualitative and quantitative data. The four propositions offered are one vehicle for supporting this empirical inquiry.

The next step in clarifying the relationship between culture and QM implementation involves the determination of methods and variables for measuring the values presented herein so that the interrelationships among the values, and between the values and Quality practice implementation and school effectiveness measures, can be assessed. This type of empirical research, based on a solid theoretical framework, is the only way to bring valid evidence to bear on the question of how organizational culture supports or inhibits implementation of QM (and other systemic school improvement initiatives).

As Bright and Cooper (1993) aptly noted, "There is a gap between making overall statements about the need for cultural change and detailing what would characterize organizational culture at higher levels of QM." In the spirit of QM itself, let us continue the work of replacing anecdotes, intuition, and vague statements with theory and empirical evidence.

Note

1. This chapter is an abbreviated version of J. Detert, K.S. Louis, and R. Schroeder (2001) "A culture framework for education: Defining quality values for U.S. High schools." *Journal of School Effectiveness and School Improvement* 12(2): 183–212.

References

Amundson, S., B. Flynn, A. Rungtusanatham, and R. Schroeder (1997) "The relationship between Quality management values and national and organizational culture." Unpublished paper.

Anderson, J.C., M. Rungtusanatham, and R.G. Schroeder (1994) "A theory of quality management underlying the Deming management method." *Academy of Management Review* 19(3): 472–509.

Argyris, C. and D.A. Schon (1974) *Theory in Practice: Increasing Professional Effectiveness.* San Francisco: Jossey Bass.

Barth, R. (1990) *Improving Schools from Within.* San Francisco: Jossey Bass.

Beck, L.G. (1994) *Reclaiming Educational Administration as a Caring Profession.* New York: Teachers College Press.

Becker, S.W. (1993) "QM does work: Ten reasons why misguided attempts fail." *Management Review* (May): 30–3.

Bright, K. and C.L. Cooper (1993) "Organizational culture and the management of Quality." *Journal of Managerial Psychology* 8(6): 21–7.

Cameron, K.S. and S.J. Freeman (1991) "Cultural congruence, strength, and type: relationships to effectiveness." *Research in Organizational Change and Development* 5: 23–58.

Chang, S.L. (1996) "Organizational culture and Quality Management." Unpublished PhD thesis, University of Missouri-Rolla, Rolla.

Christenson, S. (1992) "Family factors and student achievement: an avenue to increase students' success." *School Psychology Quarterly* 7(3): 178–206.

Coleman, J. and T. Hoffer (1987) *Public and Private High Schools: The Impact of Communities*. NY: Basic Books.

Cuttance, P. (1994) "Quality assurance in education systems." *Studies in Educational Evaluation* 20(1): 99–112.

Davies, B. and L. Ellison (1995) "Improving the quality of schools – Ask the clients?" *School Organization* 15(1): 5–12.

Deal, T.E. and K.D. Peterson (1991) *The Principal's Role in Shaping School Culture*. Washington, DC: US Government Printing Office.

Dean, J.W., Jr. and D.E. Bowen (1994) "Management theory and total quality: Improving research and practice through theory development." *Academy of Management Review* 19(3): 392–418.

Deming, W.E. (1986) *Out of the Crisis*. Cambridge, MA: MIT Center for Advanced Engineering Study.

Denison, D. and A. Mishra (1995) "Toward a theory of organizational culture and effectiveness." *Organization Science* 6(2): 204–24.

Duffy, F.M. (1997) "Knowledge work supervision: Transforming school systems into high performing learning organizations." *International Journal of Educational Management* 11(1): 26–31.

Dyer, W.G., Jr. (1985) "The cycle of cultural evolution in organizations." In R.H. Kilmann, M.J. Saxton, and R. Serpa (eds), *Gaining Control of the Corporate Culture*. San Francisco: Jossey Bass.

Erickson, F. (1987) "Conceptions of school culture: An overview." *Educational Administration Quarterly* 23(4): 11–24.

Firestone, W.A. and R. Herriott (1982) "Prescriptions for effective elementary schools do not fit secondary schools." *Educational Leadership* 40: 51–3.

—— and K.S. Louis (1999) "Schools as cultures." In J. Murphy and K.S. Louis (eds), *Handbook of Research on Educational Administration*: 297–322. San Francisco: Jossey Bass.

Flynn, B.B., S. Sakakibara, and R.G. Schroeder (1994) "A framework for Quality Management research and an associated measurement instrument." *Journal of Operations Management* 11(4): 339–66.

Geertz, C. (1973) *The Interpretation of Cultures*. New York: Basic Books.

Gross, N., J. Guiaquinta, and M. Bernstein (1969) *Innovation in Education*. New York: Basic

Hackman, J.R. and R. Wageman (1995) "Quality Management: Empirical, conceptual, and practical issues." *Administrative Science Quarterly* 40(2): 309–42.

Heck, R.H. and G.A. Marcoulides (1996) "School culture and performance: Testing the invariance of an organizational model." *School Effectiveness and School Improvement* 7(1): 76–95.

Hofstede, G. (1991) *Culture and Organizations: Software of the Mind*. London: McGraw-Hill, Inc.

——, B. Neuijen, D.D. Ohayv, and G. Sanders (1990) "Measuring organizational cultures: A qualitative and quantitative study across twenty cases." *Administrative Science Quarterly* 35: 286–316.

Hopkins, D. (1993) *A Teacher's Guide to Classroom Research*. Philadelphia: Open University Press.

Hord, S.M. and V. Boyd (1995) "Professional development fuels a culture of continuous improvement." *Journal of Staff Development* 16(1): 10–15.

Hoy, W.K. and C.G. Miskel (1996) *Educational Administration: Theory, Research, and Practice*. New York: McGraw-Hill.

Juran, J.M. (1988) *Juran on Planning for Quality*. New York: Free Press.

Keith, Timothy Z. (1993) "Does parent involvement affect 8th grade student achievement?" *School Psychology Review* 22(3): 474–96.

Kerchner, C., J. Koppich, and J. Weeres (1997) *United Mind Workers: Unions and Teaching in the Knowledge Society*. San Francisco: Jossey Bass.

Kohn, A. (1993) "Turning learning into a business: Concerns about total quality." *Educational Leadership* 51(1): 58–61.

Kroeber, A.L. and C. Kluckhohn (1952) *Culture: A Critical Review of Concepts and Definitions*. New York: Vintage Books.

Leithwood, K. and R. Aitken (1995) *Making Schools Smarter: A System for Monitoring School and District Progress*. Thousand Oaks, CA: Corwin.

—— and K.S. Louis (eds) (1998) *Organizational Learning in Schools*. Lisse: Swets and Zeitlinger.

——, D. Jantzi, and R. Steinbach (1995) "An organizational learning perspective on school responses to central policy initiatives." *School Organization* 15(3): 229–52.

Leonard, P. E. (1997) "Understanding the dimensions of school culture." Paper presented at the Annual Meeting of the American Educational Research Association, Chicago, IL.

Lieberman, M. (1993) *Public Education: An Autopsy*. Cambridge, MA: Harvard University Press.

Little, J.W. (1990) "The persistence of privacy: Autonomy and initiative in teachers' professional relations." *Teachers College Record* 91(4): 509–36.

Lortie, D. C. (1975) *Schoolteacher: A Sociological Study*. Chicago: The University of Chicago Press.

Louis, K.S. and S.D. Kruse and associates (1995) *Professionalism and Community: Perspectives on Reforming Urban Schools*. Thousand Oaks, CA: Corwin.

—— and S. Kruse (1998) "Creating community in reform: Images of organizational learning in urban schools." In K. Leithwood and K.S. Louis (eds), *Organizational Learning in Schools*. Lisse: Swets and Zeitlinger.

—— and H. Marks (1999) "The problem of high schools in the US." Paper presented at the annual meetings of the American Educational Research Association, Montreal.

—— and M.B. Miles (1990) *Improving the Urban High School: What Works and Why*. New York: Teachers College Press.

——, J. Toole, and A. Hargreaves (1999) "Rethinking school improvement." In J. Murphy and K.S. Louis (eds), *Handbook of Research on Educational Administration*: 251–75. San Francisco: Jossey Bass.

Manley, R.J. (1996) "Coalescing a school community around total quality: A superintendent's perspective." *School Administrator* 53(7): 29–32.

Marks, H.M. and K.S. Louis (1997) "Does teacher empowerment affect the classroom? The implications of teacher empowerment for instruction practice and student academic performance." *Educational Evaluation and Policy Analysis* 19(3): 245–75.

Martin, J. (1992) *Cultures in Organizations: Three Perspectives*. New York: Oxford University Press.

Masland, A.T. (1985) "Organizational culture in the study of higher education." *The Review of Higher Education* 8(2): 157–68.

Nadler, D.A. and M.L. Tushman (1980) "A congruence model for organizational assessment." In E.E. Lawler III, D.A. Nadler, and C. Cammann (eds), *Organizational Assessment: Perspectives on the Measurement of Organizational Behavior and the Quality of Work Life*: 261–78. New York: John Wiley & Sons.

National Institute of Standards and Technology (1999) *Malcolm Baldrige National Quality Award 1998 Education Criteria for Performance Excellence*. Washington, DC: Department of Commerce.

Newmann, F. and associates (1996) *Authentic Achievement: Restructuring Schools for Intellectual Quality*. San Francisco, Jossey Bass.

O'Reilly, C.A., III, J. Chatman, and D.F. Caldwell (1991) "People and organizational culture: A profile comparison approach to assessing person-organization fit." *Academy of Management Journal* 34(3): 487–516.

Osigweh, C. (1989) "Concept fallibility in the social sciences." *Academy of Management Review* 14(4): 579–94.

Peck, K.L. and A.A. Carr (1997) "Restoring confidence in schools through systems thinking." *International Journal of Educational Reform* 6(3): 316–23.

Pettigrew, A.M. (1990) "Conclusion: Organizational climate and culture: Two constructs in search of a role." In B. Schneider (ed.), *Organizational Climate and Culture*: 413–34. San Francisco: Jossey Bass.

Prawat, R. (1996) "Learning community, commitment and school reform." *Journal of Curriculum Studies* 28: 91–110.

Quinn, R.E. and J. Rohrbaugh (1981) "A competing values approach to organizational effectiveness." *Public Productivity Review* 5: 122–40.

Rago, W. (1993) "Struggles in transformation: A study in QM, leadership, and organizational culture in a government agency." *Public Administration Review* 56(3): 227–34.

Reger, R.K., L.T. Gustafson, S.M. DeMarie, and J.V. Mullane (1994). "Reframing the organization: Why implementing Total Quality is easier said than done." *Academy of Management Review* 19(3): 565–84.

Reynolds, P.D. (1986) "Organizational culture as related to industry, position, and performance: A preliminary report." *Journal of Management Studies* 23(3): 333–45.

Rigsby, K.L. (1994) "Quality Management and the culture of a model elementary school: A case study". EdD thesis: University of South Florida.

Riley, P. (1983) "A structurationist account of political culture." *Administrative Science Quarterly* 28: 414–37.

Rinehart, G. (1993) "Building a vision for quality education." *Journal of School Leadership* 3(3): 260–8.

Rist, M.C. (1993) "TQM in Tupelo." *Executive Educator* 15(6): 27–9.

Rokeach, M. (1973) *The Nature of Human Values*. New York: The Free Press.

Rossman, G.B., H.D. Corbett, and W.A. Firestone (1988) *Change and Effectiveness in Schools: A Cultural Perspective*. Albany, NY: SUNY Press.

Salisbury, D.F., R.K. Branson, W.I. Altreche, F.F. Funk, and S.M. Broetzmann (1997) "Applying customer dissatisfaction measures to schools: You'd better know what's wrong before you try to fix it." *Educational Policy* 11(3): 286–308.

Saphier, J. and M. King (1985) "Good seeds grow in strong cultures." *Educational Leadership* (March): 67–74.

Sarason, S.B. (1996) *Revisiting "The Culture of the School and the Problem of Change."* New York: Teachers College Press.

Sashkin, M. (1990) *School Culture Assessment Questionnaire*. Washington, DC: Graduate School of Education and Human Development, George Washington University.

—— and M.G. Sashkin (1993) "Principals and their school cultures: Understandings from quantitative and qualitative research." In M. Sashkin and H.J. Walberg (eds), *Educational Leadership and School Culture*. Berkeley, CA: McCutchan Publishing.

Scheerens, J. (1992) *Effective Schooling*. London: Cassell.

Schein, E.H. (1992) *Organizational Culture and Leadership*. San Francisco: Jossey Bass.

Smart, J.C. and E.P. St John (1996) "Organizational culture and effectiveness in higher education: A test of the 'culture type' and 'strong culture' hypotheses." *Educational Evaluation and Policy Analysis* 18(3): 219–41.

Smircich, L. (1983) "Concepts of culture and organizational analysis." *Administrative Science Quarterly* 28: 339–58.

Snyder, K. and M. Acker-Hocevar (1995) "Managing change to a quality philosophy: A partnership perspective." Paper presented at the Annual International Conference of the Association of Management, Vancouver, British Columbia.

Stringfield, S. (1995) "Attempting to enhance students learning through innovative programs: The case for schools evolving into high reliability organizations." *School Effectiveness and School Improvement* 6(1): 67–96.

Sweeney, J.E. (1986) "Developing a strong culture: The key to school improvement." *National Forum of Education and Supervision Journal* 3(3): 134–43.

Trice, H.M. (1985) "Rites and ceremonials in organizational culture." *Research in the Sociology of Organizations* 4: 221–70.

—— and J.M. Beyer (1984) "Studying organizational cultures through rites and ceremonials." *Academy of Management Review* 9(4): 653–69.

Tucker, R.W. and W.J. McCoy (1988) "Can questionnaires measure culture: Eight extended field studies." Paper presented at the Annual Convention of the American Psychological Association, 12–16 August, Atlanta, GA.

Van de Ven, A.H. and A.L. Delbecq (1972) "The Nominal Group as a research instrument for exploratory health studies." *American Public Health Association Journal* (March): 337–42.

Van Maanen, J. and S.R. Barley (1984) "Occupational communities: Culture and control in organizations." In B. Staw and L. Cummings (eds), *Research in Organizational Behavior*, Vol. 6: 287–365. Greenwich, CT: JAI.

Weller, S.J. and L.D. Weller (1997) "Quality learning organizations and continuous improvement: Implementing the concept." *NASSP Bulletin* 81(591): 62–70.

Wilson, E.K. (1971) *Sociology: Rules, Roles, and Relationships*. Homewood, IL: Dorsey.

Wilson, K.G. (1994) "Wisdom-centered learning: Striking a new paradigm for education." *School Administrator* 51(5): 26–33.

Zammuto, R.F. and J.Y. Krakower (1991) "Quantitative and qualitative studies of organizational culture." *Research in Organizational Change and Development* 5: 83–114.

14

The Impact of Mental Models, Professional Community, and Interdisciplinary Teaming on Classroom Practice[1]

Introduction

This chapter investigates change in teachers' classroom practice. Using data from a 2001 survey of teachers in a large district's elementary schools, we examine how teachers' work environment and conceptions of practice influenced their adoption of arts-infused practices. This analysis represents our effort to understand the way in which an externally funded initiative combines with individual professional beliefs and the social organization of the school to encourage improved pedagogy. While our analysis focuses on teachers' responses to a particular initiative, our analytic model emphasizes three factors that are part of the change process: the individual assumptions that practitioners bring to a change initiative, their daily interactions with colleagues, and the collaborative relationships that they may develop with others as they try to improve their practice. All three of these factors are among the building blocks of school culture with which change advocates must work if they are to improve student learning and all three can, to a greater or lesser extent, be built into the design of school improvement initiatives.

The Change Initiative

In 1999, The Minneapolis Public Schools received a $3.2 million Challenge Grant from the Annenberg Foundation, whose focus was on the role of the arts as a means for overall academic improvement. To accomplish this goal, schools would increase integration of the arts into the "core curriculum" and would develop strong partnerships with artists and arts organizations. The vision was that ultimately every child would experience and learn from the richness, diversity, and life-changing truths that are found in theatre, music, visual arts, and other art forms. As with other major improvement initiatives, the primary criterion for judging success or failure was increased student learning and, based on analyses of standardized test scores, the project was a success, particularly with students whose personal characteristics placed them at risk of falling behind (Ingram and Louis 2003). The summative evaluation results also found that it was not merely the *presence* of the program in a school, but the *intensity* of its realization within classrooms that accounted for increased learning. This paper focuses on the core question that always follows from the finding of variable success in implementation: what factors account for the fact that some teachers in some schools changed a great deal, while others participated but did not make the changes in pedagogy that appeared to lead to increased student learning?

Related Literature

To answer this question, this chapter looks at elementary-school teachers who were employed in schools that were participating in the Annenberg Project, and is influenced by earlier analyses of elementary-school implementation (Freeman and Louis 2002) as well as case studies of implementation in high schools (see Chapter 10, this volume). We frame our study in the context of research on organizational culture (Hatch 1993), more particularly the culture of schools (Firestone and Louis 2000), and draw on recent cognitive psychology and sociological studies. Three concepts that increasingly appear in this literature are *mental models* (also referred to as cognitive maps or schemata), *professional community*, and *teacher interdisciplinary teaming*.

Mental Models

The term mental models has emerged as a shorthand for capturing a central tenet of recent cognitive research, namely that people always interpret their environment through a set of "cognitive maps" that summarize ideas, concepts, processes or phenomena in a coherent way. That people have mental models to serve as internal representations of the world is not new (Carley and Palmquist 1992), but the incorporation of the concept into cultural studies is more recent. The convergence of cognitive psychology and cultural sociology is based on the assumption that culture presents a "toolkit" (Swidler 1986) of mediated images and validated actions that individuals and groups draw on, often with little explicit thought, to guide their daily behavior (DiMaggio 1997). Mental models are important because decision-makers, whether CEOs or working mothers, need them in order to simplify the chaotic environments and multiple logical options that they face (Porac and Thomas 1990; Thomas *et al.* 1993). Reliance on mental models may be particularly prevalent in the case of busy professionals such as teachers, whose work requires them to make hundreds of rapid decisions each day as they search for the best way of encouraging their students to absorb and interpret the material that they are presenting.

Mental models are, in part, a consequence of the range of cultural (socially constructed and recognized) elements that any group develops, and partly a result of how any given individual organizes the cultural information for their own use (DiMaggio 1997: 268). In education, this means that each teacher carries their own set of images about what constitutes good pedagogy, but that this image is drawn from a limited bank of options that are generated by common expectations, collective experience, and shared professional practice, as well as "their biases, expectations, and explanations about how people think and how they learn" (Spillane and Louis 2002: 395). The common bank of images from which mental models are drawn is influenced by the "microculture" of a school or a local community, but also by the broadly shared professional or "macroculture" (Abrahamson and Fombrun 1994). In particular, teachers are faced with alternative schemata for good teaching, ranging from practices that are often collected under the rubric of "direct instruction" (which, in this chapter, we choose to call contemporary teacher-centered pedagogy) to those that are based on constructivist or progressive education principles (which, in this chapter, we choose to call student-directed learning). Newmann and his colleagues also point to the importance of pedagogic mental models that emphasize connections between the classroom and the real world (Newmann and associates 1996).

Mental models serve as guides to making both big and little decisions, but they are also constraints because they are the first screen through which new information must pass. DiMaggio (1997) notes that people pay more attention to information that is relevant to their current schemata, and they are less likely to have correctly remembered information that is inconsistent. The more widely shared the individual mental models are, the more likely it is that challenging information will be readily accepted – or rejected and reinterpreted (Meyer and Rowan 1977; Giddens 1984). Thus, when individuals use their mental models as a way of making sense of new information or ideas from their environment, they can lead to creativity and innovation, or inhibit it (Ford 1996).

Making an effort to use arts–infused lessons requires a significant change in pedagogy, and represents a real challenge for those who are most comfortable with conceptions of knowledge that emphasize teaching a single discipline at a time, or thinking about learning as equivalent to acquiring stronger basic skills and facts (Wahlstrom 2003). Thus, research suggests that teachers' mental models may hold the key to determining whether they make significant changes in their practice, or pour the new wine of the arts into existing teaching strategies (Toole 2001).

Professional Community

A key sociological contribution to the study of school culture and change has emerged in the concept of professional community. Although they have been around for some time, Westheimer (1999) argues that theories of teacher communities are "under conceptualized." Furman (1999) calls them "confusing," a "mismatch" with postmodern life, and providing "little guidance for practice." Adding to the confusion, researchers use a variety of terms to describe how to organize schools for teacher community and learning: *collegiality* (Little 1990; Barth 2001), *collaboration* (Zellermeyer 1997; Nias *et al.* 1999), *professional community* (Hargreaves 1993; Kruse *et al.* 1995), *discourse communities* (Putnam 2000), *professional learning community* (Chapter 10, this volume), and *schools that learn* (Leithwood 2002).

By using the term *professional learning community*, we signify our interest not only in discrete acts of teacher sharing, but in the establishment of a school-wide culture that makes collaboration expected, inclusive, genuine, ongoing, and focused on critically examining practice to improve student outcomes. The term integrates three robust concepts: a school culture that emphasizes professionalism is "client oriented and knowledge based" (Darling-Hammond 1990); one that emphasizes learning places a high value on teachers' inquiry and reflection (Toole 2001); and one that is communitarian emphasizes personal connection (Kruse *et al.* 1995). The hypothesis is that what teachers do together outside of the classroom can be as important as what they do inside in affecting school restructuring, teachers' professional development, and student learning.

Kruse *et al.* (1995) designate five interconnected variables that describe what they call genuine professional communities in such a broad manner that they can be applied to diverse settings. The variables are: shared norms and values, a focus on student learning, deprivatized practice, reflective dialogue, and collaboration. Researchers can and do vary on the exact list and number of key variables, and those variables can only act as general descriptors. Little (2000) points out that there is no simple checklist or template that will ever adequately guide the construction of professional learning communities. But the central idea of the model is the existence of a social architecture to school organizations that helps shape teachers' attitudes toward new pedagogies (Toole 2001), and recent research using professional learning community as a variable has shown powerful associations with teacher practice (Bryk *et al.* 1999; Pounder 1999; Scribner 1999; Toole 2001).

Interdisciplinary Teams

A final variable in our analysis deals with a central effort on the part of the Minneapolis Annenberg Challenge to change the culture of collaboration by promoting classroom-based *interdisciplinary teaming*. Introducing teams is a strategy that has often been used in schools to foster teacher leadership for innovation and improvement, and is currently being promoted under the general label of Small Learning Communities (SLCs). The results of such structural changes have been mixed. Formal teams may have limited effects on student achievement (Hackmann *et al.* 2002; Supovitz 2002), and may even undermine collaboration on a school-wide basis (Kruse and Louis 1997), although in other cases they create profound change in practice (Detert *et al.* 2001). Some researchers and practitioners emphasize semi-formal teamwork and collaboration in efforts to raise achievement (Polite 1994; Kanthak 1995). Our inquiry is focused on voluntary, informal pairing of an artist and a teacher to work in a classroom. (For a more extensive discussion of how teaming worked in the Arts for Academic Achievement program, see Freeman and Louis (2002).)

Teamwork, innovation, and changes in practice can be fostered by sustained, high-quality professional development (Desimone *et al.* 2002). While greater emphasis is currently placed on whole-school professional development, often to create professional community (Desimone 2002), there is also a consensus that professional development must consistently reinforce the basic focus on teaching and learning (Newmann *et al.* 2002; Spillane and Louis 2002). This is where team work fits in, because it is in smaller groups, working around new curriculum and pedagogy, that the greatest professional growth through reflective practice is likely to occur (Kruse and Louis 1997; Freeman and Louis 2002).

An Integrated Model of School Improvement

Mental models, professional community, and interdisciplinary teaming are, theoretically, distinct dimensions of school culture. On the one hand, teachers hold individual and collective images of pedagogic practice that steer both individual decisions in classrooms and collective decisions about how best to work with students in the school and joint curriculum work. These mental models may support or inhibit change. On the other hand, individual teachers work in settings that may be characterized by more-or-less supportive environments that encourage collective action and nurture professional improvement. Finally, teachers may take steps to counter the disciplinary culture of autonomy and individualism by accepting professional partners within their classroom, or they may choose to work on changing their pedagogy on their own. If we think of improvement practices and more effective school organization as the goal, all three can be expected to contribute.

A comprehensive model of change must, of course, take into account other important and empirically verified approaches, which emphasize extra-school environmental conditions, such as policies, leadership styles, available resources, parental expectations, and so on, as well as the characteristics of the students who populate the school. In addition, psychological predispositions of teachers will affect their behavior above and beyond the cultural features that we have noted. In this paper, however, we will focus exclusively on mental models, professional community, and interdisciplinary teaming to answer four questions:

1. To what extent do teachers' mental models predict their use of arts-infused pedagogies in their classrooms?
2. To what extent do teachers' experiences of professional community in their school predict their use of arts-infused pedagogies in their classrooms?
3. To what extent do teachers' direct experiences of interdisciplinary teaming predict their use of arts-infused pedagogies in their classrooms?
4. To what extent does the combined effect of all cultural variables, considered simultaneously, affect the use of arts-infused pedagogies in classrooms?

Research Methods

This paper is based on survey data collected in the spring of 2001 from all teachers working in 41 Minneapolis schools funded by the Annenberg Project.[2] Research staff administered the survey during a regularly scheduled staff meeting at each site during April and May of 2001. The survey was designed to capture teachers' perspectives on arts integration and their school community; interests in the arts; beliefs about teaching; the extent of their use of integration and partnering; and demographic information. All teachers were asked to complete the survey even if they had not been directly involved in any project activities during the year. Teachers were informed that their responses were confidential and the survey results would not be used to determine future funding. A conservative estimate of the response rate at each site varied from 23 per cent to 94 per cent, or 62 per cent overall.[3]

For the purpose of this paper, we were interested in responses from educators who taught in grades 1–6. From the original dataset of $N = 1,369$, we selected schools that were either K–5 or K–8 configurations ($N = 30$). From these sites, we chose teachers who were not arts specialists and who taught in grades 1–6. The final number of subjects was 725.[4] Descriptive information for demographic variables, as well as the dependent and outcome measures used in this study, may be found in Table 14.1.

Measurement and Scaling

Mental Models
Mental model (MM) measures were based on an instrument previously developed by Toole (2001). The fifteen mental models items were completed on a four-point Likert-type scale (1 = Strongly Disagree, 4 = Strongly Agree). These items were submitted to a Principal Components Factor Analysis with Varimax Rotation. The analysis revealed three components with Eigen values greater than 1. Factor 1 appears to represent variance related to Contemporary Teacher-centered schemas, while Factor 2 represents variance representing Real World Connections, and Factor 3 Student-Directed Learning. Together these three factors account for 50 per cent of the variance. Alpha reliability coefficients for each of the three factors were 0.81, 0.74, and 0.60, respectively. Scales were created by adding together individuals' responses to items loading on each factor. Descriptive information about the scales may be found in Table 14.1, while additional information regarding the individual items and their loadings on each factor is located in Appendix A.

Professional Community
Professional community (PC) measures were based on an instrument previously used by Louis et al. (1999). The twelve professional community items were completed on a four-point Likert-type scale (1 = Not at all true, 2 = Not very true, 3 = Somewhat true, and 4 = Very true). Although Louis et al. used a single scale of professional community, these items were submitted to a Principal Components Factor Analysis with Varimax Rotation, which yielded two components with Eigen values greater than 1. Factor 1

Table 14.1 Descriptive Information for Demographic/Control, Dependent, and Independent Variables

	N	%		
Gender				
Male	135	18.6		
Female	590	81.4		
Special focus teaching (ELL or Special Education)	96	13.2		
Grade Level				
Primary (1–3)	302	41.7		
Upper Elementary (4–6) or Both	423	58.3		
	Mean	SD	Median	Range
Mental Model Scales				
Contemporary Teacher Centered	20.20	2.28	20	6–24
Real World Connections	15.55	1.89	15	5–20
Student-directed Learning	11.51	1.58	11	4–16
Professional Community Scales				
Professional Behavior	20.70	3.68	21	7–28
Professional Belief System	16.29	2.75	16	5–20
Interdisciplinary Teaming	2.76	3.52	0	0–12
Arts Integration	5.21	3.97	6	0–12

represents variance related to professional behaviors, while Factor 2 represents variance associated with professional belief systems. The alpha reliability coefficient for Factor 1 and Factor 2 was 0.85. As with the mental models scales, the professional community scales were computed by adding together responses to items that loaded on Factor 1 and Factor 2, respectively (see Table 14.1). A table of the professional community items and factor loadings may be found in Appendix B.

Interdisciplinary Teaming

In one section of the survey, teachers were asked whether they worked with an arts partner to integrate the arts, and were then asked about the number of times they engaged in a number of activities with the arts partner. Because a major focus of the project was to give teachers and artists the opportunity to develop new ways of working together we included survey items that would allow us to distinguish between teachers who may have had an artist in their classroom as part of a typical artist-in-residency program and teachers who collaborated with artists on interdisciplinary teams to develop and deliver arts-integrated instruction. Many of the activities that were listed were typical of artist-in-residency programs and involved no interdisciplinary teaming as we have defined it. For example, an artist may have taught the class an arts activity with no participation by the regular teacher, or they may have taught an in-service lesson for several teachers in the school.

The following activities, which were embedded in the longer list of ways in which the arts partner may have worked with the teacher, were intended to measure interdisciplinary teaming: co-developed an arts-integrated curriculum, co-developed an arts-integrated assessment, and co-taught students in the teacher's classroom. Response options for these items were:

- 1 = Never;
- 2 = 1–2 times;
- 3 = 3–4 times; and
- 4 = 5 or more times.

These items were aggregated to create an "extent of partnering" or interdisciplinary teaming scale. A score of "0" on this scale indicates that the individual did not have an arts partner, while a score of 3 means that, although the individual had an arts partner, he or she did not participate in any of these activities. Table 14.1 contains descriptive information for the interdisciplinary teaming scale.

Arts Integration

The extent, or level, of each teacher's use of arts integration in the classroom was obtained from four survey items in which teachers rated their use of arts integration on a 4-point scale (not at all, very little, some, a lot) in English/reading, math, history/social studies, and science. As with the interdisciplinary teaming variable, these items were aggregated to create an arts integration scale (see Table 14.1).

Individual Level Control Variables

Individual characteristics and specific work settings and roles are always reasonable predictors whose effects could outweigh the individual, cultural, and program variables that we examine. We include three teacher characteristics as controls:

- *Gender.* Measured as a dichotomous variable, we include gender because it is an established correlate of teachers' job satisfaction and experience of professional community.
- *Special-focus teaching.* The roles of special-education teacher and second-language teachers (ELL) have a special character in the elementary schools in this study: they do not see the same group of children for the whole day, and have specific and much more prescribed learning objectives for the students that they do work with. Special-education and ELL teachers were coded as "1"; all other teachers with specific grade assignments were coded as "0".
- *Grade level.* We include attention to the grade level taught because, in this district, the nature of other policies and innovative programs affected the two groups differently. While the primary teachers (1–3) were focused on a major district effort to increase the reading skills of all students, upper elementary teachers (4–6) were also deeply involved in district-sponsored mathematics and science innovations. In our view (based on qualitative data collected in the schools), there was considerably more pressure on upper elementary teachers to work on disciplinary knowledge of all types, in addition to beginning to prepare students for important standardized and state tests. Teachers who taught at the primary level were coded as "1", while those teaching at upper elementary, or both primary and upper elementary, were coded as "0".

The simple correlations of the variables used in the analysis are presented in Table 14.2.

Table 14.2   Correlation Matrix

	Gender	Special Populations Teacher	Elementary Level	Partnering	MM: Teacher Centered	MM: Real World Connections	MM: Student Directed	PC: Behavior	PC: Beliefs
Gender									
Special Pop. Teacher	0.08*								
Elementary Level	0.11**	0.17***							
Partnering	0.00	−0.24***	0.16***						
MM: Teacher Centered	0.12**	−0.004	−0.02	0.136***					
MM: Real World Connections	0.09**	0.05	−0.06†	0.10**	0.60***				
MM: Student Directed	0.07†	−0.04	−0.05	0.13***	0.55***	0.47***			
PC: Behavior	0.11**	0.05	−0.05	0.11**	0.19***	0.18***	0.18***		
PC: Beliefs	0.12**	−0.01	0.002	0.13***	0.215***	0.19***	0.17***	0.61***	

MM, mental models; PC, professional community.

$†P < 0.01$, $*P < 0.05$, $**P < 0.01$, $***P < 0.001$.

Data Analysis And Results

Question 1 asked: *To what extent do teachers' mental models predict their use of arts-infused pedagogies in their classrooms?* To answer this question, we conducted separate two-stage regressions of the measure of reported arts integration on the three mental-models variables. In the first step, the control variables were entered, while in the second, third, and fourth, a single MM variable was added. Finally, the three MM variables were entered simultaneously. These regressions are summarized in Table 14.3.

The results indicate that teachers' personal and professional characteristics contribute significantly to the prediction of using arts integration in the classroom. In particular, "regular" classroom teachers who and primary-grade teachers were the most likely to use arts-infused models. Teacher gender had no effect on reported arts integration.

These relationships, as measured by the standardized regression coefficients (β), are not dramatically altered in Model 2 by introducing the MM Teacher-Centered variable. However, the latter added substantially to the variance explained by the model

Table 14.3 Multiple Regression of Level of Arts Integration on Mental Models

	Model 1 β	Model 2 β	Model 3 β	Model 4 β	Model 5 β
Covariates					
Gender	0.051	0.019	0.034	0.033	0.018
Special Populations Teacher	−0.225***	−0.220***	−0.231***	−0.213***	−0.215***
Elementary Level (Lower/ Upper)	0.249***	0.258***	0.262***	0.264***	0.265***
R^2	0.136				
Adjusted R^2	0.132				
F	37.76***				
MM: Teacher Centered		0.243***			0.168***
R^2		0.19			
Adjusted R^2		0.19			
F		43.30***			
MM: Real World Connections			0.172***		0.013
R^2			0.165		
Adjusted R^2			0.160		
F			35.52***		
MM: Student Directed				0.220***	0.123**
R^2				0.184	
Adjusted R^2				0.179	
F				40.50***	
Full Model R^2					0.21
Adjusted R^2					0.20
F					30.86***

**P < 0.01; ***P < 0.001.

(R^2 = 0.136 for Model 1 and R^2 = 0.19 for model 2). In addition, MM Teacher Centered was also a significant predictor of arts infusion (β = 0.243, significant at the 0.000 level). The comparable regression model for the second MM variable, MM Connections, produced similar but weaker results. In other words, the MM Real World Connections variable increased the percentage of variance explained slightly in step 2 (from R^2 = 0.136 for Model 1 to R^2 = 0.165), but achieved a significant beta coefficient in the regression model (β = 0.172, $P < 0.001$). The fourth regression model used the MM Student-directed variable, with results that were more similar to Model 2 (MM Teacher Centered). The R^2 increased from 0.136 in step 1 to 0.184 in step 2, and the standardized coefficient for the variable was β = 0.22 – the largest after the coefficient associated with being a primary (1–3) teacher. The full Model 5, which includes all three MM variables, is slightly more effective at explaining the dependent variable, increasing the amount of variance explained to 21 per cent. Both the teacher-centered MM variable and the student-directed MM variable are significant in the model.

To summarize, all three MMl variables contribute significantly to predicting teachers' use of arts-infused pedagogy in their classrooms, but the teacher-centered and student-centered mental models are most powerful.

The second question, *To what extent does teachers' experience of professional community predict their use of arts-infused pedagogies in their classrooms?*, was addressed using a similar regression model. The results of the regressions are presented in Table 14.4.

Table 14.4 Multiple Regression of Level of Arts Integration on Professional Community

	Model 1 β	Model 2 β	Model 3 β	Model 4 β
Covariates				
Gender	0.051	0.036	0.034	0.031
Special Populations Teacher	−0.225***	−0.230***	−0.224***	−0.227***
Elementary Level (Lower/Upper)	0.249***	0.256***	0.251***	0.255***
R^2	0.136			
Adjusted R^2	0.132			
F	37.76***			
Professional Behavior		0.139***		0.085*
R^2		0.156		
Adjusted R^2		0.150		
F		32.96***		
Professional Belief System			0.140***	0.088*
R^2			0.155	
Adjusted R^2			0.150	
F			33.04***	
Full Model				
R^2				0.160
Adjusted R^2				0.154
F				27.32***

**$P < 0.01$; ***$P < 0.001$.

We turn directly to Model 2, since the first model, which introduces the covariates, has been described in conjunction with Question 1. This model shows that PC Behavior increases the multiple R^2 from 0.136 to 0.156. While the increase is not great, the variable exhibits a standardized regression coefficient of $\beta = 0.139$, which is significant at the 0.001 level. The effect of PC-Beliefs is similar, as shown in Model 3. The introduction of the PC variables does not impact the large negative effect of being special populations teachers or the large positive effect of working in the primary grades. In the fourth full model, both the professional behavior and professional beliefs scales were significant predictors of arts integration. The R^2 increase is similar to that observed for the two scales separately – from 0.136 to 0.16, and both of the PC variables are significant at the 0.05 level. As in the other regressions, the introduction of the PC variables does not change the significant effects associated with grade level or being a special populations teacher.

To summarize, the PC variables significantly affect the degree to which teachers actively infuse the arts into their regular classroom practice, although they do not outweigh the importance of the teachers' role within the structure of elementary-school settings.

The third question asks: *To what extent do teachers' direct experiences of interdisciplinary teaming predict their use of arts-infused pedagogies in their classrooms?* A two-step regression model with the extent of partnering variable entered as the second step is shown in Table 14.5. The partnering variable has a more profound effect on the use of arts-infused pedagogy than either the MM or PC variables. The amount of variance explained increased from 0.136 in Step 1 to 0.323 in Step 2, with a corresponding increase in the F statistic from 37.69 to 85.89 ($P < 0.001$). The standardized regression coefficient for the teaming variable is $\beta = 45$ ($P < 0.001$). Further, the addition of the teaming variable substantially reduces the beta coefficients associated with being a special populations teacher (from $\beta = -23$ to $\beta = -0.13$) and working with lower elementary students (from $\beta = 0.25$ to $\beta = 0.19$). This contrasts markedly with the limited effects of the MM and PC variables on the covariates.

To summarize, it appears that teachers who are involved in interdisciplinary teaming with an arts partner are more likely to use arts-infused models in their teaching. Although teaming was voluntary in all schools, teachers who engaged in classroom-based teaming learned new pedagogies.

Our final question, *To what extent does the combined effect of all cultural variables, considered simultaneously, affect the use of arts-infused pedagogies in classrooms?*, was addressed with a structural equation model. The model used all the indicators involved in the regression models with the exception of gender, which had previously shown no relationship with any of the other indicators including the arts integration scale. The model explored the possibility of direct effects of mental models and professional community on arts integration and indirect effects on arts integration through interdisciplinary teaming. Grade level was modeled as having a direct impact on arts integration, while special-focus teaching was thought to have an indirect impact through interdisciplinary teaming. Special-focus teaming, grade level, interdisciplinary teaming, and arts integration are all measured by single indicators. The model imposes the assumption that single indicators

Table 14.5 Multiple Regression of Level of Integration on Interdisciplinary Teaming

	Model 1 β	Model 2 β
Covariates		
Gender	0.051	0.049
Special Populations Teacher	−0.225***	−0.125***
Elementary Level (Lower/Upper)	0.249***	0.193***
R^2	0.136	
Adjusted R^2	0.132	
F	37.76***	
Partnering		0.450***
R^2		0.323
Adjusted R^2		0.319
F		85.89***

***$P < 0.0$.

are measured without error. Mental model is a construct measured by the three mental-model scales (teacher centered, real world, student directed). Professional community is a construct measured by the two professional community scales (professional beliefs, professional behavior). Given the differing types of variables involved, the input data are an asymptotic covariance matrix based on polychoric, polyserial, and Pearson R correlations between the indicators. The model was estimated with LISREL 8.52 (Jöreskog and Sörbom 1979) (see Figure 14.1).

The model achieves a good fit to the data based on several fit measures. It has a chi-square ratio to degrees of freedom equal to 4.1, which is considered acceptable (Wheaton et al. 1977). It has a root mean square error of approximation (RMSEA) equal to 0.064, which is considered acceptable (Browne and Cudeck 1993). The Goodness of Fit Index (GFI) and the Adjusted Goodness of Fit Index (AGFI) are both high at 0.99 and 0.95, respectively. The model shows the central role interdisciplinary teaming plays in determining the level of arts integration. The impact of professional community is indirect on arts integration as is that of mental model. Professional community affects mental model, which in turn is a significant predictor of interdisciplinary teaming. Professional community also impacts interdisciplinary teaming directly. Neither professional community nor mental model had direct effects on arts integration. Whether a teacher works with a special population has a positive impact on interdisciplinary teaming in contrast to its negative relationship to arts integration seen in the regression models. Grade level does not have a significant impact on arts integration in this model, however.

Discussion and Conclusion

We summarize briefly, noting that our analysis suggests that the integrated model proposed at the beginning of the paper is supported by the data. Mental models, which

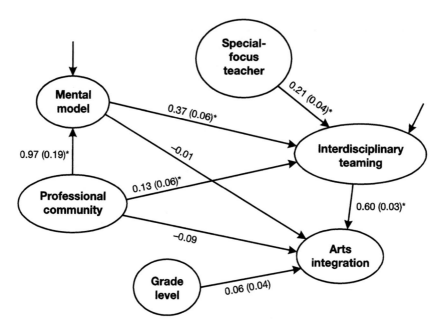

Figure 14.1   Structural Path Coefficients Predicting Arts Integration

*Statistically significant coefficient ($P < 0.05$). Coefficients are standardized coefficients with standard errors in parentheses. $N = 725$. Chi square with 12 degrees of freedom = 49.20. Root mean square error of approximation (RMSEA) = 0064. Adjusted Goodness of Fit Index (AGFI) = 0.95.

are individually held "schema" or maps that teachers draw on to guide their professional practice, professional community, which measures the supportive learning environment for adults, and interdisciplinary teaming, which provides significant cognitive stimuli for change, all contribute to elementary teachers' reported efforts to introduce arts-infused pedagogical approaches in their classrooms.

The implications of these findings go beyond the identification of three variables that have an effect on a particular pedagogical innovation. We believe that they represent the three supporting legs of efforts to create learning organizations in schools, and that they direct our attention to the importance of cognitive approaches to school reform.

Learning organizations depend on the willingness of individual members to be open to challenges and experimentation. As many authors have noted, without actors who are both willing and able to actively make sense of new ideas and demands, change cannot occur in contexts where discretion and judgment are needed to carry out the work at hand. This is particularly true where the change requires a significant shift from past practices – which is almost always the case when teachers are asked to alter how they teach as well as what they teach (Spillane *et al.* 2002: 398). Our analysis supports Toole's (2001) research, which suggests that mental models can predict whether teachers will change.

In this case, we also add to the theoretical debates about what kinds of mental models are most conducive to reflective pedagogical practice. While our measures of "teacher-centered" and "student-directed" pedagogy are imperfectly related to the "direct instruction"-"constructivist pedagogy" debate, our findings suggest that it may be more important for teachers to have a clearly held mental model that incorporates contemporary knowledge about teaching and learning than to have a consistent theoretical position. It is indecisive teachers – those who do not score high on either or both of these mental models – who seemed to be the least likely to be able to take advantage of the opportunities for change presented by the Arts for Academic Achievement program.

Learning organizations are also dependent on a culture that supports talking about and exploring new ideas and their impacts in schools. While this may, in part, be considered as an aggregation of the situated cognition or mental models of all members of the organization, most people who study schools as learning organizations view the culture as greater than the sum of its parts (Firestone and Louis 2000). We have looked here at one way of framing school culture – professional community – that has been explicitly linked to the way in which schools learn (Bryk *et al.* 1999; Leithwood 2002). Our analysis suggests that professional community has a role to play in changing classroom practice, but its effects are less than those suggested by some previous studies. One possible explanation for this, put forward by Toole (2001), is that mental models determine whether a teacher is ready to change, while professional community is more powerful in determining whether pedagogical changes persist over time on a school-wide basis.

The third leg of the stool is the teachers' opportunity to learn. In this case we have used the collaboration between an artist and a teacher in the classroom as the source of powerful learning experiences. Through teaming and collaboration, teachers both participate in and observe very different ways of teaching, and are able to extrapolate from these experiences to other instructional activities. Unlike most forms of professional development, teaming with a partner who approaches instruction and learning in a very different way provides both immediate and longer-term challenges. It also provides an opportunity to experiment with a low cost of failure or loss of face, since there is no supervisory or peer-coaching role implied in the partnership. Clearly there are powerful learning opportunities other than teaming that can occur in schools, but in this case it seems that the opportunity to work closely with another person who approached both content and instruction very differently provided a particularly important boost to learning. Thus we suggest that creating significant change in classrooms must involve sustained engagement with ideas and practices that challenge teacher's taken-for-granted assumptions about themselves, their students, and how best to stimulate learning.

Appendix A Mental Models Items and Factor Loadings

	Factor 1: Contemporary Teacher Centered	Factor 2: Real World Connections	Factor 3: Student Directed Learning
Teachers should prompt students to explain and justify their ideas to others.	0.53		
Teachers should design lessons that provide students with choices.	0.59		
I regularly incorporate student interests into lessons.			0.55
I often allow students to shift the direction and content of my lessons.			0.58
Students learn best when they are actively involved in exploring things, inventing and trying out their own ways of doing things.	0.68		
In order to learn complex material, students need information presented to them in several different ways.	0.76		
Students should help establish criteria on which their work will be assessed.			0.45
Hearing other classmates' ideas is essential for student learning.	0.59		
Most students in my class are capable of taking charge of their own learning.			0.77
If students can't apply what they learn to the real world, they don't really understand it.		0.67	
It is important that students study real life problems that they are likely to encounter outside of the classroom.		0.67	
If students have an audience besides the classroom teacher, they will often work harder and produce better academic results.		0.64	
Students should be given opportunities to take on adult roles (e.g. as artists or scientists) to produce original work and knowledge.		0.59	
Students need to address subjects in depth to explore connections and produce complex understandings.		0.58	
By trying different teaching methods, I can significantly affect my students' achievement levels.		0.66	

Appendix B Professional Community Items and Factor Loadings

	Factor 1: Professional Behavior	Factor 2: Professional Belief System
We frequently talk about past activities or projects and what made them work well or not so well.	0.66	
We continuously look for the most recent programs and research that can improve student learning.	0.69	
We spend a lot of time planning how to improve curriculum and instruction.	0.77	
We frequently discuss how the school can best be organized to improve learning.	0.74	
We often observe each other teach.	0.54	
Most teachers here take responsibility for improving the school.		0.68
We frequently collaborate in developing curriculum, materials, or activities that will improve the school.	0.68	
We frequently talk about how to assess student learning.	0.66	
Teachers share high standards for each other; there is peer pressure to teach well.		0.67
Most teachers in this school feel responsible that all students learn.		0.82
In this school most teachers help maintain discipline in the entire school.		0.76

Notes

1. This chapter was co-authored with Amy R. Anderson and Eric Riedel. See Chapter 10 for another article based on this research project.
2. Three schools were unable to schedule a time for group administration of the survey.
3. A discussion of the issues and method of calculating the response rates from the AAA surveys may be found in Anderson and Ingram (2002).
4. For the purpose of the larger project, the factor analyses described in the next section were conducted on the full data set of $N = 1,369$.

References

Abrahamson, E. and C.J. Fombrun (1994) "Macrocultures: Determinants and consequences." *Academy of Management Review* 19(4): 728–55.

Anderson, A.R. and D. Ingram (2002) *Arts for Academic Achievement: Results from the 2000–2001 Survey*. Minneapolis: Center for Applied Research and Eduational Improvement, University of Minnesota.

Barth, R. (2001) *Educating by Heart*. San Francisco: Jossey Bass.

Browne, M.W. and R. Cudeck (1993) "Alternative ways of assessing model fit." In K.A. Bollen and J.S. Long (eds), *Testing Structural Equation Models*: 136–62. Newbury Park, CA: Sage.

Bryk, A., E. Camburn, and K.S. Louis (1999) "Promoting school improvement through professional communities: An analysis of Chicago elementary schools." *Educational Administration Quarterly* 35(4): 707–50.

Carley, K. and M. Palmquist (1992) "Extracting, representing and analyzing mental models." *Social Forces* 70(3): 601–36.

Darling-Hammond, L. (1990) "Teacher professionalism: Why and how?" In *Schools as Collaborative Cultures: Creating the Future Now*, Vol. 3. Bristol, PA: The Falmer Press.

Detert, J., K.S. Louis, and R. Schroeder (2001) "A culture framework for education: Defining quality values for U.S. high schools." *Journal of School Effectiveness and School Improvement* 12(2): 183.

DiMaggio, P. (ed.) (1997) *Culture and Cognition*, Vol. 23. Washington, DC: American Sociological Association.

Desimone, L. (2002) *The Role of Teachers in Urban School Reform* (ERIC Digest). New York: ERIC Clearinghouse on Urban Education.

——, A. Porter, and M. Garet (2002) "Effects of professional development on teachers instruction: Results from a three-year longitudinal study." *Educational Evaluation and Policy Analysis* 24(2): 81–112.

Firestone, W. and K.S. Louis (2000) "Schools as cultures." In J. Murphy and K.S. Louis (eds), *Handbook of Research on Educational Administration*: 297–322. San Francisco: Jossey Bass.

Ford, C. (1996) "A theory of individual creative action in multiple social domains." *The Academy of Management Review* 21(4): 1112–42.

Freeman, C. and K.S. Louis (2006) "Teacher teaming and high-school reform." In K.S. Louis (ed.), *Organizing for School Change*: 175–92. Abingdon, Oxon: Routledge.

—— and K.S. Louis (2002) *Models of Implementing Arts for Academic Achievement: Challenging Contemporary Classroom Practice*. Minneapolis, MN: Center for Applied Research and Educational Improvement.

Furman, G. (1999) "School as community: Editor's forward." *Educational Administration Quarterly*, 35(1): 6–12.

Giddens, A. (1984) *The Constitution of Society; Outline of a Theory of Structuration*. Berkeley: University of California Press.

Hackmann, D., V. Petzko, J. Valentine, J. Clark, and D.C. Nori (2002) "Beyond interdisciplinary teaming: Findings and implications of the NASSP national middle level study." *NASSP Bulletin* 86(632): 33–47.

Hargreaves, A. (1993) "Individualism and individuality: Reinterpreting the teacher culture." In J.W. Little and M.W. McLaughlin (eds), *Teachers Work: Individuals, Colleagues, and Contexts.* New York: Teachers College, Columbia University.

Hatch, M.J. (1993) "The dynamics of organizational culture." *Academy of Management Review* 18(4).

Ingram, D. and K.S. Louis (2003) *Arts for Academic Achievement: Summative Evaluation Report* (final evaluation report). Minneapolis: Center for Applied Research and Educational Improvement, University of Minnesota.

Jöreskog, K.G. and D. Sörbom (1979) *Advances in Factor Analysis and Structural Equation Models.* Cambridge, MA: Abt Associates.

Kanthak, L.M. (1995) "Teamwork: Profile of high achieving schools and their leaders." *Schools in the Middle:* 5(2): 27–30.

Kruse, S. and K.S. Louis (1997) "Teacher teaming in middle school: Dilemmas for school-wide community." *Educational Administration Quarterly* 33(3): 261–81.

——, K.S. Louis, and A. Bryk (1995) "An emerging framework for analyzing school-based professional community." In K.S. Louis and S. Kruse (eds), *Professionalism and Community: Perspectives on Reforming Urban Schools.* Thousand Oaks, CA: Sage.

Leithwood, K. (2002) *Organizational Learning and School Improvement.* Greenwich, CT: JAI.

Little, J.W. (1990) "The persistence of privacy: Autonomy and initiative in teachers' professional relations." *Teachers College Record* 91(4): 503–36.

—— (2000) "Organizing schools for teacher learning." In L.D. Hammond and G. Sykes (eds), *Teaching as a Learning Profession: Handbook of Policy and Practice.* San Francisco: Jossey Bass.

Louis, K.S., H. Marks, and S. Kruse (1996) "Teachers' professional community in restructuring schools." *American Educational Research Journal* 33(4): 757–98.

Meyer, J. and B. Rowan (1977) "Institutionalized organizations: formal structure as myth and ceremony." *American Journal of Sociology* 83(4): 340–63.

Newmann, F. and associates (1996) *Authentic Achievement: Restructuring Schools for Intellectual Quality.* San Francisco: Jossey Bass.

——, B. Smith, E. Allensworth, and A. Bryk (2002) "Improving Chicago's schools: School instructional program coherence." *ERS Spectrum* 20(2): 38–40.

Nias, J., G. Southworth, and R. Yeomans (1999) *Staff Relationships in Primary Schools.* London: Cassell.

Polite, M. (1994) "Team negotiation and decision-making: Linking leadership to curricular and instructional innovation." *Research in Middle Level Education* 18(1): 65–81.

Porac, J.F. and H. Thomas (1990) "Taxonomic mental models in competitor definition." *Academy of Management Review* 15(2): 224–40.

Pounder, D.G. (1999) "Teacher teams: Exploring job characteristics and work-related outcomes of work group enhancement." *Education Administration Quarterly* 35(3): 317–48.

Putnam, R.D. (2000) *Bowling Alone: The Collapse and Revival of American Community*. New York: Simon & Schuster.

Scribner, J. (1999) "Professional development: Untangling the influence of work context on teacher learning." *Educational Administration Quarterly* 35(2): 238–66.

Spillane, J. and K.S. Louis (2002) "School improvement processes and practices: Professional learning for building instructional capacity." In J. Murphy (ed.), *Challenges of Leadership: Yearbook of the National Society for the Study of Education*. Chicago: University of Chicago Press.

——, B.J. Reiser, and T. Reimer (2002) "Policy implementation and cognition: Reframing and refocusing implementation research." *Review of Educational Research* 72(3): 387–431.

Supovitz, J. (2002) "Developing communities of instructional practice." *Teachers College Record*, 104(8): 1591–626.

Swidler, A. (1986) "Culture in action: Symbols and strategies." *American Sociological Review* 51(2): 273–86.

Thomas, J.B., S.M. Clark, and D.A. Gioia (1993) "Strategic sensemaking and organizational performance: Linkages among scanning, interpretation, action and outcomes." *The Academy of Management Journal* 36(2): 239–70.

Toole, J. (2001) "Mental Models, Professional Learning Community, and the Deep Structure of School Improvement: Case Studies of Service Learning." Unpublished PhD thesis, University of Minnesota, Minneapolis.

Wahlstrom, K. (2003) *Images of Arts Infusion in Elementary Classrooms*. Minneapolis: Center for Applied Research and Educational Improvement.

Westheimer, J. (1999) "Communities and consequences: An inquiry into ideology and practice in teachers' professional work." *Educational Administration Quarterly* 35(1): 71–105.

Wheaton, B., B. Muthen, C. Alwin, and G. Summers (1977) "Assessing reliability and stability in panel models." In D.R. Heise (ed.), *Sociological Methodology*: 84–136. San Francisco: Jossey Bass.

Zellermeyer, M. (1997) "When we talk about collaborative curriculum-making, what are we talking about?" *Curriculum Inquiry* 27(2): 187–214.

Section IV
Educational Knowledge
in Action

This volume begins with a chapter that addresses knowledge use and the change process. Issues of how schools use knowledge emerge periodically throughout chapters in other sections, particularly in the way in which teachers get and use knowledge to change their practices, and how knowledge is created and disseminated in organizational learning. In this last section, I include three chapters that highlight my enduring interest in the relationship of knowledge and change more clearly.

My involvement in evaluating school improvement interventions began as a graduate student in the mid-1970s and coincided with the emergence of evaluation research as a distinct field in the social sciences. Carol Weiss, one of the founders of the field, offered me my initial job as a graduate research assistant, helping to develop an annotated bibliography for one of the first practical guides for program evaluators. This was an optimistic time of exuberant investment in education, where federal initiatives were expected to shake up a complacent system. There was great anticipation that evaluation research and policy analysis would emerge as significant tools for creating closer linkages between funded programs and the needs of schools: good applied research *would* make the world of education a better place.

By the beginning of the 1980s, with several large-scale evaluations under my belt, I was more skeptical. Chapter 15, "Policy Research in a Policy Vacuum," looks at some of the institutional reasons why government agencies, no matter how well-intentioned, may be incapable of using the research that they have commissioned. This chapter draws on Ron Corwin's and my observations of the knowledge-use history of two interventions and their associated evaluations. While this paper was narrowly focused on a single federal agency, my subsequent experience has validated the issues originally raised here. While there are always political reasons for using or not using research knowledge (which I and others have analyzed elsewhere), there are also clear organizational variables that influence whether new knowledge falls on fallow or barren ground.

A policy vacuum can be thought of as an organization that fails to provide the minimal conditions for reasonable policy initiatives to survive. The characteristics of a policy vacuum – lack of an organized constituency of "users," lack of agreement about a clear set of problems to be addressed, inconsistent policy and competing policy options, unclear decision-making responsibilities, and the rapid cycling of programs – are not confined, as we assumed when I wrote this paper, to large federal agencies. Over the last decade, I have observed that policy vacuums seem to be inherent in a variety of command and control systems, not just the largest and most bureaucratic. I have witnessed parallel problems at the school and district level, as well as on my occasional forays into the innovation literature in the fields of medicine and business.

Many of these characteristics echo my discussion in Chapter 5 of the constraints on organizational learning in schools. The lack of effective knowledge use is not a consequence of short-sighted individuals or weak groups, but is inherent in the weak linkages between parts of what has come to be recognized as a "loosely coupled system." In Chapter 16, "Improving Urban and Disadvantaged Schools: Dissemination and Utilization Perspectives," I argue that weak linkages are inequitably distributed within the larger educational system. Just as there are isolated teachers who are out of the social and innovation loop in many schools, so are there knowledge-marginalized systems – and these are often the systems that serve the neediest students. It is as if the struggle to survive, to produce the minimal standards of success, takes precedence over innovation, even when innovation might provide a more efficient and elegant solution. This can be likened to bailing water out of the boat at an ever faster rate, while ignoring the hole that needs to be plugged.

Until very recently, even universities and laboratories located in the center of urban areas tended to work most closely with schools located in the more affluent suburbs. Although many colleges of education have stepped up to their role as specialists in urban schooling, now they tend to affiliate with a few magnet or professional development schools within a larger district. The last decade has seen this problem addressed with an increased concentration on the knowledge and professional development needs of urban schools in many countries, and initiatives to reduce the information gap exist in cities such as London, Rotterdam, and Stockholm as well as in some of the troubled inner cities of the USA. That said, the organizational and social conditions cited in this paper, drafted back in the early 1990s, still limit the impact of new networks and innovations in the schools that serve children who need the greatest support.

The final chapter in this section, "Reconnecting Knowledge Utilization and School Improvement" emerged from a request by David Hopkins to undertake a literature review of the "state of the art" on knowledge use. My first instinct was to say no – I felt that my feet were so firmly planted in school improvement work that this task would be a distraction. After a few days of puzzling about how to gracefully decline had passed, it suddenly occurred to me that many of my nascent ideas about school improvement actually had their roots in my old work on knowledge use. *Voilà!* – a focus that challenged me enormously, and has reignited my interest in the connection between knowledge use and school structures at all educational levels.

So, I approach the last decade of my career with a renewed interest in many of the same questions that initially drew me into educational research. I wish, of course, that I had found the educational equivalent of penicillin. However, the process of putting this book together (which required me to read material that I hadn't looked at in decades) reminds me of the progress we have all made in grappling with the complex moving targets that educational systems represent.

15

Policy Research in a Policy Vacuum[1]

Introduction

The purpose of policy or applied research is presumably to improve the design and implementation of social programs. However, many argue that applied research typically does not have clearly discernable impacts on practice (Lindblom and Cohen 1979). The explanations for the weak linkage often focus on:

1. the "politics" of decision-making;
2. the primitive state of the research art; or
3. personal flaws in the individual policy-makers or in the researchers.

This chapter presents a case based on a recent policy research study that illuminates another fundamental reason for lack of immediate research impacts upon practice. We have called this phenomenon the "policy vacuum." It should be emphasized that, while we have taken case examples from one agency, we do not believe that our cases are substantially different from some others that we have observed less closely in this and similar types of agencies, and that the concept of the policy vacuum is one that can be applied to a variety of decision settings and research projects at federal, state, and local levels.

Dominant Knowledge Utilization Models

The ideal-typical model of policy research features several critical components. First, there is an operating program and/or a clear set of policy options about which a "policy-maker" wishes to have more information. Second, there are clear and delimited information objectives, which are agreed upon by the policy-maker and the researcher. Third, the research or evaluation is conducted by a well-trained social scientist, who has ample time and resources to do a technically competent job, and who is in a position to be objective about both the data being collected and their policy implications (Guttentag 1977). Finally, the research produces clear-cut results that can be readily translated into desirable policy changes.

There are instances when this neat, linear pattern of applied knowledge production and utilization does occur. However, more typically, policy research tends to be diffuse and out of synchronization with decision timeliness, and to have only vague policy implications, and virtually no short-term impact on policy decisions (Cohen and Garet 1975).

Some Reasons why Policy Research does not Impact Practice

For purposes of this chapter, we have identified five reasons to help account for the relatively weak ties between policy research and policy decisions.

Evaluation and Ritual

As the resources and responsibilities allotted for social programs have increased in recent years, the public has come to demand more formal accountability from the people responsible for them. The policy-makers can point to the mere existence of any form of policy research to satisfy accountability requirements. Sometimes, intimidated by the evaluation connotations of policy research, policy-makers are easily tempted to transform the research into a ritual, insulated from the decision-making process (Downs 1965; Knorr 1977). Also, legislators desiring to please their constituents tend to select evidence to coincide with popular demand. But even when policy-makers are sincere about using policy research, its impact can be blunted when it is treated as a ceremonial activity commissioned on the blind faith that the results might magically "help" in some unspecified way (McGowan 1976).

Cooptation and Legitimation

A second closely related reason why policy research may not have direct impact on practice occurs when policy-makers co-opt the research to serve their own limited interests. Controversies over research techniques and theoretical paradigms and constraints imposed by limited resources all make policy research easy prey for reluctant users seeking to exploit findings for their public relations value – that is, to legitimate their program through publicizing its positive aspects (Cook et al. 1980).

The temptation to co-opt policy research is enhanced by the absence of clear priorities concerning the purpose of the research and who is to be the intended beneficiary (Brickell 1978). For example, managers of funding agencies want information to weed out bad programs, whereas the directors of operating programs want information to help them improve their local operations (McGowan 1976). Also, everyone wants evidence that will help to obtain additional funding. Researchers are often more interested in the theoretical significance of the program than in being of assistance to the policy-makers. And yet, in our experience, "Requests for Proposals" (RFPS) often blithely state that the research is intended to "serve practitioners, program managers, and scholars," which only serves to promote struggles to control priorities during the course of the research.

Enlightenment

Recently, another explanation for the lack of impact of policy research has been advanced by some observers who question the appropriateness of holding policy research accountable for specific decisions because of the difficulty of tracing the sources of specific pieces of legislation, regulations, or program plans. Weiss (1980), for example, claims that applied knowledge serves a variety of potential functions, only one of which is to inform immediate decisions specific to a program or a given policy setting. Another, equally important use is to inform diffuse decisions. That is, results of a policy study are entered into the realm of discussion and debate, and serve to subtly alter perspectives over time – in other words, the way in which policy-makers view alternatives. In this regard, a broad study such as the Rand Study of Federal Programs Supporting Educational Change (Berman and McLaughlin 1975, 1979) is likely to have a diffuse long-range effect on program planning even if it does not in itself produce new legislation regulating the separate programs included in that study.

Each of the reasons mentioned thus far in one way or another attributes the weak tie between research and practice to tendencies for policy research to be used for purposes other than affecting specific policy decisions. There are, however, some other explanations that seek to account for the shortcomings of policy research even when it is sincerely intended to affect policy decisions.

State of the Art

The research community has been faulted on many counts. One of policy-makers' most frequent complaints about applied research is that researchers are more concerned about the theoretical interests of a discipline than about the particular program being studied. Others have noted that the quality of evaluation methods is often sufficiently low to militate against a clear-cut interpretation of the researchers' results (Bernstein and Freeman 1975). Moreover, researchers are accused of ignoring the "usability" of the research product (Patton 1978; Lindblom and Cohen 1979). Poor understanding of the policy content and range of possible decisions, and the importance of presenting highly technical analyses and material in a form that can be digested by bureaucrats and congressional staff members (who may be reluctant to pick up a fifty-page single-spaced "executive summary" unless they can be assured of finding something of interest to them) represent clear impediments to use. The preoccupation with individual characteristics of researchers and "key decision-makers" is clear (Bernstein and Freeman 1975;

Patton *et al*. 1977). But a more fundamental problem arises from the balance among resources and expectations. While the social sciences are filled with controversies over the validity and reliability of certain techniques, we believe that a far more serious problem than the technical capacity of social science is the ambitious expectations of decision-makers.

The Policy Vacuum

Finally, we propose still another explanation for why policy research findings frequently are not used: the policy vacuum. We sense that even when policy-makers are totally sincere in their efforts to use the research to guide current decision choices, they are unable to match the available information to decision settings because of the structure of the policy environment. What we define below as the policy vacuum is a distinct organizational feature of many policy agencies. While distinct, it is nonetheless integrally related to the other reasons for lack of impact of policy research that have already been cited. Thus, on the one hand, the state of the art is not always robust. On the other hand, given a policy vacuum, policy research will be even more susceptible to being used for legitimation and ritual, co-optation, and enlightenment.

The Policy Vacuum: A Definition

A policy vacuum occurs when:

- there is no organized constituency of policy-makers to whom the research is directed;
- there is no agreement among significant constituents as to a set of clear research questions that need to be addressed;
- there is no consistent policy over a given area, and hence no clear-cut policy options to be decided;
- there is no clear interagency division of labor over policy development; and
- there are no concrete, ongoing programs to be affected by the research.

These conditions are, of course, not mutually exclusive. They are overlapping and mutually reinforcing, and they can be present or absent in varying degrees. Nevertheless, it will be useful to consider some of the conditions separately and in more detail.

Multiple Constituencies

Ideally, responsibility for particular policy decisions is clearly lodged with a given individual or office. However, in practice, responsibility for decision-making is usually diffused throughout an agency and shared by a number of policy-makers. In this instance, in the ideal situation, the policy researcher is able to deal with a well-integrated system of policy-makers, each of whom wants better information about an issue or a program. This set of policy-makers should include a congressman or an entire committee, significant appointed directors at an agency where the research is being funded, and the upper-level civil service staff members who have responsibility for defining and monitoring the research (Hill 1980). In practice this situation often does not prevail for a variety of reasons. In many cases, the only person with a sustained level of concern about the research is not a policy-maker at all, but a researcher-cum-civil servant, whose primary responsibility is to supervise technical quality. Because the "technical project officers" who monitor large-scale research studies are not policy-makers per se, they themselves may not understand what it would take to make a study more useful (Cowden and Cohen 1979). In some agencies there are also restrictions on the interaction between policy actors. For example, Department of Education employees are not permitted to deal directly with congressional staff. This restriction is intended to reduce "lobbying" by program staff, but it also prevents the development of more coherent policy constituencies.

In addition, the various actors may simply have diverse interests and priorities. This possibility is promoted by agency reorganizations, turnover of key officials, and a changing political climate which produces vague or shifting policy priorities, as well as by "slippage," or misunderstandings that arise among individuals at different levels of the hierarchy concerning one another's needs and intentions. This last condition, slippage, can become particularly critical when a research program is initiated by program officials in subordinate bureaucratic levels acting on vague notions of what will please or displease their administrative and legislative superiors.

No Clear Set of Research Questions

All the conditions mentioned contribute to the indeterminate focus of much policy research. But whatever the reasons, many policy researchers have found that at the end of their study the questions they labored to answer are no longer of interest to the client. This situation is made even more problematic in larger and longer studies, where the quixotic nature of the policy environment changes rapidly, but the design decisions made in earlier years constrain the ability of the researcher to respond.

Perhaps the fundamental problem is that the number of interesting (and even significant) questions that can be asked about any policy situation or ongoing program inevitably exceeds the resources that can be devoted to a study (McGowan 1976). Furthermore, even where resources for a study are plentiful, choices that are made about design and methods preclude answering some questions in the interest of focusing on others.

The first task of policy research is to determine which of the endless possible questions are most critical for various actors and then to design a study capable of addressing as many of them as possible. But when that task is left to the policy researchers, the client loses ownership and often interest in the questions that are being addressed.

Absence of Policy

In some cases, policy-makers at various levels may agree that a topic is important, but if there is no clear policy governing activity in that area, it is difficult for them to imagine who would use the information that a policy research study might provide, or how it would be used. One indicator that there is no clear policy is a sharp disagreement between various actors within the same agency over what the federal role should be in a given policy area; another is major "turf" battles over long periods of time between programs that have similar objectives. This, of course, indicates that vested program interests (such as Teacher Corps or Teacher Centers) may prevail over the development of higher-level policies concerning, for example, ways of providing improved staff development to teachers.

Where there is no coherent policy, and no one set of officials is responsible for developing it, it is unlikely that clear policy options will be formulated which a policy research project could compare. Consequently the research is likely to produce answers to questions that policy-makers have not posed and most likely cannot readily use.

Overlapping bureaucratic jurisdictions

The absence of a coherent policy and well formulated policy options is virtually assured by interagency rivalries. The sociologist's image of bureaucracy is often conditioned by the Weberian definition acquired in his or her professional infancy. Even where the ideal type has been challenged, a minimal vestige of the rational image is assumed to prevail, namely the relative clarity of the division of labor among agencies. The recent attempts of the federal government to rationalize still further, by separating the new Department of Education from its old partners, Health and Welfare, reinforce this imagery. However, interagency disputes are frequent, and are often precipitated by unclear divisions of labor and functions as prescribed by Congress. Thus, for example, the development of a broad "youth policy" has been distinctly hampered by the fact that part of "youth" (youth employment) has been assigned to the Department of Labor while other significant parts of "youth" (Education and Family) fall under the Department of Education and the Department of Health and Human Services. This problem has been recognized, but is unlikely to be fully resolved by the recent presidential youth initiatives, to be housed in the Department of Education.

No Program

Even more critical than the lack of a consistent policy, however, is the absence of an established, long-term program that testifies to federal investment in the particular policy area. Programs represent a commitment. They are hard to get rid of; it is often easier to turn them upsidedown in response to an evaluation than to eliminate them. But, when there is no program, competing demands for funds from influential managers of existing programs may mitigate strongly against a new effort that is a clear policy consequence of a study. As Glennen *et al.* (1978) point out, this fact has often blunted the impact of demonstration programs that are intended to help formulate policy options for the federal government.

Policy Vacuums and Garbage Cans

The concept of the policy vacuum clearly relates to other images of organizational nonrationality that have been presented in recent literature (see Corwin 1981). However, we have chosen to introduce a new imagery. Our reason stems from the fact that previously articulated concepts, such as the "garbage can" model of organizational choice (March and Olsen 1976) and the evolutionary model of program implementation (Farrar *et al.* 1980), are premised on the notion that decision settings are very complicated and "full."

Our image of the policy vacuum is, on the other hand, the opposite of the full, highly peopled landscape of the lawn party or the garbage can. Instead, the image is intended to conjure up the potential decisions that are not made, the issues that do not make it on an agenda, and the features of policy-making that are attended to either by no one or by the wrong person. Vacuum implies the absence of things, rather than the presence. March and Olsen (1976), for example, describe the garbage-can model as limiting rational choice largely because of the inability of individuals to determine the decision settings or the people who will be involved in the decisions – or even the decisions that will need to be made at a given time. Rather, people, problems, and solutions are viewed as separate streams that continuously enter into any given decision setting. Farrar *et al.* (1980) also emphasize the people-intensive quality of organizational process by likening the implementation of new organizational programs to a lawn party, at which people come and go, each with his or her own personal motivation for attending, each able to go away having accomplished some of what he or she came to do. The authors attribute the unplanned adaptation and change that occurs in any new change program to the superimposition of multiple individual agendas on the innovation plan.

These alternate images are useful mechanisms to capture some of the nature of "organized anarchy." However, in addition to the contrast between full and empty decision settings, we feel that they are limited in two additional respects. First, the focus of both the garbage can and the lawn party is upon the role of the individual in the decision-making and/or change processes. By contrast, our objective is to articulate identifiable characteristics of organizational structures that affect the policy-making process. Second, both are, in our opinion, at the extreme of nonrational views, in that they imply that it is impossible (or at least very difficult) to predict the outcomes of decision or implementation settings. On the other hand, we believe that, while specific decisions may not be predictable within a nonrationalized organizational setting, under the conditions of a policy vacuum it is possible to anticipate some of the behaviors and some of the outcomes that will occur.

The Policy Vacuum: Case Examples

In the following sections we will relate two case examples that illuminate how a policy vacuum developed and affected the research component of a large-scale demonstration project. First, we will describe the programs and the organizational context in which they developed. Then we will describe how this context affected the development of the research activities. The case analysis of the R&D Utilization (RDU) Program is based upon formal interviews with nine federal employees who were connected with the program and who participated in decisions concerning the research. The case of the Rural Experimental Schools (Rural ES) Program draws mainly upon secondary sources (Cowden and Cohen 1979; Herriott 1979; Rosenblum and Louis 1981).

In addition, we have brought to bear the participant observation of the research projects by both authors. It should be noted that our observations on the Rural ES case are relatively complete: the research project effectively ended in 1978, and current data do not suggest that the receptiveness of the policy environment to its products is changing in significant ways. The RDU research is, however, still underway, and our observations refer only to the first eighteen months of the project's life. Since that time, there has been a growing concern in the sponsoring agency for utilization and policy relevance, and it is currently unclear how that will affect the final impact of the research on policy.

The RDU Program was a $10 million effort sponsored by the National Institute of Education. Operating for three years, between 1976 and 1979, the program was intended to stimulate significant local improvement activities in schools through:

1. the provision of a set of tested programs and curriculum information (the product of federally funded research and developmental activities) relevant to locally defined problems;
2. the provision of support and training for improved (more deliberate and rational) problem-solving practices and broader participation in problem-solving; and
3. a network of relationships between a variety of organizations that had resources that would support school improvement activities at the local level (see Louis *et al.* 1978).

The program operated in over three hundred schools through seven projects. An integral part of the demonstration was a research study, which was initially intended to function throughout the life of the program, and which was to document and analyze the project and local activities that best accounted for successful information use and problem-solving.

Although limited in scope, the RDU Program was ambitious by most standards, relatively well designed, adequately funded, and soundly managed. Furthermore, it addressed a number of issues that were (and are) of significant interest both to researchers and policy-makers (such as how R&D can be made useful to local practitioners and how federal intervention programs can support local improvement efforts without subverting local autonomy, to name only two of those that were current when the program was designed). However, because of two contexts – that of the agency in which it was situated, and the way in which the demonstration component developed – it was born into a policy vacuum.

The Rural ES Program was also an ambitious, $55 million effort that originated in the Office of Education in 1971 but which was administered out of the National Institute of Education for most of its eight-year life. The objective of the ES effort was to make a major reform of the federal role in education, shifting the patterns of funding from categorical grants (which were thought to result in piecemeal change efforts that were poorly suited to the local district) to more broadly based funding which would stimulate locally planned, broadly based change activities. There were multiple components to the ES Program, including a major emphasis on urban schools.

The rural component (Rural ES) involved ten small districts, located in remote parts of the United States from Mississippi to Alaska. It ran for six years from 1972 to 1977, while the multi-million-dollar research companion study was funded for seven years. The major features of the Rural ES strategy were:

1. a locally developed plan for change;
2. comprehensive, rather than piecemeal, change;
3. five-year guaranteed but terminal funding, which was thought of as a "bubble in the budget" of the small districts; and
4. significant citizen participation in the local planning (Herriott 1979).

The Importance of Contest: The Entrepreneurial Bureaucracy

In order to understand the policy vacuum that developed in each of these programs, we must first understand the National Institute of Education (NIE) as a federal bureaucracy. The NIE was established by Congress in response to negative evaluations concerning the quality, relevance, and management of existing educational research activities, which were then being funded by the Bureau of Research in the Office of Education (Sproull et al. 1978). The NIE's mission was to:

- help solve or alleviate the problems and achieve the objectives of American education;
- advance the practice of education as an art, science, and profession;
- strengthen the scientific and technological foundations on which education rests; and
- build a vigorous and effective educational research and development system.

From the beginning the NIE did not resemble a typical bureaucracy. Sproull et al. (1978) have described its initial years as anarchic. At the very least, between the four reorganizations that it underwent in its first four years and the constant verbal battering and reduction in funding that attended its stormy relationship to Congress, the early development of the agency was chaotic.

By 1976, however, it developed a stable pattern resembling an "entrepreneurial bureaucracy." The entrepreneurial bureaucracy emerges as a result of new mandates, often to "solve" newly perceived problems (such as the poor quality of educational research). Its basic feature is the incentive system. The managerial strategy is to recruit bright, aggressive subordinate staff and give them the freedom they need to initiate and manage their own programs. They are rewarded with visibility, influence, and autonomy, which they can achieve in the field as well as in the agency. Individuals who can fulfill these specifications must also have a great deal of political savvy and ability to justify and aggressively market their new ideas both within and outside the agency.

Some contrasts between the entrepreneurial bureaucratic model and the old-line bureaucracy (more characteristic of federal agencies such as the Office of Education) are shown in Table 15.1. What is important for our purposes here is that the heavy reliance placed on personal initiative also calls for a diffuse decision-making structure and

Table 15.1   Management Strategies Used in Entrepreneurial and Old-line Agencies

	Entrepreneurial Bureaucracies	Old-line Agencies
1. Incentives	Visibility, and influence, and salary increases; increased responsibility	Predictable promotions within the agency and in the field
2. Behavior rewarded	Initiative; responsiveness to clientele; giving technical assistance and advice	Compliance; loyalty to established policies and practices; monitoring contracts to contractors
3. Abilities required	Merchandizing skills: interpersonal and political	Administrative skills; coordinating and monitoring
4. Basis of authority	Professional expertise in substantive field of the agencies' focus	Administrative experience in bureaucratic research or practice
5. Authority system	Decentralization: autonomy, discretion	Centralization: compliance, close supervision
6. Division of labor	Fluid, temporary coalitions based on shifting competition and interdependencies	Stable, clearly defined responsibilities
7. Allegiance or reference orientation	Loyalty split between a specific agency and external constituencies; personal	Loyalty to the bureaucratic system rather than to a specific agency
8. Outcome/products	New programs based upon program's current theory; discretionary; often short-term	Long-term service with established clientele

corresponding autonomy for individuals and groups. Such an agency recruits staff who are specialists and who can call upon their expertise to inspire and direct new programs. In competitive and rapidly changing fields of R&D, youth is valued over seniority.

While we have not analyzed the degree to which other agencies exhibit entrepreneurial characteristics, less systematic observations (and communications with colleagues) suggest that there are many within the federal establishment that do, including more recently formed agencies such as the Department of Energy and the National Cancer Institute.

It is important to emphasize that new agencies are designed along the entrepreneurial model largely because of the potential benefits that may accrue, which include:

- elevation of expertise over hierarchical authority;
- loyalty to an external constituency as well as to administrative superiors;
- recruitment of creative and visionary bureaucrats, which is facilitated by staff turnover and by new ideas;
- flexibility in approaches to management and problem-solving; and
- high energy, which emerges from the recruitment of risk takers (rather than those who prefer stability) and because of the emphasis on constantly rethinking priorities and directions.

On the other hand, entrepreneurial bureaucracies also have inherent weaknesses, including fragmentation of effort, difficulty of developing long-range plans, and tensions between the short-term employees who are in the midst of building careers with an audience outside the agency and long-term civil servants whose loyalties and careers look inward and toward the agency. In the following cases we will tend to highlight some of the more negative consequences of an entrepreneurial organization, but if our intent were to present a more balanced analysis of the entrepreneurial bureaucracy, many positive functions could be found.

Lack of Constituencies: Birth of the RDU Program as an Entrepreneurial Bureaucracy

The RDU Program was conceived and initiated in the above context. The fateful decision of Congress to include dissemination activities as part of the NIE responsibilities gave the agency its only opportunity to provide direct service to its clientele. As originally conceived, the NIE was not to operate "service delivery programs." However, the House Select Subcommittee on Education was convinced that it would be necessary to assign NIE responsibility for disseminating its products or they would never get into circulation. Thus, the bulk of the Office of Education dissemination programs – the ERIC information storage and retrieval system and the final stages of the Pilot State Dissemination Project – were transferred into the new agency. (The Office of Education retained the responsibility for disseminating the products related to its own programs.)

The NIE director and other senior staff members were not entirely pleased with this "gift" of dissemination programs. In fact, they were reluctant to promote dissemination at all because it was viewed as irrelevant to the broader "knowledge production" functions of the agency (Sproull et al. 1978: 132). However, there were pressures from the outside: from state Departments of Education, who were annoyed that an earlier dissemination program had been dropped despite a laudatory evaluation (Sieber et al. 1972), and from Congress, intent on holding the NIE accountable for a dissemination budget that was increased by 72 per cent between 1973 and 1974. In addition, new functions were added to the ERIC-based dissemination unit, which was consolidated in a Dissemination and Resources Group under an associate director.

The assistant director who designed the RDU Program had been recruited with a mandate to develop new directions for the emerging dissemination program. A creative, mercurial scholar, it did not take him long to grasp the fact that in this agency it would be easier to create a new program than try to reshape existing ones. There were at least three ongoing programs within the same agency that logically might have housed any new initiative, such as the one he was contemplating, namely a component that would combine reliance on high-quality, screened R&D products with an improved, locally controlled problem-solving process. (These programs were the well-established ERIC system, the recently established State Capacity Building Grants Program, and the School Problem-Solving Program.) In each case, an outside observer would be likely to conclude that the existing programs would have benefited from the addition of an experimental component of the type that the assistant director had in mind. However, in all cases there were other, equally powerful forces moderating against cooperation, not least of which was the failure of the NIE leadership to provide incentives for cooperation (Sproull *et al.* 1978) and the relatively powerful ideological conflicts that were encouraged in an agency that valued diversity and intellectual debate. Cooperation with ongoing programs in the Office of Education was hardly considered.

Thus, the program was born largely as a result of the thinking of one man and a small number of his close colleagues. It did not involve collaboration between closely related activities, even those occurring under the direction of the same division of the NIE. Furthermore, during the development of the new program, the jostling for support and monies with other similar programs and the press for a rapid implementation created new competitive tensions and reduced even further the possibility of support from others within the agency.

The implications for the policy research were played out in full over the first months of the program. The research was not viewed by many in the agency as being of general policy interest, but rather as an artifact of a program that was ideologically separate and detached from other, more basic agency activities. For at least the first three years after the program's birth, representatives of other parts of the NIE either didn't know of the research project's existence or viewed the research, like the program, as intellectually flawed and of little interest to themselves, despite the fact that it drew upon organizational research traditions that underlie their own work. The development of a ready constituency for the evaluation within the NIE was a major challenge throughout the study.

Fragmenting a Constituency: The Transfer of the Rural ES Program

The isolation of the Rural ES Program as a result of its location in an entrepreneurial bureaucracy was far more extreme than that of the RDU Program. Rural ES was conceived of and planned for within the Office of Education, prior to the creation of the NIE. The program reflected a consensus among a large group of actors in the legislature and the executive branch, and even within the White House, that major changes needed to be made in the relationship of the federal government to local schools. It was, for a discretionary program, significant both in size and duration: the underlying strategy was to develop a demonstration and a research and documentation component that would be of sufficient magnitude to be able to convincingly show the presumed superiority of locally developed comprehensive change strategies.

The support that the program enjoyed under the aegis of the Office of Education (OE) rapidly evaporated when it was transferred to the newly created NIE. The potential for friction became immediately apparent when the program director refused to move his office to the new location (Sproull *et al.* 1978). More importantly, however, the new leadership at the NIE felt no stake in the design of "inherited" programs such as ES (see also McGowan 1976), and the high costs of supporting such programs were seen as an impediment to mounting new initiatives with a sounder research base (Herriott

1979). It became clear quite early on that the NIE staff did not have any strong affection for either the assumptions or the design underlying ES – a pattern that was heavily influenced by the frustration of being held accountable for achieving the goals of the new institute based on commitments and programs that were designed in the OE. Staff distaste for Experimental Schools Programs increased as it became apparent that portions of the Urban ES Program were being mismanaged, and after the release of a report from the General Accounting Office (GAO) that was highly critical of one of the evaluation studies being conducted in conjunction with the urban program component (Herriott 1979). In addition, the notion of district-wide, comprehensive change as it was implemented in the Rural ES Program was distant from many of the growing preferences of powerful actors in the NIE (and elsewhere) for more focused change at the school level (see, for example, Kirst 1979). When the director of the NIE demanded the resignation of the original ES Program director in late 1974 (largely because of his unremitting support of the program – see also McGowan 1976), the NIE constituency that supported the program had virtually disappeared.

The impact of the fragmented constituency on the research program attached to the demonstration was not immediately apparent. In the beginning it seemed that one of the only redeeming features about the Rural ES Program would arise through its opportunities to contribute to both basic and more applied research about the process and outcomes of change in rural settings. The research team rested content in the knowledge that, whatever the problems with the program, the agency was committed to the research. The problem in the long run, however, was that the NIE support for the research activities was not based in a clear policy context. As we shall see below, this lack of policy-related grounding for the study led to shifting research agendas and directives that threatened, at times, to overwhelm the stability of the project.

The Absence of Clear Research Questions in the RDU Program: Controversies over the Role of and Appropriate Methods for the Research in RDU

The RDU study was initially considered to be an integral part of the program and was "sold" to the research-oriented NIE management this way. However, soon after the program got under way, the research was postponed. The immediate problem was that about this time Congress had issued a personnel hiring freeze, which had prevented the assistant director from recruiting staff who possessed the specialized competencies needed to supervise the research. However, in addition, a struggle arose for control over the research component, which involved both controversies over the appropriate methods and disagreements over whom the research was intended to serve.

These problems were compounded by a division of labor within the agency. The responsibility for designing the research was to be shared between the assistant director who had initiated the program and an independent evaluation coordinator who also reported directly to the associate director of the division. These two positions were irreconcilably in conflict. The assistant director wanted the study to be "formative," that is, to provide information that would be helpful to the project directors who were responsible for delivering services. In addition, he was partial to a design based on separate case studies of the many individual schools at the local sites.

The evaluation coordinator, on the other hand, had a different view – one that was supported by many of her colleagues. She believed that the study must encompass research objectives broader than providing formative evaluation information for the project directors, and that a study design based on a large number of noncomparable case studies could not fulfill this objective. She and her colleagues emphasized the need to define what kinds of program-wide impacts the RDU should have and to consider ways of measuring those impacts.

The debate was initially resolved through the exercise of relatively unsubtle power politics. The coordinator was removed and the assistant director was allowed to proceed with an interim solution, namely contracting with an NIE-funded regional laboratory to help flesh out the program director's design and to collect some "baseline" data. But the battle to control the research study was not fully resolved until eighteen months after the beginning of the program – well after the external research contractor had been selected and had become an unwitting actor in the drama. The conflict has a number of significant consequences for the research, most of which diminished its audience both within the agency and in a broader context.

First, the contractor's ability to initiate a sound study was hampered by the existence of the partially implemented interim design mentioned above. That study was not commissioned with the goal of a guiding future federal program development, and yet it was this objective, rather than an emphasis on formative improvement of the RDU projects, that came to predominate in the agency. The NIE staff wanted to make use of the work that had already been done. The need to use existing data while reorienting the study led, in the final analysis, to some interesting methodological innovations (Louis 1982), but this process was extremely costly, both in time and dollars.

Second, the controversies over who would control the study led to a gap between the interests of the external research team and the NIE staff members who actually designed and ran dissemination programs. In order to protect the development of an improved research design, the project director of the external study actively lobbied with the associate director of the Dissemination and Resources Group to assign responsibility for monitoring the study to a team other than the one that had designed and managed the RDU Program. The request was granted, but this decision precipitated a conflict with the assistant director in charge of the RDU Program. The consequence of splitting the research from the operational program was to decrease the "sense of ownership" of the program staff over the research questions. The early study objectives had emphasized information that would feed into program and project management, but the new study, no longer under their control, was perceived to be shifting more and more toward broad theoretical and policy concerns.

This organizational change in the location of the study had serious implications for the conduct of the research. The overall design initially envisioned a partnership between program managers and researchers. However, the new structure reflected not only a philosophical gap between the program management and the research study staff, but also a breakdown in actual communication. Thus, the study of the RDU Program became detached from the group of actors who represented its greatest potential users. The battle of developing a research focus on larger program-wide questions had been won, but access to one of the most significant audiences was diminished.

The Absence of Clear Questions in the Rural ES Study:
The Effects of Design Flaws

In the case of Rural ES, the problem of an absence of clear research questions articulated by the funding agency was compounded by the fact that the nature of the program was constantly refined and altered over the first years in which it was in operation. In fact, the program planners at the federal level believed that the meaning of "comprehensive-ness" – the basic intervention strategy – would become clear only as the program evolved, and that it would be defined collaboratively with the participating districts (Cowden and Cohen 1979). In addition, it was not entirely clear whether "comprehen-siveness" was a strategy or the desired outcome (Rosenblum and Louis 1981). Were the Districts to be evaluated on the basis of the degree to which they actually implemented changes in all areas of their functioning, and within all schools? Or was the effort to change comprehensively to lead to (undefined) school district improvements? Even more difficult was the assumption, which evolved over the early years of the program, that their combination of innovations into comprehensive packages would produce "synergistic" results. While some considered this to be one of the major concepts that the ES Program was designed to test, the ability of the study to do so (since all ten districts were supposedly implementing comprehensive plans approved and monitored by the NIE) was unclear. Finally, some senior NIE staff members were confused because they were unable to determine the educational questions that should be raised about ES, which struck them more as an experiment in government funding strategies than in educational structures or techniques (Cowden and Cohen 1979). The difficult-ies of trying to get federal officials to define what it was they wanted to know went deeper than just identifying questions, however. As Cowden and Cohen (1979: 47) point out:

> Federal managers wanted the evaluation to provide a "holistic" view of local change efforts. Yet they didn't know what this meant; they knew only what they didn't want, and seemed to think that by naming an alternative they had created one. But to call evaluation holistic does not provide criteria for judging what that is or is not, nor guidance for how to do it.

This situation wherein the federal client could communicate neither the precise nature of the intervention nor the desired methodological characteristics of the valuation clearly led to considerable friction between the contractor and NIE staff.

The Rural ES study project director attempted to confront the lack of clear research questions on a number of occasions. At one point, for example, he forced a meeting with NIE staff members to brainstorm about relevant policy questions that could help to focus the study. According to him, the meeting was "a complete bust. I left asking them to get back to me, but I never heard from them." When it became apparent that clear guidance would not be forthcoming from ES/Washington, the project director's explicit strategy became the protection of the core design and the professional research interests of the staff members who worked in the project. His strategy was chosen under the assumption that, at minimum, the research effort could still contribute to basic social science but that the opportunities for policy impact were fading (see Cowden and Cohen 1979: 49).

Absence of Policy or Specific Policy Options: The RFP Procurement Process

In order fully to understand why the policy issues surrounding the RDU study were not clear, we must backtrack slightly in time. Because of his inability to command the technical expertise necessary to produce an acceptable RFP from within his own division, the assistant director was forced, by necessity, to get assistance in writing an RFP. However, producing an RFP proved to be difficult because there was little time in which the individual interests could be melded: it was 1976 and the projects had been in operation for almost a year. In addition, the rationale for the study had already been formally stated and partially implemented, which acted as a constraint on the research design.

The RFP, therefore, carefully avoided some critical policy issues and adhered to the original study design. New research questions were not blended into the study. Rather, they were identified as separate, "special studies" that were to be funded in addition to the main study. Second, the RFP carefully labeled the research contract an "analysis contract," with the intent of confining any group responding to the RFP to the assumption that the existing data, design, and instruments would remain intact, and that any additional data collections would be minor and supplementary. Finally, the RFP was deliberately vague about the purposes of the study. It did not attempt to define the acceptable or expected outcomes of the RDU Program at the school level (much less for the program as a whole); nor did it even elaborate a set of policy questions that the study was expected to address. Rather, the RFP implicitly invited the proposer to help define the study questions.

Perhaps this strategy of vagueness and pro forma conformity to the original study design helped to obtain internal consensus about the RFP, but it put the burden of defining a "new" study upon the proposer. The winning proposal added new elements, attempted to integrate the "special studies" with the ongoing study of school behavior, defined a range of outcomes or impact variables at different levels, and promoted an altered data collection mechanism that would include more survey data. In addition, the proposal identified seven key policy questions – the first time that a set of specific, researchable issues had actually been firmly attached to the study. In sum, the RFP served to stimulate questions, but did not define policy issues and options to be compared. It was the winning proposal that actually set forth the policy dimensions of the study in a form that became finalized in a contract.

Later in the contract period it became clear that this process was seriously flawed from the perspective of potential policy impact: the questions were, in fact, the researchers' questions and not the NIE's. The research contractor's questions were prompted by intellectual curiosity and professional interests as well as assumptions about what would be of interest to program managers. Consequently, reports that attempted to address these questions did not necessarily meet with equal interest at the receiving end. This general problem was compounded by NIE staffing turnover. The original statement of research questions was reviewed by several NIE staff members for relevance early in the research project's life. However, none of these individuals remained when the first reports were submitted. Unfortunately the research contractor had failed to discuss the research questions with the monitors who were to review their reports.

This highlights one of the most unfortunate characteristics of the "entrepreneurial bureaucracy" from the policy researcher's perspective: there is a great deal of turnover, as employees who are not from the civil service leave on their way to other positions and new career opportunities. Because of the lack of concern within the agency for developing a consistent policy, the relevance of one group's "burning policy questions" to another that succeeds them may be very limited. It also shows naiveté in assuming that one set of policy questions has universal appeal.

The Absence of Policy Options: Turnover and the Slippery Policy Context in Rural ES

The problem of turnover and a changing policy context was even more evident in the case of the Rural ES project. Turnover occurred not only within the NIE (the director of the ES Program and the senior executives of the agency were all replaced by the end of the program, and the research project itself had eight technical project officers over the course of six years), but the more significant external constituency in the White House and legislative branch were also gone. In 1970, Experimental Schools had been a rallying concept for many who believed in changing the way in which the federal government related to schools. In 1978, when the Rural ES study drew to a close, a Democrat with very different policy views occupied the White House, and several of the most critical legislative actors were gone.

Within the NIE, the changing political environment was fully reflected in a total abandonment of interest in the program on the part of all staff in their accompanying despair and anger over their inability to access any of the funds allocated to the districts or to the research. Efforts to mold the study in different directions became very frequent, as each new technical project officer tried to negotiate new research questions *post hoc*. The further the project went the more convinced the research staff became that they were the only parties with an enduring stake in the research and the less receptive they were to discussing new policy questions. Unlike other programs, where both the researchers and the agency staff members may recognize the problem of shifting policy contexts and work together to build a more receptive audience, the perceived gulf between researchers and agency grew wider with time.

This was reinforced by the previously mentioned GAO study, which helped to affirm the growing public image of the ES research program as a boondoggle and a failure. Many external policy-makers were not aware that there were multiple study contractors and tended to tar the Rural ES study with the same brush. This tendency was reinforced as a draft version of a report criticizing the entire research effort (Cowden and Cohen 1979) began to circulate inside the NIE – a report that was admittedly written without the benefit of reviewing any of the Rural ES final reports. Within the NIE this report widened the belief that nothing of use would come from the $5 million investment in studying comprehensive change in rural schools and communities.

No Clear Jurisdiction: External Pressures on Policy in the RDI and Rural ES

The Rural ES Program engendered no major "turf battles" once it became firmly located within the NIE. However, the relatively more obscure RDU Program did. As the RDU study was being redesigned in late 1977, the NIE found itself in a painful conflict with the Office of Management and the Budget (OMB) over the RDU Program. The first indication of trouble came when the "forms clearance" branch of the OMB raised questions about possible duplication between RDU and a recently completed Rand study, Federal Programs Supporting Educational Change. While the NIE was attempting to cope with these questions, another division of the OMB, the Budget Office, raised the more fundamental policy issue of whether the NIE should be involved in an expensive technical assistance/service delivery program that seemed remotely connected to the institute's research mission. While acknowledging the NIE's legal mandate for dissemination, these OMB officials disputed the wisdom of spending so much effort on servicing school districts. It was their position that the congressional intent was that the NIE was to be a policy analysis and research organization, whose purpose (even in dissemination) was to keep the Office of Education on target, not to run operational programs that service schools. There were also some hints that adversaries of RDU – for example, directors of competing programs and some state school superintendents – were exerting pressures on the OMB.

The study commenced with the staggering burden of having to "prove" to a variety of individuals who were aware of the OMB controversy that it was a study that was worth doing, and that it had policy-relevant information to offer that would expand upon that already available. To some extent, despite efforts to publicize the unique features of the study early in the life of the program, this reputational albatross persisted. It was later compounded by the fact that in 1978 the same OMB agency approved a $2 million study of the National Diffusion Network and other related programs sponsored by the Office of Education that focused on the same set of general questions and issues covered by the RDU study. As a consequence, many of the policy-makers who might have been interested in the RDU results began to appear confused at the presence of two similar studies. While some NIE staff members were concerned about the lack of coordination between the research staff in the Office of Education and their own staff over the Office of Education Dissemination Study, they were unable to negotiate an environment in which steps could be taken to make the studies complementary in the design phase.

Isolation from a Continuing Program: Rural ES and RDU

The number of publications emerging from the Rural ES study was vast (a total of sixteen reports, five of which were commercially published as books, and forty-five published articles, in addition to numerous conference presentations – see Herriott 1980). However, the gap between the information in these reports and a policy audience was complete by the end of the study. To our knowledge, only a few people in the NIE have read the reports that were finally produced, and most are convinced a priori that they have little to say to policy-makers. Since "comprehensive change" had disappeared as a policy agenda item, so had any interest in the policy conclusions that could be drawn from the study. Concerted efforts by the few remaining staff members in the agency who feel that the reports are of value in illuminating other policy may minimize this detachment. However, the process of redeeming the relevance of ES is likely to be slow at best.[2]

The RDU study, on the other hand, has charted a somewhat different course. Generalizing from the consistent praise of the RDU project directors, the NIE managers provided support and were facilitative throughout the project. In this aspect the RDU program contrasts with some other federal programs in which the responsible agencies have played an intrusive or nonsupportive role (Corwin 1977; Zigarmi et al. 1980). However, the program managers did not give equal attention to publicizing the Program. Indeed, a year after the program was funded, there was still no brochure or any other publicity that described the program to interested audiences. An unattractive mimeographed handout prepared as the only program description available was sadly out of date. Interviews conducted by the research staff in 1978 revealed that the RDU Program had not gripped the interest of highly placed federal people. In many cases, they had not heard of the program, and they were hard-pressed to find any direct relevance to their own highest priorities. In one or two other instances we met with some actual hostility and skepticism – the program was viewed as jargon-filled, impractical, atypical NIE "pie in the sky." Slowly, the relevant officials at NIE began to realize that it would be desirable to promote better public relations for the program. Their intent to make RDU more visible and more relevant to ongoing programs within the agency, through a commendable effort to reduce the policy vacuum, affected the research project in significant ways.

First, the research contractor was sought out as a possible solution to the low profile of the RDU project. Some public-relations functions had been built into the contract, namely a "glossy" report that was to tie the RDU study questions to policy issues in federal and local government. When the contractor finally produced this report in mid-1978 (Chabotar and Kell 1978), it became the first polished description of the program, its purposes, and structures. While 500 copies of this report were distributed, the desire for an improved public image persisted within the agency. After protracted discussions with the NIE, another polished glossy report (Louis et al. 1978) was substituted for a set of "working papers" that were intended only for review within the agency. The main purposes of these brief and expensively produced reports was to create a constituency for the program by urging "policy-makers" or "managers of change at the local level" to think about ways in which RDU could feed into their own upcoming decision needs.

Thus, it turned out that the main function of the study contract during its first year was to assist the NIE in publicizing the existence of a temporary program. The assumption of these functions occurred because neither the program nor the study was tied to policy decisions relevant to ongoing programs either within the NIE or within the Office of Education as a whole. Since the study was not in a position to illuminate well-defined policy questions, it was necessary to engage in defining, legitimizing, and publicizing a set of questions that might appeal to a larger constituency. The primary problem was that when RDU terminated there would be no program to affect and, moreover, no steps had been taken to formally link the RDU efforts to related ongoing programs. Indeed, not only had the original competition among federal programs contributed to isolation, but also, over the course of time, NIE managers decided against undertaking additional initiatives comparable to the scale of the RDU Program. The agency's policy toward research funding shifted markedly away from multi-million dollar demonstration studies. Instead, the agency began developing a large number of focused grants programs for research, most of which encourage research and/or demonstration projects at levels of $100,000 or less. Thus, not only was there no program to affect, but there were no obvious future policy developments within the NIE or the dissemination division to which the research could clearly be tied.

Conclusions

The imagery of a vacuum embodies the notion of a continuum – one can have a partial as well as a total vacuum. Our two cases illustrate some diversity along the different indicators of a policy vacuum. The Rural ES project – plagued with much less clear policy questions, disappearing policy options, high levels of agency-staff turnover, and isolation within the funding agency – might be characterized as falling into almost a total vacuum. The RDU research, on the other hand, is not yet over, and there are indications that the funding agency is cognizant of the problems that have been presented here. Relevant NIE officials are attempting to construct a salient policy context for the research reports, including building bridges with other divisions within NIE, sharpening the focus of reports to policy-makers, and building a communication network with potential information users in the Department of Education, which houses continuing programs that might benefit from the findings from RDU. As researchers, we have also learned some lessons from observing and participating in these two cases about the ways to avoid sending a good research or evaluation project into the oblivion of a policy vacuum. Some of these lessons are outlined below.

No Organized Constituency

Most federal employees have an appreciation of the loose integration of federal policy. In many cases, little can be done to circumvent the factionalized policy constituencies, at least in the short term. However, steps can be taken to make policy debates within an agency such as the NIE more constructive. As Farrar et al. (1980) have noted, policy development situations may be viewed as a lawn party to which different constituencies bring different interests and from which all may go away satisfied. We have portrayed the process of program and research development using a conflict model in this chapter, because the conflict model fits the particular situations that we have described most closely. However, both "feds" and researchers may, with active effort, reduce conflicts and promote a more evolutionary approach through briefing workshops and explicit negotiation and compromise.

Even where formal summit talks or treaties cannot iron out differences in a federal agency, staff members can assist in building a climate of mutual interest through low-key methods. We have noticed, for example, that horizontal dissemination inside federal agencies is extremely poor. (In this regard, of course, federal agencies resemble other bureaucracies.) We believe that improved internal communications, both formal and informal, would be extremely helpful in preventing extreme policy vacuums.

The internal marketing associated with the entrepreneurial bureaucracies is often simply associated with the initial "selling" of a new idea. Once a project or idea is funded, continued marketing may be necessary if the impact from a policy study is to be maximized. This is particularly important since, in many cases, utilization of policy research may occur before any formal report is available. (In our experience, it is often six months to a year before a "finding" is available in a report. Yet in the interim there are usually many decisions being made that might be improved through knowledge of that research.)

One of the ways to improve the circulation of ideas before they are finalized is to change the reporting structure that is associated with policy research. In many cases, projects have numerous reports. Often, however, interim reports are treated like final reports: they are long, highly technical, and subject to the detailed review processes that final reports engender. It might, for example, be preferable to develop occasional papers, which are more speculative and less finished. These would require less effort on the part of the researcher to produce and the federal government to review. As they should be shorter, they may also be more readable and therefore more easily circulated within the agency.

We also sense that policy researchers frequently pay too little attention to building constituencies, and instead spend most of their time developing close relationships with the federal project officer who monitors their work. Based on our observations, however, a more active stance in developing constituencies should be considered a part of the policy researchers' work. Because researchers are outside the system, it is often easier for them to gain access to different individuals who hold opposing views. In addition, if they are perceived as neutral, it may also be easier for them to determine how the interests and concerns of different groups may be attended to through the research. There is a tendency on the part of researchers to define the internal dissemination of their results as outside their job and possibly a suspect activity that is incompatible with the objective scientific status that they hope to give to their work. However, if they wish to have an impact, they may have to lobby for funding that they believe in.

No Clear "Research Questions"

Under most conditions it is assumed that the funding agency develops the research questions and the policy researcher attempts to answer them. This model is, of course, only one possibility. Clearly much policy research has gone in the opposite direction: a researcher poses a "policy question," and policies are later developed to take whatever findings have emerged around that question into consideration.

Wherever the policy questions originate, they should be clarified on a relatively continuous basis. We believe that the major responsibility for the continuous clarification of research questions must rest with the researcher, but with guidance from the funding agency. This is true largely because it is the researcher who is most highly trained to think in terms of questions that are at once answerable through available or obtainable data and which may have some relevance to the constituencies. Nevertheless, without continual renegotiation or reaffirmation of the relevance of the questions, particularly where there is any turnover within the funding agency or any formal or informal reorganization of constituencies, the risk of irrelevant reports is considerably increased. The responsibility of the federal government should be to encourage this type of activity both by mandating it within RFPs and by facilitating interaction between the researcher and potential users.

No Clear Bureaucratic Jurisdictions

Just as the negotiation of research questions requires primary activity on the part of the researcher, so the negotiation of bureaucratic jurisdictions should usually be spearheaded by the agency rather than the researcher. One of the main issues at stake here is the reluctance of most researchers to put themselves in a position of being advocates for one agency that is in a boundary dispute with another. Thus, the research information is likely to be a background rather than a foreground for the development of agency agendas. Nevertheless, as the authority of the OMB or other competing agencies grows and questions of duplication or overlap emerge more frequently, it seems very likely that federal employees will (and should) call more frequently upon researchers to provide evidence on a case. Thus, for example, in the conflict between RDU and the OMB, the research team could have provided the NIE with considerable ammunition that would have allowed the NIE representatives to substantially strengthen their arguments about the unique contributions to knowledge that could be made through a study of the RDU Program.

Lack of a Program

The lack of an ongoing program to affect is perhaps one of the most serious of the policy vacuum issues. The review of the literature by Glennan *et al.* (1978), for example, suggests that major mandated demonstration programs typically have relatively little impact upon congressional decision-making. As we have a better understanding of the demonstration as a policy-relevant liability, however, we must also begin to think of ways to compensate for this. Perhaps the most important is to design at least a few more modest demonstrations. Thus, for example, much of the lack of interest in the study of the Rural ES Program seemed to stem from the fact that the demonstration appeared to be designed to produce maximal results rather than to be "institutionalizable" (see Herriot 1979, 1980; Louis and Rosenblum 1981). The criticisms of the RDU Program (and of the study) also run in the same vein: the program had too many resources, it couldn't be replicated on a continuing basis, it wasn't politically realistic, and so forth. We have also noted the same phenomenon within the RDU Program: in general, those projects that built upon existing structures and developed objectives of slightly lower scope were more likely to endure after federal funding than those which hired new staff, attempted to build more significant new structures, and tried for more clear-cut or experimental interventions. We are not arguing here for the notion that a program that ventures little will produce much change. We are, however, arguing that the federal program designers and the policy researchers must strike a balance between pointing out what may be the best of all possible worlds and what might be done to incrementally improve the world we currently live in. Both types of information are necessary to encourage healthy debate and political action.

Acknowledgement

This chapter profited from the comments of our colleagues John Egermeier, Robert Herriott, Mike Kane, and Sheila Rosenblum. A previous version of this chapter was presented at the 1980 meeting of the American Sociological Association.

Notes

1. This chapter was published as K.S. Louis and R.G. Corwin (1982) "Policy research in a policy vacuum." In *Sociology of Education and Socialization Research, Vol. 3: Policy Research*. Greenwich, CT: JAI. Dated chapter notes were eliminated.
2. A view from 2004: in the latter part of the 1990s policy emphasized whole-school or comprehensive reform (The New American Schools and related efforts), but no effort was made to look at the many research reports from the ES study.

References

Berman, P. and M. McLaughlin (1975) *Federal Programs Supporting Educational Change*. Vols 2 and 7 (1979). Santa Monica, CA: Rand Corporation.

Bernstein, I. and H. Freeman (1975) *Academic and Entrepreneurial Research*. New York: Russell Sage Foundation.

Brickell, H. (1978) "The influence of external political factors on the role and methodology of evaluation." In T. Cook (ed.), *Evaluation Studies Review Annual*, Vol. 3. Beverly Hills, CA: Sage.

Chabotar, K. and D. Kell (1978) *Linking R&D With Local Schools: A Federal Program and Its Policy Context.* Cambridge, MA: Abt Associates.

Cohen, D. and M. Garet (1975) "Reforming educational policy with applied social research." *Harvard Educational Review* 45(l):17–43.

Cook, T.D., J. Levinson-Rose, and W. Pollard (1980) "The misutilization of evaluation research: some pitfalls of definition." *Knowledge: Creation, Utilization, Dissemination* 1 (June): 477–98.

Corwin, R. (1977) *Patterns of Federal Local Relationships in Education: A Case Study of the Experimental Schools Program.* Cambridge, MA: Abt Associates.

—— (1981) *The Politics of Program Design.* Cambridge, MA: Abt Associates.

Cowden, P. and D. Cohen (1979) *Divergent Worlds of Practice: The Federal Reform of Local Schools in the Experimental Schools Program.* Cambridge, MA: The Huron Institute.

Downs, A. (1965) "Some thoughts on giving people economic advice." *American Behavioral Scientist* 9 (September): 30–2.

Farrar, E., J. DeSanctis, and D. Cohen (1980) "Views from below: implementation research in education." *Teachers College Record* (fall): 77–100.

Glennan, T., W. Hederman, L. Johnson, and R. Rettig (1978) *The Role of Demonstrations in Federal R&D Policy.* Santa Monica, CA: Rand Corporation.

Guttentag, M. (1977) "Evaluation and Society." In M. Guttentag (ed.), *Evaluation Studies Review Annual*, Vol. 2. Beverly Hills, CA: Sage.

Herriott, R. (1979) "The federal context: planning, funding and monitoring." In R. Herriott and N. Gross (eds), *The Dynamics of Planned Educational Change*: 49–73. Berkeley, CA: McCutchen.

—— (1980) "Federal Initiatives and Rural School Improvement: Findings from the Experimental Schools Program." Cambridge, MA: Abt Associates.

Hill, P. (1980) "Evaluating education programs for federal policymakers: lessons from the NIE compensatory education study." In J. Pincus (ed.), *Education Evaluation in the Public Policy Setting*: 48–74. Santa Monica, CA: Rand Corporation.

Kirst, M. (1979) "Strengthening federal-local relationships supporting educational change." In R. Herriott and N. Gross (eds), *The Dynamics of Planned Educational Change*: 274–97. Berkeley, CA: McCutchen.

Knorr, K.D. (1977) "Policy makers' use of social science knowledge: symbolic or instrumental?" In C. Weiss (ed.), *Using Social Research in Federal Policy Making*: 165–82. Lexington, MA: Lexington Books.

Lindblom, C. and D. Cohen (1979) *Useable Knowledge.* New Haven, CT: Yale University Press.

Louis, K. and S. Rosenblum (1981) *Designing and Managing Interorganizational Networks.* Cambridge, MA: Abt Associates.

——, J. Molitor, G. Spencer, and R. Yin (1978) *Linking R&D With Local Schools: An Interim Report.* Cambridge, MA: Abt Associates.

McGowan, E.F. (1976) "Rational fantasies." *Policy Studies* 7: 439–54.

March J. and J. Olsen (1976) *Ambiguity in Organizations.* Bergen: Universitetsforlaget.

Patton, M. (1978) *Utilization Focused Evaluation.* Beverly Hills, CA: Sage.

—— et al. (1977) "In search of impact: An analysis of the utilization of federal health evaluation research." In C. Weiss (ed.), *Using Social Research in Federal Policy Making*: 141–64. Lexington, MA: Lexington Books.

Rosenblum, S. and K. Louis (1981) *Stability and Change: Innovation in an Educational Context*. New York: Plenum Press.

Sieber, L., K. Louis, and L. Metzer (1972) *The Use of Educational Knowledge*. New York: Bureau of Applied Social Research, Columbia University.

Sproull, L., S. Weiner, and D. Wolf (1978) *Organizing an Anarchy*. Chicago: University of Chicago Press.

Weiss, C. (1980) "Knowledge creep and decision accretion." *Knowledge: Creation, Diffusion, Utilization* 1(4): 381–404.

Zigarmi, P., B. Turnbull, A. Lieberman, M. Reynolds, and D. Stedman (1980) *Strengthening Technical Assistance to the National Diffusion Network*. Washington, DC: Dingle Associates.

16

Improving Urban and Disadvantaged Schools: Dissemination and Utilization Perspectives[1]

Introduction

> The conditions in some of our schools are so bad, and the physical and social environ-
> ments in which theses schools are located are so frightful, that we may have to cross
> off some ... as expendable.

> (Halpin 1966, quoted in Englert 1993: 3)

In many countries, poor, minority or first-generation immigrant students are concen-
trated in a few schools, often in urban areas. In the USA, ambivalence about the status of
urban schools goes back to the early part of this century, coinciding with the first wave
of "foreigners" from Eastern Europe. But the problem of knowledge utilization (KU)
and urban schools is not only a North American phenomenon: in many countries recent
patterns of immigration have created large and small pockets of urban poverty that are
often associated with problems within the educational system.

In most cases, targeted policies for improving urban education have been linked to
major financial or structural reforms, ranging from subsidies for schools with poorer
students, magnet schools/schools of choice, or the introduction of special structured

curriculum/testing programs. Rarely has anyone looked seriously at incremental, knowledge-based strategies for improving urban settings. This may be, in part, due to the belief that "big problems need big solutions." However, in addition, the experience of countries with well-established dissemination systems (such as the USA, Denmark and The Netherlands) has been that urban schools are harder to reach than more affluent schools in smaller cities or towns. In the USA, for example, the folklore of dissemination professionals is that unless state or regional dissemination personnel happen to be "natives," these schools may be "out of the KU loop."

In this chapter, I will discuss the organizational properties of urban schools that lead to their isolation and outline some strategies to improve dissemination and utilization. These will include political/community organizing strategies, linking dissemination to organization development, increasing the salience of ties between universities and schools, the development of teacher networks, and action research. The chapter will conclude with some principles for designing a dissemination system that will effectively promote KU in urban centers.

Redefining Dissemination and Knowledge Utilization in Schools: An Organizational Learning Perspective

As critics of dissemination and utilization (D&U) theories have pointed out, the derivation of research from studies of the transfer of new technologies to farmers, village women, or other individual "knowledge users" has only partial relevance for today's schools. The focus on the organization as the unit of change has dominated research on educational innovation since the early 1970s. In recent years, this focus has generated lines of research that attempt to integrate theories of D&U with theories of organizational change (Louis *et al.* 1981; Louis and Dentler 1988; Weiss 1993). I will argue that the characteristics of urban schools, and the nature of the strategies that seem to be working to promote KU in urban schools, suggest a more radical theoretical departure from the knowledge/product driven models.

In particular, D&U models for urban schools need to take into account the extensive need for integrating "organizational learning" frameworks into the D&U strategies (Senge 1990; Louis 1992). The definition that I use here is that *organizational learning involves the creation of socially constructed interpretations of facts and knowledge that enter the organization from the environment, or are generated from within.* What differentiates an organizational learning approach from more traditional theories about D&U is the emphasis on the socially constructed nature of "useable knowledge" – and the low likelihood of any meaningful change in an institutionalized school setting in the absence of efforts to reach an internalized consensus in the school about how any new information contributes to a more powerful vision of how urban children should be educated. At its best, organizational learning is defined by the ability of the organization to challenge its own assumptions (at least on a regular basis) in order to improve performance (Daft and Huber 1987). I will return to the organizational learning theme at the end of the paper.

Why is it Hard to Reach Urban Schools?

Field reports suggest that such schools tend to be bureaucratic, politicized, and isolated from the most up-to-date information about educational innovations that may improve the educational opportunities for disadvantaged children. This isolation, in turn, makes them less able to adopt and implement innovations (Natriello *et al.* 1990). Here I will focus not on the characteristics of urban schools that may make them less effective for children (see Cibulka *et al.* 1992; Englert 1993), but only on those that may affect their ability to become learning organizations. In addition, I have made no effort to be exhaustive, but point primarily to characteristics that have emerged in recent research, including my own, on restructuring and reform in urban schools.

Socio-economic Conditions

The characteristics of urban communities have significant implications for issues of knowledge use and reform. In a study of a federally funded R&D Utilization Program, Louis *et al.* (1981) found that the larger the proportion of disadvantaged students in a school, the less effective were the school's capacities to engage in an effective problem-solving process. Wealthy communities have a richness of intellectual and social capital that supports education, while less wealthy communities frequently lack such resources. Pallas *et al.* (1989) observe that schools are not the sole educators of children, and that communities, as well as families, vary in terms of the educational experiences that they provide to supplement what is learned more formally. This assumption is corroborated by research in Scotland, which shows that children in low-income communities perform less well than similarly disadvantaged peers who live in communities of a higher socio-economic status (SES), even when the SES composition of the school is controlled for.

In the USA, at least, demographic projections suggest that the number of children who come from educationally disadvantaged settings will rise very rapidly over the next few decades. For example, Pallas *et al.* (1989: 20) estimate that the number of children living with mothers who have not completed secondary school will increase by 56 per cent by 2020, while the number whose primary language is not English will increase from about 2.5 per cent in 1982 to 7.5 per cent of all students in 2020. Thus, educational failure cannot be addressed only through formal schooling. This assumption underlies the recent effort to reform the Chicago Public Schools, which emphasizes the need to involve the community directly in the education of the young. Similarly, Central Park East Secondary School in New York, for example, has a student body that is predominantly poor and minority, but a significant component of the curriculum involves students working in the community, during which they both learn and help.

In spite of efforts to link community development to educational improvement, disadvantaged communities currently lack the resources to help schools find and take advantage of new ideas. It is not simply that middle-class parents possess "knowledge" that helps children do well and that supports school improvement and innovation; it is also that the knowledge that is possessed by lower-SES parents tends to be devalued and excluded from a definition of what should be learned. Put more simply, urban schools often lack the resources and the networks of more advantaged communities' schools that help to create an environment that supports knowledge use – yet the demands and need for innovation are much higher. Currently, no country has policies that address this issue, and serious efforts to permanetly redistribute resources, including knowledge connections, to disadvantaged urban schools are controversial in an era of limited increases in educational budget.

Educational dissemination and KU strategies, even when targeted at schools rather than individuals as users, have not addressed the issue of how to incorporate or develop social and cultural capital that can support knowledge use in schools. While focusing on the school as the unit of change may be appropriate in a middle-class community, it may be as limited in some urban settings as the dissemination models of the late 1960s, which assumed that we could change the educational system by making individual teachers into knowledge users.

Cultural Conditions

Urban schools are hard to reach because many of them are poorly linked to the natural professional networks through which ideas are diffused. Dissemination research has established that communication of new ideas across cultural boundaries is extremely difficult (Rogers 1982). Because urban schools are viewed as part of the "dominant culture" by the government agencies that fund them, attention to cultural barriers as a problem in innovation is rare. However, this perspective – "we own them, and they are therefore part of us" – is shortsighted, as there is plenty of evidence that cultural factors may play a part in impeding KU.

One feature of urban school systems in the USA is that, just as poor communities are socially isolated from mainstream knowledge, so are many urban schools culturally isolated from broader streams of educational thought. For example, efforts to assess the number of improvement programs being carried out in urban high schools during the mid-1980s indicated that only a tiny fraction were basing any efforts on the "effective schools" literature (Louis and Miles 1990). Rollow and Bryk (1993) note that the Chicago Public School System tends to recruit teachers who went through that system and who, in addition, received their teacher training at a single Chicago-based institution whose faculty members also tend to be local. While the Chicago case may be extreme, there are many stories about the "inbred" quality of urban systems. This differentiates them from other smaller communities, where teacher-training students leave at least for the duration of their programs, and where recruitment patterns are more likely to bring in "outsiders." However, even outsiders may be socialized to working conditions that sap professional creativity, and become acclimated to pervasive dullness of instruction and low expectations: if they do not become socialized to accept the situation more or less as it is, they are likely to leave.

The fact that some urban schools are located in undesirable neighborhoods in which middle-class people feel uncomfortable reinforces their cultural isolation. Visitors from universities don't "pop in," opportunities for student teaching are limited, and even district staff may prefer to stay in the office rather than spending time "in the trenches." Teachers in urban districts are less likely to engage in cross-school curriculum development efforts (which, because of larger bureaucracies are more likely to involve district office staff) than are teachers in suburban settings. Cultural isolation is thus further reinforced.

Political Conditions

All schools exist in a political environment, because the goals and means of educating our young arc hotly contested everywhere. In urban settings, however, interest-group politics tend to mix with educational politics in a more volatile way than in smaller towns (Peterson 1985; Reese 1986). As Louis (1991) notes, many urban settings display fragmented values with regard to education. Some may also be extreme "policy vacuums" characterized by an absence of clear, organized constituencies, a clear understanding of policy issues and choices, consistency in policy initiatives, and coordination between overlapping or complementary policies (Corwin and Louis 1982). This is often true in the many urban districts that have had instability in the superintendent's office (Louis and Miles 1990). There is more likely to be antagonism between professional educators and parents, and there are more parent and community groups that form distinctive perspectives on what should happen to schools. Most would agree, however, that efforts to devolve authority into smaller districts within the central district have not been effective, as they tend to simply add an additional layer of bureaucracy or even create new and Balkanized interest groups. Union militancy has often been the response both to bureaucratization and political pressures. Although unions are often the scapegoat, there is more evidence that urban unions are eager to collaborate in school reform than to the contrary (McDonnell and Pascal 1988; Hill et al. 1989).

There are more calls for Chicago- or Kentucky-like efforts to dismantle district control and create a more powerful relationship between the local community and the school, while increasing the direct relationship between the state and schools. It is often assumed that this will reduce the volatility of educational politics by breaking up city-wide interest groups and reducing the control of powerful unions. Ravitch (1974) points out, however, that the centralization versus decentralization question is cyclical and that neither extreme appears to be effective in the long run.

Any discussion of the politics of education and its impact on innovation cannot ignore the politics of race and poverty. As city schools have become increasingly minority dominated, many decisions are made about education that have less to do with educational quality than the achievement of other social goals, ranging from desegregation to the retention of white, middle-class students. As Lytle (1990) notes, the current educational reform movements in the USA (and in developed other countries as well) are inherently conservative, driven by economic and employment rhetoric rather than by issues of equity, and many urban school systems are touting their ability to improve student learning outcomes with minimal changes in structure and financial resources. Another dimension of urban politics according to Apple (1991) concerns curriculum. As Apple has observed, control over curriculum lies outside of the school, and is held by relatively conservative interests. In schools where children are frequently from relatively powerless communities, the lack of influence over the content of curriculum is of profound importance. In particular, the curriculum in many urban settings is focused on basic skills and is unconnected with the experiences of the students who attend.

Apple points to urban experiments in which control over the curriculum has been taken back from textbook manufacturers; my own observations suggest that under the right conditions, urban schools (with little to lose in terms of public confidence) may be willing to experiment freely.

Fragmented and politicized environments make the development of a learning community more difficult, in part because all outsiders may come to be viewed as potential sources of problems for the school. Recent studies of innovation in urban schools have emphasized the importance of a stable policy environment (Louis and Miles 1990), which cannot occur where interest group politics are fierce. In addition, the absence of serious discussion about the possible need for a fundamentally different approach to curriculum and instruction for poor, disadvantaged urban youth inhibits the development of dialogue inside the school. Organizational learning theory suggests that such dialogue about change conditions is a necessary prerequisite for KU and improvement.

Organizational Conditions

There are many organizational conditions that need to be addressed before urban schools can be effective. The Carnegie Foundation (1988), for example, pointed to the need for school-based management, clear accountability standards, and intervention procedures when schools are not meeting their objectives. While these are probably necessary for renewal, there are other characteristics that have a bigger impact on knowledge use and reform, such as size, teachers' working conditions, and decision-making structures.

Urban school districts are, almost by definition, large, and urban schools also tend to be larger than average (although they are not, especially at the high-school level, the largest in the USA). Recent efforts to look at the combined effects of district and school size (which are associated) suggest that big is more bureaucratic and also bad for children – at least where students are of lower socio-economic status (Wahlberg 1989). With reference to teachers and knowledge use, however, larger schools in lower SES communities tend to have a lower "sense of community" among teachers (Bryk and Driscoll 1988) – and sense of community is a critical ingredient for collectively grappling with issues related to knowledge use and reform (Louis 1994). This is, perhaps, the reason why larger schools have also been found to have less effective problem-solving and knowledge-utilization processes (Louis et al. 1981).

With increasing federal and state mandates, bureaucratization of urban school districts has grown, and individual schools have become reliant on regulations and special programs to improve their functioning. There is plenty of evidence to suggest that more bureaucratic and centralized organizations are less effective at using knowledge than less bureaucratic, decentralized ones (Leavitt and March 1988). Goldring's (1990) study of principals' attitudes toward parents suggests that bureaucratization interferes with building community: among principals in low-SES settings in the Chicago metropolitan area, those working in settings that were less bureaucratic had more positive attitudes toward parents. Many writers have suggested that solving the size problem is central to breaking the bureaucratic mentality that seems to afflict many urban schools (Ruffin 1989; Wahlberg 1989). Size is associated with fragmented delivery of services, which, in turn, makes using knowledge to fundamentally improve more difficult (Englert 1993: 28). When schools are involved with multiple programs, serviced by multiple professionals, and these programs have no relationship with each other, opportunities for synergistic improvement are often overlooked.

Urban schools have more difficulty than others in recruiting and retaining the most talented teachers (Englert 1993: 38). This is, perhaps, not surprising when we note that teachers' working conditions in urban schools are often less conducive to energetic involvement in knowledge use and reform than those in newer and/or smaller districts. It is not simply that the buildings in urban centers tend to be older, but that teachers are less involved in policy decisions, are treated less respectfully by administrators, have fewer opportunities to engage in significant work with each other, and are generally treated less professionally (Corcoran et al. 1988). Teacher turnover may be either too high (where seniority rights encourage "bumping") or too low (in schools with poor reputations) to support effective social construction of knowledge for reform. Each of these features has been shown to be related to teachers' sense of efficacy and commitment – and inversely related to negative attitudes about the students they teach (Rosenblum et al. 1994). Teachers who encounter these circumstances are unlikely to develop the professional community that is critical to active knowledge use and improvement (Kruse and Louis 1993).

But the nature of work in urban schools has an additional character (which is shared to some extent with teaching in other contexts); namely it is hurried, focused on the short-term, and subject to interruption. No matter what we would like them to be, few teachers and administrators are "reflective practitioners" who eagerly seek complex information to improve their work. Rather, they tend to be harassed, and looking for information that will solve today's problem – today. In addition, schools lack basic information that would encourage reflection and experimentation. Urban districts rarely have information-management systems that permit them to gain access to useable data, much less information and ideas that are less familiar (Cibulka 1992: 37).

Finally, traditional patterns of KU are a barrier. First, it is common to refer to schools as "loosely coupled" organizations, in which safe experimentation and KU occurs in quasi-autonomous individual classrooms. However, when more extensive organization-wide reform is an issue, traditional forms of loose coupling (teacher autonomy and zoning of decisions) may prevent the development of consensus about the nature of the needed changes (Rosenblum and Louis 1981; Louis and Miles 1990). Second, few schools have extensive, cosmopolitan staff-development opportunities, and typically the principal acts as a screen that filters knowledge as it enters the school (Wahlstrom and Louis 1994). Even in restructured urban schools, for example, principals are likely to have more influence over "what's on the agenda" than individual teachers, but the evidence suggests that typical principals do not take active postures with respect to knowledge use (Rosenblum et al. 1994).

Dissemination Theory and Practice: Does Conventional Wisdom Fail to Address the "Urban Problem?"

In the following section I will describe the US dissemination system, and will argue that both the theory and practice of dissemination are based on a "technology push" model that is not appropriate for urban educational systems.

The Land Grant/Extension System Model

The US pioneered the role of research as a means of improving practice when the federal government fostered the land grant college system, and its associated tradition of "extension services" that linked the funded institutions to the needs of agricultural and rural communities in the state. The notion that research knowledge can be used to answer specific questions of practice was, for a long time, a peculiarly American phenomenon. The extension system model operates, of course, on the belief that there is a need for intermediate, locally available offices that are delegated the responsibility for increasing communication between the university and "the field." Extension agents answer questions raised by individuals through consulting research findings and researchers located at the state's land grant university. Researchers, on the other hand, have a vehicle through which new, applied findings can be rapidly communicated to "the field."

While it has left us with a system of universities and a model that had proven, over the years, to be highly effective, the extension model has also constrained the way in which we think about dissemination and KU (Patton 1988). The extension system, until recently, has been set up largely to serve the needs of individuals; the problems of education, however, are invariably tied up with the functioning of schools as organizational units. In addition, because urban schools exist in highly politicized environments, the elegant simplicity of the extension's technology transfer model is complicated by the constant independent streams of actors, problems, competing solutions, and crises (March and Olsen 1976). In addition, the "problems" that the extension system was so admirably set up to solve were typically concrete, and the results of adoption were visible. In contrast, the problems of urban education are complex, interrelated, and the availability of clear solutions is unlikely.

The Development of ERIC

The ERIC system was developed in response to the deeply held (and accurate) belief that one of the problems with the low levels of research utilization in education that were routinely discussed in the 1950s and early 1960s was the inaccessibility of research. But ERIC was developed without any corresponding thought given to how educators would actually use the system. ERIC, as designed, was not, and is still not "user friendly." But, since so much was invested in creating it, the need to build ERIC into any further dissemination policies was unquestioned. Indeed, the first efforts of the federal government to get into more active dissemination postures (the Pilot State Dissemination Project, designed in the late 1960s and funded from 1970 to 1972) was specifically intended to focus on proving that ERIC could be useful to teachers and administrators. The need to justify and maintain ERIC still drives dissemination policy. This has an unintended consequence of skewing dissemination policy in general toward a knowledge-base driven approach, rather than a problem-solving approach. This is clearly reflected in Klein's (1992) model design for a new US dissemination system, which makes no mention of the characteristics of the "user systems."

In addition, ERIC lacks good, solid information for urban educators. In preparation for this paper I did an ERIC search (for material entered since 1988). Although there were over 400 entries in response to the descriptor "urban education," I judged few of them to be both readily available and suitable for urban practitioners.

The Regional Laboratory System

The regional laboratories, which were initiated in the mid-1960s, were intended as a mechanism to renew education through development. Inherently intended as research-utilizing agencies, the regional laboratory system has become the backbone of the "general purpose dissemination system" of the federal government – for example, dissemination activities that serve the broad needs of schools rather than the special needs of a targeted program. Nevertheless, despite their central position, they have been systematically bypassed in a number of the most critical KU/school improvement experiments – including the Pilot State Dissemination Project, the R&D Utilization Program, the National Diffusion Network, and others. This isolation of the Regional Laboratories from other federal thrusts in school improvement is typical of the tendency of federal policies to promote competition and experimentation rather than integration of activities to support improvement. The emphasis in federal policy on the "with and through" role of laboratories – that they are not to work directly with schools in most instances, but to work with other agencies, such as state departments of education, to provide services – additionally underscores their position as providers of knowledge rather than as activists in reform.

Several of the Regional Laboratories are located in major urban centers. However, up until the mid-1990s none had chosen to specialize in issues of urban school improvement, and even some of those located in urban settings had no special urban strategy.

Special Purpose Assistance

One of the major competitions in federal support policies is between "general purpose dissemination" and "special purpose assistance," the latter being funded out of programs such as Title I/Chapter I, desegregation funds, bilingual program, and so on. These programs have often funded "assistance centers" that provide technical help regarding the special needs of program recipients. Because they are funded by the programs, rather than by a general program for the support of school change and improvement, coordination between them is non-existent. Because these special purpose activities are often targeted to low-income students, urban centers are an obvious target. However, because they are uncoordinated, they are unable to focus their services collectively on a school's information needs. Rather than promoting organizational learning, they contribute to the fragmented character of many change strategies in urban schools.

Summary
These brief background remarks are intended to illustrate a number of characteristics of the emergent US support system:

1. It is deeply indebted to the extension model developed in the agricultural tradition;
2. It has traditionally focused on the dissemination side of the equation, rather than on the knowledge use/local development side;
3. It has grown up as a set of uncoordinated – and even competitive – activities;
4. It is inattentive to the contextual characteristics of urban schools that affect their desire and ability to take advantage of opportunities to use and apply knowledge.

The result is an approach that is largely top-down, research-to-practice focused rather than bottom-up, problem-solving focused. None of these characteristics permits the D&U system in the USA to have a concerted effort to reach urban schools.

Strategies to Reach Urban Schools: What Kinds of Agents? What Kinds of Support?

A growing number of individuals and organizations in the USA are developing to address the problems of urban education. Before I turn to a discussion of principles and dissemination/utilization theory, I would first like to describe some of the successful approaches that are being taken – most of which are occurring outside of the formal research, development, dissemination, and utilization (RDD&U) structures described above.

Coordinating Multiple Agencies
A number of large foundations have taken an interest in dealing with the problem of KU and coordination of multiple agencies dealing with the wide variety of problems faced by urban schools. Not all of these have been successful in improving classroom practices (Wehlage 1992; White and Wehlage 1994), but what they have done is focused attention on education as a community development problem. In doing so, efforts that fall into this category are trying to support urban schools by addressing the significant socio-economic issues that interfere with the development of effective schools.

One might not, on the face of it, think of the co-location of key social and health services for families and children within a school building as an issue of knowledge dissemination and utilization – but I would argue strongly that it is. Far more than in previous years, educators need access to information about the non-educational factors that affect their students' lives and their ability to learn. By locating other "experts" in child and family development close to teachers, they have access that would otherwise not be available from the formidably large and fragmented bureaucracies that provide non-educational services to children.

University-School Linkages

The chasm between the university and the schools, and problems of spanning differences in culture, language, and goals are viewed as contributing to the "problem of utilization." Recent research (Huberman 1990) suggests that this is not inevitable, and that if schools are involved in faculty research throughout its conduct, the chances of utilization are greatly increased, as are the probabilities of future collaboration and exchange. Of particular interest in this study is that "spillover effects" – long considered in the industrial technology transfer literature to be critical to economic development – are strongly related to sustain linkages during the research.

There has also been a growth of school-university collaboratives in urban settings (Ascher 1989; Harkavy and Puckett 1992), most of which apparently emphasize collegiality and equality among the members. Aside from those relationships that focus directly on KU (staff development; curriculum development and delivery), they address enduring rather than episodic exchanges and encourage "spillover effects" through informal consultation and exchange of ideas. When universities become involved in schools for mutual research, to help with policy changes, to provide curriculum support, or to facilitate college study for students still in high school, there is a common focus on improving achievement that creates more permanent bonds and may lead to systemic reform. Professional Development Schools are an example of a particular type of university-school collaborative that has become more common. The relationships initially conceived of as a way of improving teacher training and delivering staff development are sustained through mutual benefits beyond this limited goal (Metcalf 1993). Metcalf concludes that, although these relationships may be productive, they are difficult to sustain. Clearly, since professional practice schools are, by definition, involved in teacher training, the least advantaged schools are not suitable sites. However, in a number of instances, they have been successfully developed in urban schools that have, at least initially, not been viewed as instructionally outstanding.

Organization Development

Sustained, long-term organization development (OD) has always been viewed as a strategy for changing schools (Schmuck and Rankel 1985), but most OD projects have been too short, and have relied too heavily on internal capacities to be viewed as a "good strategy" for working with urban schools (Miles *et al.* 1978). Furthermore, the traditional focus of OD on improving climate and interpersonal relationships fell out of favor in the late 1970s and 1980s, where policy tended to focus on KU strategies that could clearly be linked to classroom or student experiences. However, more recently a number of efforts have developed that have a curriculum "product" or strategy, and which provide a modified OD approach to school change in urban settings. One of these is the Consortium for School Change in Chicago, whose strategy has evolved to argue that *only* intensive OD over a long period of time will be able to develop the internal capacities of severely disadvantaged schools to develop professional learning communities (Rollow and Bryk 1993). The Consortium offers a participating school a choice of working on reading or math, a limited number of strategies within that, and requires the school to support an internal facilitator, while it provides an external facilitator for a three-year period. Henry Levin's "accelerated schools" model is another example, as are the dissemination activities that have been launched in Chicago by James Comer. In each case, the strategy involves limited or no choice of "the knowledge base," but active training and support available from a single source, typically university-based.

Networks
The emergence of school networks that involve urban schools, such as the Coalition of Essential Schools, The Urban Math Network, or the Center for Collaborative Education in New York City is a notable phenomenon of the last few years. Most of these, like the organization development efforts, are supported by foundation grants, rather than by federal agencies. They differ from the OD approaches in several ways:

1. they are typically less dominated by a single university faculty member/group;
2. they involve knowledge exchange between schools that share a particular orientation to reform, either of their subject matter or of the school's curriculum and pedagogy; and
3. they are less focused on the implementation of a particular model of reform.

Because these are voluntary groups, they are good vehicles for enlarging the KU networks for urban schools that are already committed to reform. They are less likely to reach schools that are culturally isolated, or deeply disadvantaged.

Action Research
Action research may be used as a strategy for improving KU alone, or as a vehicle that accompanies organization development or other university-school linkages. Action research requires that the teacher or a group of teachers examine their own practice reflectively and systematically, and it thus promotes a demand for more information. It may, if it focuses on the relationship between classroom practice and context (Carr and Kemmis 1986), promote political awareness on the part of the staff, changing their notions of how schooling relates to the urban setting. Action research is frequently advocated as a strategy for encouraging organizational learning. However, given the often discouraging working conditions in which urban teachers find themselves, maintaining a sustained commitment to the very hard work of action research may be difficult.

Summary

What are some of the commonalities among the above strategies for working with urban schools, and how are these different from the dominant paradigm for RDD&U?

First, all of these approaches are highly contextualized. They begin from a set of assumptions about what urban schools need, and how they operate. In many cases, they begin with assumptions about a specific urban setting and how it functions. Thus, the emphasis is on what might work in a particular place. This is less true of networks than the other strategies, but even here the effort is to group schools that are "alike," and networks typically promote a flexible interpretation of what would constitute an authentic variation on the model or set of concepts that holds the network together.

Second, the knowledge being transmitted is often urban specific, or is made urban specific. That is, it is tailored to the issues that truly trouble urban teachers and students – poverty, low skill levels, hopelessness, and so on. By being tuned into the cultural assumptions of the urban school, it is made more accessible.

Third, knowledge is viewed as conditional and constructed. Rather than thinking about educational knowledge as if it were analogous to a new technology, the strategies focus on the need for "social processing" of information over time, and the development of a site-specific interpretation of both the knowledge and its consequences. Teachers and administrators are involved as makers of knowledge and reform, rather than as passive recipients, and making time to talk about knowledge is a key part of the strategies.

Fourth, with the exception of some networks and action research, the emphasis is typically on school-wide reform. Even where the knowledge is initially targeted at individuals or a group within a school, the goal is to change the experiences of all teachers and all students.

Fifth, there is a high degree of equity between disseminator and receiving school, particularly where the knowledge is "owned" or "developed" by a "researcher." Teachers are viewed as learners and teachers of each other, and "craft knowledge" is typically celebrated as part of the process of adapting knowledge to the school site.

Sixth, there is not one D&U strategy, but many. Each of these may work for some schools, at some times. Each relies on different actors to make it work. Thus, opportunities to engage schools with different characteristics – not only those who are already attuned to the need for improvement, but also those whose capacities for change are very limited – are multiplied.

Seventh, they are all decentralized, and all avoid becoming involved with authorities and/or bureaucracies outside the school. Even in some instances where a district might sponsor or validate the appropriateness of a strategy, control by the district over knowledge and information flow is minimized.

Eighth, the emerging "urban D&U system" is not only complex, it is largely uncoordinated, and there is no expectation for coordination. Although most parts of the system draw on university-generated knowledge, this is not systematic. Most of the actors are entrepreneurial, in the sense that they believe that they have a good strategy for promoting knowledge use and improvement in urban education, they have found financial support, and have searched for schools that they can work with. The result from the school's perspective is vast confusion over where (or even whether) to get help. Because the system is so complex, it cannot be converted to a user-driven (or even user-friendly) system without major changes. Elsewhere (Louis 1992), I have argued that *unmanaged* complexity in a dissemination system will have the effect of excluding less sophisticated users – or the very schools that are most in need of improvement.

Discussion

As urban educators make serious efforts to address the problems that impede their effectiveness, they face many obstacles, both outside and within. A policy vacuum in the area of school improvement at the federal level appeared to be continuing under the Clinton administration, particularly in the area of D&U and school improvement (which was being viewed as largely synonymous with the development of curriculum guidelines and high stakes tests). What was observed was the virtual elimination of federally funded programs that promote school improvement, and the episodic resurgence of interest in dissemination did not yet appear to have picked up the major thrusts that were associated with the focus on school problem-solving and change that emerged in the 1970s. Instead, interest in D&U emphasized the need for more research syntheses, and technologically based communication networks. Although there was much research information on what makes schools become both more innovative and more likely to be active knowledge users, there had been little interest among educational policy-makers both in Washington and at the state level for developing initiatives that would build real KU into the current efforts to reform urban education.

In an earlier paper I used existing literature to define a number of conditions that may support organizational learning, or the capacity of schools to engage with and use knowledge. These are:

- decentralization, or the perceived empowerment of individuals to make a difference through KU;
- dense communication networks that provide opportunities for members to discuss ideas and develop a working consensus about how knowledge fits the specific context;
- "visionary leadership," or the willingness of an individual or group to help the school to define and redefine its central objectives (this provides a sieve through which the rich variety of available information can be diffused and sifted);
- an available knowledge base with useful, credible information; and
- an environment that provides useful feedback on performance and the effects of knowledge use.

These seem, in the context of the present chapter, to provide a framework for evaluating current efforts to provide KU support to urban schools, and to consider what needs to be done.

First, there are political issues related to governance that lie outside of what is generally considered to be the KU perspective; namely the decentralization of some choices to the school, and within the school the elimination of benevolent dictatorships in favor of enabling, but strong leadership (Rosenblum *et al.* 1994).

Second, the community and organization development strategies, which focus on the development of dense communication networks through which the "social processing" of knowledge occurs have considerable (albeit resource-intensive) potential. I would argue that, at least for the most disadvantaged schools, there is no alternative strategy other than the political/community development approach discussed above.

Third, the issue of performance feedback has been poorly addressed by all of these strategies. In general, performance feedback in urban settings is divorced from KU and other improvement efforts. As I have noted elsewhere (Louis 1992), this interrupted feedback cycle tends to produce faddish KU, in which innovations cycle through so rapidly that they have little potential for demonstrating powerful effects. Current efforts to give feedback on performance are dysfunctional, because the kinds of tests that are used are viewed by teachers, most researchers, and administrators as inappropriate.

Fourth, some of the most popular interventions – networks and action research – are, as currently practiced, weak tools in generating an organizational learning capacity in disadvanged urban schools. Action research, and networks that involve individuals or small groups of teachers, may contribute significantly to KU for the autonomous teacher in a highly disadvantaged school, and may be extremely important sources of individual and school development in schools that already function reasonably well. However, in fragmented and dysfunctional environments it may add up to little in the way of solid improvement in school functioning.

In sum, new models of KU in urban schools demand attention to organizational and organization-environment characteristics, and a commitment to a marriage between organizational change models and KU models that has virtually disappeared from the policy agenda since the mid-1970s. If organizational learning is accepted as a basis for a new direction in KU theories, we are lead almost inevitably back to reinvent the older traditions related to KU, namely those articulated by Kurt Lewin, Robert Merton, and others when they examined the influence of social groups – both artificial and natural – on attitudes and behavior. Knowledge utilization for the purposes of significant reform is not an individual act, but reflects the existing patterns of communication and influence that exist within a community. These may be reinforced with subject/discipline-specific networks and projects, but to hope for serious, effective KU in poorly structured, socially disorganized, centralized, and leaderless settings is unrealistic.

Note

1. This is an edited version of K.S. Louis (1995) "Improving urban and disadvantaged schools: Dissemination and utilization perspectives." *Knowledge and Poligy* 13: 287–304.

References

Apple, M. (1991) "The politics of curriculum and teaching." *NASSP Bulletin* (February): 39–50.

Ascher, C. (1989) "School-college collaborations: A strategy for helping low-income minorities." *The Urban Review* 21: 181–91.

Bryk, A.S. and M.W. Driscoll (1988) *The High School as Community: Contextual Influences and Consequences for Students and Teachers.* Madison: National Center on Effective Secondary Schools, University of Wisconsin-Madison.

Carnegie Foundation for the Advancement of Teaching (1988) *An Imperiled Generation: Saving Urban Schools.* Princeton, NJ: Carnegie Foundation.

Carr, W. and S. Kemmis (1986) *Becoming Critical: Education, Knowledge and Action Research.* London: Falmer.

Cibulka, J. (1992) "Urban education as a field of study: Problems of knowledge and power." In J. Cibulka, R. Reed, and K. Wong (eds), *The Politics of Education in the United States.* Washington, DC: Falmer Press.

Corcoran, T., L. Walker, and J.L. White (1988) *Working in Urban Schools.* Washington, DC: Institute for Educational Leadership.

Corwin, R. and K.S. Louis (1982) "Organizational barriers to the utilization of research." *Administrative Science Quarterly* 27: 623–40.

Daft, R. and G. Huber (1987) "How organizations learn," in N. DiTomaso and S. Bacharach (eds), *Research in the Sociology of Organizations*, Vol. 5: 1–36. Greenwich, CT: JAI.

Englert, R. (1993) "Understanding the urban context and conditions of practice of school administration." In P. Forsyth and M. Tallerico (eds), *City Schools: Leading the Way.* Newbury Park, CA: Corwin.

Goldring, E. (1990) "The district context and principals' sentiments toward parents." *Urban Education* 24: 391–403.

Harkavy, I and J. Puckett (1992) "Universities and the inner cities." *Planning for Higher Education* 20: 27–33.

Hill, P., A. Wise, and L. Shapiro (1989) *Educational Progress. Cities Mobilize to Improve their Schools.* Santa Monica, CA: RAND.

Huberman, M. (1990) "Linkage between researchers and practitioners: A qualitative study." *American Educational Research Journal* 27: 363–91.

Klein, S. (1992) "A framework for redesigning an R&D based national educational dissemination system in the United States." *Knowledge* 13: 256–86.

Kruse, S.D. and K.S. Louis (1993) "A framework for analyzing school-based professional community." Paper presented at the annual meeting of the American Educational Research Association, Atlanta.

Leavitt, B. and J.G. March (1988) "Organizational learning." *Annual Review of Sociology* 14: 319–40.

Louis, K.S. (1991) "Social and community values and the quality of teachers' work life." In M. McLaughlin, J. Talbert, and N. Bascia (eds), *The Context of Teachers' Work in Secondary Schools*13–22. New York: Teachers College Press.

—— (1992) Comparative perspectives on dissemination and knowledge use policies: Supporting school improvement. *Knowledge*, 13, 287-304.

—— (1994) "Beyond managed change: Rethinking how schools change." *School Effectiveness and School Improvement* 5: 1–22.

—— and R.A. Dentler (1988) "Knowledge use and school improvement." *Curriculum Inquiry* 18: 32–62.

—— and M. Miles (1990) *Reforming the Urban High School: What Works and Why*. New York: Teachers College Press.

——, S. Rosenblum, and J. Molitor (1981) *Strategies for Knowledge Use and School Improvement*. Washington, DC: National Institute of Education.

Lytle, J. (1990) "Reforming urban education: A review of recent reports and legislation." *The Urban Review* 22: 199–220.

McDonnell, L. and A. Pascal (1988) *Organized Teachers in American Schools*. Santa Monica, CA: RAND.

March, J. and J. Olsen (1976) *Ambiguity and Choice in Organizations*. Oslo: Universitetsforlaget.

Metcalf, P. (1993) "Toward establishing professional development schools: faculty perceptions in colleges and schools of education." Unpublished PhD. dissertation. Minneapolis, MN: University of Minnesota.

Miles, M., M. Fullan, and G. Taylor (1978) *Organization Development in Schools: The State of the Art*. New York: Center for Policy Research.

Natriello, G., A. Pallas, and E. McDill (1990) *Schooling Disadvantaged Children: Racing Against Catastrophe*. New York: Teachers College Press.

Pallas, A., G. Natriello, and E. McDill (1989) "The changing nature of the disadvantaged population: Current dimensions and future trends." *Educational Researcher* (June–July): 16–22.

Patton, M. (1988) "Extension's future: Beyond technology transfer." *Knowledge* 9: 476–91.

Peterson, P. (1985) *The Politics of School Reform: 1870–1940*. Chicago: University of Chicago Press.

Ravitch, D. (1974) *The Great School Wars*.

Raywid, M. (1993) "Finding time for collaboration." *Educational Leadership* 51: 30–4.

Reese, W. (1986) *Power and the Promise of School Reform: Grassroots Movements During the Progressive Era*. Boston: Routledge & Kegan Paul.

Rogers, E. (1982) *Diffusion of Innovations*. New York: Free Press.

Rollow, S. and Bryk, A. (1993) "Catalysing professional community in a school reform left behind." Paper presented at the annual meeting of the American Educational Research Association, Atlanta, Georgia.

Rosenblum, S. and K.S. Louis (1981) *Stability and Change*. New York: Praeger.

——, K.S. Louis, and R. Rossmiller (1994) "School leadership and teacher quality of work life in restructuring schools." In J. Murphy and K.S. Louis (eds), *Leadership and Restructuring*: 110–29. Newbury Park, CA: Corwin.

Ruffin, S. (1989) "Improving urban communities and their schools: A national emergency." *NASSP Bulletin* (May): 61–70.

Schmuck, R. and P. Rankel (1985) *The Handbook of Organization Development in Schools*. Prospect Heights, IL: Waveland Press.

Senge, P. (1990) The *Fifth Dimension: The Art and Practice of the Learning Organization*. New York: Doubleday.

Wahlberg, H. (1989) "District size and learning." *Education and Urban Society* 21: 154–63.

Wahlstrom, K. and K.S. Louis (1993) "Adoption revisited: Decision-making and school district policy." In S. Bacharach and R. Ogawa (eds), *Advances in Research and Theories of School Management and Educational Policy, Vol. 1*: 61–119. Greenwich, CT: JAI.

Wehlage, G. (1992) "Restructuring urban schools: The New Futures experiment." *American Science Quarterly* 21: 1–19.

Weiss, C. (1993) "Structuring the field: Designing and teaching a course in knowledge use." Paper presented at the annual meetings of the American Educational Research Association, Atlanta.

17

Reconnecting Knowledge Utilization and School Improvement[1]

Introduction

Theories of knowledge utilization and educational improvement have been closely linked since Havelock's (1969) classic literature review. This connection is also apparent in practice. On the one hand, school improvement depends on the implementation of new ideas about school organization and instruction; on the other, the refinement of theories about how schools use knowledge depends on having schools that serve as natural loci of experimentation and change. In recent years, however, explicit attention to dissemination and knowledge utilization has dropped from the agenda of most scholars interested in school reform. The purpose of this paper is to review emerging theories that may help to reconnect research on knowledge utilization with research on educational improvement. The analysis presented below assumes that the reader is familiar with the broad outlines of both school improvement and school effectiveness research (for example, Fullan and Stiegelbauer 1991), but less familiar with research traditions related to knowledge utilization.

In the first section of this paper I briefly review the current "state of the art" in knowledge utilization theory, and discuss how it is connected both to school effectiveness and improvement research streams. I then go on to look at some of the challenges to traditional theories of knowledge use that have been posed by postmodernists. Finally, I will briefly discuss why both the dominant and the challenging paradigms are not adequate to explain observed phenomena relating to dissemination and knowledge utilization in education.

In the second section of the paper I examine some new perspectives that have the potential for altering the way in which we analyze and interpret the observed phenomena discussed in the first section. In reviewing new ideas that can contribute to our under-standing of knowledge utilization, it is critical that we maintain the thoroughly interdisci-plinary base of this field. While various writers may approach the problem of putting knowledge to work for the betterment of individuals, and/or societies, with different lenses, major reviews of the field, such as Rogers (1982) or Glaser (1976), demonstrate that high-quality research and ideas come from disciplines ranging from agriculture to political science. This paper cannot, of course, range as broadly as these synthetic reviews, and since my objective is primarily to stimulate thinking about theory, I will confine myself to a few viewpoints from political, historical, organizational, and cognitive learning theory. In each case, I will briefly illustrate how the knowledge utilization perspective is reflected in current school improvement or school reform issues. I then turn to some elements of an intersection between knowledge utilization theories and school improve-ment theories that may drive us forward to a synthetic model of dissemination and utiliza-tion (D&U) that represents a paradigm shift rather than a paradigm revolution (Kuhn 1970). Some suggestions about practical implications will also be made.

State of the Art

A recent issue of *Knowledge and Policy*, which emerged from a 1993 conference in Haifa on the topic of D&U in education, contains very timely reviews of both the state of the art in more traditional theory (Huberman 1994), and a postmodernist critique of that perspective (Watkins 1994). Because these are both thoughtful and reasonably compre-hensive essays, I will review some of the main features of their arguments rather than to reinvent them. In addition, I will suggest some of the implications of traditional and postmodernist theories for school effectiveness and school improvement research.

Traditional D&U Theory Renewed

Huberman's review of the state of the art begins with the common assumption that there is a gap between research knowledge and practitioner knowledge that cannot be bridged without calculated interventions. Early efforts to do so have long been viewed as hyper-rational due to their assumptions that:

1. the flow of knowledge should be largely one-way, from the research community to the practice community; and
2. that more sophisticated forms of knowledge packaging and communication strategies would reduce, if not eliminate, the gap between what was known and what people did.

However, this body of research was never as simplistic as latter-day critics contend. As Havelock (1969) notes, scholarly work led to the conclusion that there was no simple, direct line between knowledge production and utilization. Early on, for example, there was attention to systemic and organizational barriers, to and facilitators, of knowledge utilization – as, for example, in the long line of work that started in the 1940s at Teachers College, which emphasized organizational and community factors in the spread of educational innovations, or the network analysis used to study the spread of medical and educational innovations (Mort 1963; Carlson 1965; Coleman *et al.* 1966). While these and other studies operated within a positivist frame, in that they studied the spread of identifiable, research-based innovations within a defined population of practitioners, they foreshadow many of the more recent themes that look at situated or contextually specific reasons for learning and knowing.

Huberman (1994) notes the many challenges to a rational model of knowledge use but chooses to review the subtleties of the existing paradigm as it has emerged in the 1980s and early 1990s. He argues that five factors, at least in education, have demonstrated strong empirical relationships with knowledge utilization. These include:

1. the context of research, including characteristics of the knowledge base and the motivation of the researcher to disseminate to practitioners;
2. the user's context, including factors ranging from perceived needs to the perception of the value of the research information;
3. linkage mechanisms – a major focus of Huberman's own research – such as the "sustained interactivity" between researchers and practitioners during the production and utilization phases;
4. the impacts of context and linkages on the resources, including attention, time, and acceptability of the research; and
5. the amount of effort expended creating an appropriate environment for use, which includes both the amount and quality of dissemination effort, the "useability" of the knowledge, and the quality of planning and execution in the "using site."

Huberman focuses on the role of reciprocally influential relationships in the process of knowledge utilization, but his perspective is consistent with the main lines of D&U research, which emphasize the dispersion of knowledge to multiple sites of practice. For example, beginning in the late 1970s in the USA, there were a number of efforts to develop research-to-practice models that translated the results of the "effective schools" and "effective teaching" research into training and support programs for local schools. Similar experiments involving collaboration between schools, trainers, and researchers have been conducted in The Netherlands. Policy-makers in most countries believe that, with proper sticks and carrots, schools can be encouraged (or required) to become better consumers of "good research results." Popular documents, funded by a variety of agencies and teacher associations (US Department of Education 1990; Fullan and Hargreaves 1991) are intended to pave the way toward a better understanding of the connection between research knowledge and good school practice. Individual researchers who believe that they have found a key to improved student performance may also "package" their ideas with materials, models, and training or support, as in Slavin's "Success for All" or Levin's "Accelerated Schools."

While Huberman's review is centered in this tradition, he makes a bridge to alternative perspectives in an important regard: he ties his own research findings regarding the importance of mutual influence to the notion of *social constructivism*. Huberman notes that researchers and practitioners may have a reciprocal influence on each other, and suggests that the need for sustained interactivity to promote research/knowledge utilization is consistent with some elements of the contemporary constructivist approach to teaching. The latter asserts that teachers' practitioner knowledge is constructed, largely by individuals, through both reflective practice (Schön 1983) and through more disciplined inquiry, such as action research (Carr and Kemmis 1986). This perspective is more consistent with emerging ideas about D&U that are associated with school improvement research: an emphasis on the uniqueness of schools, on the importance of local development activity, and on the centrality of school culture and leadership to improvement (and even effectiveness) (Newmann and Wehlage 1995).

Challenges from Postmodernist Thinking

Andy Hargreaves recently noted that one may wholeheartedly agree that we live in a postmodern era, defined by a radical shift in the nature of economies, employment and social relations, and disagree with many of the propositions put forward by self-styled postmodern thinkers (personal communication). This point should be borne in mind when reading this chapter.

Watkins (1994) presents a succinct critique of the current theoretical mainstream from a variety of different perspectives within the broad postmodernist frame. He begins where Huberman leaves off, with the observation that teachers construct knowledge as they go about their work, particularly when they engage in professional discussions around their own practice. Like many postmodernists, he then goes on to equate daily efforts to solve classroom problems with research – research that is highly contextualized because it is grounded in many years of "experience, training, problem-solving, reflection and the struggle to make sense ... " (p. 56). The school's process may appear nonlinear and random to outsiders, but a constructivist perspective accepts that:

1. all knowledge is "local" (Geertz 1983):
2. all knowledge is contested and partial, and there is no clear way to differentiate whether one knowledge claim is better than another; and
3. all knowledge is political, and influenced by the interests of those who develop and/ or use it.

Watkins' discussion is grounded in philosophical debates about the nature of knowledge, which range at one extreme from a positivist argument for the objectivity of some forms of knowledge (scientific knowledge, for example) to interpretivism, which argues that all knowledge is socially or individually constructed, and that the dominance of some ideas (ideologies) is largely a result of the power that groups may exert in promoting their perspectives. While Watkins distinguishes his own view, "critical realism," from extreme interpretivism (he acknowledges objective realities, but argues that we cannot perceive them directly or fully), he argues that "If [knowledge] meets scientific criteria, if it is generalizable, objective and theoretical, it is necessarily disembodied from its cognitive and social matrix, and no longer constitutes valid knowledge ... it is intrinsically meaningless in other contexts" (Watkins 1994: 65).

Since it is obvious that people communicate with others every day, and that these communications have a clear impact on behavior (for example, utilization), the apparent dilemma of observations of use and the theoretical impossibility of use can be resolved in two ways. The critical perspective espoused by Watkins, on the one hand, emphasizes the hegemony of particular groups who are able to make their interpretations of facts and information prevail. To avoid being a knowledge oppressor, the research community must, at minimum, give up control over the production of knowledge by creating learning communities with others and, at maximum, eliminate any distinction between researcher and user (Watkins 1994: 69).

On the other hand, a "non-critical theory" approach might differentiate between *knowledge* and *information*: information can be easily transferred, but until it is interpreted, either by the individual or the group, it does not become useable knowledge (Louis 1994). This position is consistent with a long line of mainstream sociological research that emphasizes the importance of socially constructed frames of reference that make learning at both the individual and group level possible – a position that predates the current wave of postmodernist thinking by several decades (Berger and Luckmann 1966). It does not, however, demand adherence to Watkins' assumption that "knowledge is ... not disseminateable per se ... [but] will need to be reconstructed in any use setting" (Watkins 1994: 72).

Just as traditional views of knowledge utilization are alive and well in public policy arenas, so are modified postmodernist perspectives. A paper recently commissioned by the US Office of Education (Campbell 1994) suggests that teachers and other educational practitioners will only "buy"our scholarly research if they contribute to it in meaningful ways. The paper goes on to propose a variety of techniques that could be used to involve practitioners in the process of research, and of testing and developing practices based on scholarly knowledge. Permeating the paper is the assumption that knowledge produced "outside" the practitioner's own system is legitimately viewed as invalid, or "non-knowledge." Some forms of action research also adopt a similar position, arguing that teacher creation of knowledge within their own classrooms is the preferred strategy for creating renewed educational settings. The notion that local invention occurs in response to local conditions is part of the persistent policy thrust in several countries toward decentralization. The "charter schools movement" in the USA, for example, is promoted as an antidote to centrally managed effectiveness programs that "don't work." Proponents of charter schools, which are typically new schools founded by groups of teachers and parents, assume that improving educational performance requires invention at the lowest level, not the diffusion of centrally developed and approved ideas. This assumption has been adopted as a public policy option in Sweden, where the National Board of Education was disbanded, the national curriculum simplified, and funding for education decentralized to municipalities (most of whom pass it through to individual schools).

A Critique

The so-called debate between "objectivist modernists" and "constructivist postmodernist" is, in my view, useful but limited. The debates are based in competing assumptions about science and the nature of knowledge, in which both modernists and postmodernists fail to fully reflect the conditions of inquiry or practice that are related to the development and utilization of knowledge in schools. In fact, there are also some similarities between the two. Both focus on the nature of knowledge and the relationship between knowledge production and knowledge utilization. Both assume, for the most part – even though the postmodernist perspective is critical of this situation – that formal knowledge is currently produced by researchers, and knowledge utilization, whether formal or informal, takes place in the work of practice. In other words, as Huberman posits, there is "a gap." In fact, as both acknowledge, the picture is more complex. However, neither has built a theoretical base that incorporates the complexity that they acknowledge.

Postmodernism appears to be more flawed than the revisionist versions of traditional theory. Most basic scientists have long ago given up the straw man of radical empiricism, which claims that research knowledge is entirely objective and capable of trust tests in a cross-cultural, value-free context (Duening 1991). Similarly, it is hard to imagine even the most anti-research practitioners accepting the contention that the only knowledge that exists to guide what they do in their classroom is their own interpreted experience. Furthermore, some observational empirical evidence suggests that, although there *is* a gap between what researchers think they know and how users and practitioners of various sorts behave, there is also considerable activity around knowledge utilization that does not obviously involve dark efforts to impose ideas on a passive audience.

One thing is clear: even if postmodern philosophy is correct, it has not damaged science at all. In a number of disciplines, for example, scholars are eagerly sought out for the potential commercial value of their ideas (Blumenthal *et al.* 1995). Rather than bemoaning lack of utilization, the research community debates where to draw the line between science and development of valuable ideas. The value of a scholar's "sticky knowledge" – Von Hippel's (1994) term for the insights from research that are not published, but can be communicated – is also apparent in education, where the work of some researchers leads them to be in high demand among the practitioner community (for example, US researchers who have developed cooperative learning, or the university-based scholars who have new strategies for reading instruction). There is also clear evidence that people in normal positions and regularized circumstances seek and use knowledge that they believe to be, if not objective in the philosophical sense, at least useful, comprehensible, and applicable. This knowledge is not always purveyed by social scientists and educational developers, but the fact that some of "our knowledge" is not viewed as "useable" (Lindblom and Cohen 1979) does not obviate observations of knowledge use in educational practice.

If we see many examples of educators looking for or using externally generated knowledge as if it had real meaning, then postmodernism's argument that all knowledge is local must be flawed. Similarly, if we see that most knowledge from the outside is viewed as suspect – or at least imperfect – until other additions have been made to it, then the modernist/positivist view is also problematic. Although the revisions to traditional theory suggested by Huberman attempt to address the problematic and contingent nature of knowledge, and to suggest ways in which dissemination activities may take account of this, his discussion does not address the other issues raised by postmodernists, namely that all knowledge is local, contested, and political. In addition, there is an emerging body of theory and research that suggests a middle ground for dissemination scholars between the modernist extremes articulated by Popper (1972), on the one hand, and Geertz's (1983) more recent postmodernist work on the other. Furthermore, these middle-ground positions are more helpful in thinking about the problem of D&U and efforts to reform education than either of the more extreme positions. Some of these will be reviewed below.

New Perspectives

The new perspectives on dissemination and knowledge utilization, described briefly below, can be viewed like layers on an onion of the problem of knowledge and practice. While it is clear that philosophers – and most Western individuals – accept Descartes' dictum of "I think, therefore I am," which encapsulates the individual and psychological perspective on knowledge use, there has been a long recognition that thinking and subsequent knowing is constrained by context. Scholars have recently begun to examine these layers at a number of different levels: societal, organizational, and cognitive. Each of these will be briefly examined below, and the relationship of theoretical ideas to the problem of school improvement will be suggested.

Societal

At the societal level, two problems emerge from the current theoretical debates. The first has to do with the notion of research inquiry as hegemonic, while the second poses a fundamental problem of how knowledge becomes socially constructed/institutionalized if it is, by definition, local. Both of these issues are clearly related to current debates about how to reform schools, although they do not intersect neatly with the theoretical and practical perspectives of school effectiveness and school improvement scholars.

Political Perspectives

The notion that knowledge use is constrained by political contexts is not new. In the late 1980s, when evaluation research was well established on the policy scene, observers began to notice that publicly funded research was often used primarily because it "fit" a set of partisan purposes that were formed prior to the availability of the results. Legislative staff members did not read research to find out how their elected bosses should vote; instead they often combed research to find results that would fit the policy-maker's preferred stance. Thus, for example, even the most rigorous multi-million-dollar educational evaluations relating to supplementary educational services for less advantaged children in the USA were ignored or embraced depending on personal perspectives.

Weiss and Bucuvalas (1980) were among the first to propose that knowledge produced through more-or-less rigorous inquiry needs to pass two types of tests before it is used: there is a truth test, which helps the individual or group looking at the information to decide whether it is a reasonable approximation of reality, but there is also a utility test, by which the same groups determine whether or not it can be applied given a set of constraints, which could range from financial to potential negative consequences not considered in the research. Thus, for example, educational researchers wonder why policy-makers continue to advocate for large schools and large districts when cumulative research evidence suggests strongly that size is negatively related to student achievement (Wahlberg 1989; Lee and Smith 1994). Yet local school boards and superintendents can present compelling evidence to support bigger institutions that range from obvious (cost savings) to symbolic (large schools are more likely to have comprehensive programs, which increases public support for education). The research may be true, but does not yet pass the utility test.

Weiss views knowledge as value laden, but, unlike the critical theorists, her perspective does not emphasize hegemony and explicit power interests, but the chaotic nature of knowledge and social cognition that make both dissemination and knowledge utilization uncertain activities. Research ideas can pop up and rejuvenate public discourse long after their initial proponents have forgotten them (Weiss 1980). Knowledge that at least partially passes a truth test may creep into the public consciousness through the accretion of small decisions, producing a slow but nonlinear movement towards consistency. Thus, for example, the "small school" perspective is now beginning to shape US public debates in a different form, through current efforts to create "charter schools" and alternative learning environments for special populations.

A recent analysis by Vickers (1994) compares Weiss's theory of semi-ordered chaos and the hegemonic, critical perspective in two cases where "outside" knowledge was incorporated into Australian educational policy. In one instance, she shows that in the school-to-work transition policies used knowledge produced by the Organization for Economic Cooperation and Development (OECD) in ways that are consistent with the "knowledge creep" process, gradually producing a new social consensus. In a second, a single policy-maker used OECD knowledge to justify a decision already reached rather than to engender a public discussion. In both cases there was a paradigm shift in policy, but in one the process of utilization was decentralized and focused on changing meanings among a broad set of actors, while in the other it represented legitimation for a policy arrived at among a small group. As Vickers points out, both of these cases support

Weiss's basic assumptions that the meaning of knowledge use is not simple, and that, while "knowledge is power," that power can take on different forms, not all of which involve imposing one world-view upon another.

These contrasting political perspectives on knowledge utilization are clearly related to problems of school improvement today. On the one hand, in many countries we observe devolution or decentralization policies that place the responsibility for knowledge utilization and change more clearly in the hands of schools, where teachers and school leaders struggle together to create better learning conditions for students. The assumption that localized processes of knowledge utilization can contribute to educational improvement is a distinct paradigm shift that has occurred on an international basis, propounded by an increasing consensus among teacher associations, politicians and parents in countries as diverse in educational tradition as Sweden, The Netherlands, and the USA. On the other hand, political actors continue, even in these settings, to make decisions that involve centralized, hegemonic decisions that are intended to shock parts of the system into change – for example, efforts to introduce new standards-based reforms in both the USA and The Netherlands, and to argue for more central control over a "high stakes" examination system in Sweden. The fact that these are international trends, often involving the borrowing of language and ideas between countries, suggests a strong currency for an international flow of political perspective about educational reform. Ideas about effective schools and effective teaching have also been widely diffused through international research networks, and later, within countries, have been influential in affecting policy discourse.

Historical Perspectives

The problem of determining how, under the constructivists/local knowledge assumptions, technologies become used over a wide area is addressed in a creative study by Turnbull (1994). Turnbull begins with a basic assumption of constructivism and postmodernism, namely that all knowledge is local. However, he points out that the localness of knowledge refers to its production, and not to its distribution and/or use by others. Turnbull points out that modern science is not the only example of knowledge produced at one site being broadly shared. He goes on to explore the processes by which this occurred in historical situations: the Anasazi Indians of the American Southwest, the Incas of Central and South America, the Micronesian navigators, and the stonemasons who were responsible for the building of the medieval cathedrals. His analysis of the strategies that were used by earlier cultures, to transmit theories and "useable knowledge" across groups that were loosely connected and, in some cases, did not even share a base of common language, is instructive for our current understanding of how knowledge becomes widely shared and acted on. One of his more powerful examples is the example of how illiterate craftsmen shared "templates of practice" across decades and even centuries in order to build the massive European cathedrals. His analysis of historical systems also suggests that the boundaries of the movement of knowledge are affected by power: at some boundary, the "owners" of the knowledge, whether stonemasons or priests, lose their communication influence, and the knowledge system that they represent becomes culture bound. However, it is not only formal power but the utility of the knowledge across sites that accounts for its spread.

Turnbull's analysis focuses on the implications of communications technology for the hegemony of ideas in modern science. I interpret his data from another perspective: although all knowledge may be local, local knowledge can be shared under conditions where there are both limited and elaborate infrastructures and communication vehicles. Although remote from the issues of educational improvement, Turnbull's perspective is pertinent to adjudicating the traditional and postmodernist perspectives on the role of practitioner in the development of educational knowledge. A romantic view of school practice argues that teachers, as artists, must invent, reflect, and study in their own settings. Unlike artists, the teacher does not have a concrete artifact of their developmental work that can be easily shared. However, we increasingly see ideas about practice spreading through networks of teachers with a communication infrastructure (journals, professional meetings, and books) that is very limited. This is particularly evident in the networks of innovative schools that have been initiated in both the USA and other countries, where there is an explicit effort to ensure that the development and flow of knowledge is controlled by teachers and not scholars. The flow of ideas across organizational and even cultural boundaries suggests that even when teachers create their own knowledge, there is a strong desire to share and spread under largely non-hegemonic conditions.

Organizational

Two recent developments in organizational studies seem to have profound implications for D&U and school reform. Each also contributes to the debate between the modernists and postmodernists. The first builds on the work of institutional sociologists of the 1950s and early 1960s, but takes a more radical stance in terms of the degree to which external influences condition internal stabilities in organizations, and thus affect the knowledge that will or will not be used. This school of thought, which emerged in the early 1980s, is referred to as the "new institutionalism" (DiMaggio and Powell 1991). A second line of work, which is more recent, examines organizations as systems that learn. This perspective is consistent with traditional open-systems theory as it applies to organizations (Katz and Kahn 1966; Scott 1981), but pays more attention to the mechanisms that foster or inhibit the ability of organizations to take advantage of knowledge that is generated locally or from outside.

The "New Institutionalism"

The new institutionalism perspective begins with the assumption that the patterned regularity of organizational behavior, which is particularly noticeable within sectors or industries, is a major social phenomenon that requires explanation. The assumption that repetitive social relations are "facts" that cannot be reduced to individual explanations is as old as the field of sociology itself. What is new about the current perspectives, however, is the emphasis placed on explaining lack of variation in organizational patterns – for example, why do all modernized countries have a higher education system that is increasingly similar both in terms of types of institutions, length of study, and the names of courses of study? Why are school classrooms remarkably similar whether one is in California or Illinois?

The answer, according to institutional theory, is that the emergence of an organizational field, or a collection of organizations in the same line of business, becomes both an opportunity to influence the environment, but also a normative environment. This has tremendous implications for dissemination and utilization of knowledge, because:

> in the long run, an organization's actors making rational decisions construct around themselves an environment that constrains their ability to change in later years. *Early adopters of organizational innovations are commonly driven by a desire to improve performance. But ... as an innovation spreads [within the field] a threshold is reached beyond which adoption provides legitimacy rather than improves performance* ... Thus organizations may try to change constantly; but after a certain point in the structuration of an organizational field, the aggregate effective of individual [organizational] change is to lessen the extent of diversity within the field.
>
> (DiMaggio and Powell 1991: 65; italics added)

The spread of the community college system throughout the USA after its initial "invention" in California is an example. Particularly striking is its institutionalization as a system that contains both academic and vocational programs and the similarity of programs between units that avowedly respond to local needs (Brint and Karabel 1989).

The similar nature of individual organizations within an institutionalized field is maintained not by rational choices, but by the dominance of the norms and symbols that come to exemplify "the best of what we do." Through their participation in symbolic rituals, organizational actors reinforce the order of the institution and its relationship to society (Friedland and Alford 1991: 250). To give just a small example, the use of bells in US high schools to signify the end of classes has little practical significance. Yet, just a few years ago, efforts to eliminate the use of bells raised intense passion: bells are an important symbol of the orderliness of schooling, as contrasted with the chaos of adolescence. Resistance to change is not a consequence of individual concerns, but of environmental pressures from the organizational field, and, especially in the case of public sector organizations, from other constituencies who reinforce the norms and symbols. These may range from the general public (who expect bells) to the government and accrediting associations or inspectorates, who demand visible regularity.

In spite of the rigidities introduced into an institutionalized organizational field, change and knowledge utilization do, of course, occur. However, reforms often occur in a mimetic fashion, and become quickly institutionalized (DiMaggio and Powell 1991). A clear example is the recent wave of "accountability reforms" of undergraduate liberal education requirements at major US universities – a response to public concerns about the rigor and breadth of this highly institutionalized aspect of our higher education system. The notion of liberal education requirements was not challenged during the course of this wave of reform (although few other countries' higher education systems have a liberal education requirement), but most institutions made significant changes to simplify, focus, and update the commitment to liberal education. In doing so, institutions typically relied on information from others in their field: rates of knowledge dissemination and utilization were high, and research about liberal education and its effects were circulated broadly to the relevant committees on university campuses. In this case, the institutional interests of the organizational field in preserving public confidence in their programs stimulated modest reform that was based on both local traditions and cosmopolitan knowledge from similar institutions, and on scholarly writing. The "middle-school movement" in the USA is another example of the diffusion of institutional change based on a mixture of scholarly research, information about practices in other schools, and "local knowledge" of what will work given district customs and constraints. What began as a series of local efforts to improve lower secondary education has become identified with key structural elements, such as teacher teams, interdisciplinary curriculum, and cooperative pedagogical styles. Having these changed structures and practice becomes prima facie evidence that the school has reformed.

To summarize, the institutional perspective picks up the postmodernist themes of hegemony of particular ideas and forms of knowledge, but argues that these are created within the organizational field (often in response to external pressure) and are self-sustaining. Rather than emphasizing the "localness" of knowledge construction and use, they point to empirical evidence suggesting the impossibility of local change in the absence of similar pressures and needs to change throughout the field. Furthermore, they point to the mimetic nature of organizations within an institutionalized field as a determinant of what knowledge will be used. Traditional D&U concerns with communication, packaging of knowledge, and so on, are relatively unimportant in this perspective, as are postmodernist concerns about "whose knowledge is it?" Educational reform within the broad organizational field is not dependent on the availability of specific externally developed models complete with training and support, although these may support change in individual schools. More important to determining whether there will be broadly based reform is the intersection between pressures for change from outside, local development activities, and the rapid spread of workable ideas between adopting units.

Organizational Learning

If the new institutionalism examines the environment for dissemination and knowledge utilization activities that affect whether information will spread within an organizational field, the organizational learning model moves into the interior of the school, looking at features that affect the adaptability of individual units. Organizational learning begins with a social constructivist perspective: knowledge is not useable at the local site until it has been "socially processed" through some collective discussion and agreement on its validity and applicability (Louis 1994). Organizations that are more effective in using knowledge have certain characteristics – for example, they have denser internal communication networks, and more individuals serve in boundary-spanning roles where they legitimately bring in new ideas from the outside (Daft and Huber 1987;

Senge 1990). Conversely, organizations that don't learn – even from information that they request – are characterized by internal boundaries, competition, excessive individual entrepreneurship, and lack of continuity in personnel (Corwin and Louis 1982). Three features of school culture and practice – memory, knowledge base and development, and information distribution and interpretation – can also have a big impact on teachers' ability to sustain openness to learning (see Chapter 12).

But an information base is not enough. Teachers must also interpret and distribute information before it becomes knowledge that is applicable across classrooms. Joint efforts to interpret information must provide a foundation for challenging existing beliefs about the school, or previous views of teaching and learning remain unchanged (Louis *et al.* 1996). Genuinely understanding an innovation or the basis on which it rests is necessary if teachers are to make the new information applicable in the classroom.

The organizational learning perspective is critical when we consider the relationship of D&U and improvement theories in education. It suggests that the possibility for reaching a school with new knowledge is dependent not on where the knowledge comes from or the linkage mechanism, but on characteristics of the school and its ability to process information. While "sustained interaction" with a researcher might enhance utilization, it cannot produce it in the absence of the structures and culture that encourage the development of a shared knowledge base that will guide collective action. In this respect, Huberman's (1994) focus on school characteristics as a factor mediating knowledge use intersects clearly with emerging ideas about school development and improvement.

Cognitive Learning Theory

At the most micro-level, new advances in cognitive theory suggest many directions for theories about dissemination and knowledge utilization. Many of these are consistent with postmodernist perspectives, but they assume that individuals not only create their own knowledge, but also incorporate knowledge from outside. Since few postmodernists attend to cognitive psychology, assumptions about individual learning are not well reflected in their work. However, the new traditionalists, such as Huberman, have made considerable progress in thinking about ways that emergent findings related to how both children and adults learn should affect how we think about dissemination and knowledge utilization (Huberman and Broderick 1995).

Huberman and Broderick argue that "the most hopeful new avenue of inquiry in the D&U literature emerges when dissemination takes place … through … sustained interactions between researchers and practitioners" (1995: 3–4), a point that is central to the renewed traditional theory. They go on, however, to explore the cognitive and structural conditions under which sustained interaction may result in increased meaning on the part of both. Central to their argument is the idea of socially shared cognition that has begun to dominate the field of cognitive development (Brown 1994). This perspective is based in the assumption that individuals learn best when they interact with peers and relate new ideas to an existing core of shared knowledge. This occurs most frequently when peers challenge their assumptions and provide them with incentives to rethink their previous ideas. However, this process works best when the learner has reached a minimal level of understanding of the content, and the challenges are not too great. While Huberman and Broderick do not note this, it also assumes that the group has certain characteristics: that there is some shared culture, and that there is a level of familiarity that permits communication of challenges in ways that are not excessively threatening. Their perspective differs from organizational learning theory discussed above in that it also draws on Vygotsky (1986), who argues that interpersonal processes must be translated into intrapersonal processes before learning can be said to have occurred. Thus, their emphasis is largely on the way in which individual researchers and practitioners enter into relationships that cause them, as individuals, to change their assumptions and even their behaviors.

The notion that thinking is irreducibly a social practice implies that dissemination and utilization are best thought of as a process of reflection, in which people with different but overlapping knowledge and culture meet to consider their common concerns (Huberman and Broderick 1995: 21). Researchers find that engaging in dissemination leads to greater clarity about their own work, just as young students obtain greater mastery of concepts when they are obliged to teach them to others. Because researchers and practitioners in education share some assumptions, but have divergent experiences on most dimensions, "opportunities for cognitive discrepancy are good; they are fed by attempts to reconcile the conflicting versions of what those issues now mean" (Huberman and Broderick 1995: 30). By creating some shared meanings and language through discussion of cognitively dissonant ideas, a new reality is created that did not previously exist:

> Thus, cognitive shifts are not activated "within the person" or "within the setting" but rather within the mediating activity itself, dynamically and dialectically – a bit like Leontiev's concept of a continuously shifting "construction zone" or Schön's notion of "reflecting in practice" and Dewey's idea of "knowing in action."
>
> (Huberman and Broderick 1995: 31)

Thus, while retaining the notion of the valid-yet-different perspectives of research knowledge and practice knowledge, Huberman and Broderick argue that it is at the intersection between the two (or between any two sets of "local knowledge" for that matter) that cognitive progress is made at the individual level.

Paradigm Evolution or Revolution?

This review points to two issues: first, there is a proliferation of research and theory bearing on the intersection of knowledge dissemination and utilization and school improvement (although many authors quoted in this paper do not explicitly consider this issue) and, second, much of this research already incorporates elements of a postmodernist position, although none of the new approaches discussed, with the exception of Turnbull, is consciously postmodernist. The convergence taking place around the key elements of postmodernist views of knowledge will be considered first, and then the implications for school improvement practice:

- *All knowledge is local.* The above discussions assume that local knowledge is a key feature of the landscape of change, but most would agree that there is important knowledge that is not local. Knowledge created elsewhere must, according to all theories, be compatible with existing belief structures, diffuse rapidly throughout the organization field so that it becomes legitimized, have utility in local sites, and be "processed" in ways that make it fit with local preferences. The "new institutionalism" adds another wrinkle: knowledge that is widely diffused is itself institutionalized so that it can be easily shared within the "field." Although a great deal of important knowledge may come from outside the organization, the above theories also suggest that this information is always combined with local knowledge.

- *All knowledge is contested and partial.* This feature of postmodernism is supported by most new theoretical advances. At the cognitive learning level, for example, the contesting of knowledge is central to the learning process. The "new institutionalism" argues that it is the incontestability of many features of an organizational field that make it difficult to change: only where there are chaotic events that cause either insiders or outsiders to question the knowledge will change or knowledge utilization occur. The contested nature of knowledge is a key element of political theory, and the primary element that leads both Weiss and Vickers to conclude that there are many ways of using knowledge, depending on the degree to which it meets truth and utility tests. In the organizational learning model, it is the debate and discussion around contested or partial knowledge that leads to a new consensus about how to solve problems or change modus operandi, a perspective that is consistent with emergent cognitive learning theory.

- *All knowledge is political.* Insofar as the newer theories address power, there is a tendency to follow Macauley's assumption that "knowledge is power" and that the creation of knowledge creates powerful settings (including constraints). None of the perspectives reviewed here adopts, however, the critical postmodernist perspective, in which the power associated with knowledge is viewed as an instrument of oppression. Cognitive psychologists, for example, do not find that children who temporarily have knowledge that others lack use this to dominate. Turnbull, who applies a postmodernist frame, assumes that knowledge becomes less powerful at the periphery of the social group. Nevertheless, political contexts are critical to understanding knowledge use, as is demonstrated by the analysis of knowledge utilization among policy-makers, and the new institutionalist observation that knowledge use is constrained as the organizational field becomes defined both by internal norms or patterns and external expectations or regulation.

While all of the perspectives reviewed are consistent with some of the basic tenets of postmodernist views of knowledge, they also assume that knowledge has some realist qualities, and that it can be used by individuals who have not created it. The use process is complex and difficult to predict: there will be no production function D&U models emerging from this set of scholars. But messy cannot be equated with impossible. Postmodernist theory has taken us two steps forward, demanding that we examine a wide variety of assumptions that we make about the nature of knowledge and its effects on ourselves and our settings. However, we must also take one step back and realize that the most profound of these insights are compatible with revised versions of existing theories, particularly if we broaden where we look for research to inform dissemination practice. In addition, as I have argued throughout this chapter, the modifications to theories about knowledge and knowledge utilization are compatible with what we know about educational improvement and the directions of educational reform policies in a variety of settings.

Some Implications for Practice

"But is there any there, there?" – this is the bitter query of the disillusioned postmodernist. If we think of "there" as D&U applications in pursuit of educational change, there are many implications of the layered approach to D&U theory proposed in this paper. In particular, I would argue that there is a self-conscious need to reintegrate our understanding of the nature of three arenas of knowledge: research results related to educational goal achievement (school effectiveness, broadly conceived), educational change processes (school improvement, broadly conceived), and the knowledge-use strategies that can be pursued both inside and outside schools to improve student learning and development. None of these is inconsistent with Huberman's reformulation of traditional dissemination theory, but they suggest an expanded context for thinking about D&U. In particular, we need to draw upon the research about political, historical, and organizational contexts affecting knowledge use to enrich the micro-level perspectives that are emphasized in Huberman's formulation. While it is beyond the scope of this paper to suggest a model for D&U and school development that fully incorporates these theories, a few examples can demonstrate the practical connections:

- *Research knowledge is only one source of knowing, and its use must be negotiated during a dissemination process. This fluid relationship – and even co-dependence – between research and practice must be acknowledged, and researchers must be prepared to be open to involvement in the development process at the user level.* If this is true for "gold standard" science, it is particularly true for social science and educational research, which is less likely to be "gold standard." Best practice in education is not often generated by scholars in laboratories, but by teachers and school leaders in actual settings. On the other hand, the invention and spread of new practices in education is frequently aided by research, which may codify and extend practice-based knowledge as well as making independent contributions to it. In many cases, researchers may not be as well equipped to engage in field-based development over long periods of time (they have students and new research projects to carry out), but the others may fulfill this function *if* they have a deep understanding of the emerging nature of the negotiated knowledge.
- There has been a trend in many countries to involve practitioners in setting research agendas (for example, serving on peer-review panels), and even as co-participants in

carrying out research. This is thought to make research more grounded and, hence, usable. However, *involving "users" in research will not necessarily make the research more usable – except at a particular site or among those who have been directly involved.* While it may be good for researchers to become more connected to practice settings and vice versa, the power of site or place when it comes to change is strong. Thus, involvement of practitioners as researchers should occur for its own direct benefits, and not because it improves the possibility of dissemination and utilization.

- The main barriers to knowledge use, at least in the public sector, are not at the level of individual resistance, but lie in the *rigidities induced in institutionalized organizational fields, organizational designs that do not foster learning, and political agendas that are not consistent with the information.* Changing these organizational rigidities in the short term may be extremely difficult. The motto under these circumstances is not to engage in Sisyphysian efforts, but to "try again another day" because contextual circumstances change for reasons that have nothing to do with research or educational policy.

- The barriers to knowledge utilization are often to be found in organizational design. This suggests that *redesigning the organization should be part of any effort to engage in "sustained interactivity"* around research utilization. The emphasis on developing school capacities for self-management that is emerging in many countries should be shaped around those capacities that not only augment the ability to manage budgets and personnel policies, but that also attend to the creating of schools that can learn from knowledge generated inside and outside the school. This objective will require policies, direct training, and support to schools that have previously not engaged in these efforts.

- *Some forms of useful knowledge will spread with little dissemination effort* – due to organizational field compatibility or because the field develops an infrastructure to assess and legitimate the type of knowledge. We do not always need elaborate infrastructures or sustained interactivity to ensure the incorporation of new ideas in practice.

- *Utilization and impact can only be assessed over the long haul.* Short-term efforts to foster major utilization are likely to appear shallow and hegemonic to practitioners, and to fail to disrupt the interorganizational rigidities of the field. Policy-makers and disappointed researchers are likely to view these efforts as "failures" and to pronounce schools as impossible to change. Thus, research-based efforts to create school reform must be based on an extended time-line.

- Creating sustained interactivity is not a solution to the D&U problem but, if it becomes a norm, it may well increase the scholarly impact because it *enlarges the organizational field.* We should not limit the idea of sustained interactivity to the relationship between a "knowledge producer/researcher" and "knowledge consumers/ practitioners" but focus also on formal and informal networks for transmitting knowledge between units. These networks, to be successful, must involve practice templates that combine research knowledge and practice knowledge.

These are only a few suggestions. The main point of this chapter has been to argue that we do not need to throw away our theories about school reform processes and D&U, but to merge and enlarge them. The fact that enlarged perspectives have reasonable practical implications is only one of many criteria that need to be applied to determine whether the analysis presented above is valid.

Note

1. A slightly longer version of this chapter was published in A. Hargreaves, D. Hopkins, M. Fullan, and A. Lieberman (eds), *International Handbook of Educational Change*: 1074–95. Dordrecht: Kluwer.

References

Berger, P. and T. Luckmann (1966) *The Social Construction of Reality*. New York: Doubleday.

Blumenthal, D., N. Causino, E. Campbell, and K.S. Louis (1996) "Relationships between academic institutions and industry in the life sciences: An industrial survey." *New England Journal of Medicine* 334(6): 368–73.

Brint, S. and J. Karabel (1989) *The Diverted Dream: Community Colleges and the Promise of Educational Opportunity in America: 1900–1985*. New York: Oxford University Press.

Brown, A. (1994) "The advancement of learning." *Educational Researcher* 7(8): 4–12.

Campbell, P. (1994) *Whose Knowledge Is it?: Involving Teachers in the Generating and Using of Information on Educational Innovations*. Washington, DC: USOE/OERI.

Carlson, R. (1965) *The Adoption of Education Innovations*. Eugene: Oregon Press.

Carr, W. and S. Kemmis (1986) *Becoming Critical: Education, Knowledge and Action Research*. London: Falmer.

Coleman, J., E. Katz, and H. Menzel (1966) *The Diffusion of Medical Innovations*. Indianapolis, IN: Bobbs-Merrill.

Corwin, R.G. and K.S. Louis (1982) "Organizational barriers to knowledge use." *Administrative Science Quarterly* 27: 623–40.

Daft, R. and G. Huber (1987) "How organizations learn." In N. DiTomaso and S. Bacharach (eds), *Research in the Sociology of Organizations*, Vol. 5: 1–36. Greenwich, CT: JAI.

DiMaggio, P. and W. Powell (1991) "The iron cage revisited: Institutional isomorphism and collective rationality in organizational fields." In W. Powell and P. DiMaggio (eds), *The New Institutionalism in Organizational Analysis*. Chicago: University of Chicago Press.

Duening, T. (1991) "Rorty's Liberal Ironist: A Model for Information Age Undergraduate Education." Unpublished PhD Dissertation: University of Minnesota.

Friedland, R. and R. Alford (1991) "Bringing society back in: Symbols, practices and institutional contradictions." In W. Powell and P. DiMaggio (eds), *The New Institutionalism in Organizational Analysis*. Chicago: University of Chicago Press.

Fullan, M. and A. Hargreaves (1991) *What's Worth Fighting For? Working Together for Your School.* Ottawa: Ontario Public School Teachers' Federation.

—— and S. Stiegelbauer (1991) *The New Meaning of Educational Change.* New York: Teachers College Press.

Geertz, C. (1983) *Local Knowledge: Further Essays in Interpretive Anthropology.* New York: Basic Books.

Glaser, E. (1976) *Putting Knowledge to Use: A Distillation of the Literature Regarding Knowledge Transfer and Change.* Los Angeles: Human Interaction Research Institute.

Havelock, R. (1969) *Planning for Innovation through the Dissemination and Utilization of Knowledge.* Ann Arbor, MI: CRUSK, Institute for Social Research, University of Michigan.

Huberman, M. (1994) "Research utilization: The state of the art." *Knowledge and Policy* 7(4): 13–33.

—— and M. Broderick (1995) "Research utilization: An exploration into new territories." Unpublished manuscript, University of Geneva.

Katz, R. and R. Kahn (1966) *The Social Psychology of Organizations.* New York: Wiley.

Kuhn, T. (1970) *The Structure of Scientific Revolutions.* Chicago: University of Chicago Press.

Lee, V. and J. Smith (1994) "Effects of restructured teacher worklife on gains in achievement and engagement for early secondary school students." Paper presented at the annual meeting of the American Educational Research Association, New Orleans.

Lindblom C. and D. Cohen (1979) *Usable Knowledge: Social Science and Social Problem-Solving.* New Haven, CT: Yale University Press.

Little J. (1993) "Teachers' professional development in a climate of educational reform." *Educational Evaluation and Policy Analysis* 15(2): 129–51.

Louis, K.S. (1994) "Beyond managed change: Rethinking how schools improve." *School Effectiveness and School Improvement* 5: 1–22.

——, S. Kruse, and M. Raywid (1996) "Putting teachers at the center of reform: Learning schools and professional communities." *NASSP Bulletin* 80: 9–22.

Mort, P.R. (1963) "Studies in educational innovation from the Institute of Administrative Research: An overview." In M.B. Miles (ed.), *Innovation in Education*: 317–28. New York: Teachers College Press.

Newmann, F. and G. Wehlage (1995) *Effective School Restructuring.* Madison: Center for Educational Research, University of Wisconsin.

Popper, K. (1972) *Objective Knowledge: An Evolutionary Approach.* Oxford: Clarendon Press.

Rogers, E. (1982) *The Diffusion of Innovations.* New York: The Free Press.

Schön, D. (1983) *The Reflective Practitioner: How Professionals Think in Action.* New York: Basic Books.

Scott, W. R. (1981) *Organizations: Rational, Natural, and Open Systems.* Englewood Cliffs, NJ: Prentice Hall.

Senge, P. (1990) *The Fifth Dimension: The Art and Practice of the Learning Organization.* New York: Doubleday.

Turnbull, D. (1994) "Local knowledge and comparative scientific traditions." *Knowledge and Policy* 8: 29–54.

US Department of Education (1990) *What Works*. Washington, DC: US Department of Education.

Vickers, M. (1994) "Cross-national exchange, the OECD and Australian education policy." *Knowledge and Policy* 7: 24–47.

Von Hippel, E. (1994) "'Sticky Information' and the locus of problem solving: Implications for innovation." *Management Science* 40(4): 429–37.

Vygotsky, L.S. (1986) *Thought and Language*. Cambridge, MA: MIT Press.

Wahlberg, H. (1989) "District size and learning." *Education and Urban Society* 21: 154–63.

Watkins, J. (1994) "A postmodern critical theory of research use." *Knowledge and Policy* 7(4): 55–77.

Weiss, C. (1980) "Knowledge creep and decision accretion." *Knowledge: Creation, Dissemination, Utilization* 1: 381–404.

—— and M. Bucuvalas (1980) *Social Science Research and Decision Making*. New York: Columbia University Press.

Index

Note: the names of several schools have been changed in the text; the names listed in the index are those given in the text, which are not necessarily the real names.

CONTEXTS OF LEARNING